Pear and Gorgonzola Cheese
Pizza, page 178

Lettuce with Hot Bacon Dressing,
page 235

Thai Coconut
Chicken, page 137

Lemonade Cake, page 88

all recipes™
dinner tonight

Oxmoor House®

Allrecipes.com, Inc.
President: Bill Moore
Senior VP Development: Tim Hunt
Vice President Marketing: Esmée Williams
Production Managers: Jill Charing, Jenni Johns
Senior Recipe Editor: Sydny Carter
Senior Food Editor: Jennifer Anderson
Recipe Editors: Emily Brune, Richard Kozel,
    Leslie Peterson, Britt Swearingen
Creative Direction: Yann Oehl, Jeff Cummings

Allrecipes.com, Inc.
400 Mercer Street, Suite 302
Seattle, WA 98109
(206) 292-3990
www.Allrecipes.com

Oxmoor House, Inc.
Editor-in-Chief: Nancy Fitzpatrick Wyatt
Executive Editor: Susan Carlisle Payne
Art Director: Cynthia R. Cooper
Copy Chief: Allison Long Lowery

Allrecipes Dinner Tonight
Editor: Allison Long Lowery
Assistant Editor: McCharen Pratt
Copy Editor: Donna Baldone
Editorial Assistants: Terri Laschober, Diane Rose
Senior Photographer: Jim Bathie
Photographer: Brit Huckabay
Senior Photo Stylist: Kay E. Clarke
Photo Stylist: Ashley J. Wyatt
Director, Test Kitchens: Elizabeth Tyler Luckett
Assistant Director, Test Kitchens: Julie Christopher
Recipe Editor: Gayle Hays Sadler
Test Kitchens Staff: Kristi Carter, Nicole Lee Faber,
    Kathleen Royal Phillips, Jan A. Smith, Elise Weis,
    Kelley Wilton
Publishing Systems Administrator: Rick Tucker
Director of Production: Phillip Lee
Production Manager: Theresa L. Beste
Production Assistant: Faye Porter Bonner

Contributors:
Designer: Carol Damsky
Indexer: Mary Ann Laurens
Photographer: Lee Harrelson
Editorial Intern: Danielle McClure

Table of Contents

Welcome from the Staff of Allrecipes!

Dear Friends:

We all face the proverbial question—What's for dinner tonight? Whether you're preparing meals for a large family or whipping up a simple dinner for one, many times figuring out what to prepare poses more of a dilemma than actually doing the cooking. The online community of **Allrecipes.com** has the answer to your question, and we guarantee that dinner doesn't get any better than this. We've searched our vast collection of America's best community recipes from **Allrecipes.com** and have pulled together simple, reliable, family-pleasing menus and recipes to make mealtime a pleasure. For this all-new volume, we've selected over 400 top-rated recipes—rated and reviewed by over 6 million home cooks on **Allrecipes.com**—and organized them into an easy-to-follow book that will keep one-of-a-kind, blue-ribbon winning recipes at your fingertips. Check out some of our favorite features:

- **15 "Six-O'Clock Solution" menus deliver weeknight meal ideas, complete with prep plans and serving suggestions. With menus that feature 30-minute meals, slow-cooker fare, quick-and-easy gourmet cuisine, and budget-friendly suppers, you have the flexibility to find a menu that suits your needs.**
- **15 menus for "Casual Entertaining" provide complete meal plans to help with last-minute guests, holidays, and family gatherings. You'll be able to cherish your holidays and special events with simple recipes prepared with love—and without any panic.**
- **Reader reviews from** *Allrecipes.com* **supplement each recipe with valuable tips, serving suggestions, and substitution ideas from people who tested the recipe in their own home.**
- **48 pages of enticing new photography showcases these best-loved recipes in style.**
- **Each recipe comes with its own set of information that's invaluable to the home cook. Prep and cook times, nutritional analysis, and recipe banners such as Quick & Easy, Kid-Friendly, and Make-Ahead make finding exactly what you want for dinner tonight trouble-free.**

We welcome you to this treasury of recipes that will give you more time—time for sitting around the dinner table with family and friends, time for a home-cooked meal, and time for yourself. Join in the fun the next time you're online and become a part of the **Allrecipes** family. Share your time-honored recipes and make them a part of the world's largest community cookbook.

Happy Cooking,

The Staff of Allrecipes

What is Allrecipes.com?

Six years ago, we created a place for home cooks to share their favorite recipes via the Internet. As word spread, others joined in, and in no time, **Allrecipes.com** grew into the world's largest community of home cooks—over 6 million strong—and became the number-one source for online recipes. On the website, recipes are posted for everyday home cooks to put them to the test and then rate and review them online. It's an interactive recipe swap that's helping over 6 million people get dinner on the table with confidence.

About the recipes

Every recipe in this book includes a brief **comment from the contributor.** This may be a serving suggestion, where the recipe came from, or other valuable information about the dish. We always preserve the character of the contributed recipe, but we make slight changes where necessary to ensure consistency, accuracy, and completeness in the published version.

On **Allrecipes.com,** visitors post **recipe reviews,** and for this book, we've included the most helpful reviews alongside the recipes. Look for **"What other cooks have done"** in the box beside every recipe for these reviews that give serving suggestions and cooking tips.

Veterans of the website know to look not only to the **highest-rated, but also the most-rated recipes** when they're looking for winners. This means that lots of people have tried these recipes at home and rated them online. We've included the rating for each recipe—for this book only 4 or 5, out of a possible **5 star recipes** were selected. Once you've made a few of these recipes, go online and share your thoughts. Look on the next two pages for a list of the most rated and reviewed recipes from this book.

You may wonder why some of the recipe titles have **Roman numerals** attached to them, like Reuben Sandwich II on page 234 or Buttermilk Pancakes II on page 284. Contributors submit multiple recipes with these titles, so we assign them a number to help keep up with all the variations. In this book, you'll find only one of the variations—the highest-rated, most-reviewed version—but you can find all the different takes on classic recipes online.

Prep and cook times are included as a basic guide with each recipe to help you plan meals. Remember that these times are approximate. How fast you chop, the accuracy of your oven's temperature, humidity, and other variations can affect your prep and cook time.

Need more information?

You'll find helpful tip boxes and charts throughout the book to help you with basic cooking and baking questions, and you can visit us online if you need more information. Check out the "Cooking Advice" section at **Allrecipes.com** where you can browse through articles and step-by-step cooking tutorials.

Recipe Hall of Fame

Check out the best of the best from this year's Allrecipes Dinner Tonight cookbook. We've pulled together this all-star list of recipes with the most ratings and reviews from the website. The following recipes (in order of appearance in the book) received 150 or more ratings from the online community and come with the testimonials of home cooks everywhere who have made these their all-time favorites. Listen to what people are saying about these best-of-the-best recipes.

▶ **Barbecued Beef** (page 22)
"One of the best barbecued beef recipes I've ever had! We made this for dinner, and the kids were scrambling to claim seconds for lunch the next day. We made a bigger roast for a get-together at our house, and everyone requested the recipe. I'm still emailing it to friends and family."

▶ **Awesome Honey Pecan Pork Chops** (page 34)
"This has become a favorite 'need a last minute dinner idea' meal in our family. My husband, who normally does not cook, actually enjoys making this recipe."

▶ **Pan-Fried Asparagus** (page 76)
"A wonderful change from steamed asparagus! Served with grilled chicken and new potatoes, it makes an elegant, easy dinner!"

▶ **Day-Before Mashed Potatoes** (page 94)
"I first made this for Thanksgiving—one less thing to do at the last minute and one less thing to take up a burner on the stove! Now I make these anytime I have a big meal planned, so I'm not mashing potatoes and trying to finish everything else at the same time. My family loves this recipe, and my husband likes the less-frazzled me at dinnertime!"

▶ **Burgundy Pork Tenderloin** (page 125)
"Wonderful flavor, quick to prepare, great presentation— what more could you want? I'll be using this as my new favorite tenderloin recipe."

▶ **Caramel-Apple Pork Chops** (page 128)
"The sweet cinnamon-spiked sauce and warm apples give these pork chops a very nice flavor. The dish is simple to make, and you'll probably have all the ingredients on hand in your pantry."

▶ **Anniversary Chicken** (page 133)
"I was looking for a different way to prepare chicken and found this. It's one of the most magnificent chicken recipes around! We now make it all the time. It's quick to put together yet special enough for company."

▶ **Aimee's Quick Chicken** (page 133)
"I love how quick this is—it's perfect for a workday supper. While it was baking, I tossed together a salad, steamed some vegetables, and supper was ready!"

▶ **Chicken Breasts Pierre** (page 136)
"I prepared this dish late in the evening and served it the next day for supper. The sauce was flavorful and the aroma filled the house. I have five kids who loved it."

▶ RamJam Chicken (page 143)

"Thanks, RamJam. Because of this marinade, I've now been promoted from 'appetizer' to 'main course' at our family BBQ's. Everyone loved it!"

▶ Addictive Sweet Potato Burritos
(page 163)

"Addictive is right! I found the recipe when planning a dinner with vegetarian guests. Now we don't need a vegetarian in attendance for an excuse to make them."

▶ Seven-Layer Tortilla Pie (page 168)

"Boy, was this delicious and just perfect for my Super Bowl party! Even though it was very easy to prepare, the presentation was quite impressive."

▶ Exquisite Pizza Sauce (page 170)

"This pizza sauce is great to make in a big batch and freeze for future use. It beats anything store-bought, and it makes pizza night extra special!"

▶ Absolutely Ultimate Potato Soup
(page 218)

"Words can't sufficiently describe how good this soup is. Do yourself a favor and save it for the next snowy or rainy day, and make sure you have a loaf of good crusty bread, a baguette of sourdough, or some good croutons. It's definitely a Hall of Famer in my book."

▶ Oven-Roasted Red Potatoes
(page 266)

"These potatoes are so good! They came out crispy on the outside and cooked perfectly inside."

▶ Grilled Potatoes and Onion
(page 267)

"Be sure to put aside a serving of these potatoes for yourself! They'll be gone before you finish putting everything else on the table!"

▶ Gourmet Sweet Potato Classic
(page 269)

"I made this for Thanksgiving, and it's a definite keeper. My family went crazy over this one. It was so delicious with its sweet, nutty texture and flavor that I was able to convert confirmed sweet potato haters into fans! Now I've been asked to make this for every family gathering!"

▶ Best-Ever Muffins (page 276)

"The best basic muffin recipe I've tried yet. You can add anything you want to these or just eat them plain. Very moist and easy to make. I like to add a little cinnamon-sugar mixture on top before baking. Makes a great breakfast or snack."

▶ Buttermilk Pancakes II (page 284)

"My daughter and I made these pancakes, and we could not believe how delicious they were! They turned out perfectly—light and fluffy with just a hint of sweetness. This recipe will definitely go in my 'best of the best' file. No more boxed mixes in our home!"

▶ Chocolate Cavity Maker Cake
(page 305)

"Look no further for the perfect 'make-people-melt' chocolate cake. Make this cake and be prepared to receive all compliments. It's extremely moist and rich. Don't forget your glass of cold milk with this one."

Recipe Highlights

Every single recipe in Allrecipes Dinner Tonight *has a banner to help you identify favorite features. Here's a guide to all the banners that are scattered throughout the book. Look for them in the index for more help in finding the perfect recipe for your needs.*

Around-the-World Cuisine ▼

Open your mind and your palate with these recipes that feature exotic flavors from around the globe.

Blue Ribbon Winner ▼

Contributors share some of their special prizewinning fare from around the country.

Classic Comfort Food ▼

Chicken and Dumplings, Meatloaf, Macaroni and Cheese, Bread Pudding . . . need we say more?

Company is Coming ▼

When you need a meal to impress your guests, look for this banner to fill your entertaining needs.

Covered-Dish Favorite ▼

Whether it's a church potluck or a family reunion, you'll have the right dish to carry along.

Crowd-Pleaser ▼

These recipes yield enough for a large party and are fit for all kinds of celebrations.

Family Favorite ▼

When it's reliable, family-pleasing recipes you're looking for, try these foolproof picks.

From the Grill ▼

Add a little spice to backyard barbecuing with these new approaches to grilling your favorite meals.

Healthy ▼

These guilt-free recipes are low in fat and calories and don't sacrifice flavor.

Holiday Fare ▼

We've made it easy to find the best recipes to celebrate the holidays with your family and friends.

Holiday Gift Giving ▼

Give a gift of the heart with these recipes for wonderful homemade gifts from your kitchen.

Hot & Spicy ▼

Hot and spicy fans can find their next indulgence here. Remember you can adjust the seasonings to taste.

Kid-Friendly ▼

Pull out these recipes for surefire hits with little ones and adults alike. Everyone will clean their plates.

Make-Ahead ▼

For parties or weeknight meals, plan ahead and make life easier with recipes that can be made ahead.

Meatless Main Dish ▼

Looking for a break from meat and potatoes? These vegetarian delights will please even die-hard meat-eaters.

One-Dish Meal ▼

Dinner can't get much easier than a whole meal in one dish. You'll enjoy all the flavor without all the fuss.

Out-of-the-Ordinary ▼

Shake up things at the dinner table with recipes that turn everyday meals into extraordinary feasts.

Party Food ▼

Put on your party hat and get cooking. You'll set the mood for your next gathering with style.

Quick & Easy ▼

These recipes save the day when you're on the run and there are hungry mouths to feed.

Restaurant Fare ▼

Make standout dishes from your favorite restaurant at home with these classic recipes.

Slow-Cooker Creation ▼

Delicious dinners will be waiting on you when you use these slow-cooker concoctions.

Six O'Clock Solutions
Weeknight Meal Planning Made Easy

1. Prepare barbecue chicken pizza topping, assemble pizza, and bake.

2. Prepare dressing and chill while pizza bakes. Stir in cilantro and dress prewashed, prepackaged salad greens just before serving.

3. Prepare milkshakes just before serving.

Prep Time: 15 minutes

Cook Time: 15 minutes

Average Rating: ★★★★☆

What other cooks have done:

"I used a homemade pizza crust for this recipe instead of store-bought and cooked it on a pizza stone. If you're using homemade pizza crust, cook it longer. This is excellent served with a crisp green salad and root beer. It's also excellent heated up for lunch the next day with some fresh cilantro on top."

Shortcut Menu

Slash your time in the kitchen by using convenience products like prewashed salad greens, a prebaked pizza crust, and bottled barbecue sauce to create this down-home meal. Top it off with homemade milkshakes made with your family's favorite ice cream.

BBQ Chicken Pizza *(pictured on page 38)*

Submitted by: **Nivola**
"This is an easy, not-too-sweet, delicious alternative to tomato sauce pizzas! It's sure to satisfy everyone. Use any kind of barbecue sauce, and it'll still be a winner!"

3 skinless, boneless chicken breast halves, cooked and cubed	½ bunch fresh cilantro, chopped
1 cup hickory-flavored barbecue sauce	1 (12 inch) prebaked pizza crust
1 tablespoon honey	1 cup shredded mozzarella or smoked Gouda cheese
1 teaspoon molasses	1 cup thinly sliced red onion
⅓ cup packed brown sugar	

1. Preheat oven to 425°F (220°C). In a saucepan over medium–high heat, combine chicken, barbecue sauce, honey, molasses, brown sugar, and cilantro. Bring to a boil; remove from heat.

2. Spread chicken mixture evenly over pizza crust and top with cheese and onions. Bake in the preheated oven for 10 to 15 minutes or until cheese is melted. **Yield:** 4 servings.

Per serving: About 708 calories, 46g protein, 85g carbohydrate, 22g fat, 4g fiber, 106mg cholesterol, 1398mg sodium

Casa Dressing *(pictured on page 38)*

Submitted by: **Denyse**

"This creamy dressing reminds me of the house dressing at Mexican restaurants."

⅔	cup mayonnaise	1	teaspoon ground black
⅓	cup milk		pepper
2½	tablespoons lime juice	1	tablespoon chopped fresh
1	teaspoon ground cumin		cilantro
1	teaspoon salt		

1. In a small bowl, whisk together mayonnaise, milk, and lime juice. Season with cumin, salt, and pepper. Cover and chill until ready to serve. Stir in cilantro just before serving. **Yield:** 1 cup.

Per 2 tablespoons: About 141 calories, 1g protein, 2g carbohydrate, 15g fat, 0g fiber, 12mg cholesterol, 402mg sodium

◄ **Restaurant Fare**

Prep Time: 5 minutes

Average Rating: ★★★★★

What other cooks have done:

"I have been looking for this recipe a very long time. I used to get this dressing in those little bagged salad kits, but they don't sell it on the shelf anymore. Try dipping veggies or chips in this creamy dressing. I added a few drops of hot sauce because I like it hot, but it's wonderful alone as well."

Chocolate Mug Milkshakes *(pictured on page 300)*

Submitted by: **Sue**

"If you like chocolate and you have a sweet tooth, then this is your drink. It tastes like hot chocolate but it's cold!"

4	cups chocolate ice cream, divided	¼	cup white sugar, divided
2	cups milk, divided	¼	teaspoon ground cinnamon, divided
¼	cup packed brown sugar, divided		

1. In a blender, combine half each of ice cream, milk, brown sugar, white sugar, and cinnamon. Blend until smooth. Pour into glasses. Repeat procedure and serve. **Yield:** 4 servings.

Per serving: About 447 calories, 9g protein, 70g carbohydrate, 17g fat, 5g fiber, 55mg cholesterol, 167mg sodium

◄ **Kid-Friendly**

Prep Time: 15 minutes

Average Rating: ★★★★☆

What other cooks have done:

"I died when I tasted this! I added vanilla ice cream and chocolate milk mix because that's all I had on hand. It was great!"

Getting Your Greens Ready ▼

Choosing, Preparing, and Storing

Choose greens that are free of blemishes and that look lively and fresh picked. To clean, separate the leaves from their base. Fill the sink with cold water. Plunge the leaves into the cold water and gently swish them around with your hands. Let stand in the cold water for a few minutes; then either place them in a salad spinner or lay on paper towels and blot dry. Be sure your greens are completely dry before storing or making your salad. Store greens by loosely wrapping in paper towels and sealing in airtight plastic bags or containers. They will stay fresh for up to a week in your refrigerator.

Dressing Your Greens

When you're ready to make your salad, either tear or cut the leaves into chunks. Mixes of baby lettuces and the greens that have small leaves don't need to be torn or chopped. Now you can combine them with other ingredients like tomatoes, cucumbers, fruit, meats, or whatever strikes your fancy. Remember to always add the vinaigrette or dressing at the last minute or to serve it on the side. This will prevent the fresh crisp greens from becoming limp and wilted.

- *Jennifer Anderson*
For more information, visit **Allrecipes.com**

Fast and Fresh

Who says a quick meal can't be chock-full of nutritious veggies and fresh flavor? Even takeout isn't this quick! Try using precut vegetables for the stir-fry to speed things up even more, and add an authentic touch to the meal by serving Egg Drop Soup. It can be ready in 20 minutes.

Ginger Veggie Stir-Fry

Submitted by: **Karla**

"I just whipped this up one day with veggies I had on hand. Try it with any seasonal veggies. It has a mild ginger flavor that can be enhanced according to taste, and it's filling yet light on the tummy! Tofu may be added. Serve over a bed of steamed jasmine rice."

1	tablespoon cornstarch	¾	cup julienned carrots
1½	cloves garlic, crushed	½	cup halved green beans
2	teaspoons chopped fresh ginger root, divided	2	tablespoons soy sauce
¼	cup vegetable oil, divided	2½	tablespoons water
1	small head broccoli, cut into florets	¼	cup chopped onion
½	cup snow peas or sugar snap peas	½	tablespoon salt
			Hot cooked rice

1. In a large bowl, blend cornstarch, garlic, 1 teaspoon ginger, and 2 tablespoons vegetable oil until cornstarch is dissolved. Mix in broccoli, snow peas, carrots, and green beans, tossing to lightly coat.

2. Heat remaining 2 tablespoons oil in a large skillet or wok over medium heat. Cook vegetables in oil for 2 minutes, stirring constantly to prevent burning. Stir in soy sauce and water. Mix in onion, salt, and remaining 1 teaspoon ginger. Cook until vegetables are tender but still crisp. Serve over hot cooked rice. **Yield:** 6 servings.

Per serving: About 116 calories, 2g protein, 7g carbohydrate, 9g fat, 2g fiber, 0mg cholesterol, 905mg sodium

Chi Tan T'ang (Egg Drop Soup)

Submitted by: **Brian Gillette**
"The best egg drop soup I've ever had! Reheats well in microwave."

8	chicken bouillon cubes	3	tablespoons white vinegar
6	cups hot water	3	eggs, beaten
2	tablespoons cornstarch	1	green onion, minced
2	tablespoons soy sauce		

1. In a large saucepan, dissolve bouillon in hot water. Mix cornstarch with a small amount of water and stir into bouillon. Add soy sauce and vinegar. Bring to a boil and simmer, stirring occasionally. Gradually pour the beaten eggs into the saucepan while stirring soup. Sprinkle with green onions. Serve immediately. **Yield:** 6 servings.

Per serving: About 64 calories, 4g protein, 5g carbohydrate, 3g fat, 0g fiber, 107mg cholesterol, 1880mg sodium

◄ **Restaurant Fare**

Prep Time: 10 minutes

Cook Time: 10 minutes

Average Rating: ★★★★★

What other cooks have done:
"This simple recipe makes an impressive soup. I've found that using only egg whites makes a better swirl."

Mango Cream

Submitted by: **Jacqueline J. Guadalupe**
"This simple recipe makes a wholesome and refreshing summer dessert. Garnish with sliced mango and a sprig of mint."

3	mangoes, unpeeled	¼	cup honey
½	cup heavy cream		

1. In a medium saucepan, place whole, unpeeled mangoes in boiling water and simmer 30 minutes. Remove mangoes from water; let cool until mangoes are cool enough to handle.
2. Remove the skin and pits from the mangoes. Place fruit in a blender and puree until smooth.
3. Beat the cream and honey in a medium bowl until light and fluffy. Fold mango puree into cream mixture until well blended. (Mixture should be thick and smooth.) Pour into dessert bowls; cover and chill at least 2 hours before serving. **Yield:** 6 servings.

Per serving: About 179 calories, 1g protein, 30g carbohydrate, 8g fat, 2g fiber, 27mg cholesterol, 10mg sodium

◄ **Make-Ahead**

Prep Time: 15 minutes

Cook Time: 30 minutes

Chill Time: 2 hours

Average Rating: ★★★★★

What other cooks have done:
"Those who love creamy desserts will rave over this recipe. Here's a tip: It looks fab when garnished with a single maraschino cherry."

Menu

Cuban Midnight Sandwich

Black Bean Soup II

Easy Lemon Bars

Serves 4

Menu Prep Plan

1. Bake Easy Lemon Bars, cool, and store in refrigerator.

2. Prepare and simmer soup until ready to serve.

3. Assemble sandwiches and cook just before serving.

Around-the-World Cuisine ▶

Prep Time: 5 minutes

Cook Time: 5 minutes

Average Rating: ★★★★★

What other cooks have done:

"These are wonderful, the whole family loved them! I used mozzarella cheese and it was just as good as Swiss. I used soft hoagie rolls and spread the mayo mixture on one side, then topped with the cheese, turkey, dill pickle, and ham, then spread the mustard on the side that touched the ham. When pressed in the skillet, the outside gets slightly crusty and the middle is hot and soft."

Soup-and-Sandwich Night

Nothing is more comforting than a soup-and-sandwich feast at the end of a busy day. This mile-high sandwich is packed full of ham, turkey, Swiss cheese, and pickles, making it a feast by itself! And Black Bean Soup starts with canned beans as a big time-saver. Tangy-sweet lemon bars make a nice dessert and will be good packed in lunches the rest of the week.

Cuban Midnight Sandwich

Submitted by: **Maruchy Ramos-Lachance**

"This sandwich is called a 'Media Noche' which translates to 'Midnight.' It makes a wonderful dinner sandwich because it's served hot. A nice side dish is black bean soup or black beans and rice and plantain chips."

½	cup mayonnaise	½	pound thinly sliced cooked ham
2½	tablespoons Italian dressing	½	pound thinly sliced Swiss cheese
4	hoagie rolls, split lengthwise and toasted		
¼	cup prepared mustard	1	cup dill pickle slices
½	pound thinly sliced cooked deli turkey	¼	cup olive oil

1. In a small bowl, mix together mayonnaise and Italian dressing. Spread mixture on bottom half of toasted hoagie rolls. Spread each roll with mustard. On each roll, arrange layers of turkey, ham, and cheese. Top each with dill pickle slices. Add tops and brush tops and bottoms with olive oil.

2. Heat a nonstick skillet over medium–high heat. Place sandwiches in skillet. Cook sandwiches for 2 minutes, pressing down with a plate covered with aluminum foil. Flip and cook for 2 more minutes or until cheese is melted. Remove from heat, place on plates, and cut in half diagonally. **Yield:** 4 servings.

Per serving: About 1068 calories, 45g protein, 38g carbohydrate, 81g fat, 3g fiber, 117mg cholesterol, 2477mg sodium

Black Bean Soup II

Submitted by: **Kathy**

"My family has enjoyed this easy recipe for years and hopefully yours will, too. Garnish with garlic bread, croutons, or chopped cilantro."

1	onion, chopped	1	teaspoon salt
2	cloves garlic, chopped	½	teaspoon ground black pepper
1	green bell pepper, chopped		
1	teaspoon olive oil	⅛	teaspoon ground cumin
2	(15 ounce) cans black beans, rinsed and drained		Olive oil
			Sour cream (optional)
1	cup water		

1. In a Dutch oven, sauté onion, garlic, and green pepper in oil over medium heat until tender. Add beans and water and season with salt, pepper, and cumin. Stir well and simmer for 15 minutes.
2. Pour soup into blender and puree to desired consistency. Return to Dutch oven and reheat over medium-low heat.
3. Pour a few drops of olive oil in bowl for added flavor before serving. Top with sour cream, if desired. **Yield:** 4 servings.

Per serving: About 209 calories, 12g protein, 32g carbohydrate, 3g fat, 12g fiber, 0mg cholesterol, 660mg sodium

◄ **Quick & Easy**

Prep Time: 10 minutes
Cook Time: 30 minutes
Average Rating: ★★★★★
What other cooks have done:
"This is an easy and tasty recipe for a quick black bean soup. I used chicken broth instead of water. I also added a bit of cayenne pepper."

Easy Lemon Bars *(pictured on page 44)*

Submitted by: **Peggy**

"These bars are great and easy to make. Hope you like them!"

1	(18.25 ounce) package lemon cake mix with pudding	1	(8 ounce) package cream cheese, softened
		⅓	cup white sugar
1	egg	1	tablespoon lemon juice
½	cup vegetable oil		

1. Preheat oven to 350°F (175°C).
2. Pour cake mix into a large bowl. Add the egg and oil; mix until well blended. (Mixture will be slightly dry.) Reserve 1 cup for the topping and pat the rest into a greased 9x13 inch pan. Bake in the preheated oven for 15 minutes. Set aside to cool.
3. Meanwhile, in a medium bowl, beat the cream cheese with the sugar and lemon juice until smooth. Spread mixture evenly over the baked crust. Crumble the reserved cake mix mixture over the top.
4. Bake in the preheated oven for 20 to 22 more minutes or until filling is set and the topping is lightly toasted. Cool before cutting into bars. Refrigerate leftovers. **Yield:** 15 servings.

Per serving: About 284 calories, 4g protein, 30g carbohydrate, 17g fat, 0g fiber, 39mg cholesterol, 295mg sodium

◄ **Crowd-Pleaser**

Prep Time: 20 minutes
Cook Time: 37 minutes
Average Rating: ★★★★★
What other cooks have done:
"Yummy! I couldn't find a cake mix with the pudding inside, so I bought a lemon cake mix and added lemon pudding. So tangy and sweet! Everyone at the office loved them!"

Menu

Chicken Tetrazzini
for a Crowd

Blue Ribbon Overnight
Rolls

Toffee Cake

Serves 8

Menu Prep Plan

1. Prepare cake and chill 24 hours.

2. Prepare dough for rolls and chill overnight.

3. Assemble tetrazzini; bake or cover and freeze up to 1 month before baking.

4. Bake rolls and pie just before serving.

Covered-Dish Favorite ▶

Prep Time: 20 minutes

Cook Time: 45 minutes

Average Rating: ★★★★★

What other cooks have done:

"I made two casseroles and served one at home and the other at a school luncheon. I used turkey in place of chicken because I cooked a small bird. The dark and white meat were mouth-watering. The faculty raved and everyone requested a copy of the recipe. My family—5 kids, husband, and myself—inhaled it. Twenty people couldn't be wrong. I added a tablespoon of dry sherry and grated Parmesan on the top with the Cheddar."

Comforting Casserole Dinner

Dive into this make-ahead meal that's nothing short of magic! You can prepare all these dishes ahead—even the rolls—and have an impressive, delectable meal waiting for you.

Chicken Tetrazzini for a Crowd

Submitted by: **Lois Shaw**
"This recipe makes 2 casseroles—you can eat one and freeze the other. You can also use turkey breast."

1 pound spaghetti, broken into pieces	4 cups (16 ounces) shredded Cheddar cheese, divided
2 (8 ounce) packages sliced fresh mushrooms	6 cups cooked and shredded chicken
2 teaspoons olive oil	1 (4 ounce) jar diced pimentos, drained
3 (10.75 ounce) cans condensed cream of mushroom soup	1 cup chicken broth

1. Preheat oven to 350°F (175°C). Bring a large pot of salted water to a boil. Add spaghetti and cook for 8 to 10 minutes or until al dente. Drain and set aside.

2. In a large saucepan, sauté mushrooms in oil over medium-high heat. Add soup and heat over low heat. Add 3 cups shredded cheese and stir together. In a large bowl, combine mushroom soup mixture, the chicken, pimentos, and cooked spaghetti; stir together. Add broth and mix together.

3. Pour mixture into 2 greased 9x13 inch baking dishes. Sprinkle ½ cup shredded cheese on top of each dish and bake in the preheated oven for 25 to 35 minutes or until bubbly. **Yield:** 16 servings.

Per serving: About 374 calories, 31g protein, 27g carbohydrate, 16g fat, 1g fiber, 87mg cholesterol, 1290mg sodium

Blue Ribbon Overnight Rolls

Submitted by: **Pam Vienneau**

"Easy, tasty recipe! There are never any left when I make them."

1	(.25 ounce) package active dry yeast	2	eggs, beaten
1	cup warm milk (110°F/45°C)	½	cup butter, melted
½	cup white sugar	1	teaspoon salt
		3¾	cups all-purpose flour

1. In a large bowl, mix together yeast, milk, and sugar. Let stand at room temperature for 30 minutes.

2. Mix eggs, butter, and salt into yeast mixture. Mix in flour, 2 cups at a time. Cover dough and chill overnight or up to 24 hours.

3. Let dough stand at room temperature 15 minutes. Punch dough down and divide in half. Roll each half into a 12 inch round circle. Cut each round into 12 pie shaped wedges. Roll up each wedge, starting from wide end to the tip. Place on greased baking sheets. Cover and let rise 30 minutes or until doubled.

4. Preheat the oven to 400°F (200°C). Bake in the preheated oven for 10 to 12 minutes or until golden brown. **Yield:** 24 servings.

Per serving: About 138 calories, 3g protein, 21g carbohydrate, 5g fat, 1g fiber, 29mg cholesterol, 147mg sodium

◀ **Classic Comfort Food**

Prep Time: 30 minutes

Cook Time: 12 minutes

Chill Time: 24 hours

Average Rating: ★★★★★

What other cooks have done:

"I made these rolls last year for my first holiday with the future in-laws, and they were a big success—not one left! I brushed mine with melted butter and sprinkled garlic powder on top before baking for a little extra flavor."

Toffee Cake

Submitted by: **Nina**

"With three simple ingredients, you can have a knockout dessert. It takes only minutes to make and is light and delicious. If you're in a rush, you can serve it right away, but it's best if refrigerated for 24 hours to allow the flavors to blend."

1	(10 inch) angel food cake	6	(1.4 ounce) bars chocolate covered English toffee, crushed
1	(12 ounce) container frozen whipped topping, thawed		

1. Split angel food cake in half horizontally.

2. Stir together the whipped topping and the crushed toffee bars. Use to fill and frost cake. Cover and refrigerate cake. **Yield:** 12 servings.

Per serving: About 270 calories, 3g protein, 34g carbohydrate, 14g fat, 1g fiber, 10mg cholesterol, 271mg sodium

◀ **Make-Ahead**

Prep Time: 10 minutes

Chill Time: 24 hours

Average Rating: ★★★★★

What other cooks have done:

"I hollowed out an angel food cake and added toffee bits and mini chocolate chips to the whipped topping. I frosted the top with remaining whipped topping and added crushed toffee candy bars to the top."

Menu Prep Plan

1. Prepare Raspberry Cupcakes and freeze at least 5 hours or overnight.

2. Add ingredients to slow cooker for Barbecued Beef. Cook on High 1 hour; reduce heat to Low and cook 7 to 8 hours. Shred meat and cook 1 more hour on Low.

3. Assemble slaw and chill at least 1 hour.

Slow-Cooker Creation ▶

Prep Time: 20 minutes

Cook Time: 10 hours

Average Rating: ★★★★★

What other cooks have done:

"I put the sauce in a container in the freezer while I'm shredding the beef. The grease hardens on top, and then I can skim it off. Then I return the sauce to the slow cooker with the shredded beef. Excellent!"

Slow-Cooking Creation

Every busy home cook has a best friend—the slow cooker. Throw in your ingredients and forget about it all day until those dinnertime hunger pangs kick in. Make Barbecued Beef in the beginning of the week and you'll have leftovers for sandwiches later in the week. Make the slaw and Raspberry Cupcakes ahead of time too for a truly stress-free meal.

Barbecued Beef

Submitted by: **Corwynn Darkholme**
"This dish is zesty and yummy! Spoon meat onto toasted sandwich buns and top with additional barbecue sauce."

1½ cups ketchup	½ teaspoon salt
¼ cup packed brown sugar	¼ teaspoon ground black pepper
¼ cup red wine vinegar	¼ teaspoon garlic powder
2 tablespoons prepared Dijon-style mustard	1 (4 pound) boneless chuck roast, cut in half
2 tablespoons Worcestershire sauce	
1 teaspoon liquid smoke flavoring	

1. In a slow cooker, combine ketchup, brown sugar, red wine vinegar, Dijon-style mustard, Worcestershire sauce, liquid smoke, salt, pepper, and garlic powder; stir well.
2. Place chuck roast halves in slow cooker. Turn meat to coat with ketchup mixture. Cover and cook on High for 1 hour. Reduce heat to Low and cook 7 to 8 hours.
3. Remove roast, shred with two forks, and return to slow cooker. Stir meat to evenly coat with sauce. Continue cooking on Low approximately 1 hour. **Yield:** 12 servings.

Per serving: About 278 calories, 19g protein, 14g carbohydrate, 17g fat, 0g fiber, 65mg cholesterol, 589mg sodium

Spicy Southwestern Slaw

Submitted by: **Dinah**

"Great topping for tacos—also a nice side dish for any type of Mexican or Tex-Mex entrée! Use green or red cabbage, or a combination of the two."

3	cups shredded cabbage	½	cup canola oil
1	large carrot, shredded	2	tablespoons apple cider vinegar
1	onion, diced		
1	red bell pepper, diced	1	tablespoon white sugar
1	jalapeño pepper, seeded and diced	1	teaspoon cayenne pepper
1	tablespoon chopped fresh cilantro		Salt and pepper to taste

1. In a large bowl, toss together the cabbage, carrot, onion, red pepper, jalapeño, and cilantro. Set aside.

2. In a small bowl, whisk together the oil, vinegar, sugar, cayenne pepper, salt, and pepper. Pour over vegetable mixture and toss to combine. Cover and refrigerate for at least 1 hour. **Yield:** 8 servings.

Per serving: About 152 calories, 1g protein, 7g carbohydrate, 14g fat, 2g fiber, 0mg cholesterol, 156mg sodium

◀ **Make-Ahead**

Prep Time: 15 minutes
Chill Time: 1 hour
Average Rating: ★★★★☆
What other cooks have done:
"Excellent side dish with Mexican main dishes. My family does not like cilantro, so I substituted fresh parsley."

Raspberry Cupcakes

Submitted by: **William "Uncle Bill" Anatooskin**

"Like mini, no-bake cheesecakes. Frozen raspberries can also be used. When thawed, drain some of liquid and use in the raspberry puree."

¾	cup graham cracker crumbs	1	(14 ounce) can sweetened condensed milk
¼	cup chopped pecans		
3	tablespoons butter, melted	1	cup frozen whipped topping, thawed
¾	cup fresh raspberries, crushed		Whole fresh raspberries
½	(8 ounce) package cream cheese, softened		

1. Line a 12 cup muffin pan with paper cup liners. In a medium bowl, combine graham cracker crumbs, pecans, and melted butter, mixing well to blend. Spoon mixture evenly into cup liners. Press mixture with a spoon to firm bottom. Puree crushed raspberries; set aside.

2. Beat cream cheese until fluffy. Add condensed milk and ¼ cup of the raspberry puree and mix until well blended. Fold in whipped topping.

3. Spoon cream cheese mixture evenly into baking cups. Freeze for at least 5 hours. When ready to serve, remove paper liners. Invert cakes onto individual serving plates. Drizzle remaining raspberry puree over cakes. Garnish with whole raspberries. Serve frozen. **Yield:** 12 servings.

Per serving: About 228 calories, 4g protein, 25g carbohydrate, 13g fat, 1g fiber, 29mg cholesterol, 133mg sodium

◀ **Make-Ahead**

Prep Time: 15 minutes
Freeze Time: 5 hours
Average Rating: ★★★★★
What other cooks have done:
"I used the mini-graham cracker crusts, and these were gobbled up in less than an hour!"

Easy Sausage Strata
Bran Muffins
Easy Fruit Dip
assorted fruit
Serves 8

Menu Prep Plan

1. Prepare batter for muffins and chill overnight or up to one week.

2. Assemble strata and chill overnight.

3. Wash fruit and prepare fruit dip; chill until ready to serve.

4. Remove strata from refrigerator 30 minutes before baking; bake and let stand 10 minutes.

5. Bake muffins and serve immediately.

Holiday Fare ▶

Prep Time: 20 minutes

Chill Time: 8 hours

Cook Time: 1 hour

Average Rating: ★★★★★

What other cooks have done:

"I made several of these for a huge holiday brunch. I used sausage in two of them, ham in two, and a smaller vegetarian version. They were the hit of the party! Very simple to make and very tasty, too!"

Breakfast for Dinner

Switch things up for dinner tonight and serve this hearty breakfast-style meal. It would also make a nice weekend brunch for a holiday or special occasion.

Easy Sausage Strata

Submitted by: **Lisa Rosenkrans**
"This strata is really easy to make. Put it together the day before, then just remove from the refrigerator and bake. Ham or bacon can be substituted for the sausage. Sometimes I add chopped cooked broccoli for a change of pace."

1	pound pork sausage	6	eggs
6	(1 ounce) slices bread, cubed	2	cups milk
		1	teaspoon salt
2	cups shredded Cheddar cheese	1	teaspoon powdered mustard

1. Place sausage in a large, deep skillet. Cook over medium–high heat until evenly brown. Drain and set aside.

2. Layer bread cubes, sausage, and Cheddar cheese in a lightly greased 7x11 inch baking dish. In a bowl, beat together the eggs, milk, salt, and mustard. Pour the egg mixture over the bread cube mixture. Cover and refrigerate at least 8 hours or overnight.

3. Remove the casserole from the refrigerator 30 minutes before baking. Preheat oven to 350°F (175°C).

4. Bake 50 to 60 minutes in the preheated oven or until a knife inserted in the center comes out clean. Let stand 10 minutes before serving. **Yield:** 8 servings.

Per serving: About 404 calories, 23g protein, 15g carbohydrate, 27g fat, 1g fiber, 227mg cholesterol, 1165mg sodium

Bran Muffins

Submitted by: **Tammy Elliott**
"This muffin batter can be mixed up ahead of time and kept in the refrigerator for up to one week before baking."

2	cups raisin bran cereal	4	eggs
4	cups whole bran cereal	4	cups buttermilk
2	cups boiling water	5	cups all-purpose flour
1	cup shortening	5	teaspoons baking soda
3	cups white sugar	1½	teaspoons salt

1. Mix cereal and boiling water together in a metal bowl and cool.
2. Cream shortening, sugar, and eggs in a large bowl. Add buttermilk and cooled cereal mixture. Combine flour, baking soda, and salt; stir into the creamed mixture just until flour is moistened. Batter should be lumpy. Cover and chill overnight or up to 1 week.
3. Preheat oven to 375°F (195°C). Spoon batter into muffin tins, being careful not to mix or stir batter. Bake in the preheated oven 15 minutes. Remove muffins from pans immediately and cool on wire racks. **Yield:** 36 servings.

Per serving: About 218 calories, 4g protein, 36g carbohydrate, 7g fat, 2g fiber, 25mg cholesterol, 352mg sodium

◄ Family Favorite

Prep Time: 30 minutes
Chill Time: 8 hours
Cook Time: 15 minutes
Average Rating: ★★★★★
What other cooks have done:
"For a great variation, we added a spoonful of raspberry jam near the middle of the muffins as we were filling the cups with batter. The cooking time is the same, but you end up with a sweet surprise in every muffin."

Easy Fruit Dip

Submitted by: **Natalie L.**
"This easy and delicious fruit dip is always a hit, and the kids love it. Slice up a selection of fruit and snacks to serve with the dip. My family likes apples, strawberries, cantaloupe, grapes, pretzels, raisin bread, or muffins."

1	(8 ounce) package cream cheese, softened	1	tablespoon maraschino cherry juice
2	(7 ounce) jars marshmallow cream		

1. Place cream cheese and marshmallow cream in a microwave-safe bowl. Place in microwave and cook on medium-high in 20 second intervals until softened.
2. Stir cherry juice into the cream cheese mixture. Cover and refrigerate until chilled. **Yield:** 12 servings.

Per serving: About 117 calories, 1g protein, 29g carbohydrate, 7g fat, 0g fiber, 21mg cholesterol, 76mg sodium

◄ Quick & Easy

Prep Time: 5 minutes
Average Rating: ★★★★★
What other cooks have done:
"Sinfully delicious! I added a container of raspberry yogurt since I didn't have cherry juice. I also whipped the cream cheese in my mixer, heated the marshmallow cream alone for 20 seconds in the microwave, and then poured it into the mixer."

**Restaurant–Style
Chicken Nachos**

salad greens

Vinaigrette

ice cream

Sue's Hot Fudge Sauce

Serves 4

Menu Prep Plan

1. Assemble nachos and bake.

2. Prepare greens and vinaigrette.

3. Prepare hot fudge sauce and serve with ice cream or chill until ready to serve.

Party Food ▶

Prep Time: 30 minutes

Cook Time: 10 minutes

Average Rating: ★★★★★

What other cooks have done:

"These really did taste like they were from a restaurant. I seasoned the chicken with taco seasoning, added some refried beans, and served with sour cream! My hubby and I ate them for a meal."

Nacho Night

Friday night supper has never been this fun! Serve up a hearty helping of nachos topped with leftover shredded chicken, cheese, tomatoes, and onions. A side salad completes the meal. And don't forget simple, homemade hot fudge sauce over ice cream for dessert. Have fun and let everyone make their own sundaes.

Restaurant-Style Chicken Nachos

Submitted by: **Laura**

"This delicious and simple recipe is hearty enough for a meal. The key is the meat filling—it also makes a great filling for tacos and quesadillas. This recipe can be modified to meet your taste. I recommend serving it with sour cream and guacamole. Be creative!"

3	cloves garlic, crushed	2	cups salsa
8	green onions, sliced, white parts and tops separated	1	(12 ounce) package tortilla chips
3	tablespoons canola oil	1	(8 ounce) package shredded Cheddar/Monterey Jack cheese blend
2	boneless, skinless chicken breasts, cooked and shredded	1	large tomato, diced
	Salt and pepper to taste		

1. Preheat oven to 350°F (175°C).

2. In a 12 inch skillet over medium heat, cook and stir the garlic and white parts of the green onions in canola oil until tender. Mix in shredded chicken, salt, and pepper. Toss until well coated with oil. Stir in the salsa.

3. Arrange tortilla chips on large baking sheets. Spoon the chicken mixture over tortilla chips. Top with cheese and tomato. Bake in the preheated oven 10 minutes or until cheese has melted. Remove from heat and sprinkle with green onion tops before serving. **Yield:** 4 servings.

Per serving: About 873 calories, 35g protein, 70g carbohydrate, 53g fat, 9g fiber, 92mg cholesterol, 1913mg sodium

Vinaigrette

Submitted by: **Karen Castle**

"This is simple to make and delicious, especially if you like garlic."

½	cup red wine vinegar	2	teaspoons white sugar
½	cup vegetable oil	2	teaspoons salt
1	clove garlic, crushed		

1. In a jar with a tight fitting lid, combine vinegar, oil, garlic, sugar, and salt. Shake well and refrigerate until ready to use. **Yield:** 1 cup.

Per 2 tablespoons: About 130 calories, 0g protein, 2g carbohydrate, 14g fat, 0g fiber, 0mg cholesterol, 581mg sodium

Sue's Hot Fudge Sauce

Submitted by: **Lisa Kreft**

"Decadently thick and delicious hot fudge sauce. Simple to make and so much better than store-bought!"

1	cup butter	1	(12 ounce) can evaporated milk
⅓	cup unsweetened cocoa powder	1	teaspoon vanilla extract
3	cups white sugar		

1. Combine butter, cocoa, sugar, and evaporated milk in a saucepan over medium heat. Bring to a boil and boil for 7 minutes. Remove from heat; stir in vanilla. Carefully pour hot mixture into a blender and blend for 2 to 4 minutes. Serve immediately and store any leftovers in refrigerator. **Yield:** 16 servings.

Per serving: About 280 calories, 2g protein, 41g carbohydrate, 13g fat, 1g fiber, 37mg cholesterol, 140mg sodium

◄ **Quick & Easy**

Prep Time: 5 minutes

Average Rating: ★★★★★

What other cooks have done:

"This vinaigrette has become my absolute favorite. I particularly like it on romaine lettuce with tomatoes, red or yellow peppers, red onion, feta cheese, and toasted almonds. Every time I've made this salad I've had rave reviews."

◄ **Kid-Friendly**

Prep Time: 4 minutes

Cook Time: 7 minutes

Average Rating: ★★★★★

What other cooks have done:

"Wow! I've tried a number of hot fudge sauces and this one beats them all. The cocoa made it so easy, and it has such a smooth, velvety texture. I purchased canning jars at the neighborhood hardware store, added a piece of holiday fabric under the lid, and gave them to neighbors as a Christmas treat."

Farfalle with Asparagus and Smoked Salmon

Tomato Cucumber Salad

Lemon Ice

Serves 4

Menu Prep Plan

1. Prepare Lemon Ice and freeze until ready to serve.

2. Assemble Farfalle with Asparagus and Smoked Salmon and chill at least 2 hours. Let stand until room temperature before serving.

3. Prepare tomato salad and chill until ready to serve.

Healthy ▶

Prep Time: 10 minutes

Cook Time: 20 minutes

Chill Time: 2 hours

Average Rating: ★★★★☆

What other cooks have done:

"This is a great dish for a dinner party—no muss, no fuss, and it can be made a bit ahead so the cook can enjoy the company. I threw in some cherry tomatoes for added color and flavor."

Light and Easy Leftovers

Fresh herbs and vegetables take center stage in this deceptively simple meal. Take last night's smoked salmon and give it a face-lift as it's mixed with pasta, asparagus, pistachio nuts, and fresh basil. And enjoy the bounty of your summer garden with a simple tomato cucumber salad that serves as a fitting side to the meal. Refreshingly cool Lemon Ice caps off this summertime meal in style.

Farfalle with Asparagus and Smoked Salmon

Submitted by: **Myra**

"This is a light summer pasta salad that utilizes only a few ingredients, but is very tasty. I eat it year-round because it's low fat and super tasty!"

1	(8 ounce) package farfalle (bow tie) pasta	1	tablespoon chopped fresh basil
½	cup fresh asparagus tips	1	tablespoon extra virgin olive oil
2	ounces smoked salmon, chopped		Salt and pepper to taste
1	lemon, juiced		
1	tablespoon chopped pistachio nuts		

1. In a large pot of salted boiling water, cook pasta until al dente; rinse under cold water and drain.

2. Steam the asparagus over boiling water and cook until tender but still firm. Drain, cool, and coarsely chop.

3. In a large bowl, combine the pasta, asparagus, smoked salmon, lemon juice, pistachios, basil, olive oil, salt, and pepper. Mix well and refrigerate for 2 hours. Remove from refrigerator and serve at room temperature. **Yield:** 4 servings.

Per serving: About 272 calories, 11g protein, 44g carbohydrate, 6g fat, 2g fiber, 3mg cholesterol, 392mg sodium

Tomato Cucumber Salad

Submitted by: **Sowmya**

"A simple, refreshing salad that accompanies any type of food."

2	tomatoes, chopped		Ground black pepper to taste
1	cucumber, peeled and diced		
1	onion, chopped	1	tablespoon lemon juice
	Salt to taste		

1. Combine tomatoes, cucumber, and onion in a salad bowl. Season to taste with salt and black pepper. Sprinkle with lemon juice; cover and chill. **Yield:** 4 servings.

Per serving: About 33 calories, 1g protein, 7g carbohydrate, 0g fat, 2g fiber, 0mg cholesterol, 9mg sodium

◄ **Quick & Easy**

Prep Time: 10 minutes

Average Rating: ★★★★★

What other cooks have done:

"This is a delicious salad that tastes great with Indian food. I like to add some chopped fresh cilantro or mint leaves."

Lemon Ice

Submitted by: **Barbara**

"An easy citrus ice. I often use oranges instead."

1	lemon, zested and juiced	2	cups white sugar
1	lemon, juiced	4	cups milk

1. In a medium bowl, stir together lemon juice and zest with sugar until smooth. Stir in milk. Pour into a 9x9 inch dish; cover and freeze, stirring once when it begins to harden, until firm (about 2 hours). **Yield:** 10 servings.

Note: You can also pour the lemon mixture into the freezer canister of an ice cream maker and freeze according to manufacturer's directions.

Per serving: About 208 calories, 4g protein, 47g carbohydrate, 2g fat, 1g fiber, 8mg cholesterol, 50mg sodium

◄ **Family Favorite**

Prep Time: 10 minutes

Freeze Time: 2 hours

Average Rating: ★★★★★

What other cooks have done:

"Here's a tip for zesting a lemon: Use a vegetable peeler to remove the paper-thin layer of lemon peel. Put these strips of lemon peel in a food processor along with the sugar from the recipe. Pulse the food processor until the lemon peel is in bits. Works great and is extremely quick. No more grated knuckles!"

Menu

Busy Night Turkey Taco Soup with Avocado Cream

Mexican Cornbread II

Double Layer Chocolate Peanut Butter Pie

Serves 4

Menu Prep Plan

1. Prepare pie and chill at least 4 hours.

2. Prepare cornbread batter and bake.

3. Prepare and simmer soup until ready to serve. Top with Avocado Cream just before serving.

Classic Comfort Food ▶

Prep Time: 10 minutes

Cook Time: 20 minutes

Average Rating: ★★★★★

What other cooks have done:

"If you like Tex-Mex style food, you'll love this recipe! Like others, I modified the recipe slightly—spicing it up a bit by adding jalapeños and green chiles. For a fresher taste, I added more cilantro. I found it to be easy to make, and my family found it to be very tasty—going back for seconds and thirds."

Tired of Turkey-and-Dressing Dinner

Tired of Thanksgiving leftovers and turkey sandwiches for days on end? Look no further. This winning soup will add the zip back into your culinary repertoire and get you out of that holiday rut. Serve with spicy cornbread and irresistible peanut butter pie for dessert and watch everyone come back for seconds.

Busy Night Turkey Taco Soup with Avocado Cream

Submitted by: **Janice Elder**

"My family loves Tex-Mex dishes, and I love quick and convenient but healthy and interesting dishes, so this soup fits the bill in every way. No one can believe that this hasn't simmered for a long time, as the flavors blend beautifully. If I don't have guacamole on hand, I blend green chiles with the sour cream—it's very adaptable. Serve with tortilla chips!"

1	(11 ounce) can Mexican-style corn	2½	cups cooked, chopped turkey
1	(16 ounce) can chili beans, undrained		Salt and pepper to taste
2	(14.5 ounce) cans chicken broth	¼	cup chopped fresh cilantro
1	(16 ounce) jar chunky salsa	½	cup low-fat sour cream
		2	tablespoons guacamole

1. In a large pot over medium heat, combine corn, chili beans, broth, and salsa. Bring to a boil and reduce heat; stir in cooked turkey. Season with salt and pepper. Cover and cook 5 to 10 minutes more until heated through. Stir in cilantro.

2. In a bowl, stir together sour cream and guacamole until smooth.

3. Ladle soup into bowls and top with guacamole mixture.

Yield: 4 servings.

Per serving: About 410 calories, 38g protein, 44g carbohydrate, 12g fat, 9g fiber, 79mg cholesterol, 2209mg sodium

Mexican Cornbread II

Submitted by: **Bea**
"Moist, spicy cornbread that's so simple to make and tastes so good!"

1	(8.5 ounce) package self-rising cornmeal mix	1	cup shredded Monterey Jack cheese
1	egg	1	(4.5 ounce) can chopped green chiles, drained
½	cup milk		
1	(8 ounce) can cream-style corn		

1. Preheat oven to 400°F (200°C). Lightly grease a 9x9 inch baking pan.
2. Place cornmeal mix in a large bowl. Stir in egg, milk, corn, cheese, and chiles. Spread batter into prepared pan.
3. Bake in the preheated oven for 25 minutes or until golden brown and cornbread pulls away from sides of pan. **Yield:** 12 servings.

Per serving: About 128 calories, 5g protein, 18g carbohydrate, 4g fat, 2g fiber, 27mg cholesterol, 471mg sodium

◄ Family Favorite

Prep Time: 10 minutes
Cook Time: 25 minutes
Average Rating: ★★★★☆
What other cooks have done:
"This was very good and easy. For more sweetness, try adding a little sugar! And, to spice it up a bit, add some diced jalapeño pepper."

Double Layer Chocolate Peanut Butter Pie

Submitted by: **R. Johnson**
"This is a very easy pie to whip up. It tastes great and is always a favorite with children and adults alike!"

½	(8 ounce) package cream cheese, softened	2	(3.9 ounce) packages instant chocolate pudding mix
1	tablespoon white sugar	2	cups cold milk
1	tablespoon cold milk	4	peanut butter cups, chopped
1	cup peanut butter		
1	(8 ounce) container frozen whipped topping, thawed		
1	(9 ounce) prepared graham cracker crust		

1. In a large bowl, mix cream cheese, sugar, 1 tablespoon milk, and peanut butter until smooth. Gently stir in 1½ cups of whipped topping. Spread mixture on bottom of pie crust.
2. In a second bowl, stir pudding mix with 2 cups milk until thick. Immediately stir in remaining whipped topping. Spread mixture over peanut butter layer.
3. Scatter chopped peanut butter cups over pie. Cover and refrigerate for at least 4 hours. **Yield:** 8 servings.

Per serving: About 646 calories, 14g protein, 66g carbohydrate, 38g fat, 3g fiber, 21mg cholesterol, 811mg sodium

◄ Kid-Friendly

Prep Time: 20 minutes
Chill Time: 4 hours
Average Rating: ★★★★★
What other cooks have done:
"Great recipe! And for a low-fat version, I used reduced-fat peanut butter and sugar-free, fat-free pudding mix, and it still tasted great. Thanks for the recipe!"

Menu

**Spinach Salad
with Peaches and Pecans**

Quick Gnocchi

Gorgonzola Sauce

Easiest Focaccia

Serves 4

Menu Prep Plan

1. Prepare focaccia and bake.

2. Make Gorgonzola Sauce and simmer over low heat while preparing gnocchi.

3. Prepare gnocchi and boil.

4. Toast pecans for salad; assemble and dress salad just before serving.

Out-of-the-Ordinary ▶

Prep Time: 10 minutes

Cook Time: 10 minutes

Average Rating: ★★★★★

What other cooks have done:

"I also make a variation of this using strawberries and pink grapefruit sections. The color of the peaches against the spinach was beautiful."

Restaurant Fare ▶

Prep Time: 20 minutes

Cook Time: 15 minutes

Average Rating: ★★★★★

What other cooks have done:

"Awesome comfort food—very quick and easy. I didn't even have to make a trip to the store. Try it with some caramelized onions and butter for a deeper flavor."

Easy Gourmet

Step out of the usual and turn dinnertime into a grand dining experience. These quick recipes promise sublime flavor without lengthy ingredient lists required of many gourmet recipes.

Spinach Salad with Peaches and Pecans

Submitted by: **Robin Durawa**

"A perfect summer salad with ripe peaches, baby spinach, and roasted pecans."

¾　cup pecans
2　ripe peaches
4　cups baby spinach, rinsed
　　and dried

¼　cup poppy seed salad
　　dressing

1. Preheat oven to 350°F (175°C). Arrange pecans in a single layer on a baking sheet and roast in the preheated oven for 7 to 10 minutes or until they just begin to darken. Remove from oven and set aside.
2. Peel peaches and slice into bite-size segments. Combine peaches, spinach, and pecans in a large bowl. Toss with dressing until evenly coated, adding additional dressing, if desired. **Yield:** 4 servings.

Per serving: About 262 calories, 3g protein, 14g carbohydrate, 23g fat, 4g fiber, 5mg cholesterol, 130mg sodium

Quick Gnocchi

Submitted by: **Sandy Metzler**

"An easy version of an Italian favorite, using instant mashed potatoes."

2　cups dry potato flakes
2　cups boiling water
2　eggs, beaten
2　teaspoons salt

¼　teaspoon ground black
　　pepper
3　cups all-purpose flour

1. Place potato flakes in a medium-size bowl. Pour in boiling water; stir until blended. Let cool.
2. Stir in eggs, salt, and pepper. Blend in enough flour to make a fairly stiff dough. Turn dough out on a well-floured board. Knead lightly.
3. Divide dough in half. Shape each half into a long thin roll. With a knife dipped in flour, cut into bite-size pieces.
4. Place a few gnocchi in boiling water. As the gnocchi rise to the top of the pot, remove them with a slotted spoon. Repeat until all are cooked. **Yield:** 4 servings.

Per serving: About 468 calories, 15g protein, 90g carbohydrate, 4g fat, 4g fiber, 123mg cholesterol, 1233mg sodium

Gorgonzola Sauce

Submitted by: **Amy**

"This extremely easy and quick pasta sauce is also good with cooked chicken or shrimp. For a lower fat version, substitute half-and-half for the cream and add a teaspoon of cornstarch for thickening."

1½	cups dry white wine	4	ounces Gorgonzola cheese, crumbled
1¼	cups heavy cream		Pinch ground nutmeg
2	tablespoons grated Parmesan cheese		Black pepper to taste

1. In medium saucepan, cook white wine over high heat until reduced by half. Add cream, reduce heat, and cook until reduced by one-third. Add Parmesan, Gorgonzola, nutmeg, and pepper to taste. Stir until cheeses melt and sauce is creamy. **Yield:** 4 servings.

Per serving: About 432 calories, 9g protein, 4g carbohydrate, 36g fat, 0g fiber, 134mg cholesterol, 362mg sodium

◄ Company is Coming

Prep Time: 10 minutes

Cook Time: 20 minutes

Average Rating: ★★★★★

What other cooks have done:

"This was very good. It was balanced and light, not overpowering like some Gorgonzola sauces. I used half-and-half, and it came out fine."

Easiest Focaccia

Submitted by: **Sam**

"Great for sandwiches and snacks. You can use more or less olive oil or salt if you wish."

1	teaspoon white sugar	2	cups all-purpose flour
1	(.25 ounce) package active dry yeast	2	tablespoons olive oil
½	cup warm water (110°F/45°C)	½	teaspoon salt

1. In a small bowl, dissolve sugar and yeast in warm water. Let stand until creamy, about 10 minutes.
2. In a large bowl, combine the yeast mixture with flour; stir well to combine. Stir in additional water, 1 tablespoon at a time, until all of the flour is absorbed. When the dough has pulled together, turn it out onto a lightly floured surface and knead briefly for about 2 minutes.
3. Place dough in a lightly oiled bowl and turn to coat dough with oil. Cover with a damp cloth and let rise in a warm place until doubled in volume, about 25 minutes.
4. Preheat oven to 475°F (245°C). Punch the dough down and turn it out onto a lightly floured surface; knead briefly. Pat or roll the dough to ¼ inch thickness into a 9x13 inch rectangle and place on a lightly greased baking sheet. Brush the dough with olive oil and sprinkle with salt.
5. Bake in the preheated oven for 12 to 15 minutes. **Yield:** 4 servings.

Per serving: About 296 calories, 7g protein, 49g carbohydrate, 7g fat, 2g fiber, 0mg cholesterol, 296mg sodium

◄ Family Favorite

Prep Time: 10 minutes

Rise Time: 25 minutes

Cook Time: 15 minutes

Average Rating: ★★★★☆

What other cooks have done:

"I have made this delicious recipe numerous times. I have mixed in Italian seasoning and garlic powder in the flour mixture for some extra flavor. I've even mixed in olives with the dough and put cheese and veggies on top."

Menu Prep Plan

1. Prepare Apple Delight and bake.
2. Boil potatoes and mash before serving.
3. Prepare pork chops and sauce.

Classic Comfort Food ▶

Prep Time: 15 minutes

Cook Time: 10 minutes

Average Rating: ★★★★☆

What other cooks have done:

"I like to grill the chops. Then I melt the butter in a saucepan and add the honey and pecans. Generously spoon the sauce over the grilled chops."

Holiday Fare ▶

Prep Time: 10 minutes

Cook Time: 30 minutes

Average Rating: ★★★★★

What other cooks have done:

"We love nutritious sweet potatoes, and this one is flavorful and easy to prepare. You can also replace the maple syrup with ¼ cup of brown sugar and ½ cup of honey!"

Budget-Friendly Meal

Comfort food at a comforting price—what could be better? With just a few ingredients, many of which you probably have on hand, you can have a family-style meal that will taste like a million bucks.

Awesome Honey Pecan Pork Chops

Submitted by: **Karena**
"This recipe is both unbelievably easy and indescribably delicious. It takes only a few minutes to prepare. Just cook the chops in butter, and then heat honey and pecans in the drippings to make the sauce."

½ cup all-purpose flour	2 tablespoons butter
Salt and pepper to taste	¼ cup honey
1¼ pounds boneless pork chops, pounded thin	¼ cup chopped pecans

1. In a shallow dish, mix together flour, salt, and pepper. Dredge pork chops in the flour mixture.
2. In a large skillet, melt butter over medium–high heat. Add chops and brown both sides. Transfer to a warm plate.
3. Mix honey and pecans into the pan drippings. Heat through, stirring constantly. Pour sauce over chops. **Yield:** 4 servings.

Per serving: About 523 calories, 31g protein, 30g carbohydrate, 31g fat, 1g fiber, 101mg cholesterol, 119mg sodium

Mashed Sweet Potatoes

Submitted by: **Rainspirit**
"You're just four ingredients away from sweet potato heaven!"

6 sweet potatoes, peeled and cubed	¾ cup maple syrup
½ cup butter	¾ cup milk

1. Bring a large pot of salted water to a boil. Add potatoes and cook 20 to 30 minutes or until tender.
2. With an electric mixer on low, blend potatoes. Add butter and maple syrup. Blend until smooth. Slowly add enough milk until desired consistency. Serve warm. **Yield:** 6 servings.

Per serving: About 391 calories, 3g protein, 60g carbohydrate, 16g fat, 2g fiber, 44mg cholesterol, 192mg sodium

Apple Delight

Submitted by: **Paula Anderson**

"For a quick-to-make excellent treat, try this yummy apple dessert that melts in your mouth."

2	(21 ounce) cans apple pie filling	¼	cup butter, melted
1	(18.25 ounce) package yellow cake mix		

1. Preheat oven to 350°F (175°C).
2. Pour apple pie filling into a lightly greased 9x13 inch pan. Sprinkle cake mix over apples. Drizzle melted butter on top. Bake in the preheated oven for 30 minutes. Serve hot or cold. **Yield:** 18 servings.

Per serving: About 213 calories, 1g protein, 40g carbohydrate, 6g fat, 1g fiber, 7mg cholesterol, 244mg sodium

◀ **Quick & Easy**

Prep Time: 5 minutes

Cook Time: 30 minutes

Average Rating: ★★★★★

What other cooks have done:
"Here's another variation. I make this recipe with 2 large cans of peaches with light syrup. The syrup from the peaches bubbles through the cake mix and butter, forming a crust on top. I always serve mine warm with vanilla ice cream!"

Rediscover Sweet Potatoes ▼

There's at least one day of the year when sweet potatoes will grace every table. Thanksgiving dinner almost always brings with it a sweet potato dish—usually a casserole adorned with loads of sugar, butter, and perhaps marshmallows, too. Don't relegate sweet potatoes to purely Thanksgiving fodder, though! Once you discover some new preparations for these nutritious, sweet spuds, you'll want to incorporate them into your everyday cooking.

Yam I Am—Not!

There's a lot of confusion about the difference between sweet potatoes and yams. Some sweet potatoes have a yellow flesh that's dry and crumbly—similar to that of a Russet potato. What many of us refer to as yams—the ones with the moist, sweet, bright orange flesh—are actually just another variety of sweet potato. Real yams are not even related to sweet potatoes, and yams don't taste particularly sweet.

Picking Potatoes

Sweet potatoes are packed with nutrition: They're high in vitamins A and C, not to mention iron, potassium, and fiber. Available from mid-fall to mid-winter, sweet potatoes do not store as well as white potatoes, so buy them when they're in season and enjoy them within a week. Choose sweet potatoes that are firm, with unwrinkled skin and no bruises or soft spots. Store them in a cool, dry place in a container that's open to the air. Never refrigerate raw sweet potatoes, or they will develop a hard core in the middle and their flavor will deteriorate.

Beyond the Marshmallow

The innate sweetness of sweet potatoes makes them a natural match for ingredients we usually associate with desserts, like brown sugar, vanilla, cinnamon, honey, maple syrup, ginger, coconut, nutmeg, pineapple, pecans, and fruit juices. In addition to the traditional casseroles, sweet potatoes make delicious pies, puddings, and quick breads. Their inherent sweetness also makes them a delicious contrast to savory ingredients like cumin, coriander, lime juice, beans, cheese, herbs, garlic, and onions.

Sweet Potato Possibilities

You can use sweet potatoes in just about any place you would use white potatoes: Try them mashed, toss them in a pot of soup, bake them and top with sour cream and chives, use them in potato salad, make them into French fries, use them for latkes—have fun with all the possibilities! For a quick side dish, peel and shred some sweet potatoes and sauté them with a little butter or olive oil. Season simply with salt and pepper, and maybe a splash of balsamic vinegar or a sprinkle of herbs or shredded cheese. Eat them as a side dish with any meat, or toss them with pasta. Sweet potatoes also taste great raw! Cut them into sticks for a new addition to the veggie platter, or shred them for salads. - *Jennifer Anderson*

For more information, visit **Allrecipes.com**

Menu Prep Plan

1. Puree fruit for soup and chill until ready to serve with crumbled cookie topping.

2. Prepare tuna and assemble salad.

Healthy ▶

Prep Time: 10 minutes

Cook Time: 8 minutes

Average Rating: ★★★★★

What other cooks have done:

"Easy, fast, and delicious! A new spicy favorite! My husband and I had it with rice and a citrus salad for a complete meal! Try it grilled, too!"

Super Quick Dinner

When you're short on time, you don't have to sacrifice great flavor and nutrition for your hectic schedule. So, throw away those take-out boxes and get ready for a handsome meal that will be ready in a flash. Tuna steaks that are quickly blackened adorn a bed of colorful salad greens. For dessert, the natural sweetness of melon and blueberries flavors a silky-smooth soup that gets a fun topping of crunchy oatmeal cookies.

Blackened Tuna *(pictured on facing page)*

Submitted by: **Denys**
"It may seem simple, but it's my favorite way to have tuna. Seared fish steaks are a Cajun tradition."

1½	pounds (1-inch-thick) fresh tuna steaks	2	tablespoons olive oil
¼	cup Cajun seasoning	2	tablespoons butter

1. Coat tuna with Cajun seasoning.
2. Heat oil and butter in a large skillet over high heat. When oil is nearly smoking, place steaks in pan. Cook on 1 side for 3 to 4 minutes, or until blackened. Turn steaks, and cook for 3 to 4 minutes, or to desired doneness. **Yield:** 6 servings.

Per serving: About 243 calories, 27g protein, 1g carbohydrate, 14g fat, 0g fiber, 54mg cholesterol, 557mg sodium

Blackened Tuna, facing page, and
Salad de Colores, page 45

BBQ Chicken Pizza, page 14, and
Casa Dressing, page 15

Chocolate Earthquake Cake II, page 49

Beef and Parmesan Pasta, page 48, and
Garlic Croutons, page 49

Easy Cajun Jambalaya,
page 46

Oaxacan Tacos, page 89, and
Santa Fe Rice Salad, page 90

Hot Spiced Cider, page 60,
and Cinnamon-Roasted Almonds,
page 62

Totally Groovy Chocolate Fondue,
page 63

Chutney Baked Brie,
page 61

Cranberry Bars, page 64, and
Pecan Tassies, page 62

Easy Lemon Bars, page 19

Salad de Colores *(pictured on page 37)*

Submitted by: **L. Stafford**
"This kaleidoscope of a salad is bursting with color and nutrients! Use organic whenever possible and a balsamic vinaigrette salad dressing."

1	(10 ounce) bag fresh spinach	3	tablespoons balsamic vinaigrette salad dressing
½	medium head red cabbage, shredded (about 3 cups)	3	tablespoons pumpkin seeds or slivered almonds (optional)
2	large carrots, sliced		
1	red bell pepper, chopped		

1. In a large bowl, combine the spinach, cabbage, carrots, and bell pepper. Add enough salad dressing to coat. Toss and sprinkle with pumpkin seeds, if desired. **Yield:** 5 servings.

Per serving: About 92 calories, 5g protein, 17g carbohydrate, 2g fat, 5g fiber, 0mg cholesterol, 213mg sodium

Honeydew-Blueberry Soup

Submitted by: **J. Carlson**
"A cold soup of honeydew and blueberries. Top with whipped topping, if desired."

1	honeydew melon	6	oatmeal cookies
1	pint blueberries		

1. Cut the melon into chunks. Puree in a food processor or blender until smooth. Pour into a large bowl; gently stir blueberries into pureed melon. Chill until cold.
2. To serve, ladle soup into individual bowls and crumble an oatmeal cookie over each serving. **Yield:** 6 servings.

Per serving: About 180 calories, 2g protein, 39g carbohydrate, 3g fat, 4g fiber, 0mg cholesterol, 83mg sodium

Menu

**Easy Cajun Jambalaya
crusty bread
Bread Pudding with
Whiskey Sauce**
Serves 6

Menu Prep Plan

1. Prepare bread pudding and bake. Pour sauce over pudding 5 minutes before serving.

2. Prepare jambalaya and serve with bread.

Crowd-Pleaser ▶

Prep Time: 15 minutes

Cook Time: 26 minutes

Average Rating: ★★★★☆

What other cooks have done:

"My husband and I loved it! I substituted turkey kielbasa for the real thing in order to cut down on some fat. I also added a tablespoon of Cajun seasoning for that New Orleans kick!"

Cajun Creation

Head South for the full-bodied flavors of Cajun cuisine with this unforgettable meal. Served with crusty bread, jambalaya is a one-dish meal that will satisfy the biggest appetites from here to Cajun country. Finish off the meal with a classic dessert—bread pudding that's drenched in a creamy whiskey sauce.

Easy Cajun Jambalaya *(pictured on page 40)*

Submitted by: **Grant Michel**

"I have always loved Cajun foods but my wife doesn't like the 'kick.' In response to this, I made my traditional jambalaya without the heat. Everyone loved this recipe, and I hope you will, too. Enjoy!"

2	teaspoons olive oil	½	teaspoon onion powder
2	skinless, boneless chicken breasts, cut into bite-size pieces	¾	teaspoon salt
		¼	teaspoon ground black pepper
8	ounces kielbasa, diced	2	cups uncooked white rice
1	onion, diced	4	cups chicken broth
1	green bell pepper, diced	3	bay leaves
½	cup diced celery	4	teaspoons Worcestershire sauce
2	tablespoons chopped garlic		
¼	teaspoon cayenne pepper	2	teaspoons hot pepper sauce

1. Heat oil in a large saucepan over medium–high heat. Sauté chicken breasts and kielbasa until lightly browned, about 5 minutes. Stir in onion, bell pepper, celery, and garlic. Season with cayenne, onion powder, salt, and pepper. Cook 3 minutes or until onion is tender and translucent.

2. Add rice; stir in chicken broth, bay leaves, Worcestershire sauce, and hot pepper sauce. Bring to a boil, reduce heat, cover, and simmer 18 minutes or until rice is tender. Discard bay leaves before serving.

Yield: 6 servings.

Per serving: About 500 calories, 30g protein, 59g carbohydrate, 15g fat, 2g fiber, 71mg cholesterol, 1174mg sodium

Bread Pudding with Whiskey Sauce

Submitted by: **Cherry**

"This is the best bread pudding I've ever eaten! My husband wants me to make it every weekend for Sunday brunch."

2 eggs, beaten	1 cup chopped pecans
3 tablespoons butter, melted	½ cup white sugar
2 tablespoons vanilla extract	½ cup butter
2½ cups milk	½ cup heavy cream
¼ cup white sugar	¼ cup whiskey
1 (1 pound) loaf French bread, cut into 1 inch cubes	

1. Preheat oven to 325°F (165°C). Lightly grease a 9x13 inch pan.

2. In a large bowl, stir together eggs, 3 tablespoons butter, vanilla, and milk. Gradually add ¼ cup sugar and mix thoroughly until sugar is dissolved.

3. Place bread cubes in prepared pan. Pour liquid over bread, fully saturating all bread. Sprinkle pecans on top.

4. Bake in the preheated oven for 1 hour or until golden. Meanwhile, combine ½ cup white sugar, ½ cup butter, cream, and whiskey in a small saucepan. Warm over medium-low heat, stirring constantly, until sauce is gently boiling. Pour sauce over baked bread pudding. Let stand 5 minutes before serving. **Yield:** 8 servings.

Per serving: About 604 calories, 11g protein, 55g carbohydrate, 36g fat, 3g fiber, 122mg cholesterol, 562mg sodium

◄ **Classic Comfort Food**

Prep Time: 20 minutes

Cook Time: 1 hour

Average Rating: ★★★★★

What other cooks have done:

"I thought this was absolutely fabulous but I added raisins, cinnamon, and nutmeg to the recipe. These additions definitely made the recipe terrific. I especially liked the whiskey sauce!"

Menu

Beef and Parmesan Pasta

tossed salad

Garlic Croutons

Chocolate Earthquake Cake II

Serves 6

Menu Prep Plan

1. Prepare and bake cake and let stand until ready to serve.

2. Prepare pasta and simmer; meanwhile, assemble and bake croutons.

3. Top pasta with Parmesan cheese and serve; dress salad greens and serve with croutons.

Family Favorite ▶

Prep Time: 30 minutes

Cook Time: 30 minutes

Average Rating: ★★★★★

What other cooks have done:

"It's always nice to find some really good meals that the whole family will enjoy! Feel free to substitute other vegetables for the zucchini."

Perfecto Pasta

Your whole family will cheer for this pleasing pasta meal. Sliced zucchini add a new element to everyday tomato sauce, and homemade Garlic Croutons dress up packaged salad greens. Shake things up for dessert with an over-the-top Chocolate Earthquake Cake that heightens chocolate, coconut, and pecans to new levels of chocolate pleasure.

Beef and Parmesan Pasta *(pictured on page 39)*

Submitted by: **Corwynn Darkholme**
"This is a great main dish, and it makes a nice side dish, too."

1½	pounds lean ground beef	2	cups sliced zucchini, (¼ inch thick)
1	(14 ounce) can beef broth	¾	cup grated Parmesan cheese, divided
1	(14.5 ounce) can Italian-style diced tomatoes, undrained		
2	cups uncooked farfalle (bow tie) pasta		

1. In a large skillet over medium-high heat, brown the ground beef until crumbled and no longer pink. Remove beef with a slotted spoon to a bowl. Pour off the drippings.

2. Return the skillet to the heat and add the beef broth, tomatoes, and pasta. Stir to coat all of the pasta. Bring to a boil and reduce heat to medium.

3. Cook, uncovered, for 15 minutes stirring frequently. Add zucchini and continue cooking for 5 more minutes or until pasta is tender.

4. Return beef to the skillet and stir in ½ cup of the cheese; heat through. Sprinkle the remaining cheese over each serving. **Yield:** 6 servings.

Per serving: About 344 calories, 30g protein, 13g carbohydrate, 18g fat, 2g fiber, 84mg cholesterol, 722mg sodium

Garlic Croutons *(pictured on page 39)*

Submitted by: **Cathy Hofmann**
"These croutons are good for a Caesar's salad or any tossed green salad."

¼ cup butter	3 (¾ inch thick) slices French
1 clove garlic, minced	bread, cut into cubes

1. Preheat oven to 350°F (175°C).
2. In a large sauté pan, melt butter over medium heat. Stir in garlic; cook and stir for 1 minute. Add bread cubes and toss to coat. Spread on a baking sheet.
3. Bake in the preheated oven for 15 minutes or until crisp and dry. Check frequently to prevent burning. Cool. **Yield:** 6 servings.

Per serving: About 88 calories, 1g protein, 4g carbohydrate, 8g fat, 0g fiber, 21mg cholesterol, 122mg sodium

Chocolate Earthquake Cake II *(pictured on page 39)*

Submitted by: **P. Price**
"This is a wonderfully rich chocolate cake and very easy to make."

1 cup flaked coconut	1 (16 ounce) package
1 cup chopped pecans	confectioners' sugar
1 (18.25 ounce) package	½ cup butter, melted
devil's food cake mix	1 teaspoon vanilla extract
with pudding	
1 (8 ounce) package cream	
cheese, softened	

1. Preheat oven to 325°F (165°C). Spray a 9x13 inch pan with cooking spray.
2. Spread coconut and pecans in pan.
3. Mix cake mix according to package directions. Pour over the pecans and coconut.
4. Beat cream cheese with an electric mixer until smooth; add confectioners' sugar, butter, and vanilla until combined. Drop by teaspoonfuls over the batter.
5. Bake in the preheated oven for 1 hour or until set. **Yield:** 18 servings.

Per serving: About 378 calories, 4g protein, 49g carbohydrate, 20g fat, 1g fiber, 33mg cholesterol, 311mg sodium

---

◄ **Restaurant Fare**

Prep Time: 5 minutes
Cook Time: 20 minutes
Average Rating: ★★★★★
What other cooks have done:
"This is a fantastic way to use stale bread! I used garlic powder instead of fresh garlic and sprinkled Parmesan cheese and Italian herbs over the bread cubes before baking them. They're so good—you can snack on them all by themselves."

◄ **Crowd-Pleaser**

Prep Time: 20 minutes
Cook Time: 1 hour
Average Rating: ★★★★★
What other cooks have done:
"This cake was an instant hit. The first time I made it, it scored a 10 on the Richter scale with taste to match! I used ¼ cup of butter."

Ken's Spicy Curry Chicken
hot cooked rice
Kulfi
Serves 6

1. Prepare Kulfi and freeze overnight.
2. Prepare curry and serve over hot cooked rice.

Restaurant Fare ▶

Prep Time: 10 minutes

Cook Time: 15 minutes

Average Rating: ★★★★★

What other cooks have done:

"This was absolutely delicious! It tasted like I had ordered it from a Thai restaurant! I suggest experimenting by adding more vegetables to the dish and maybe a tad of cornstarch to thicken the sauce. Delicious!"

Out-of-the-Ordinary ▶

Prep Time: 20 minutes

Freeze Time: 8 hours

Average Rating: ★★★★★

What other cooks have done:

"This is the best kulfi I have had in years! My kids love it. I have improvised on the basic process by adding crushed pistachios and rose water to the mixture."

Curry in a Hurry

Cross the globe and indulge in this exotic, one-dish meal that can be ready in under 30 minutes.

Ken's Spicy Curry Chicken

Submitted by: **Ken**
"This chicken curry tastes just like the curries you order at Thai restaurants."

2	(14 ounce) cans coconut milk	1	green bell pepper, cut into 1-inch pieces
2	tablespoons green curry paste	1	cup sliced fresh mushrooms
⅔	cup chicken broth	3	skinless, boneless chicken breasts, cut into 1-inch pieces
1	(8 ounce) can sliced water chestnuts, drained		
1	(8 ounce) can sliced bamboo shoots, drained	3	tablespoons fish sauce
		¼	cup chopped fresh basil

1. In a large saucepan, whisk coconut milk and curry paste together. Simmer over medium heat for 5 minutes.
2. Stir in broth, water chestnuts, bamboo shoots, bell pepper, mushrooms, and chicken. Season with fish sauce and basil. Simmer for 10 more minutes or until chicken is cooked, yet still tender. **Yield:** 6 servings.

Per serving: About 420 calories, 29g protein, 13g carbohydrate, 34g fat, 4g fiber, 61mg cholesterol, 828mg sodium

Kulfi (Indian Ice Cream)

Submitted by: **Simmi Gupta**
"This is a simple but delicious recipe from my sister-in-law."

1¼	cups evaporated milk	4	slices white bread, torn into pieces
1¼	cups sweetened condensed milk	½	teaspoon ground cardamom
1	(16 ounce) container frozen whipped topping, thawed		

1. Combine evaporated milk, condensed milk, whipped topping, and bread in a blender until smooth.
2. Pour mixture into a 9x13 inch baking dish or 2 plastic ice cube trays, sprinkle with cardamom, and freeze for 8 hours or overnight. **Yield:** 24 servings.

Per serving: About 140 calories, 3g protein, 17g carbohydrate, 7g fat, 0g fiber, 10mg cholesterol, 62mg sodium

Casual Entertaining
15 Menus For No-Fuss Fun

Easy Meatloaf

Suzy's Mashed Red Potatoes

Buttery Cooked Carrots

Easy Chocolate Chip Pound Cake

Serves 8

Menu Prep Plan

1. Prepare and bake meatloaf.

2. Cook carrots and potatoes while meatloaf bakes. Dress carrots and mash potatoes. Prepare batter for chocolate chip pound cake.

3. Let pound cake bake during dinner.

Family Favorite ▶

Prep Time: 10 minutes

Cook Time: 1 hour

Average Rating: ★★★★★

What other cooks have done:

"I added about a tablespoon of Worcestershire sauce to the meat mixture and sautéed the onions in a little butter and garlic for just a few minutes until the onions were softened. It was delicious."

Quick & Easy ▶

Prep Time: 10 minutes

Cook Time: 10 minutes

Average Rating: ★★★★★

What other cooks have done:

"Wow—what a way to jazz up your red potatoes. I melted the butter in the milk over low heat, which worked well."

Meat and Potatoes

Treat your family to a filling meal of meatloaf and mashed potatoes. Still hungry? Enjoy a slice of pound cake for dessert.

Easy Meatloaf

Submitted by: **Janet Caldwell**

"This is a very easy and no-fail recipe for meatloaf. It's quite good!"

1½ pounds ground beef	2 tablespoons brown sugar
1 egg	2 tablespoons prepared
1 onion, chopped	mustard
1 cup milk	⅓ cup ketchup
1 cup dried breadcrumbs	
Salt and ground black pepper to taste	

1. Preheat oven to 350°F (175°C). Lightly grease a 5x9 inch loaf pan or 9x13 inch baking dish.

2. In a large bowl, combine the beef, egg, onion, milk, and breadcrumbs. Season with salt and pepper to taste. Place in prepared loaf pan or form into a loaf and place in prepared baking dish.

3. In a small bowl, combine the brown sugar, mustard, and ketchup. Mix well and pour over the meatloaf.

4. Bake in the preheated oven for 1 hour. **Yield:** 8 servings.

Per serving: About 373 calories, 18g protein, 19g carbohydrate, 25g fat, 1g fiber, 101mg cholesterol, 361mg sodium

Suzy's Mashed Red Potatoes

Submitted by: **B.T.**

"These are the best I've had! Red potato skins are full of flavor!"

2 pounds small red potatoes, scrubbed and quartered	¼ cup sour cream
½ cup butter	Salt and ground black pepper to taste
½ cup milk	

1. Bring a large pot of lightly salted water to a boil. Add potatoes; cook until tender but still firm, about 10 minutes. Drain and set aside.

2. Add butter, milk, sour cream, and salt and pepper to taste to potatoes; mash together until smooth. **Yield:** 8 servings.

Per serving: About 214 calories, 3g protein, 22g carbohydrate, 13g fat, 2g fiber, 35mg cholesterol, 133mg sodium

Buttery Cooked Carrots

Submitted by: **Rebecca**

"Sweet cooked carrots that even my carrot-hating family loves. There are never leftovers."

2	pounds baby carrots	⅔	cup packed brown sugar
½	cup butter or margarine		

1. Cook carrots in a large pot of boiling water until tender. Remove carrots with a slotted spoon and drain off most of the liquid, leaving bottom of pot covered with water.

2. Stir butter and brown sugar into pot. Simmer and stir until the butter melts. Return carrots to pot and toss to coat. Cover and let sit for a few minutes to allow flavors to mingle. **Yield:** 8 servings.

Per serving: About 188 calories, 1g protein, 21g carbohydrate, 12g fat, 2g fiber, 0mg cholesterol, 175mg sodium

◀ **Family Favorite**

Prep Time: 15 minutes

Cook Time: 10 minutes

Average Rating: ★★★★

What other cooks have done:

"I steamed the carrots. I used a squeeze of lemon, ½ teaspoon cinnamon, and ¼ teaspoon nutmeg. I also had the carrots marinate in the sauce for about 20 minutes before serving; I just covered the dish with a lid. This recipe was a favorite in my house!"

Easy Chocolate Chip Pound Cake

Submitted by: **T's mom**

"Very easy, very rich, and very good! You can substitute vanilla pudding for a less chocolaty cake or semisweet chocolate chips for a more intense chocolate flavor."

1	(18.25 ounce) package yellow cake mix	4	eggs, lightly beaten
1	(3.9 ounce) package instant chocolate pudding mix	1	(8 ounce) container sour cream
½	cup white sugar	½	cup milk chocolate chips
¾	cup water	2	tablespoons confectioners' sugar
¾	cup vegetable oil		

1. Preheat oven to 325°F (165°C). Lightly grease and flour a 10 inch Bundt pan.

2. In a medium bowl, stir together cake mix, instant pudding, and sugar. Add water, oil, eggs, and sour cream; mix until well blended. Fold in the chocolate chips. Pour into the prepared Bundt pan.

3. Bake in the preheated oven for 50 to 60 minutes or until a toothpick inserted near the center of the cake comes out clean. Cool in pan for 10 minutes before inverting onto a wire rack to cool completely. Dust with confectioners' sugar before cutting and serving. **Yield:** 14 servings.

Per serving: About 410 calories, 5g protein, 48g carbohydrate, 23g fat, 1g fiber, 70mg cholesterol, 386mg sodium

◀ **Company is Coming**

Prep Time: 10 minutes

Cook Time: 1 hour

Average Rating: ★★★★★

What other cooks have done:

"This cake was delicious! Definitely one of the easiest cakes I've ever made. I took it to a church luncheon and everyone loved it. My chocoholic kids want more!"

Menu Prep Plan

1. Prepare tomato salad a day ahead and store in refrigerator. Cut chicken into pieces and refrigerate.

2. Prepare biscuits and let rise. Fry chicken and okra.

3. Set out tomato salad and prepare pie filling. Bake biscuits.

4. Bake pie just before the meal and let cool while finishing dinner.

Classic Comfort Food ▶

Prep Time: 10 minutes

Cook Time: 35 minutes

Average Rating: ★★★★☆

What other cooks have done:

"I was craving fried chicken, so when I came upon this recipe, I was stunned to see how simple it looked. I loved it. I did add a little more salt and pepper, and I used oil instead of shortening. I will be making this again. And the cast iron skillet is essential—the chicken didn't stick at all!"

Southern-Style Supper

You don't have to be Southern to enjoy this down-home dinner. If fried okra isn't your favorite, heat a can of green beans instead. The easy gravy recipe below complements fried chicken, Chicken Fried Steak (page 108), and mashed potatoes.

Deep-South Fried Chicken *(pictured on page 77)*

Submitted by: **Marilyn**

"This was my grandmother's and mother's recipe. If you're going to fry anything, let it be a frying size chicken. Cut your calories some other way! Start a new tradition, as I have, of fried chicken on Christmas Day!"

1 cup shortening	1 (3 pound) whole chicken,
2 cups all-purpose flour	cut into pieces
1 teaspoon salt	
1 teaspoon ground black pepper	

1. Heat shortening in a large cast iron skillet over medium-high heat.

2. In a brown paper lunch bag, combine flour, salt, and pepper. Place 2 chicken pieces in the bag and shake to coat; place them in the skillet. Repeat until all of the chicken is coated and in the skillet.

3. Fry the chicken over medium-high heat until all of the pieces have been browned on both sides. Turn the heat to medium-low, cover, and cook for 20 minutes. Remove the lid and increase heat to medium-high. Continue frying until chicken pieces are a deep golden brown and the juices run clear. **Yield:** 4 servings.

Per serving: About 1406 calories, 69g protein, 48g carbohydrate, 102g fat, 2g fiber, 306mg cholesterol, 826mg sodium

Note: Serve fried chicken with a simple gravy. Pour off all except ¼ cup drippings from skillet in which chicken was fried; place skillet over medium heat. Add ¼ cup flour; stir until browned. Gradually add 2½ to 3 cups hot milk; cook, stirring constantly, until thickened and bubbly. Add salt and pepper to taste. Serve hot. **Yield:** 2½ cups.

Chrissy's Sweet-'n'-Sour Tomato Salad

(pictured on page 77)

Submitted by: **Chrissy**
"An easy to prepare, delicious sweet 'n' sour tomato salad just right to complement any meal—or to eat alone! You can adjust the amounts of vinegar and sugar according to your taste."

7	tomatoes	½	cup vegetable oil
1	small yellow onion	½	teaspoon salt
½	cup white sugar	¼	teaspoon ground black
½	cup distilled white vinegar		pepper

1. Thinly slice the tomatoes. Cut onion in half through root end and thinly slice into half-circles. In a large bowl, toss together tomatoes, onion, sugar, vinegar, oil, salt, and pepper. Serve at room temperature. **Yield:** 6 servings.

Per serving: About 324 calories, 1g protein, 41g carbohydrate, 19g fat, 2g fiber, 0mg cholesterol, 225mg sodium

Fried Okra *(pictured on page 77)*

Submitted by: **Linda Martin**
"A simple Southern classic! Okra is dredged in seasoned cornmeal, then fried until golden."

20	pods okra, sliced into ¼ inch pieces	½	teaspoon salt
2	eggs, lightly beaten	½	teaspoon ground black pepper
2	cups cornmeal	2	cups vegetable oil

1. In a small bowl, soak okra in egg for 5 to 10 minutes. In a medium bowl, combine cornmeal, salt, and pepper.
2. Heat oil in a large skillet over medium-high heat. Dredge okra in cornmeal mixture, coating evenly. Carefully place okra in hot oil; stir continuously. When okra first starts to brown, reduce heat to medium and cook until golden. Drain on paper towels. **Yield:** 4 servings.

Per serving: About 397 calories, 5g protein, 29g carbohydrate, 29g fat, 3g fiber, 53mg cholesterol, 164mg sodium

◄ Quick & Easy

Prep Time: 30 minutes
Average Rating: ★★★★★
What other cooks have done:
"I used olive oil instead of vegetable oil and added some sliced cucumber, and it turned out delicious. Everyone loved it and raved about it. It has become a quick, easy, delicious, and always popular dish to take to picnics and gatherings."

◄ Family Favorite

Prep Time: 15 minutes
Cook Time: 15 minutes
Average Rating: ★★★★★
What other cooks have done:
"I found that a combo of ¾ cup flour and ¼ cup cornmeal works just fine. For an alternative, I soaked the okra in milk in place of the eggs; the milk mixture is as thick as beaten egg after the okra has soaked in it. With a garden full of okra, I've fried my fair share this summer!"

Angel Biscuits II *(pictured on page 77)*

Submitted by: **Karin Christian**
"A delicious cross between a roll and a biscuit."

1	(.25 ounce) package active dry yeast	3	tablespoons white sugar
¼	cup warm water (110°F/45°C)	1	tablespoon baking powder
2	cups buttermilk	1	teaspoon baking soda
5	cups all-purpose flour	2	teaspoons salt
		¾	cup shortening

1. Preheat oven to 425°F (220°C). Lightly grease baking sheets.
2. In a small bowl, dissolve yeast in warm water. Let stand until creamy, about 5 minutes. Add buttermilk and set aside.
3. In a large bowl, combine flour, sugar, baking powder, baking soda, and salt. Cut in shortening with a pastry blender until mixture resembles coarse meal. Stir in yeast mixture until dry ingredients are moistened. Turn dough out onto a floured surface and knead 4 or 5 times.
4. On a lightly floured surface, roll dough to ½ inch thickness. Cut out biscuits using a 2½ inch round cutter. Place on prepared baking sheets, barely touching each other. Cover and let rise in a warm place for 30 minutes or until almost doubled in size.
5. Bake in the preheated oven for 10 to 12 minutes or until browned.
Yield: 22 servings.

Per serving: About 181 calories, 4g protein, 25g carbohydrate, 7g fat, 1g fiber, 1mg cholesterol, 361mg sodium

Caramel Pecan Pie

Submitted by: **Corwynn Darkholme**
"Serve hot or cold with a dollop of whipped topping or vanilla ice cream."

36	individually wrapped caramels, unwrapped	3	eggs
¼	cup butter	½	teaspoon vanilla extract
¼	cup milk	¼	teaspoon salt
¾	cup white sugar	1	cup pecan halves
		1	(9 inch) unbaked pie crust

1. Preheat oven to 350°F (175°C.) In a saucepan over low heat, combine caramels, butter, and milk. Cook, stirring frequently, until smooth. Remove from heat and set aside.
2. In a large bowl, combine sugar, eggs, vanilla, and salt. Gradually stir in melted caramel mixture. Stir in pecans. Pour filling into pie crust.
3. Bake in the preheated oven for 35 to 40 minutes or until pastry is golden brown. Allow to cool until filling is firm. **Yield:** 8 servings.

Per serving: About 537 calories, 7g protein, 67g carbohydrate, 29g fat, 3g fiber, 99mg cholesterol, 387mg sodium

Springtime Feast

When friends or family are coming for dinner, dress your table with this spread to impress. Your guests will delight in family favorites like macaroni and cheese and sweet glazed ham.

Tangy Honey-Glazed Ham

Submitted by: **Sue**
"Add any leftover glaze to the pan drippings with a little flour or cornstarch and make a nice sauce to accompany the meat."

1	(10 pound) fully cooked, bone-in ham	⅓	cup honey
1¼	cups packed dark brown sugar	⅓	orange, juiced and zested
⅓	cup pineapple juice	2	tablespoons prepared Dijon-style mustard
		¼	teaspoon ground cloves

1. Preheat oven to 325°F (165°C). Place ham in a roasting pan.
2. Bake ham in the preheated oven, uncovered, for 2 hours.
3. While ham bakes, in a saucepan, combine brown sugar, pineapple juice, honey, orange juice, orange zest, mustard, and ground cloves. Bring to a boil, reduce heat, and simmer for 5 to 10 minutes.
4. After ham bakes 2 hours, remove ham from oven and brush with glaze. Bake 30 to 45 more minutes, brushing ham with glaze every 10 minutes. **Yield:** 12 servings.

Per serving: About 851 calories, 65g protein, 32g carbohydrate, 50g fat, 0g fiber, 185mg cholesterol, 3623mg sodium

Lemon Pepper Green Beans

Submitted by: **Annette Byrdy**
"These green beans are a bit tangy, spicy, and crunchy. My family's favorite!"

1	pound fresh green beans, rinsed and trimmed	¼	cup sliced almonds
2	tablespoons butter	2	teaspoons lemon pepper

1. Place green beans in a steamer over 1 inch of boiling water. Cover and cook 10 minutes or until tender but still firm.
2. Melt butter in a skillet over medium heat. Sauté almonds until lightly browned and season with lemon pepper. Stir in green beans and toss to coat. **Yield:** 6 servings.

Per serving: About 81 calories, 2g protein, 6g carbohydrate, 6g fat, 3g fiber, 10mg cholesterol, 198mg sodium

Menu

Tangy Honey-Glazed Ham

Lemon Pepper Green Beans

Fried Corn with Bacon

Easy Add-in Macaroni and Cheese

Strawberry Cake II

Serves 6

Menu Prep Plan

1. Bake ham. Meanwhile, prepare and bake cake; let layers cool completely and then frost cake.

2. While layers cool, boil macaroni, scrape corn, and string beans.

3. Prepare macaroni and cheese; bake. While it bakes, prepare green beans and corn.

◀ Holiday Fare

Prep Time: 15 minutes

Cook Time: 2 hours 45 minutes

Average Rating: ★★★★★

What other cooks have done:

"I made this for Easter and impressed everyone! Instead of the juiced zested orange, I used ⅓ cup orange juice and added dried orange peel to the glaze. The leftovers were just as good the next day!"

◀ Quick & Easy

Prep Time: 5 minutes

Cook Time: 20 minutes

Average Rating: ★★★★☆

What other cooks have done:

"I got raves at all my holiday dinners when I served this side. The kids even had seconds. Works with frozen petite beans as well as blanched fresh ones."

Fried Corn with Bacon

Submitted by: **Mary Bray**
"A side dish combining fresh corn, bacon, and green pepper. This is not a low-fat, low-calorie dish, but it sure is good. It can be made ahead and refrigerated until you're ready to 'fry' it."

1. Holding each ear of corn over a medium bowl, slice corn off cob and scrape cob to release the milk. Discard cobs and set corn aside.
2. Place bacon in a large, deep skillet. Cook over medium–high heat until evenly browned. Crumble and set aside.
3. Retain 2 tablespoons of the bacon drippings in the skillet and fry pepper until just softened. Add corn and cook until tender. Stir in crumbled bacon and cook 1 more minute. **Yield:** 6 servings.

Per serving: About 257 calories, 6g protein, 24g carbohydrate, 17g fat, 3g fiber, 19mg cholesterol, 220mg sodium

Easy Add-in Macaroni and Cheese

Submitted by: **Beth Howard**
"This recipe is super easy and it uses stuff you probably already have in the cabinet. You also can substitute most of the ingredients with similar ones that you have on hand!"

1	(7.25 ounce) package uncooked macaroni and cheese	3	tablespoons sour cream
1	(10.75 ounce) can condensed cream of mushroom soup	1	cup shredded Cheddar cheese
½	cup butter or margarine, divided	12	buttery round crackers, crushed

1. Preheat oven to 350°F (175°C).
2. Cook macaroni according to package directions. Remove from heat and drain. Add soup, ¼ cup butter, sour cream, shredded cheese, and the cheese packet from the box. (Do not use milk as directed on the box.)
3. Pour into a small casserole dish and top with crushed crackers. Melt remaining butter and pour over the crackers. Bake in the preheated oven for 25 minutes. **Yield:** 6 servings.

Per serving: About 439 calories, 12g protein, 32g carbohydrate, 30g fat, 1g fiber, 28mg cholesterol, 983mg sodium

---

Make-Ahead ▶

Prep Time: 15 minutes

Cook Time: 10 minutes

Average Rating: ★★★★★

What other cooks have done:

"I've made this recipe for ages, varying it each time. During the summer, I use fresh corn from the cob, but during the winter I've used frozen corn with good results. If I don't have bacon around, I add red peppers (in addition to the green peppers) for color and sauté them in a tablespoon of butter with some chopped onions. They go great with burgers!"

Classic Comfort Food ▶

Prep Time: 20 minutes

Cook Time: 25 minutes

Average Rating: ★★★★★

What other cooks have done:

"I use cream of chicken soup instead of the cream of mushroom. This was so easy and tasted great. I'm a big fan of homemade mac and cheese, but don't think I will go through all of the fuss now that I found this recipe."

Strawberry Cake II

Submitted by: **Judalee**

"Here's a beautiful cake for the strawberry lover. Easy to make with packaged gelatin and white cake mix. Fresh strawberries can be used when they're in season."

1	(3 ounce) package strawberry-flavored gelatin	3	tablespoons all-purpose flour
½	cup cold water	1	(10 ounce) package frozen strawberries, thawed and divided
1	(18.25 ounce) package white cake mix		
4	eggs	6	tablespoons butter, softened
1	cup vegetable oil	2	cups confectioners' sugar

1. Preheat oven to 325°F (165°C). Grease and flour 3 (9 inch) round cake pans.

2. Dissolve the gelatin in cold water. In a large mixing bowl, combine dissolved gelatin with cake mix, eggs, vegetable oil, flour, and half of the strawberries. Beat for 5 minutes. Pour batter into prepared cake pans.

3. Bake in the preheated oven for 30 to 35 minutes or until a toothpick inserted in the center of the cake comes out clean. Cool in pans on wire racks.

4. Cream butter, sugar, and remaining half of the strawberries in a mixing bowl until light and fluffy, adding additional confectioners' sugar if needed for desired consistency. Spread the frosting between layers and on the top and sides of cake. **Yield:** 12 servings.

Per serving: About 549 calories, 5g protein, 66g carbohydrate, 31g fat, 1g fiber, 86mg cholesterol, 379mg sodium

◄ **Company is Coming**

Prep Time: 30 minutes

Cook Time: 35 minutes

Average Rating: ★★★★★

What other cooks have done:

"This cake was delicious! I baked mine in a 9x13 inch pan for about 35 to 40 minutes. I used a cream cheese frosting instead, and I added about a cup of fresh strawberries. My husband is a strawberry lover and especially loved it. It was such a hit that this is what I'm using for my daughter's first birthday cake! Pink frosting and pink cake, perfect for a little girl!"

Menu Prep Plan

1. Make pecan tassies, almonds, fudge, and bars the day before.

2. Bake dip while cider brews and fondue melts. Bake Brie and pinwheels together, pinwheels on top rack, if you have only one oven.

Quick & Easy ▶

Prep Time: 5 minutes

Cook Time: 5 minutes

Average Rating: ★★★★★

What other cooks have done:

"This cider has a distinct apple flavor and a smooth texture."

Quick & Easy ▶

Prep Time: 10 minutes

Cook Time: 20 minutes

Average Rating: ★★★★☆

What other cooks have done:

"The pinwheels were light and flaky and packed with lots of flavor from the prosciutto. I used a mild lean prosciutto, thinly sliced, and Parmagiano Reggiano so that it wouldn't be too salty."

Holiday Appetizer Party

This holiday party is a breeze to throw together. Chutney Baked Brie and Prosciutto and Parmesan Pinwheels bake at the same temperature, so throw them in the oven together.

Hot Spiced Cider *(pictured on page 42)*

Submitted by: **Sara**

"Use an automatic coffee maker to brew the cider. If you don't own one, heat the cider in a slow cooker or a saucepan over medium heat. Clean coffee maker according to the manufacturer's instructions before using again."

¼	cup packed brown sugar	1	cinnamon stick
½	teaspoon whole allspice		Pinch ground nutmeg
1	teaspoon whole cloves	1	large orange, quartered
¼	teaspoon salt	2	quarts apple cider

1. Place filter in coffee basket and fill with brown sugar, allspice, cloves, salt, cinnamon stick, nutmeg, and orange wedges. Pour apple cider into coffee pot. Brew and serve hot. **Yield:** 12 servings.

Per serving: About 119 calories, 1g protein, 30g carbohydrate, 0g fat, 1g fiber, 0mg cholesterol, 51mg sodium

Prosciutto and Parmesan Pinwheels

Submitted by: **Claire Mooney**

"Very easy appetizer. Absolutely delicious."

1	(17.3 ounce) package frozen puff pastry sheets, thawed	5	ounces prosciutto, thinly sliced
4	teaspoons prepared Dijon-style mustard	5	ounces (1 cup) grated Parmesan cheese

1. Preheat oven to 350°F (175°C). Lightly grease a baking sheet.

2. Roll pastry out onto a floured surface. Cover with a layer of mustard, then prosciutto, then cheese. Roll up, beginning at the long side. Cut into 1 inch thick sections. Arrange on prepared baking sheet.

3. Bake in the preheated oven 20 minutes. **Yield:** 20 (1 inch) slices.

Per pinwheel: About 181 calories, 6g protein, 11g carbohydrate, 12g fat, 1g fiber, 11mg cholesterol, 343mg sodium

Artichoke and Roasted Red Pepper Dip

Submitted by: **Eileen**

"A hot, tasty dip that's sure to please everyone. Roasted red peppers add a pleasant zing to this mild crowd-pleaser that's perfect with crackers or bread."

2	tablespoons butter	1	(7 ounce) jar roasted red peppers, drained and chopped
1	leek, diced		
2	(6.5 ounce) jars marinated artichoke hearts, drained and chopped	¾	cup freshly grated Parmesan cheese
3	tablespoons mayonnaise		

1. Preheat oven to 350°F (175°C). Lightly grease an 8x8 baking dish.
2. Melt butter in a saucepan over medium heat. Sauté diced leek until tender. Stir together artichoke hearts, mayonnaise, roasted red peppers, and Parmesan cheese. Add leek and transfer to baking dish.
3. Bake in the preheated oven for 30 minutes or until bubbly and lightly browned. **Yield:** 24 servings.

Per serving: About 63 calories, 1g protein, 2g carbohydrate, 6g fat, 0g fiber, 6mg cholesterol, 242mg sodium

◀ Crowd-Pleaser

Prep Time: 10 minutes

Cook Time: 40 minutes

Average Rating: ★★★★

What other cooks have done:

"Absolutely yummy! It was easy to make and tasted great. Mine was a little runny though; I might try to add more mayo next time to thicken it for a nicer presentation."

Chutney Baked Brie *(pictured on page 43)*

Submitted by: **Hillary Quinn**

"This round wheel of Brie is dusted with curry powder, then spread with a mango chutney, studded with chopped cashews, and baked until the cheese is melted. The sweet/savory combination is so delicious."

3	teaspoons ground curry powder	1	cup chopped cashews
		1	French baguette, cut into ½ inch slices
1	(9 ounce) jar mango chutney		
3	(13.2 ounce) wheels Brie cheese		

1. Preheat oven to 350°F (175°C).
2. Sprinkle curry powder over top and sides of Brie; rub the curry powder into the rind to thoroughly coat the surface. Place each Brie wheel in a large pie plate or ovenproof dish. Spread a generous layer of chutney on top of Brie and evenly sprinkle with cashews.
3. Bake in the preheated oven 15 minutes or until cashews are slightly golden and cheese inside the rind is melted. Serve with baguette slices. **Yield:** 15 servings.

Per serving: About 206 calories, 9g protein, 14g carbohydrate, 13g fat, 1g fiber, 31mg cholesterol, 286mg sodium

◀ Out-of-the-Ordinary

Prep Time: 10 minutes

Cook Time: 15 minutes

Average Rating: ★★★★★

What other cooks have done:

"Great flavor contrasts with the curry and the chutney. For a different presentation, I wrapped this one in phyllo pastry. Turned out great."

Holiday Gift Giving ▶

Prep Time: 15 minutes

Cook Time: 1 hour

Average Rating: ★★★★★

What other cooks have done:

"I gave these in Christmas bags with other goodies, and they were the biggest hit. People raved about them! I couldn't stop eating them either. Almonds can be pricey, especially around the holidays, but if you catch a good sale, buy lots; they freeze well."

Holiday Fare ▶

Prep Time: 25 minutes

Cook Time: 25 minutes

Average Rating: ★★★★★

What other cooks have done:

"These are fantastic. I also made them substituting chopped walnuts when I realized I didn't have any pecans—also very good. And I dusted them with confectioners' sugar when they were cool. Definitely a favorite recipe for the holidays!"

Cinnamon-Roasted Almonds *(pictured on page 42)*

Submitted by: **BJ**

"Here's an easy snack idea to serve at any holiday party."

1	egg white	½	cup white sugar
1	teaspoon cold water	¼	teaspoon salt
4	cups whole almonds	½	teaspoon ground cinnamon

1. Preheat oven to 250°F (120°C). Lightly grease a 10x15 inch jelly-roll pan.

2. In a large bowl, combine egg white and water and beat until frothy but not stiff. Add nuts and stir until well coated. Mix the sugar, salt, and cinnamon; sprinkle over the nuts. Toss to coat and spread evenly on the prepared pan.

3. Bake in the preheated oven for 1 hour or until golden, stirring occasionally. Allow to cool and store nuts in an airtight container.

Yield: 16 servings.

Per serving: About 231 calories, 8g protein, 13g carbohydrate, 18g fat, 4g fiber, 0mg cholesterol, 40mg sodium

Pecan Tassies *(pictured on page 43)*

Submitted by: **Carla**

"These little tarts are a great hit—and look beautiful on a holiday tray!"

2	cups butter or margarine, softened	2½	cups packed brown sugar
4	(3 ounce) packages cream cheese, softened	3	tablespoons melted butter
		½	teaspoon vanilla extract
4	cups all-purpose flour	¼	teaspoon salt
3	eggs	1½	cups chopped pecans

1. Preheat the oven to 350°F (175°C). Lightly grease miniature muffin pans.

2. In a medium bowl, mix together butter and cream cheese until well blended. Beat in flour, 1 cup at a time, until mixture forms a smooth dough. Roll into small balls and press into the bottoms and up sides of miniature muffin pans.

3. In a medium bowl, mix together eggs, brown sugar, butter, vanilla, and salt. Stir in pecans. Use a spoon to fill each of the crusts ⅔ full (about 2 teaspoons) with the filling mixture.

4. Bake in the preheated oven for 20 to 25 minutes or until shells are light brown and the filling has puffed up. Cool and carefully remove from pans. **Yield:** 5 dozen.

Per tassie: About 167 calories, 2g protein, 16g carbohydrate, 11g fat, 1g fiber, 35mg cholesterol, 100mg sodium

Raspberry Truffle Fudge

Submitted by: **Leeza**

"An unforgettable double-layer confection that's absolutely perfect for your true love!"

3 cups semisweet chocolate chips
1 (14 ounce) can sweetened condensed milk
1½ teaspoons vanilla extract
Salt to taste
¼ cup heavy whipping cream
¼ cup raspberry-flavored liqueur
2 cups semisweet chocolate chips

1. Lightly grease a 9x9 inch square pan with cooking spray and line with wax paper.
2. In a microwave-safe bowl, combine 3 cups chocolate chips and sweetened condensed milk. Heat in microwave until chocolate melts, stirring occasionally. Be careful not to let chocolate scorch. Stir in the vanilla and salt. Spread in pan and cool to room temperature.
3. In a bowl, combine cream, liqueur, and 2 cups chocolate chips. Heat in microwave until chocolate melts; stir until smooth. Cool to lukewarm, then pour over fudge layer. Refrigerate until both layers are completely set, about 1 hour. Cut into 1 inch pieces. **Yield:** 2½ pounds or 40 servings.

Per serving: About 149 calories, 2g protein, 20g carbohydrate, 8g fat, 1g fiber, 5mg cholesterol, 13mg sodium

◄ Crowd-Pleaser

Prep Time: 10 minutes
Cook Time: 10 minutes
Average Rating: ★★★★★
What other cooks have done:
"This recipe is addicting. I used ⅓ cup raspberry preserves (heated and the seeds strained out) instead of the raspberry liqueur. It was a great hit at our Christmas party."

Totally Groovy Chocolate Fondue

(pictured on page 43)

Submitted by: **Staci Mondell**

"This totally awesome chocolate fondue is served with your favorite fruits or snack foods—strawberries, bananas, apples, oranges, pineapple, and pretzels."

2 cups milk chocolate chips
3 tablespoons heavy whipping cream
2 tablespoons cherry brandy
1 tablespoon strong brewed coffee
⅛ teaspoon ground cinnamon
Dippers: strawberries, bananas, orange sections, pound cake cubes

1. Combine chocolate, cream, brandy, coffee, and cinnamon in a fondue pot over a low flame or a heavy saucepan over low heat. Heat until melted, stirring occasionally. Serve at once with dippers. **Yield:** 10 servings (about 1⅓ cups).

Per serving: About 317 calories, 4g protein, 36g carbohydrate, 19g fat, 0g fiber, 10mg cholesterol, 42mg sodium

◄ Party Food

Prep Time: 5 minutes
Cook Time: 10 minutes
Average Rating: ★★★★★
What other cooks have done:
"A slow cooker and a low flame would be best for this fondue—I had to watch the metal pot like a hawk."

Prep Time: 30 minutes

Cook Time: 1 hour

Average Rating: ★★★★★

What other cooks have done:

"This is a great recipe! But the trick to getting the bars out of the pan without them turning into a gooey mess is to let them cool for at least an hour! The cranberry mixture needs to gel. My husband and kids really loved these—even my picky four-year-old!"

Cranberry Bars *(pictured on page 43)*

Submitted by: **TWILLIAMS05**

"A yummy bar that's tart and sweet at the same time. Easy to put together, and your home will smell wonderful while they're baking!"

1	(12 ounce) package whole cranberries	2	eggs
1	cup white sugar	1	cup regular oats
¾	cup water	¾	cup packed light brown sugar
1	(18.25 ounce) package yellow cake mix	1	teaspoon ground ginger
¾	cup butter, melted	1	teaspoon ground cinnamon

1. Preheat oven to 350°F (175°C).

2. In a saucepan over medium heat, combine the cranberries, white sugar, and water. Cook, stirring occasionally, until all of the cranberries have popped and the mixture is thick, about 19 minutes. Remove from heat and set aside to cool.

3. In a large bowl, mix together the cake mix, melted butter, and eggs. Stir in the oats, brown sugar, ginger, and cinnamon. Chill 1½ cups of the mixture and spread the rest in a 9x13 inch baking dish. Pack down to form a solid crust, getting it as even as possible. Spread the cooled cranberry mixture over the crust. Crumble the remaining crust mixture evenly over the cranberry layer.

4. Bake in the preheated oven for 35 to 40 minutes or until the top is lightly browned. Cool in the pan for about 40 minutes before slicing into bars. **Yield:** 24 servings.

Per serving: About 229 calories, 2g protein, 36g carbohydrate, 9g fat, 1g fiber, 34mg cholesterol, 209mg sodium

Super Bowl Bash

A spread of tasty dips and snacks is perfect for the big game. Serve up bowlfuls of hearty chili and make sure everyone saves room for cake.

Hot Onion Dip

Submitted by: **Tracie**

"This is the first thing to be eaten at every party, and it's sinfully easy! If you're not a big onion fan, don't be afraid. Onion is not the dominant flavor of the dish. Serve with crackers or cocktail toast."

3 (8 ounce) packages cream cheese, softened	2 cups grated Parmesan cheese
1 onion, finely chopped	½ cup mayonnaise

1. Preheat the oven to 400°F (200°C). Lightly grease a medium baking dish.
2. In the prepared dish, mix the cream cheese, onion, Parmesan cheese, and mayonnaise.
3. Bake in the preheated oven for 30 minutes or until bubbly and lightly browned. **Yield:** 24 servings.

Per serving: About 170 calories, 6g protein, 2g carbohydrate, 16g fat, 0g fiber, 40mg cholesterol, 264mg sodium

Reuben Dip

Submitted by: **Karen**

"A party favorite! Everyone fights over the pan as soon as it comes out of the oven! Serve it with wheat crackers or small pieces of rye bread."

½ cup mayonnaise	8 ounces shredded corned beef
½ cup Thousand Island dressing	16 ounces shredded Swiss cheese
16 ounces sauerkraut, rinsed and squeezed dry	

1. Preheat oven to 350°F (175°C).
2. In a small bowl, combine mayonnaise and dressing.
3. Spread sauerkraut in a 9x13 inch baking dish. Layer corned beef, Swiss cheese, and mayonnaise-dressing mixture over sauerkraut.
4. Bake in the preheated oven for 20 to 25 minutes. **Yield:** 9 servings.

Per serving: About 392 calories, 22g protein, 6g carbohydrate, 32g fat, 1g fiber, 79mg cholesterol, 842mg sodium

---

Menu

Hot Onion Dip
Reuben Dip
Nacho Cheese Sauce
The Ultimate Chili
Bacon-Cheddar Jalapeño Poppers
Texas Sheet Cake
Serves 6

Menu Prep Plan

1. Start chili in the morning. Layer Reuben Dip and chill. Bake cake; frost cake when cool.

2. Prepare jalepeño poppers. Bake Reuben Dip while cheese sauce melts.

3. Bake onion dip. Broil poppers.

◀ Crowd-Pleaser

Prep Time: 10 minutes

Cook Time: 30 minutes

Average Rating: ★★★★★

What other cooks have done:

"I used 2 blocks of cream cheese, 1 medium-size sweet onion, and sprinkled the dip with seasoned breadcrumbs and paprika for a pretty presentation."

◀ Make-Ahead

Prep Time: 5 minutes

Cook Time: 25 minutes

Average Rating: ★★★★★

What other cooks have done:

"This can be layered easily ahead of time and then refrigerated until ready to bake. But remember to bake it a few minutes longer if it's cold when you put it in the oven."

Party Food ▶

Prep Time: 10 minutes

Cook Time: 15 minutes

Average Rating: ★★★★★

What other cooks have done:

"This is wonderful! I needed a cheese sauce for a recipe. It doesn't need the salt. I love mixing it with rice and broccoli, then baking it. It makes a great dip, too. White American cheese and pimentos give it a heavenly color."

Slow-Cooker Creation ▶

Prep Time: 5 minutes

Cook Time: 8 hours

Average Rating: ★★★★★

What other cooks have done:

"Very good chili! I added the following ingredients, and if you like it spicy, try adding these: 2 tablespoons garlic powder, 1 tablespoon cayenne pepper, 1 tablespoon salt, 3 tablespoons brown sugar, 2 tablespoons honey, and 1 extra tablespoon of chili powder. To thicken the chili, use 2 tablespoons cornstarch with 4 tablespoons water. Hats off to Wendy for creating this dish."

Nacho Cheese Sauce

Submitted by: **Mary Ann Putman**

"Here's a simple cheese sauce to spread over tortilla chips. Add some jalapeños to spice things up a bit."

¼	cup butter	14	slices processed American cheese
¼	cup all-purpose flour	1	teaspoon salt
2	cups milk		

1. In a medium saucepan over medium heat, melt butter; stir in flour. Add milk and stir until the mixture thickens. Stirring constantly, mix in cheese and salt. Continue to cook and stir until cheese has melted and all ingredients are well blended, about 15 minutes. **Yield:** 8 servings.

Per serving: About 282 calories, 14g protein, 7g carbohydrate, 23g fat, 0g fiber, 67mg cholesterol, 1089mg sodium

The Ultimate Chili

Submitted by: **Wendy**

"Easy recipe with little preparation time. This can also be made with ground turkey, and it tastes even better the next day!"

1	pound lean ground beef	1	red bell pepper, chopped
	Salt and ground black pepper to taste	¼	cup red wine vinegar
3	(15 ounce) cans dark red kidney beans	2	tablespoons chili powder
		1	teaspoon ground cumin
3	(14.5 ounce) cans Mexican-style stewed tomatoes	1	teaspoon dried parsley
		1	teaspoon dried basil
			Dash Worcestershire sauce
2	stalks celery, chopped	½	cup red wine

1. In a large skillet over medium-high heat, cook ground beef until evenly browned. Drain off grease and season beef with salt and pepper to taste.

2. In a slow cooker, combine the cooked beef, kidney beans, tomatoes, celery, red bell pepper, and red wine vinegar. Season with chili powder, cumin, parsley, basil, and Worcestershire sauce. Stir to distribute ingredients evenly.

3. Cook on High for 6 hours or on High for 1 hour and Low for 7 hours. Add wine during the last 2 hours. **Yield:** 6 servings.

Per serving: About 416 calories, 28g protein, 51g carbohydrate, 11g fat, 17g fiber, 50mg cholesterol, 1280mg sodium

Bacon-Cheddar Jalapeño Poppers

Submitted by: **Meg**

"Quick and easy! Only three ingredients required. The men in my family are crazy about these yummy treats. My husband often eats them as a meal!"

1	(16 ounce) package Cheddar cheese	12	slices bacon
6	jalapeño peppers, seeded and halved		

1. Preheat the oven to Broil.
2. Cut Cheddar cheese into 12 slices long enough to fit inside the jalapeño halves. Insert cheese slices into the halves. Wrap the jalapeño halves with the bacon slices, securing with a toothpick, if necessary. Place on a lightly greased baking sheet.
3. Broil 5 to 10 minutes or until bacon is brown. **Yield:** 12 servings.

Per serving: About 308 calories, 12g protein, 1g carbohydrate, 29g fat, 0g fiber, 58mg cholesterol, 436mg sodium

◀ **Hot & Spicy**

Prep Time: 10 minutes

Cook Time: 10 minutes

Average Rating: ★★★★★

What other cooks have done:

"These were good. I used precooked bacon and broiled it only 2 to 3 minutes. I have also made them with cream cheese. I mixed shredded sharp Cheddar, 4 ounces cream cheese, and a few seeds from the jalapeño for some heat. By using precooked bacon and broiling for only 3 minutes, the cheese didn't melt all over the pan."

Texas Sheet Cake

Submitted by: **Chantal**

"Perfect potluck cake! Serves a crowd."

1	cup butter	1	teaspoon baking soda
1	cup water	½	cup butter
¼	cup unsweetened cocoa powder	¼	cup unsweetened cocoa powder
2	cups all-purpose flour	5	tablespoons milk
2	cups white sugar	4	cups confectioners' sugar
½	teaspoon salt	1	teaspoon vanilla extract
2	eggs	1	cup chopped walnuts
½	cup sour cream		

1. Preheat oven to 375°F (190°C). Grease a 10x15 inch jellyroll pan.
2. Bring 1 cup butter, water, and ¼ cup cocoa to a boil in a large saucepan. While still hot, remove from heat and add 2 cups flour, 2 cups white sugar, and salt. Mix well. Beat in eggs, sour cream, and baking soda. Do not beat too long.
3. Pour batter into prepared jellyroll pan. Bake in the preheated oven for 20 to 25 minutes or until a toothpick inserted in the center of the cake comes out clean.
4. Bring ½ cup butter, ¼ cup cocoa, and 5 tablespoons milk to a boil. Remove from heat and add confectioners' sugar, vanilla, and nuts. Beat well. Ice cake while icing is still hot. **Yield:** 20 servings.

Per serving: About 405 calories, 4g protein, 56g carbohydrate, 20g fat, 2g fiber, 61mg cholesterol, 275mg sodium

◀ **Crowd-Pleaser**

Prep Time: 30 minutes

Cook Time: 30 minutes

Average Rating: ★★★★★

What other cooks have done:

"I love this cake! I made it yesterday for my son's birthday. It came out very tender and moist and had a delicious, delicate flavor. I added a teaspoon of almond extract, too. It has a nice icing that's easy for decorating. This is my new favorite cake recipe, and I will plan on making it whenever the occasion arises."

Menu Prep Plan

1. Assemble frozen dessert and layered and potato salads the day before.

2. Prepare chicken casserole. While casserole bakes, prepare pasta salad and dump cake. Put cake in oven just before dinner.

Family Favorite ▶

Prep Time: 15 minutes

Cook Time: 45 minutes

Average Rating: ★★★★★

What other cooks have done:

"This takes awhile to prepare, but it's good. I omitted the onion and used brown rice. I also used cream of chicken soup since my husband isn't fond of mushrooms. The water chestnuts, celery, and almonds give it a nice texture. I also added some minced parsley for more color."

Family Reunion

Picky eaters are no match for this menu. Make-ahead salads and a sinfully delicious frozen dessert come together with family classics like chicken casserole and fruit cobbler to create a crowd-pleasing dinner your entire family will enjoy.

Almond Chicken Casserole

Submitted by: **Behr Kleine**

"Refrigerates well, so it can be prepared a day ahead and stored. Add the topping just before baking."

1½ cups uncooked long-grain white rice	3 tablespoons chopped onion
3 cups water	1 (8 ounce) can water chestnuts
5 cups diced, cooked chicken	1½ cups sliced almonds, divided
½ cup mayonnaise	1 cup chopped celery
½ cup plain yogurt	2 teaspoons ground white pepper
1 (10.75 ounce) can condensed cream of mushroom soup	1 tablespoon salt
2 cups chicken broth	3 cups cornflakes cereal
2 tablespoons lemon juice	1 cup butter, melted

1. Combine rice and water in a saucepan and bring to a boil. Reduce heat, cover, and simmer for 20 minutes.

2. Preheat oven to 350°F (175°C). Lightly grease a 9x13 inch baking dish.

3. In a large bowl, stir together the cooked rice, diced chicken, mayonnaise, yogurt, cream of mushroom soup, and chicken broth. Mix in the lemon juice, onion, water chestnuts, 1 cup sliced almonds, and celery. Season with white pepper and salt. Transfer mixture to the prepared baking dish.

4. In a bowl, toss the cornflakes cereal and remaining ½ cup sliced almonds with the melted butter. Spread evenly over the casserole.

5. Bake in the preheated oven 35 to 45 minutes or until lightly browned. **Yield:** 12 servings.

Per serving: About 547 calories, 23g protein, 34g carbohydrate, 36g fat, 3g fiber, 91mg cholesterol, 1263mg sodium

Spinach and Tortellini Salad

Submitted by: **Linda Vich**

"Enjoy this salad on a warm summer evening with garlic breadsticks."

3	(9 ounce) packages cheese-filled tortellini	3	(2.25 ounce) cans sliced black olives
3	(10 ounce) packages frozen chopped spinach, thawed and drained	1	(16 ounce) bottle Italian-style salad dressing Salt and ground black pepper to taste
1	cup grated Parmesan cheese		
6	cups cherry tomatoes, halved		

1. Cook pasta in a large pot of salted boiling water until al dente; rinse pasta under cold water and drain.
2. In a large bowl, combine the tortellini, spinach, cheese, tomatoes, and olives. Add enough salad dressing to coat. Toss and season with salt and pepper. **Yield:** 12 servings.

Per serving: About 371 calories, 11g protein, 29g carbohydrate, 25g fat, 4g fiber, 15mg cholesterol, 687mg sodium

Layered Salad

Submitted by: **Anonymous**

"This is a wonderful recipe that you can adjust to suit your taste. If there are only two of you, don't decrease the recipe because I'm sure you'll want more."

4	eggs	2	cups mayonnaise
1	large head lettuce, torn	2	teaspoons white sugar
1	onion, chopped	1	teaspoon seasoned salt
1	(8 ounce) can water chestnuts	¼	teaspoon garlic powder
1	(16 ounce) package frozen green peas	½	pound bacon, cooked and crumbled
		1	large tomato, chopped

1. Place eggs in a large saucepan and completely cover with water. Bring to a boil; cover and remove from heat. Let stand for 12 minutes. Remove eggs and chill.
2. In a 9x13 inch dish or large glass bowl, layer the lettuce, onion, water chestnuts, and peas.
3. In a medium bowl, combine the mayonnaise, sugar, seasoned salt, and garlic powder. Mix until smooth. Spread evenly over the top of the peas. Cover and refrigerate overnight.
4. Peel and chop hard cooked eggs. Remove salad from refrigerator; top with eggs, bacon, and tomato. Serve immediately. **Yield:** 10 servings.

Per serving: About 493 calories, 12g protein, 8g carbohydrate, 45g fat, 2g fiber, 124mg cholesterol, 785mg sodium

Edie's Patatosalata

Submitted by: **Irene**

"Red potato salad with a light oil, vinegar, and herb dressing. No mayonnaise. My kids love it! If you like, you can leave the skins on the potatoes for a more colorful dish."

1	cup extra virgin olive oil	2	red onions, thinly sliced
6	tablespoons red wine vinegar	10	large red potatoes
2	teaspoons dried oregano		Salt and ground black pepper to taste
¼	cup chopped fresh parsley		

1. In a small bowl, combine olive oil, vinegar, oregano, parsley, and onion. Mix and set aside.

2. Add potatoes to a large pot of lightly salted boiling water. Boil for about 20 minutes or until potatoes are tender. Drain and let cool.

3. Peel and dice cooled potatoes. Place in a large bowl, add dressing, and season with salt and pepper to taste. Toss to coat. Cover bowl and refrigerate for several hours or overnight. **Yield:** 10 servings.

Per serving: About 357 calories, 3g protein, 36g carbohydrate, 23g fat, 4g fiber, 0mg cholesterol, 10mg sodium

Make-Ahead ▶

Prep Time: 15 minutes

Cook Time: 20 minutes

Average Rating: ★★★★★

What other cooks have done:

"Very good, although a little oily. I added extra potatoes, and I'll cut the olive oil back to ⅔ cup next time. Great with lightly steamed green beans added to it as well."

Dump Cake V

Submitted by: **Barbara**

"This recipe for dump cake is more like a cobbler than it is a cake. I serve it in a bowl with whipped cream, ice cream, or frozen whipped topping. It's quick to prepare and it's delicious."

1	(21 ounce) can cherry pie filling	1	cup butter or margarine, melted
1	(20 ounce) can crushed pineapple, drained	1	cup flaked coconut
1	(18.25 ounce) package yellow cake mix	½	cup chopped walnuts

1. Preheat oven to 350°F (175°C). Lightly grease a 9x13 inch baking dish.

2. In the prepared dish, layer pie filling over crushed pineapple. Sprinkle cake mix over the top, covering evenly. Pour melted butter over cake mix and sprinkle the top with the coconut and chopped walnuts.

3. Bake in the preheated oven 50 to 60 minutes or until browned and bubbly. **Yield:** 18 servings.

Per serving: About 311 calories, 2g protein, 39g carbohydrate, 17g fat, 1g fiber, 1mg cholesterol, 322mg sodium

Quick & Easy ▶

Prep Time: 15 minutes

Cook Time: 1 hour

Average Rating: ★★★★★

What other cooks have done:

"This is a wonderful and easy dessert! It's very sweet, so it definitely needs to be served with vanilla ice cream! If you sprinkle the coconut and nuts under the cake mix, it keeps them from getting too brown, or you could sprinkle them on towards the end of baking. Try it with different nuts, different fruit fillings, and different cake mix flavors."

Hot Fudge Ice Cream Bar Dessert

(pictured on page 304)

Submitted by: **Connie West**
"An incredibly easy, rich, and satisfying ice cream dessert made with ice cream sandwiches and fudge sauce. This keeps in the freezer very well and can be eaten straight from the freezer."

1	(16 ounce) jar chocolate syrup	1	(12 ounce) container frozen whipped topping, thawed
¾	cup peanut butter	1	cup salted peanuts
19	ice cream sandwiches		

1. Pour syrup into a medium microwave–safe bowl and microwave 2 minutes on high. Do not allow syrup to boil. Stir peanut butter into syrup until smooth. Allow to cool to room temperature.
2. Line the bottom of a 9x13 inch dish with 9½ ice cream sandwiches. Spread half the whipped topping over the sandwiches. Spoon half the chocolate mixture over whipped topping. Top with half the peanuts. Repeat layers. Freeze 1 hour or until firm. Cut into squares to serve. **Yield:** 18 servings.

Per serving: About 384 calories, 8g protein, 47g carbohydrate, 19g fat, 2g fiber, 21mg cholesterol, 172mg sodium

We All Scream for Ice Cream ▼

The ice cream dessert above uses store-bought ice cream sandwiches, but if you're feeling adventurous, consider making your own ice cream instead.

Ice Cream Styles
Ice cream is divided into two basic categories: custard style and Philadelphia style. With custard ice cream, lots of egg yolks are whisked together with cream and milk and sugar, and cooked gently until the mixture becomes thick enough to coat the back of a spoon. All those egg yolks help make an ice cream that's remarkably smooth and incredibly rich. Philadelphia style ice cream contains no egg yolks and does not require cooking. It's based purely on cream and sugar. This kind of ice cream can be a little simpler to make than custard, because it doesn't require the same precision in cooking a custard, and you can use heavy cream, half-and-half, whole milk, skim milk, sour cream, or yogurt in your recipe.

Do Your Ice Cream a Flavor
Once you see how easy homemade ice cream is to make, you might want to invent your own favorite flavor, and we have some pointers for adding treats to your basic ice cream mix. For exceptional fruity flavor, choose fruit that's perfectly ripe, and then sprinkle it with sugar and smash it up with a potato masher before mixing it into the ice cream base. Fruit ice cream made this way will taste much better than a batch in which you just toss chunks of fruit into the mix. If you wish to add anything chunky like nuts or bits of cookie, cake, brownie, or candy, stir the chunks in by hand once the ice cream is the consistency of soft-serve. Then freeze it until it has the texture of traditional, scoopable ice cream.

Ladies and Gentlemen, start your freezers!

- Jennifer Anderson
For more information, visit **Allrecipes.com**

Menu Prep Plan

1. Layer tiramisu through Step 6 and refrigerate.

2. Prepare salad ingredients, but do not toss. Prepare artichokes. While artichokes steam, cook Chicken Marsala Florentine.

3. Toss salad just before dinner.

4. Finish tiramisu just before serving.

Restaurant Fare ▶

Prep Time: 10 minutes

Cook Time: 25 minutes

Average Rating: ★★★★☆

What other cooks have done:

"The sun-dried tomatoes add a great flavor. I used tomatoes packed in oil so I cut the butter almost in half, and it still turned out perfect! I also added a clove of garlic and a green onion to the sauce for a little more kick. This was fantastic!"

Anniversary Meal

A special meal for a special night, this dinner is designed just for two. Skip the fancy restaurant and impress your loved one with delicious dishes from your own kitchen.

Chicken Marsala Florentine

Submitted by: **Shannon**
"This is a gorgeous chicken dish with sun-dried tomatoes, spinach, and mushrooms. It's wonderful served with garlic mashed potatoes. It tastes fantastic!"

4	skinless, boneless chicken breast halves	¾	cup butter
¼	cup all-purpose flour	3	cups sliced portobello mushrooms
	Salt and ground black pepper to taste	¾	cup sun-dried tomatoes
1	tablespoon dried oregano	1	cup Marsala wine
2	tablespoons olive oil	½	cup packed fresh spinach

1. Place chicken breasts between 2 pieces of wax paper and pound to ¼ inch thickness. Dust chicken with flour, salt and pepper to taste, and oregano.

2. In a skillet, fry chicken in hot olive oil over medium heat. Cook until done, turning to cook evenly. Remove chicken; set aside and keep warm.

3. In the skillet, melt butter over medium heat; add mushrooms, sun-dried tomatoes, and Marsala wine. Cook for approximately 10 minutes, stirring occasionally. Stir in spinach and cook for about 2 minutes. Serve over chicken. **Yield:** 4 servings.

Per serving: About 667 calories, 32g protein, 23g carbohydrate, 43g fat, 3g fiber, 162mg cholesterol, 799mg sodium

Garlic Sautéed Artichokes

Submitted by: **John Donivan**

"Artichokes are sautéed in garlic butter before steaming. A simple and delicious way to use artichokes!"

2	large artichokes (about 1 pound each)	3	cloves garlic, chopped
2	tablespoons butter	¼	cup water

1. Rinse artichokes under cold water and use a sharp knife to cut the top third off each one. Trim the stems to about 1 inch and remove the smaller leaves from around the base. Use scissors to remove any remaining leaf tips. Cut each artichoke in half lengthwise, then use a spoon to scrape out the hairy choke. Rinse again to remove any residual choke.

2. Melt butter in a large skillet over medium heat. Add garlic and sauté for about 1 minute to flavor the butter. Arrange artichoke halves, cut side down, in the skillet. Sauté for about 5 to 10 minutes or until lightly browned. Reduce heat to low and pour in water; cover and let steam for 15 to 20 minutes or until the artichokes are tender. A fork should easily pierce the stem. **Yield:** 2 to 4 servings.

Per serving: About 92 calories, 3g protein, 9g carbohydrate, 6g fat, 4g fiber, 16mg cholesterol, 135mg sodium

Beet and Balsamic Vinaigrette Salad

Submitted by: **Lori Lee**

"A light and refreshing salad that needs to be eaten as soon as you add the dressing."

3	slices bacon	½	red onion, sliced in rings
2	romaine hearts, rinsed and torn	¼	cup grated Parmesan cheese
1	(15 ounce) can julienned beets, drained	½	cup balsamic vinaigrette salad dressing

1. Place bacon in a large, deep skillet. Cook over medium-high heat until evenly browned. Drain, crumble, and set aside.

2. In a large bowl, toss together the romaine, beets, onion, cheese, and dressing until evenly coated. Sprinkle with the crumbled bacon and serve immediately. **Yield:** 3 servings.

Per serving: About 152 calories, 6g protein, 21g carbohydrate, 5g fat, 3g fiber, 10mg cholesterol, 1024mg sodium

Strawberry Tiramisu for Two

Submitted by: **Linda Miranda**

"Tiramisu is Italian for 'pick me up.' This roll-your-eyes, taste-bud tantalizer has become a traditional wedding anniversary dessert treat that I've been making for my husband and me for 17 years. You might call it a happy hubby dessert! This is my easy version of a classic because it's made without eggs. It has a wonderful fresh strawberry layer and puree base. It's delicioso! It's made to accommodate two extra large portions."

Around-the-World Cuisine ▶

Prep Time: 30 minutes

Average Rating: ★★★★★

What other cooks have done:

"I wasn't sure how this would turn out with strawberries—I was stuck on the more classic variation of this dessert. I'm sure glad I made this, and my hubby loved it as well."

1	pint fresh strawberries, divided	2	tablespoons coffee-flavored liqueur
½	cup confectioners' sugar, divided	18	ladyfingers
1	cup mascarpone cheese	⅓	cup chilled espresso
½	cup heavy whipping cream, divided	½	teaspoon unsweetened cocoa powder

1. Cut tops off strawberries and slice berries lengthwise. Reserve 2 large whole berries for garnish.

2. In a blender, combine 2 cups of strawberries and 2 tablespoons confectioners' sugar; blend to puree and set aside.

3. In a medium bowl, combine mascarpone cheese, ¼ cup cream, ¼ cup sugar, and liqueur; beat with an electric mixer on medium-high speed for 1 to 1½ minutes or until thickened.

4. Place 6 ladyfingers on a serving plate and brush each with about 1 teaspoon cold espresso. Spread or pipe half of cheese mixture over the ladyfingers and layer with half of the sliced strawberries.

5. Repeat layers with the next 6 ladyfingers, espresso, remaining cheese mixture, and sliced strawberries; top with remaining 6 ladyfingers.

6. In a small mixing bowl, combine remaining ¼ cup heavy cream with 2 tablespoons sugar; beat with an electric mixer on medium-high speed until just whipped, approximately 1 minute. Spread cream evenly over top layer of ladyfingers.

7. Dust cocoa over whipped cream and garnish with 2 reserved strawberries. Pour strawberry puree onto 2 serving plates. Cut tiramisu in half and place onto puree. **Yield:** 2 servings.

Per serving: About 1290 calories, 21g protein, 113g carbohydrate, 84g fat, 5g fiber, 587mg cholesterol, 241mg sodium

Valentine's Dinner

Field Salad makes a light, flirty, and fun start to dinner, while Chocolate-Covered Strawberries (on page 81) finish it with style.

Field Salad *(pictured on page 79)*

Submitted by: **Candice Brosnan**
"This easy salad recipe will thrill all of your guests! Adorn this salad with fresh herbs and edible flowers for an extra special treat."

4	ounces mixed salad greens	1	tart green apple, cored and thinly sliced
⅓	cup chopped walnuts, toasted	¼	cup bottle raspberry vinaigrette salad dressing
4	ounces Gorgonzola cheese, crumbled		Garnish: edible flowers

1. In a large bowl, combine salad greens, walnuts, cheese, and apple. Toss with raspberry vinaigrette. Garnish, if desired. **Yield:** 2 servings.

Per serving: About 414 calories, 17g protein, 23g carbohydrate, 31g fat, 4g fiber, 60mg cholesterol, 913mg sodium

Filet Mignon with Rich Balsamic Glaze

(pictured on page 78)

Submitted by: **Linda W**.
"Here's an elegant and quick romantic dinner for two. Wonderful served with steamed asparagus and baby red potatoes."

	Salt to taste	¼	cup balsamic vinegar
½	teaspoon freshly ground black pepper	¼	cup dry red wine
2	(4 to 6 ounce) beef tenderloin steaks		

1. Sprinkle salt to taste and pepper over both sides of each steak.
2. Heat a nonstick skillet over medium–high heat. Place steaks in hot pan and cook for 1 minute on each side or until browned. Reduce heat to medium–low and add balsamic vinegar and red wine. Cover and cook for 4 minutes on each side, basting with sauce when meat is turned.
3. Remove steaks to 2 warmed plates and spoon 1 tablespoon of glaze over each. Serve immediately. **Yield:** 2 servings.

Per serving: About 364 calories, 20g protein, 6g carbohydrate, 26g fat, 0g fiber, 81mg cholesterol, 64mg sodium

---

Menu

Field Salad

Filet Mignon with Rich Balsamic Glaze

Bella's Rosemary Red Potatoes

Pan-Fried Asparagus

Chocolate-Covered Strawberries

Serves 2

Menu Prep Plan

1. While potatoes bake, pan-fry asparagus and assemble salad.
2. Cook filets.

◀ Quick & Easy

Prep Time: 10 minutes
Average Rating: ★★★★★

What other cooks have done:
"I used toasted almonds and sun-dried tomato dressing. It was a huge hit and looked so elegant. I'm going to experiment with various cheese, nut, and fruit combinations."

◀ Restaurant Fare

Prep Time: 5 minutes
Cook Time: 10 minutes
Average Rating: ★★★★☆

What other cooks have done:
"I bought a wonderful filet mignon the other night. I stumbled upon this recipe, and the filet was magnificent. I cooked the filet a little longer because I like my filet medium, and the glaze was even more caramelized and tasted great. I will never cook my filet any other way."

Bella's Rosemary Red Potatoes

(pictured on page 78)

Submitted by: **Bellarouge**

"The simplest, most elegant side dish ever! This is the best way to impress company without any extra effort. Bon appetit!"

3	tablespoons butter, melted	1	tablespoon chopped fresh rosemary
3	tablespoons vegetable oil	½	teaspoon salt
8	small red potatoes, scrubbed and cut into wedges	¼	teaspoon pepper

1. Preheat oven to 375°F (190°C).

2. Mix together melted butter and oil; pour into a 9x13 inch baking dish. Place the potatoes into the dish and stir until coated. Sprinkle with rosemary, salt, and pepper. Cover with aluminum foil.

3. Bake in the preheated oven for 30 minutes or until the potatoes are tender. Stir potatoes occasionally to ensure even cooking.

Yield: 4 servings.

Per serving: About 218 calories, 2g protein, 18g carbohydrate, 16g fat, 2g fiber, 23mg cholesterol, 387mg sodium

Pan-Fried Asparagus *(pictured on page 78)*

Submitted by: **Kim**

"This garlic asparagus dish is a northern Italian side dish. My family loves it! Even the kids!"

¼	cup butter	3	cloves garlic, minced
2	tablespoons olive oil	½	pound fresh asparagus spears, trimmed
½	teaspoon coarse salt		
¼	teaspoon ground black pepper		

1. Melt butter in a skillet over medium-high heat. Stir in the olive oil, salt, and pepper. Cook garlic in butter for 1 minute but do not brown. Add asparagus and cook for 5 to 10 minutes or until crisp-tender, turning asparagus to ensure even cooking. **Yield:** 2 servings.

Per serving: About 352 calories, 4g protein, 6g carbohydrate, 36g fat, 1g fiber, 61mg cholesterol, 821mg sodium

Deep-South Fried Chicken, page 54; Angel Biscuits II, page 56; Fried Okra, page 55; and Chrissy's Sweet-'n'-Sour Tomato Salad, page 55

Filet Mignon with Rich Balsamic Glaze,
page 75; Pan-Fried Asparagus, page 76;
and Bella's Rosemary Red Potatoes,
page 76

Chocolate-Covered Strawberries, page 81

Field Salad, page 75

Firecracker Burgers, page 84; Oven Fries, page 85; and Red, White, and Blue Slaw Salad, page 84

Chocolate-Covered Strawberries

(pictured on page 79)

Submitted by: **Kitten**

"This is the simplest version of chocolate-covered strawberries I know. Paraffin was originally used instead of shortening. Turn the strawberries upside down and insert by the toothpicks into a piece of Styrofoam for easy cooling, or simply place them on a sheet of wax paper. You can drizzle white chocolate over the milk chocolate for a fancier look. Serve with chilled champagne."

1 pound fresh strawberries with leaves	2 tablespoons shortening
16 ounces milk chocolate or semisweet chocolate chips	

1. Insert toothpicks into the tops of the strawberries.

2. In a double boiler, melt chocolate and shortening, stirring occasionally until smooth. Holding them by the toothpicks, dip the strawberries into the chocolate mixture.

3. Turn the strawberries upside down and insert the toothpicks into Styrofoam for the chocolate to cool. **Yield:** 24 servings.

Per serving: About 107 calories, 1g protein, 13g carbohydrate, 6g fat, 0g fiber, 0mg cholesterol, 13mg sodium

◀ Party Food

Prep Time: 15 minutes

Average Rating: ★★★★★

What other cooks have done:

"I've never made these before because I assumed they would be difficult and time-consuming, but these were simple. I don't own a double boiler so I microwaved the chocolate chips and shortening in a glass bowl for about 2 to 3 minutes at 70% power. I dipped 30 medium- to large-sized strawberries and still had quite a bit of the chocolate left over, which I tried out on pretzels and frozen bananas with great results."

Champagne 101 ▼

When stoking the flames of romance, pair your perfect menu with a few glasses of champagne. Don't let the multitude of bottles intimidate you—picking the right bottle is easier than you think.

Champagnes From Dry to Sweet

Five classifications are used to refer directly to the champagne's sweetness:

• Brut: very dry, less than 1.5% sugar
• Extra Brut: extra dry, 1.2 to 2% sugar
• Sec: slightly sweet, 1.7 to 3.5% sugar
• Demi-Sec: fairly sweet, 3.3 to 5% sugar (dessert champagne)
• Doux: very sweet, over 5% sugar (dessert champagne)

Other Wines Have Bubbles, Too

True champagne comes only from France, but the grapes used to make sparkling wine are grown all over the world—California, eastern Washington, Spain, Britain, and Italy, just to name a few areas. Sparkling wines are created by the same technique used to make champagne, the major difference being the grapes used. Sparkling wines are as delicious as many champagnes, and tend to be somewhat less expensive and more widely available.

Get More Out of Your Bubbly

Whether it's champagne or sparkling wine that you uncork, always remember to chill the bottle in the coldest part of your refrigerator. Serve the bubbly in clear, completely dry glasses with tall sides that come to a point on the inside (at the bottom). To open your champagne bottle with flair, follow these simple steps: Pat the bottle dry, grasp the cork with a dry cloth, and, holding the bottle at a 45 degree angle away from you, twist the bottle, not the cork. You should feel the cork easing itself loose. When you feel it start to go, get ready for the POP and to enjoy this rich and racy sparkling wine. Nothing says "celebrate" better or more than champagne!

- Tammy Weisberger
For more information, visit **Allrecipes.com**

**Shrimp and Mushroom
Linguine with Creamy
Cheese Herb Sauce**
Toasted Garlic Bread
Frozen Mudslide
Serves 4

Menu Prep Plan

1. Prepare and cook pasta.

2. Broil bread while pasta cooks.

3. Prepare mudslides just before serving.

Out-of-the-Ordinary ▶

Prep Time: 10 minutes

Cook Time: 15 minutes

Average Rating: ★★★★★

What other cooks have done:

"I added a chopped green onion, a chopped green bell pepper, and 1 chicken breast chopped (in addition to the shrimp) when sautéing the mushrooms. I also used cream cheese with chives. It was heavenly! I'll be making this meal again!"

Just Between Friends

Dinner with close friends is a perfect time to catch up, and with this casual but flavorful pasta, you can focus on conversation, not cooking. If you'd prefer a nonalcoholic beverage, serve chocolate smoothies or iced coffee instead.

Shrimp and Mushroom Linguine with Creamy Cheese Herb Sauce

Submitted by: **Karyn**

"This recipe is a 'gift from the gods.' You can easily substitute something else for the shrimp and mushrooms."

1 (8 ounce) package linguine pasta	1 (3 ounce) package cream cheese
½ pound fresh mushrooms, sliced	2 tablespoons chopped fresh parsley
1 tablespoon butter	¾ teaspoon dried basil
½ cup butter	⅔ cup boiling water
2 cloves garlic, minced	½ pound cooked shrimp

1. Cook linguine according to package directions; drain and set aside.

2. Sauté mushrooms in 1 tablespoon butter until tender and cooked.

3. In a sauté pan, melt ½ cup butter with the garlic. Stir in cream cheese, breaking it up with a spoon as it melts. Stir in the parsley and basil. Simmer for 5 minutes and stir in the boiling water; mix until smooth.

4. Add the cooked shrimp and mushrooms and heat through. Toss with cooked linguine and serve. **Yield:** 4 servings.

Per serving: About 552 calories, 23g protein, 44g carbohydrate, 33g fat, 3g fiber, 196mg cholesterol, 432mg sodium

Toasted Garlic Bread

Submitted by: **Clair**

"Quick and scrumptious garlic bread that will complement any Italian meal. Melted mozzarella is optional, but delicious!"

½ (1 pound) loaf Italian bread
2 tablespoons butter, softened
1 teaspoon extra virgin olive oil
2 cloves garlic, crushed
½ teaspoon dried oregano
  Salt and ground black pepper to taste
½ cup shredded mozzarella cheese

1. Preheat the oven to Broil.
2. Cut the bread into slices 1 to 2 inches thick.
3. In a small bowl, mix butter, olive oil, garlic, oregano, and salt and pepper to taste. Spread the mixture evenly on the bread slices.
4. On a baking sheet, arrange the slices evenly and broil 5 minutes or until slightly brown. Check frequently so the slices don't burn.
5. Remove from broiler. Top with cheese and return to broiler 2 to 3 minutes or until cheese is melted and bubbly. Serve immediately.
Yield: 5 servings.

Per serving: About 241 calories, 10g protein, 24g carbohydrate, 12g fat, 1g fiber, 28mg cholesterol, 428mg sodium

◄ Family Favorite

Prep Time: 10 minutes
Cook Time: 8 minutes
Average Rating: ★★★★★

What other cooks have done:
"Instead of preparing individual pieces of bread, I just slice the entire loaf once through the middle and prepare as instructed. I have some advice for future garlic bread makers: Don't try to broil the bread on a flat pan or stone! It works best in a deep dish; that way the oils don't drip out."

Frozen Mudslide

Submitted by: **Margaret**

"A frozen alcoholic drink. Feel free to drizzle glasses with additional chocolate syrup."

4 cups crushed ice
⅓ cup vodka
⅓ cup coffee-flavored liqueur
⅓ cup Irish cream liqueur
2 tablespoons chocolate syrup
½ cup whipped cream

1. In a blender, combine crushed ice, vodka, coffee liqueur, and Irish cream liqueur. Drizzle in chocolate syrup and blend until smooth. Pour into glasses and top with whipped cream. **Yield:** 4 servings.

Per serving: About 246 calories, 1g protein, 25g carbohydrate, 2g fat, 1g fiber, 6mg cholesterol, 35mg sodium

◄ Quick & Easy

Prep Time: 5 minutes
Average Rating: ★★★★★

What other cooks have done:
"Good stuff. The brain freeze took awhile to wear off, though."

Menu Prep Plan

1. Prepare and bake apple pie.

2. Shape burgers and prepare toppings. Wrap Banana Boats in foil. Cut potatoes.

3. Prepare slaw while fries bake. Grill burgers.

4. Heat Banana Boats and cook Kettle Corn after dinner.

From the Grill ▶

Prep Time: 10 minutes

Cook Time: 16 minutes

Average Rating: ★★★★☆

What other cooks have done:

"I use my hands when mixing—the ingredients are more evenly distributed this way. Add more heat to the burgers with pepper Jack cheese."

Make-Ahead ▶

Prep Time: 10 minutes

Cook Time: 15 minutes

Average Rating: ★★★★★

What other cooks have done:

"This slaw is delicious! I made one mistake—I didn't think ½ cup blue cheese was enough, so I added a bit, but it was too strong. Next time, I'll stick to the recipe."

Fourth of July Barbecue

Get ready for feasting and fireworks. Serve grilled burgers and coleslaw with ooey, gooey Banana Boats—boatloads better than sundaes.

Firecracker Burgers *(pictured on page 80)*

Submitted by: **Gail**

"A great burger—very moist and flavorful. Serve with your favorite fixings."

1 pound ground chuck	4 slices Monterey Jack cheese
1 (4 ounce) can diced green chiles, drained	4 hamburger buns
1 teaspoon beef bouillon granules	Toppings: lettuce, tomato, red onion, ketchup, mustard

1. Lightly oil grill rack and preheat grill for high heat.
2. In a medium bowl, mix ground chuck, diced green chiles, and bouillon granules. Shape into 4 patties.
3. Grill patties 4 to 8 minutes per side or to desired doneness. Top each patty with cheese about 2 minutes prior to removing from grill. Serve on buns with desired toppings. **Yield:** 4 servings.

Per serving: About 367 calories, 34g protein, 25g carbohydrate, 15g fat, 2g fiber, 85mg cholesterol, 683mg sodium

Red, White, and Blue Slaw Salad

(pictured on page 80)

Submitted by: **Marcy Baker**

"You will never go back to the 'old' way of making cole slaw!"

12 slices bacon	1 cup cherry tomatoes, halved
6 cups shredded cabbage	½ cup blue cheese, crumbled
1 cup coleslaw dressing	

1. Place bacon in a large, deep skillet. Cook over medium-high heat until evenly browned. Drain on paper towels and crumble; set aside.
2. In a large bowl, combine the cabbage and dressing. Mix well. Sprinkle with sliced cherry tomatoes, blue cheese, and reserved bacon. Refrigerate and serve chilled. **Yield:** 6 servings (about 5 cups).

Per serving: About 354 calories, 9g protein, 15g carbohydrate, 28g fat, 2g fiber, 45mg cholesterol, 1050mg sodium

Oven Fries *(pictured on page 80)*

Submitted by: **Barbara Harris**
"These French fries are made in the oven."

2½	pounds baking potatoes	1	teaspoon salt
1	teaspoon vegetable oil	⅛	teaspoon ground cayenne
1	tablespoon white sugar		pepper

1. Preheat oven to 450°F (230°C). Line a baking sheet with foil and lightly grease foil. Scrub potatoes well and cut into ½ inch thick strips.
2. In a large bowl, combine oil, sugar, salt, and cayenne pepper. Add potatoes and toss to coat. Spread on baking sheet in 1 layer.
3. Bake in the preheated oven for 30 minutes, turning after 15 minutes. Serve immediately. **Yield:** 6 servings.

Per serving: About 164 calories, 4g protein, 36g carbohydrate, 1g fat, 5g fiber, 0mg cholesterol, 401mg sodium

Kettle Corn

Submitted by: **Sue**
"Take a trip to the county fair with a bowl of old-fashioned sweet Kettle Corn. Your family will never want plain popcorn again!"

¼	cup vegetable oil	½	cup unpopped popcorn
¼	cup white sugar		kernels

1. Combine oil and sugar and pour into a large pot; add popcorn kernels. Over medium heat, begin to pop the popcorn. Constantly shake the pot to ensure that the popcorn kernels and oil do not burn. Once the popping has slowed, immediately remove popcorn to a serving bowl. **Yield:** 5 servings.

Per serving: About 209 calories, 2g protein, 25g carbohydrate, 12g fat, 3g fiber, 0mg cholesterol, 0mg sodium

---

◀ **Family Favorite**

Prep Time: 15 minutes
Cook Time: 30 minutes
Average Rating: ★★★★☆
What other cooks have done:
"These fries are the easiest and best we've ever had. They tasted like steak fries from a restaurant. I scored the potatoes with a fork after cutting them because it makes the spice stick better and gives the fries a restaurant appearance. You'll want to turn them halfway through the cooking to prevent burning and to be sure they cook evenly."

◀ **Family Favorite**

Prep Time: 5 minutes
Cook Time: 15 minutes
Average Rating: ★★★★★
What other cooks have done:
"This was really good. It did take me a couple of tries to perfect the technique though. The first few times I made it, I had a big gooey mess in the bottom of the pot. Make sure you start shaking as soon as the corn starts to pop and don't stop until it's done."

Banana Boats

Submitted by: **Kelsie**

"These are great for a campfire during a trip to the outdoors. If you don't have a fire, use the oven or grill. Serve with hot chocolate."

4 bananas	½ cup miniature
½ cup semisweet chocolate	marshmallows
chips	

1. Slit each banana lengthwise through the peel, making sure not to cut all the way through to the other side. Stuff the bananas with chocolate chips and marshmallows.

2. Wrap each banana in aluminum foil and cook over a fire on the grill or in a 300°F (150°C) oven for 8 minutes or until chocolate is melted. Eat with a spoon. **Yield:** 4 servings.

Per serving: About 253 calories, 2g protein, 37g carbohydrate, 14g fat, 3g fiber, 0mg cholesterol, 6mg sodium

All-American Apple Pie

Submitted by: **Amy**

"Quick and easy with a great noncrust topping. Try a variety of apples."

1½ cups all-purpose flour	¾ teaspoon ground cinnamon
½ cup vegetable oil	½ teaspoon ground nutmeg
2 tablespoons cold milk	6 Fuji apples, cored and sliced
1½ teaspoons white sugar	½ cup all-purpose flour
1 teaspoon salt	½ cup white sugar
¾ cup white sugar	½ cup cold butter
3 tablespoons all-purpose flour	

1. Preheat oven to 350°F (175°C).

2. In a large bowl, mix together 1½ cups flour, oil, milk, 1½ teaspoons sugar, and salt until evenly blended. Pat mixture into a 9 inch pie pan, spreading the dough evenly over the bottom and up sides.

3. Mix together ¾ cup sugar, 3 tablespoons flour, cinnamon, and nutmeg. Sprinkle over apples and toss to coat. Spread evenly in unbaked pie shell.

4. Using a pastry cutter, blend together ½ cup flour, ½ cup sugar, and butter until evenly distributed and crumbly in texture. Sprinkle over apples.

5. Put pie pan on a 10x15 inch jellyroll pan to catch the juices that may spill over. Bake in the preheated oven for 45 minutes or until golden. Let stand before serving. **Yield:** 8 servings.

Per serving: About 536 calories, 4g protein, 74g carbohydrate, 26g fat, 4g fiber, 31mg cholesterol, 411mg sodium

Grilling with Friends

Long summer days are made for grilling, so toss your normal grill-out menu in favor of this one. Guests can sample Artichoke Spread while the salmon cooks. They'll love the fish's spicy kick, and cool down with a refreshing slice of Lemonade Cake.

Grilled Salmon with Habanero-Lime Butter

Submitted by: **Mike Smith**
"Grilled salmon marinated in orange juice, lime juice, tequila, and habanero peppers, then served with a habanero-lime butter. You can take the seeds out of the peppers before preparation to tame the heat."

¼	cup vegetable oil	4	(4 ounce) salmon fillets
½	cup orange juice	¼	cup butter, softened
1	tablespoon grated lime zest	1	tablespoon lime juice
1	tablespoon tequila	2	teaspoons minced habanero pepper
3	tablespoons lime juice		
1	tablespoon minced habanero pepper	2	teaspoons grated lime zest
		¼	teaspoon garlic salt
1	clove garlic, minced		

1. In a stainless steel bowl or glass baking dish, combine vegetable oil, orange juice, 1 tablespoon lime zest, tequila, 3 tablespoons lime juice, 1 tablespoon habanero pepper, and minced garlic. Mix well. Place salmon fillets in marinade and coat evenly. Refrigerate for 2 hours, turning frequently.
2. In a mixing bowl, using an electric mixer, beat the butter until smooth. Mix in 1 tablespoon lime juice, 2 teaspoons habanero pepper, 2 teaspoons lime zest, and garlic salt. Cover and refrigerate.
3. Lightly oil grill rack and preheat grill for medium heat.
4. Place salmon fillets on grill. Cook 15 minutes or until salmon flakes with a fork, turning once and basting frequently with marinade. Serve with habanero butter. **Yield:** 4 servings.

Per serving: About 457 calories, 23g protein, 6g carbohydrate, 37g fat, 1g fiber, 97mg cholesterol, 298mg sodium

Menu

Grilled Salmon with Habanero-Lime Butter
Artichoke Spread
Lemonade Cake
Serves 4

Menu Prep Plan

1. Marinate salmon.
2. Prepare and chill cake.
3. Bake Artichoke Spread and prepare Habanero-Lime Butter. Grill salmon.

◄ Hot & Spicy

Prep Time: 20 minutes
Cook Time: 15 minutes
Average Rating: ★★★★★
What other cooks have done:
"We didn't have habaneros, so we substituted jalapeños."

Party Food ▶

Prep Time: 15 minutes

Cook Time: 15 minutes

Average Rating: ★★★★★

What other cooks have done:

"This is a great party dish! It travels well and is always a success. I recommend doubling or tripling it! I did not process the ingredients and instead coarsely chopped the artichokes and mixed all together by hand. This made for bites with bits and pieces of artichoke. Yummy! For a spicy variation, try adding a chopped jalapeño or two."

Make-Ahead ▶

Prep Time: 30 minutes

Cook Time: 20 minutes

Freeze Time: 3 hours

Average Rating: ★★★★★

What other cooks have done:

"I made this cake for a block party and everyone loved it! I used a 12 ounce can of lemonade concentrate to make it more lemony and substituted frozen whipped topping for the whipping cream and sugar."

Artichoke Spread

Submitted by: **Sarahsue**

"A yummy hot artichoke spread that's perfect for company! Smooth and cheesy win the race to your happy tummy. Serve it with bread, crackers, or veggies."

1 (14 ounce) can artichoke hearts, drained	1 cup grated Parmesan cheese
1 (8 ounce) package cream cheese	½ cup mayonnaise
	1 clove garlic, peeled
	¾ teaspoon dried dill weed

1. Preheat oven to 400°F (200°C).
2. Place artichoke hearts in a food processor and process until smooth. Add the cream cheese, Parmesan cheese, mayonnaise, garlic, and dill; process until the mixture is smooth and well blended. Transfer to a 9 inch pie pan.
3. Bake in the preheated oven 10 to 15 minutes or until bubbly and lightly browned. **Yield:** 24 servings (about 3 cups).

Per serving: About 93 calories, 3g protein, 2g carbohydrate, 8g fat, 1g fiber, 16mg cholesterol, 231mg sodium

Lemonade Cake *(pictured on page 4)*

Submitted by: **Mona**

"This is my husband's favorite cake. It's two layers of yellow cake with a lemonade-flavored ice cream center. Wonderful on a hot day."

1 (18.25 ounce) package yellow cake mix	2 cups heavy whipping cream
1 quart vanilla ice cream	2 tablespoons white sugar
1 (6 ounce) can frozen lemonade concentrate, thawed and divided	

1. Prepare and bake cake mix according to package directions for 2 (9 inch) round cake pans. Cool.
2. Stir ice cream to soften; stir in ½ cup lemonade concentrate. Spread ice cream mixture evenly in a foil lined 9 inch round cake pan. Freeze until firm, about 2 to 3 hours or overnight.
3. Arrange 1 cake layer on a serving plate, top with ice cream layer, then with second layer of cake. Put assembled cake back into freezer.
4. Beat whipping cream with the remaining lemonade concentrate and 2 tablespoons sugar until fluffy and peaks form. Frost top and sides of cake with whipped cream mixture. Return cake to freezer for at least 1 hour before serving. **Yield:** 12 servings.

Per serving: About 452 calories, 4g protein, 56g carbohydrate, 25g fat, 1g fiber, 75mg cholesterol, 334mg sodium

Mexican Fiesta

Meet Cinco de Mayo head on with beef rolled tacos, two kinds of salsa, and festive Margarita Cake.

Oaxacan Tacos *(pictured on page 41)*

Submitted by: **Lola**
"I learned how to make these tacos from a man from Oaxaca, Mexico, who lived with my family. The steak can be broiled or grilled, if you prefer."

2	pounds top sirloin steak, cut across the grain into thin strips	1	medium-size red onion, diced
	Salt and ground black pepper to taste	4	fresh jalapeño peppers, seeded and chopped
¼	cup vegetable oil	1	bunch fresh cilantro, chopped
18	(6 inch) corn tortillas	4	limes, cut into wedges

1. Heat a large skillet over medium-high heat. Fry the steak strips, stirring constantly, about 5 minutes or until browned on the outside and cooked through, but not too firm. Season with salt and pepper to taste. Remove to a plate and keep warm.
2. Heat the oil in a skillet over medium-high heat and quickly fry each tortilla 1 minute on each side or until lightly browned but still flexible. Set aside and keep warm.
3. Place tortillas on a plate and top with steak strips, onion, jalapeño, and cilantro to taste. Squeeze lime juice over each taco. Roll up and serve. **Yield:** 9 servings.

Per serving: About 381 calories, 20g protein, 29g carbohydrate, 21g fat, 4g fiber, 59mg cholesterol, 129mg sodium

Menu

Oaxacan Tacos
Santa Fe Rice Salad
D's Famous Salsa
Salsa de Tomatillo
Margarita Cake
Serves 8

Menu Prep Plan

1. Prepare salsas and set aside or chill. Prepare rice salad.
2. Put cake in oven and fry steak for tacos. Prepare cake glaze and pour over cake while warm.

◀ Hot & Spicy

Prep Time: 15 minutes

Cook Time: 15 minutes

Average Rating: ★★★★★

What other cooks have done:
"Tasted great, but wear gloves when you chop the jalapeños! I didn't know any better and chopped them up, handling them with my bare hands. My hands were burning for hours."

Santa Fe Rice Salad (pictured on page 41)

Submitted by: **Terri**
"Great black bean and rice salad!"

1⅓	cups water	⅓	cup vegetable oil
⅔	cup uncooked white rice	¼	cup vinegar
¾	cup black beans, rinsed and drained	1	tablespoon diced jalapeño peppers
1	large tomato, seeded and diced	½	teaspoon white sugar
¾	cup shredded Cheddar cheese		Salt to taste
⅓	cup sliced green onions	1	avocado, peeled, pitted, and diced

1. In a saucepan, bring water to a boil. Add rice and stir. Reduce heat, cover, and simmer for 20 minutes. Remove from heat and chill.
2. In a large bowl, mix together the rice, beans, tomato, cheese, and green onions.
3. In a small bowl, whisk together the oil, vinegar, peppers, sugar, and salt. Pour over the rice mixture and toss to coat. Cover and refrigerate for 30 minutes. Top with avocado just before serving. **Yield:** 8 servings (about 4 cups).

Per serving: About 235 calories, 5g protein, 19g carbohydrate, 16g fat, 4g fiber, 11mg cholesterol, 136mg sodium

D's Famous Salsa

Submitted by: **Denise Smith**
"I developed and refined this recipe over many years. It's very fast, easy, and I usually have everything on hand. I often give it as gifts to my family back East."

2	(14.5 ounce) cans stewed tomatoes	1	(4.5 ounce) can chopped green chiles
½	onion, finely diced	3	tablespoons chopped fresh cilantro
1	teaspoon salt		Garnish: fresh cilantro
1	teaspoon minced garlic		Tortilla chips
½	lime, juiced		

1. Place the tomatoes, onion, salt, garlic, lime juice, green chiles, and cilantro in a blender or food processor. Blend on low to desired consistency. Garnish, if desired. Serve salsa with tortilla chips. **Yield:** 16 servings (about 4 cups).

Per serving: About 17 calories, 1g protein, 4g carbohydrate, 0g fat, 1g fiber, 0mg cholesterol, 284mg sodium

---

Make-Ahead ▶

Prep Time: 20 minutes

Cook Time: 20 minutes

Average Rating: ★★★★★

What other cooks have done:

"I took this to a Cinco de Mayo party and it was great! I used diced green chiles instead of peppers (because I didn't have any peppers), and it turned out great. My family loved it and the hostess insisted on keeping the leftovers!"

Quick & Easy ▶

Prep Time: 10 minutes

Average Rating: ★★★★★

What other cooks have done:

"This is a wonderful tasting salsa, but I did make a few changes to the recipe. I used Mexican-style tomatoes, fresh jalapeños, and added about a teaspoon of chili powder. All our favorite Mexican restaurants tell us to use the chili powder."

Salsa de Tomatillo

Submitted by: **Sandy T.**

"Use this salsa as a sauce for grilled chicken, fish, or shrimp, or as a dipping sauce for chips. Delicioso!"

10 tomatillos, husked
1   small onion, chopped
3   cloves garlic, chopped
2   jalapeño peppers, chopped
¼   cup chopped fresh cilantro
    Salt and ground black
    pepper to taste

1. Place tomatillos in a nonreactive saucepan with enough water to cover and bring to a boil. Simmer until tomatillos soften and begin to burst, about 10 minutes.
2. Drain tomatillos and place in a food processor or blender with onion, garlic, jalapeño peppers, cilantro, and salt and pepper to taste. Blend to desired consistency. **Yield:** 16 servings (about 2⅓ cups).

Per serving: About 10 calories, 0g protein, 2g carbohydrate, 0g fat, 1g fiber, 0mg cholesterol, 1mg sodium

Margarita Cake *(pictured on page 299)*

Submitted by: **Carol**

"A margarita—tequila, lime juice, triple sec—is baked into a cake mix."

1   (18.25 ounce) package
    orange cake mix
1   (3.4 ounce) package instant
    vanilla pudding mix
4   eggs
½   cup vegetable oil
⅔   cup water
¼   cup lemon juice
¼   cup tequila
2   tablespoons triple sec
    liqueur
1   cup confectioners' sugar
1   tablespoon tequila
2   tablespoons triple sec
    liqueur
2   tablespoons lime juice

1. Preheat oven to 350°F (175°C). Lightly grease and flour a 10 inch Bundt pan.
2. In a large mixing bowl, combine cake mix, pudding mix, eggs, oil, water, lemon juice, ¼ cup tequila, and 2 tablespoons triple sec. Beat with an electric mixer for 2 minutes.
3. In a small bowl, combine confectioners' sugar with 1 tablespoon tequila, 2 tablespoons triple sec, and 2 tablespoons lime juice. Mix until smooth.
4. Pour batter into prepared pan. Bake in the preheated oven for 45 to 50 minutes or until a toothpick inserted in the center of the cake comes out clean. Cool in pan for 10 minutes; invert onto a wire rack and pour glaze over cake while still warm. **Yield:** 12 servings.

Per serving: About 394 calories, 4g protein, 54g carbohydrate, 16g fat, 1g fiber, 72mg cholesterol, 416mg sodium

Menu Prep Plan

1. A day ahead, prepare and bake cheesecake and prepare potatoes through Step 2; store in refrigerator.

2. Up to 6 hours ahead, toast walnuts for green beans and cook beans.

3. Prepare and roast turkey. Assemble and bake cranberry casserole.

4. Make spinach casserole and bake it alongside potatoes.

5. Cook carrots while casseroles bake. As turkey rests, prepare gravy, finish green beans, and briefly heat side dishes, if needed.

Family Favorite ▶

Prep Time: 1 hour

Chill Time: 2 hours

Cook Time: 3 hours 30 minutes

Average Rating: ★★★★★

What other cooks have done:

"This was my first Thanksgiving turkey and it turned out wonderful! It was so juicy and flavorful. I didn't have any marjoram so I used sage. I also didn't have any apple cider so I just added 1 cup of water and 1 tablespoon of brown sugar."

Thanksgiving Made Simple

Your Thanksgiving feast will be picture-perfect with roasted turkey, cranberry casserole, and other holiday classics.

Maple Roast Turkey

Submitted by: **Lipo**
"The maple adds a sweet flavor that's just divine."

2	cups apple cider	1	(12 pound) whole turkey, neck and giblets reserved
⅓	cup real maple syrup		
2½	tablespoons chopped fresh thyme, divided	2	cups chopped onion
2	tablespoons chopped fresh marjoram, divided	1½	cups chopped celery
		1½	cups chopped carrots
1½	teaspoons grated lemon zest	3	cups chicken broth
¾	cup butter, softened	¼	cup all-purpose flour
	Salt and ground black pepper to taste	1	bay leaf
		½	cup apple brandy (optional)

1. Boil apple cider and maple syrup in a large, heavy saucepan over medium-high heat until reduced to ½ cup, about 20 minutes. Remove from heat. Mix in 1 tablespoon thyme, 1 tablespoon marjoram, and lemon zest. Whisk in butter until melted and season with salt and pepper to taste. Cover and refrigerate until cold, about 2 hours.

2. Preheat oven to 375°F (190°C). Place rack in lower third of oven.

3. Rinse turkey and pat dry with paper towels. Place turkey on a rack set in a large roasting pan. Slide hand under turkey breast skin to loosen. Reserve ¼ cup maple butter for gravy; rub remaining maple butter under the skin of the breast and over outside of turkey. Tie legs together loosely to hold shape of turkey. Arrange onion, celery, carrots, and reserved turkey neck and giblets around turkey in pan. Sprinkle vegetables with 1 tablespoon thyme and remaining marjoram. Pour 2 cups broth into pan.

4. Roast turkey in the preheated oven for 30 minutes. Reduce oven temperature to 350°F (175°C). Cover turkey loosely with heavy-duty foil and roast until a meat thermometer inserted in thickest part of thigh registers 180°F (85°C), about 2 hours 25 minutes.

5. Transfer turkey to a platter. Let stand 30 minutes. Reserve mixture in pan for gravy.

6. For the gravy, strain pan juices into large measuring cup, pressing on solids with back of spoon. Spoon fat from pan juices. Add enough chicken broth to pan juices to measure 3 cups. Bring to a boil in a heavy saucepan. Mix ¼ cup maple butter and ¼ cup flour in a small bowl to form a smooth paste. Whisk into broth mixture. Add bay leaf and remaining thyme. Boil until reduced to sauce consistency, whisking occasionally, about 10 minutes. Add apple brandy, if desired. Season with salt and pepper to taste. Discard bay leaf. **Yield:** 12 servings.

Per serving: About 877 calories, 92g protein, 21g carbohydrate, 44g fat, 1g fiber, 296mg cholesterol, 611mg sodium

Green Beans with Walnuts

Submitted by: **Tina**
"Prepare this yummy dish in advance and toss with hot oil just before serving."

1 cup chopped walnuts	2 tablespoons minced fresh
2 pounds fresh green beans,	parsley
washed and trimmed	Salt and ground black
2 tablespoons butter	pepper to taste
2 tablespoons walnut oil	

1. Preheat oven to 350°F (175°C). Place the walnuts on an ungreased baking sheet. Bake in the preheated oven for 5 to 8 minutes.
2. Cook beans in large pot of boiling salted water until just tender, about 5 minutes. Drain. Rinse beans with cold water and drain well. (Beans can be prepared 6 hours ahead.) Let stand at room temperature.
3. Melt butter with oil in large skillet over high heat. Add beans; toss until heated through, about 4 minutes. Season with salt and pepper. Add walnuts and parsley; toss. Transfer to bowl and serve. **Yield:** 8 servings.

Per serving: About 189 calories, 4g protein, 10g carbohydrate, 16g fat, 5g fiber, 8mg cholesterol, 37mg sodium

◀ **Make-Ahead**

Prep Time: 15 minutes

Cook Time: 17 minutes

Average Rating: ★★★★★

What other cooks have done:
"These green beans tasted great, and they couldn't be any easier! Walnut oil was a splurge and worth it!"

Carrots in Dill Butter

Submitted by: **Michele O'Sullivan**
"Delicious with seafood."

16 carrots, peeled and sliced	2 teaspoons white sugar
into 1 inch pieces	1 teaspoon salt
1 cup water	1 teaspoon dill seed
¼ cup butter	

1. In a saucepan, bring carrots, water, butter, sugar, salt, and dill seed to a boil. Reduce heat, cover, and simmer 25 to 30 minutes or until carrots are tender and most of the liquid is absorbed. **Yield:** 10 servings.

Per serving: About 86 calories, 1g protein, 11g carbohydrate, 5g fat, 3g fiber, 12mg cholesterol, 560mg sodium

◀ **Quick & Easy**

Prep Time: 10 minutes

Cook Time: 30 minutes

Average Rating: ★★★★☆

What other cooks have done:
"My family loved this dish! I used baby carrots instead of cutting up big ones and it was excellent! I'm going to try it using fresh dill weed instead of dill seed."

Prep Time: 20 minutes

Cook Time: 30 minutes

Average Rating: ★★★★★

What other cooks have done:

"Delicious and creamy. I even used light sour cream and light cream cheese. I used Yukon Gold potatoes because I think they're better for mashing (not so dry). This is such a great way to make mashed potatoes."

Prep Time: 10 minutes

Cook Time: 25 minutes

Average Rating: ★★★★☆

What other cooks have done:

"I thought the recipe was good, but a little heavy in the sour cream. I also found that the amount of soup mix was a little much. If both the sour cream and soup mix were lessened, the dish would be beyond excellent!"

Day-Before Mashed Potatoes

Submitted by: **Erin**

"This recipe helps you plan ahead by allowing you to make the mashed potatoes in advance."

9	potatoes, peeled and cubed	2	teaspoons onion powder
2	(3 ounce) packages cream cheese, softened	1	teaspoon salt
1	(8 ounce) container sour cream	¼	teaspoon ground black pepper
		2	tablespoons butter

1. Bring a large pot of salted water to a boil. Add potatoes and cook until tender but still firm, about 15 minutes.

2. Transfer potatoes to a large bowl and mash until smooth. Mix in the cream cheese, sour cream, onion powder, salt, pepper, and butter. Cover and refrigerate 8 hours or overnight.

3. Preheat the oven to 350°F (175°C). Lightly grease a medium baking dish.

4. Spread potato mixture into the prepared baking dish and bake in the preheated oven about 30 minutes. **Yield:** 8 servings.

Per serving: About 272 calories, 5g protein, 27g carbohydrate, 16g fat, 3g fiber, 44mg cholesterol, 408mg sodium

Cheesy Creamed Spinach Casserole

Submitted by: **Sue**

"A spinach recipe you'll be proud to offer to others."

2	(10 ounce) packages frozen chopped spinach, cooked	1	(16 ounce) container sour cream
1	(1 ounce) package dry onion soup mix	½	cup shredded Cheddar cheese

1. Preheat oven to 350°F (175°C). Grease a 2 quart casserole dish.

2. Drain spinach. In a medium mixing bowl, combine spinach, soup mix, and sour cream. Spoon into prepared casserole dish and top with cheese.

3. Bake in the preheated oven for about 25 minutes or until heated through. **Yield:** 9 servings.

Per serving: About 157 calories, 5g protein, 7g carbohydrate, 13g fat, 2g fiber, 29mg cholesterol, 383mg sodium

Cranberry-Apple Casserole

Submitted by: **Christine Hanson**

"Perfect for holiday or everyday meals. Goes great with chicken, turkey, ham, or pork. Can double as a dessert served with ice cream or whipped cream."

1	(21 ounce) can apple pie filling	¼	cup butter, softened
1	(16 ounce) can whole-berry cranberry sauce	1½	cups rolled oats
		¾	cup brown sugar

1. Preheat oven to 350°F (175°C). Combine pie filling and cranberry sauce in a lightly greased shallow baking dish.
2. In a medium bowl, mix the butter, oats, and brown sugar until crumbly. Sprinkle evenly over the fruit mixture.
3. Bake in the preheated oven for 40 minutes or until browned and crisp. **Yield:** 8 servings.

Per serving: About 296 calories, 3g protein, 59g carbohydrate, 7g fat, 3g fiber, 15mg cholesterol, 93mg sodium

◄ **Quick & Easy**

Prep Time: 5 minutes

Cook Time: 40 minutes

Average Rating: ★★★★★

What other cooks have done:
"This was super fast to put together. I used whole-berry cranberry sauce, which added a nice texture, and added ¼ teaspoon cinnamon. I plan to experiment with this recipe some more by adding fresh apple or maybe a chunky homemade applesauce instead of the pie filling."

Marbled Pumpkin Cheesecake

Submitted by: **Renee**

"Wonderful pumpkin cheesecake with a gingersnap crust."

1½	cups crushed gingersnap cookies	¾	cup white sugar, divided
½	cup finely chopped pecans	1	teaspoon vanilla extract
⅓	cup butter, melted	3	eggs
2	(8 ounce) packages cream cheese, softened	1	cup canned pumpkin
		¾	teaspoon ground cinnamon
		¼	teaspoon ground nutmeg

1. Preheat oven to 350°F (175°C). In a medium bowl, mix together the crushed gingersnap cookies, pecans, and butter. Press into the bottom and about 1 inch up the sides of a 9 inch springform pan. Bake crust in the preheated oven for 10 minutes. Set aside to cool.
2. In a medium bowl, mix together the cream cheese, ½ cup sugar, and vanilla just until smooth. Mix in eggs, 1 at a time, blending well after each. Set aside 1 cup of the mixture. Blend remaining sugar, pumpkin, cinnamon, and nutmeg into the remaining mixture.
3. Spread pumpkin batter onto crust; drop reserved plain batter by spoonfuls onto the top. Swirl with a knife to create a marbled effect.
4. Bake in the preheated oven for 55 minutes or until filling is set. Run a knife around the edge of the pan. Cool before removing pan rim. Chill for at least 4 hours before serving. **Yield:** 12 servings.

Per serving: About 354 calories, 6g protein, 27g carbohydrate, 26g fat, 2g fiber, 108mg cholesterol, 235mg sodium

◄ **Holiday Fare**

Prep Time: 30 minutes

Cook Time: 1 hour 5 minutes

Average Rating: ★★★★★

What other cooks have done:
"My husband and I love pumpkin cheesecake but hate waiting until October or November to find pumpkin. I will probably be making these for Christmas because they're very easy to make and turn out beautifully. Not being an experienced cook myself, I tried smashing the gingersnaps in a plastic grocery bag with a rolling pin until I remembered—duh!—I have a food processor. That made life much easier."

Menu

Salad with Artichokes

Alysia's Basic Meat Lasagna

Potato Rosemary Rolls

Apricot Brandy Pound Cake

Chocolate Cherry Biscotti

Serves 10

Menu Prep Plan

1. A day ahead, prepare and bake biscotti. Bake pound cake and, when cooled, cover.

2. Combine ingredients for rolls and start bread machine. Cook lasagna noodles. Let the kids help shape rolls.

3. Layer lasagna and, while it bakes, assemble artichoke salad. Bake rolls.

Quick & Easy ▶

Prep Time: 15 minutes

Average Rating: ★★★★☆

What other cooks have done:

"This is now my standby recipe for salad. I've served it at several occasions, including Christmas, and it's always well received."

Fuss-Free Christmas Feast

Have an indulgent Christmas with double dessert (both recipes can be made ahead), and buck tradition when you serve the easiest (and tastiest) lasagna ever. Fluffy rolls and tangy artichoke salad are a cinch to make but look gourmet.

Salad with Artichokes

Submitted by: **Cindy**

"A friend gave me this recipe. She got it from a little pasta restaurant in her hometown. It calls for mixed greens, red onion, and artichokes with a vinegar and oil dressing."

8	cups mixed salad greens		2	teaspoons seasoned salt
1	red onion, sliced		2	teaspoons ground black pepper
2	(14 ounce) cans artichoke hearts in water, drained		2	teaspoons garlic powder
1	cup vegetable oil		6	tablespoons grated Parmesan cheese
1	cup red wine vinegar			

1. In a large bowl, combine mixed greens, onion, and artichoke hearts.
2. In a medium-size bowl, whisk together the oil, vinegar, seasoned salt, pepper, and garlic.
3. Pour enough dressing over salad to coat and toss well. Sprinkle with grated cheese and serve. **Yield:** 10 servings.

Per serving: About 243 calories, 3g protein, 9g carbohydrate, 23g fat, 1g fiber, 2mg cholesterol, 466mg sodium

Alysia's Basic Meat Lasagna

Submitted by: **Alysia**

"A very basic, very easy to make meat lasagna."

1½ pounds ground beef
 1 teaspoon garlic powder
 2 teaspoons dried oregano, divided
 1 tablespoon olive oil
 4 cloves garlic, minced
 1 small onion, diced
 1 (28 ounce) jar sausage flavored spaghetti sauce
 1 (8 ounce) can tomato sauce
 1 (8 ounce) package shredded mozzarella cheese
 8 ounces provolone cheese, shredded
 1 (15 ounce) container ricotta cheese
 2 eggs
 ¼ cup milk
 ½ teaspoon dried oregano
 9 lasagna noodles, cooked
 ¼ cup grated Parmesan cheese

1. Preheat oven to 375°F (190°C).

2. Season ground beef with garlic powder and 1 teaspoon oregano. In a skillet over medium heat, brown the meat and drain.

3. In a large saucepan, heat olive oil and sauté garlic and onion in oil for about 5 minutes. Add spaghetti sauce, tomato sauce, 1 teaspoon oregano, and meat and cook for 15 to 20 minutes.

4. Combine mozzarella and provolone cheeses in a bowl. In a separate bowl, mix ricotta cheese, eggs, milk, and ½ teaspoon oregano.

5. Layer a greased 9x13 inch baking dish with just enough sauce to cover the bottom of the pan. Place 3 lasagna noodles in the pan. Cover with one-third of sauce, then with half of ricotta mixture, then sprinkle with half of mozzarella/provolone mixture; repeat layering noodles, sauce, and cheese once. Finish with a layer of noodles and remaining third of sauce. Sprinkle with Parmesan cheese.

6. Bake, covered, in the preheated oven for 25 to 30 minutes. Uncover and bake for 15 minutes. **Yield:** 10 servings.

Per serving: About 572 calories, 36g protein, 36g carbohydrate, 32g fat, 3g fiber, 134mg cholesterol, 942mg sodium

◄ **One-Dish Meal**

Prep Time: 50 minutes

Cook Time: 70 minutes

Average Rating: ★★★★★

What other cooks have done:

"I'm sticking with this one! I made it for a dinner party and had nothing left but a smudge on the bottom of the pan. The only thing I added was some mild Italian sausage for extra bite."

Potato Rosemary Rolls *(pictured on page 262)*

Submitted by: **Anthony Theobald**

"Potato Rosemary Rolls are a favorite with all of our friends and family."

1	cup plus 2 tablespoons warm water	1	teaspoon salt
2	tablespoons olive oil	3	cups bread flour
2	tablespoons nonfat dry milk powder	1½	teaspoons bread machine yeast
½	cup dry potato flakes	1	tablespoon cornmeal
1	tablespoon white sugar	1	egg, lightly beaten
1	teaspoon dried rosemary, crushed	2	teaspoons kosher salt
			Garnish: fresh rosemary

1. Add warm water, olive oil, dry milk, potato flakes, sugar, rosemary, salt, bread flour, and yeast to your bread machine in the order listed by the manufacturer. Select Dough cycle and press Start.
2. Preheat oven to 375°F (190°C).
3. Divide dough into 12 pieces. Roll each into a 10 inch rope; coil rope and tuck in the end so that it comes up through the middle. Place coils 2 inches apart on a baking sheet dusted with cornmeal. Cover and let rise for 20 minutes.
4. Brush tops of rolls with egg and sprinkle with salt. Bake in the preheated oven for 15 to 20 minutes. Garnish, if desired. **Yield:** 12 servings.

Per serving: About 170 calories, 6g protein, 29g carbohydrate, 3g fat, 1g fiber, 18mg cholesterol, 523mg sodium

Apricot Brandy Pound Cake

Submitted by: **Joyce Carcara**

"I collect cake recipes that use a box cake mix as the base. This cake is rich, delicious, and easy! It also freezes well."

1	(18.25 ounce) package yellow cake mix	1	teaspoon vanilla extract
1	(3.5 ounce) package instant vanilla pudding mix	½	teaspoon orange extract
4	eggs	½	teaspoon lemon extract
½	cup apricot brandy	½	teaspoon almond extract
		1	cup sour cream

1. Preheat oven to 350°F (175°C). Grease and lightly flour a 10 inch Bundt pan.
2. In a large mixing bowl, using an electric mixer, beat cake mix, pudding mix, and eggs until smooth. In a separate bowl, mix brandy, vanilla, orange extract, lemon extract, almond extract, and sour cream; add to egg mixture. Beat at least 2 minutes on medium speed. Pour batter into prepared pan.

3. Bake in the preheated oven for 50 to 55 minutes or until a toothpick inserted near the center of the cake comes out clean. Cool cake in pan on a wire rack for 20 minutes. Remove from pan and cool on wire rack. **Yield:** 12 servings.

Per serving: About 306 calories, 5g protein, 42g carbohydrate, 11g fat, 1g fiber, 80mg cholesterol, 432mg sodium

Chocolate Cherry Biscotti

Submitted by: **Jennifer Wall**
"One of my favorite recipes. I make a batch every holiday season. They're great for mailing and keep for weeks!"

½	cup butter, softened	½	cup chopped candied cherries
¾	cup white sugar	½	cup miniature semisweet chocolate chips
3	eggs		
2	teaspoons almond extract	½	cup chopped white chocolate
3	cups all-purpose flour		
2	teaspoons baking powder		

1. Preheat oven to 350°F (175°C). Grease a large baking sheet.
2. In a large bowl, cream together the butter and sugar until smooth. Beat in the eggs, 1 at a time, then stir in the almond extract. In a separate bowl, combine the flour and baking powder; stir into the creamed mixture just until blended. Mix in candied cherries and chocolate chips.
3. With lightly floured hands, shape dough into 2 (10 inch) long logs. Place logs 5 inches apart on the prepared baking sheet; flatten each to 3-inch width.
4. Bake in the preheated oven for 20 to 25 minutes or until set and light golden brown. Cool 10 minutes. Using a serrated knife, cut logs diagonally into ½ inch slices. Arrange slices cut side down on a prepared baking sheet in the preheated oven.
5. Bake for 8 to 10 minutes or until bottoms begin to brown. Turn and bake 5 more minutes or until browned and crisp. Cool completely. Melt white chocolate in the microwave on medium, stirring every 20 to 30 seconds until smooth. Drizzle cookies with melted white chocolate. Store in a tightly covered container. **Yield:** 36 servings.

Per serving: About 117 calories, 2g protein, 17g carbohydrate, 5g fat, 0g fiber, 25mg cholesterol, 63mg sodium

◀ Holiday Gift Giving

Prep Time: 25 minutes
Cook Time: 40 minutes
Average Rating: ★★★★
What other cooks have done:
"We've tried a number of biscotti recipes over the years, and this one was a hit because it was so tasty and festive, yet different from all the traditional holiday-type cookies! I think these would work well for Valentine's Day, too, considering the pretty red cherries."

Easy and Elegant Pork Tenderloin

New Year's Day Black-Eyed Peas

Spicy Collard Greens

Camp Cornbread

White Chocolate Blondies

Serves 6

Menu Prep Plan

1. Prepare blondies a day ahead.

2. Prepare peas, boil, and simmer.

3. Add the bacon to collard greens and boil.

4. Coat tenderloin with breadcrumbs, and bake.

5. Bake cornbread in a separate oven or, if you only have one oven, bake cornbread ahead while collards cook.

Company is Coming ▶

Prep Time: 10 minutes

Cook Time: 35 minutes

Average Rating: ★★★★☆

What other cooks have done:

"I made this for dinner last night and everyone who tried it loved it! The only change I made was liberally sprinkling the tenderloin with freshly ground pepper and garlic powder before covering with the crumb mixture. The meat was great!"

New Year's Day Dinner

According to tradition, eating black-eyed peas on New Year's Day brings good luck all year long, so serve up hearty portions of good luck and good food this January or any cold day that requires a little comfort food. Use slices of sweet cornbread to clean your plate!

Easy and Elegant Pork Tenderloin

Submitted by: **Susan Burget**
"This main dish is beautiful in its presentation and always comes out tender and juicy. The crust of breadcrumbs holds in all the juices and adds a great look and taste to the finished product."

2 cups Italian seasoned breadcrumbs	2 pork tenderloins (2 pounds)
½ cup olive oil	

1. Preheat the oven to 425°F (220°C). Lightly grease a shallow baking dish.

2. Mix breadcrumbs and olive oil to reach consistency that would be moist enough to stick to the meat when pressed. Place the 2 tenderloins into pan. Press the crumb mixture onto all sides of the meat until there is no pink showing, about ¼ inch thick.

3. Bake in the preheated oven for 35 minutes or until a meat thermometer registers 160°F (70°C). Let the pork rest for 10 minutes, then cut into ½ inch slices. **Yield:** 6 servings.

Per serving: About 461 calories, 30g protein, 27g carbohydrate, 25g fat, 1g fiber, 71mg cholesterol, 623mg sodium

New Year's Day Black-Eyed Peas

Submitted by: **Roxanna Parks**

"Remember, black-eyed peas on New Year's Day bring good luck for the entire year!"

1 pound dried black-eyed peas	Salt and ground black
2 cups chopped cooked ham	pepper to taste
2 onions, diced	2 (8 ounce) cans whole
Pinch garlic powder	tomatoes

1. Place black-eyed peas in an 8 quart pot. Add enough water to fill pot three-fourths full. Stir in ham and diced onions, and season with garlic powder and salt and pepper to taste.

2. Place tomatoes in a blender or food processor and blend until the tomatoes are liquefied. Add tomatoes to pot. Bring all ingredients to a boil. Cover and simmer on low heat for 2½ to 3 hours or until the peas are tender. **Yield:** 12 servings.

Per serving: About 111 calories, 11g protein, 10g carbohydrate, 3g fat, 2g fiber, 36mg cholesterol, 392mg sodium

◄ Crowd-Pleaser

Prep Time: 15 minutes

Cook Time: 3 hours

Average Rating: ★★★★★

What other cooks have done:

"I've been cooking black-eyed peas for 60 years and never thought of putting tomatoes in them. It's an excellent addition!"

Spicy Collard Greens

Submitted by: **Jamie**

"These greens turn out just a little spicy, a kick even the little ones love."

6 slices bacon	Salt and ground black
1 bunch collard greens, rinsed	pepper to taste
and trimmed (about 3	Ground cayenne pepper to
pounds)	taste
⅓ cup vinegar	

1. Place bacon in a large, deep skillet. Cook over medium-high heat until evenly browned.

2. Bring a large pot of water to a boil. Add collard greens, bacon (with grease), vinegar, salt, pepper, and cayenne pepper to taste.

3. Boil until greens are tender, about 30 minutes. **Yield:** 6 servings.

Per serving: About 106 calories, 7g protein, 14g carbohydrate, 4g fat, 8g fiber, 5mg cholesterol, 147mg sodium

◄ Classic Comfort Food

Prep Time: 15 minutes

Cook Time: 45 minutes

Average Rating: ★★★★☆

What other cooks have done:

"Thank you for the great recipe. I like my greens sweet, so I added some sugar. I'm sure I'll make this again."

Camp Cornbread

Submitted by: **Laura Shank**

"A very easy cornbread recipe that children and husbands will love. It's sweet, chewy, and ready in a jiffy!"

1	(8.5 ounce) package cornbread muffin mix	1	(8 ounce) can creamed corn
⅓	cup milk	½	cup white sugar
1	egg, lightly beaten		

1. Preheat oven to 350°F (175°C). Lightly grease a 9x13 inch baking pan.
2. Place the muffin mix a large bowl. Stir in the milk and egg. Mix in corn and sugar. Pour batter into prepared pan.
3. Bake in the preheated oven for 30 minutes or until a knife inserted in the center of the cornbread comes out clean. **Yield:** 12 servings.

Per serving: About 131 calories, 2g protein, 26g carbohydrate, 3g fat, 1g fiber, 22mg cholesterol, 165mg sodium

White Chocolate Blondies

Submitted by: **Jenn Rochon**

"These bars have become an office favorite—they are naughty but oh-so-nice!"

8	ounces white chocolate, chopped	1	tablespoon vanilla extract
½	cup butter, softened	1¼	cups all-purpose flour
2	eggs	¾	teaspoon salt
⅓	cup white sugar	1	cup semisweet chocolate chips

1. Preheat oven to 350°F (175°C). Grease a 9x9 inch baking pan.
2. Melt white chocolate and butter in the top of a double boiler over barely simmering water. Stir occasionally until smooth. Set aside to cool.
3. In a large bowl, using an electric mixer, beat eggs until foamy. With the mixer still running, gradually add the sugar and vanilla. Drizzle in the melted white chocolate mixture. In a medium bowl, combine the flour and salt; fold into the white chocolate mixture, using a rubber spatula or wooden spoon. Fold in chocolate chips. Spread the batter evenly into the prepared pan.
4. Bake in the preheated oven for 25 minutes or until a toothpick inserted in the middle of the pan comes out clean. Cool in pan on a wire rack before cutting into bars. **Yield:** 12 servings.

Per serving: About 326 calories, 4g protein, 35g carbohydrate, 20g fat, 1g fiber, 60mg cholesterol, 256mg sodium

---

Family Favorite ▶

Prep Time: 5 minutes

Cook Time: 30 minutes

Average Rating: ★★★★★

What other cooks have done:

"This is the easiest and most delicious cornbread I've ever made. I'm allergic to eggs so I left it out, and it was still moist and so sweet!"

Crowd-Pleaser ▶

Prep Time: 20 minutes

Cook Time: 25 minutes

Average Rating: ★★★★★

What other cooks have done:

"I always thought that you either like white chocolate or you don't, but confirmed white chocolate haters not only gobbled up these blondies, they also asked for the recipe!"

Easy Entrées

Rump Roast au Jus

Submitted by: **Ardith Simon**

"This is a wonderful way to prepare rump roast in the slow cooker. It creates a delicious juice while it cooks; serve the juice over individual servings of beef. You'll want the roast to be between 4 and 5 pounds."

1 tablespoon ground black pepper	½ teaspoon garlic powder
1 tablespoon paprika	¼ teaspoon powdered mustard
2 teaspoons chili powder	1 (4 pound) rump roast
½ teaspoon celery salt	½ cup water
½ teaspoon ground cayenne pepper	

1. In a small bowl, mix together black pepper, paprika, chili powder, celery salt, cayenne pepper, garlic powder, and mustard. Rub mixture over the surface of the meat. Slice roast in half to ensure even cooking. Place roast in a slow cooker and add ½ cup water.
2. Cover and cook on High for 1 hour and reduce to Low for 7 to 8 hours. When meat is tender and well done, transfer roast to a serving platter. Skim fat from juices and strain; serve juices with meat. **Yield:** 8 servings.

Per serving: About 358 calories, 46g protein, 2g carbohydrate, 18g fat, 1g fiber, 121mg cholesterol, 161mg sodium

Slow-Cooker Creation ▶

Prep Time: 10 minutes

Cook Time: 9 hours

Average Rating: ★★★★★

What other cooks have done:

"Fantastic recipe. I've cooked it several times and get rave reviews every time. I reduce the cooking time a little to prevent the meat from drying out so much, and I don't strain the liquid, just scoop off the fat. Warning: This makes the jus quite spicy, but that's the way we like it."

Persian Shish Kabob

Submitted by: **Manouchehr Delshakib**

"Keep it simple is the idea in this recipe. The beef is marinated in lime juice and onion, seasoned with salt and pepper, and grilled. Serve with a Persian-style pilaf."

2 pounds beef tenderloin	Pinch ground black pepper
1 onion, chopped	2 tablespoons fresh lime juice
1 tablespoon salt	

1. Cut beef into 1x½ inch pieces. In a medium bowl, combine beef, onion, salt, pepper, and lime juice. Mix well, cover, and refrigerate 8 hours or overnight.
2. Lightly oil grill rack and preheat grill for high heat.
3. Thread beef onto skewers, 6 to 8 pieces per skewer.
4. Place kabobs on grill. Cook for 3 to 4 minutes on each side, 12 to 16 minutes in all. **Yield:** 4 servings.

Per serving: About 297 calories, 38g protein, 3g carbohydrate, 14g fat, 1g fiber, 113mg cholesterol, 1830mg sodium

From the Grill ▶

Prep Time: 20 minutes

Cook Time: 16 minutes

Marinate Time: 8 hours

Average Rating: ★★★★★

What other cooks have done:

"I used a cheap cut of beef for this recipe, and I think it was a mistake. Using tenderloin would have produced a much more tender result. It was delicious nonetheless."

Best-Ever Saucy Beef Kabobs

Submitted by: **Debbie Taber**

"Here's a five star recipe that combines the great taste of grilled beef kabobs with a delicious tomato sauce baste. I always double the sauce to top the beef and veggies over rice. A mouth-watering meal."

2	cups tomato juice		Dash hot sauce	
½	cup butter	2	pounds sirloin, cut into 1 inch cubes	
¼	cup finely chopped onion			
⅓	cup ketchup	½	pound fresh mushrooms, stems removed	
1	teaspoon powdered mustard			
1	teaspoon salt	1	pint cherry tomatoes	
½	teaspoon paprika	1	large onion, quartered	
½	teaspoon ground black pepper	1	large green bell pepper, cut into 1 inch pieces	
1	clove garlic, minced			
1	tablespoon Worcestershire sauce			

1. In a medium saucepan on low heat, combine tomato juice, butter, onion, ketchup, mustard, salt, paprika, pepper, garlic, Worcestershire sauce, and hot sauce; stir well. Simmer for 30 minutes; remove from heat and allow to cool.

2. Lightly oil grill rack and preheat grill for medium heat.

3. Thread the sirloin cubes, mushrooms, cherry tomatoes, onion, and bell pepper pieces onto skewers, alternating as desired and leaving a small space in between each piece.

4. Brush kabobs with sauce and place on the prepared grill. Grill for 10 to 15 minutes, occasionally turning kabobs and brushing with more sauce. **Yield:** 6 servings.

Per serving: About 539 calories, 32g protein, 17g carbohydrate, 39g fat, 2g fiber, 143mg cholesterol, 1114mg sodium

◄ **Party Food**

Prep Time: 30 minutes

Cook Time: 45 minutes

Average Rating: ★★★★★

What other cooks have done:

"These kabobs were delicious! I made this for a cookout recently, and instead of basting with the sauce while cooking, I marinated the beef in it overnight. When I cooked the kabobs the next day, they didn't even need basting."

Steak Tips with Mushroom Sauce

Submitted by: **Amy**

"Straightforward grilled steak tips with a slightly salty, hearty sauce that can be used with any cut of beef, and is great for dipping crusty bread into."

Company is Coming ▶

Prep Time: 10 minutes

Cook Time: 40 minutes

Average Rating: ★★★★★

What other cooks have done:

"Wonderful recipe. I cut up the sirloin into bite size pieces and served it over noodles. It was incredible! Be careful not to cook the sauce down too much. Served five with plenty to spare. Excellent flavor and easy to prepare."

2½	pounds sirloin tips, uncut	½	(750 milliliter) bottle Burgundy wine
¼	teaspoon salt		
½	teaspoon ground black pepper	2	(14.5 ounce) cans beef broth
¼	cup butter	2	tablespoons all-purpose flour
1	shallot, finely chopped		
4	portobello mushroom caps, sliced	1	clove garlic, chopped

1. Preheat grill for medium-high heat.

2. Grill the sirloin tips to desired doneness. Season with salt and pepper. Remove to a plate and set aside.

3. Melt butter in a large skillet over medium-high heat. Sauté shallot until transparent. Add mushrooms and cook, covered, about 5 minutes or until darkened. Remove mushrooms from pan and set aside. Deglaze pan with wine and 1 can beef broth. Increase heat and bring to a boil. Allow the mixture to boil until reduced by one-third.

4. When the sauce is reduced, whisk flour into remaining can of beef broth; stir broth mixture and garlic into sauce. Return to a boil and continue to cook and stir for another 5 to 10 minutes or until sauce reaches desired thickness. Taste and adjust seasoning, if necessary. Stir in mushrooms. Serve tips with mushroom sauce. **Yield:** 6 servings.

Per serving: About 567 calories, 41g protein, 9g carbohydrate, 37g fat, 1g fiber, 147mg cholesterol, 727mg sodium

The Magic Behind Marinade ▼

Cooks make marinades to fulfill three important functions for the meat that they cook: to flavor, to moisturize, and to tenderize. The fun thing about marinades is that the formula is so flexible—use just about any ingredient you fancy!

Fabulously Fragrant and Flavorful
The main role of marinades is to add flavor. The kinds of flavors you can add to your marinade are only as limited as your imagination and the contents of your pantry. These can include any fresh or dried herb or spice, fresh and dried chile peppers, onions, shallots, garlic, ginger, and citrus zest, as well as prepared condiments like mustard, ketchup, or plum sauce. Don't add salt to meat until right before you cook it. Salt can leech the moisture, turning your meal dry and tough.

Moist 'n' Juicy
Marinades also add moisture to foods, particularly when the marinade contains some sort of fat. Generally, oils are better to use than butter or margarine, because oils will remain liquid when refrigerated. And always refrigerate foods while they marinate. In the oil category, try olive, peanut, sesame, walnut, or chile. You can also use milk, coconut milk, buttermilk, or yogurt.

Love Me Tender
Marinades also are widely believed to tenderize meats. The acidic ingredients in a marinade have a tenderizing effect on proteins, but since the marinade touches only the surface of the meat, not the inside, the added tenderness is usually somewhat minimal. Powdered store-bought meat tenderizers usually contain natural enzymes that serve to break down the tissue of the meat, but when this kind of tenderizer is left on the meat too long, it can make the meat mushy, so use with caution. Interestingly, dairy products like buttermilk and yogurt are the only ingredients that have been proven to tenderize meat all the way through while at the same time preserving the texture. *- Jennifer Anderson*

For more information, visit **Allrecipes.com**

Adobo Sirloin

Submitted by: **Tracie Commins**
"Juicy sirloin marinated in a spicy chipotle chile sauce makes great fajitas!"

1 lime, juiced	1 (7 ounce) can chipotle
1 teaspoon minced garlic	peppers in adobo sauce
1 teaspoon dried oregano or	2 pounds top sirloin steak
1 tablespoon fresh oregano	Salt and ground black
1 teaspoon ground cumin	pepper to taste

1. In a small bowl, combine lime juice, garlic, oregano, and cumin. Finely chop 2 tablespoons of the chile peppers and add to the mixture. Taste for spice and add adobo sauce from the can as desired.
2. Prick the meat with a sharp knife several times. Sprinkle with salt and pepper to taste. Pour pepper mixture over meat, turning to coat evenly; cover and marinate in the refrigerator for 1 to 2 hours.
3. Lightly oil grill rack and preheat grill for high heat.
4. Grill steak over high heat until a meat thermometer inserted in thickest part of steak registers at least 145°F (63°C). **Yield:** 4 servings.

Per serving: About 362 calories, 38g protein, 6g carbohydrate, 20g fat, 2g fiber, 121mg cholesterol, 307mg sodium

◀ **Party Food**

Prep Time: 10 minutes
Marinate Time: 1 hour
Cook Time: 20 minutes
Average Rating: ★★★★
What other cooks have done:
"I made fajitas from this. I cut it into strips and cooked it with peppers and onion. My husband said they were the best fajitas that he had ever eaten."

Savory Garlic Marinated Steaks

Submitted by: **Angie Zayac**
"This beautiful marinade adds an exquisite flavor to these already tender steaks. The final result will melt in your mouth."

½ cup balsamic vinegar	1 teaspoon Worcestershire
¼ cup soy sauce	sauce
3 tablespoons minced garlic	½ teaspoon salt
2 tablespoons honey	½ teaspoon liquid smoke
2 tablespoons olive oil	flavoring
2 teaspoons ground black	Pinch cayenne pepper
pepper	2 (½ pound) beef rib eye
1 teaspoon onion powder	steaks

1. Combine vinegar, soy sauce, garlic, honey, oil, black pepper, onion powder, Worcestershire sauce, salt, liquid smoke, and cayenne pepper.
2. Place steaks in a shallow, nonporous dish and pour marinade over steaks. For optimum flavor, rub the liquid into the meat. Cover and let marinate in the refrigerator for 24 to 48 hours.
3. Lightly oil grill rack and preheat the grill for medium-high to high heat. Grill steaks for 7 to 8 minutes on each side or until a meat thermometer inserted in the thickest part of the steak registers at least 145°F (63°C). **Yield:** 2 servings.

Per serving: About 876 calories, 44g protein, 37g carbohydrate, 62g fat, 1g fiber, 152mg cholesterol, 2579mg sodium

◀ **From the Grill**

Prep Time: 15 minutes
Marinate Time: 24 hours
Cook Time: 16 minutes
Average Rating: ★★★★★
What other cooks have done:
"I've discovered that this marinade also works wonders on budget cuts like flank or skirt steak. Marinate overnight and grill or broil whole, then slice on the diagonal and serve (great in a wrap, too). Very tender and flavorful!"

Chicken Fried Steak

Submitted by: **Barbara**

"Breaded and deep fried beef cutlets are known as chicken fried steak because of the similarity in cooking method to fried chicken. This is a family recipe that we have used for years. Vegetable oil may be used in place of shortening for frying."

Prep Time: 15 minutes

Cook Time: 30 minutes

Average Rating: ★★★★★

What other cooks have done:

"As a retired Canadian truck driver, I have eaten this dish frequently in the States, but very few Canadians have heard of it. So far, they love it. I often make it for guests."

1	pound boneless beef top loin	¼	teaspoon garlic powder
2	cups shortening	1¼	cups all-purpose flour, divided
1	egg, lightly beaten	1	quart milk
1	cup buttermilk		Salt and ground black pepper to taste
	Salt and ground black pepper to taste		

1. Cut top loin crosswise into 4 (4 ounce) cutlets. Using a glancing motion, pound each cutlet thinly with a moistened meat mallet or the side of a cleaver.

2. In a large, heavy skillet, heat shortening to 365°F (185°C).

3. In a shallow bowl, beat together egg, buttermilk, salt, and pepper. In another shallow dish, mix together garlic powder and 1 cup flour. Dip cutlets in flour, turning to evenly coat both sides. Dip in egg mixture, coating both sides, then in flour mixture once again.

4. Place cutlets in heated shortening. Cook until golden brown, turning once. Transfer to a plate lined with paper towels. Repeat with remaining cutlets. Drain grease, reserving ½ cup in pan.

5. Add ¼ cup flour to reserved drippings in pan; blend to form a paste. Gradually add milk to desired consistency, stirring constantly. For a thinner gravy, stir in more. Heat through and season with salt and pepper to taste. Serve over chicken fried steak. **Yield:** 4 servings.

Per serving: About 639 calories, 48g protein, 45g carbohydrate, 29g fat, 1g fiber, 162mg cholesterol, 279mg sodium

Stuffed Flank Steak

Submitted by: **BarbiAnn**

"Delicious! The stuffing makes it much more filling, but there's never any left over! Can also be cooked in the microwave. Just cover and cook at medium setting (50%) in a microwave-safe dish for 30 minutes, rotating dish halfway through cooking. Serve with sauce from the pan."

2 cups dry stuffing mix	1 red bell pepper, chopped
1 cup boiling water	1 (10.5 ounce) can mushroom gravy
2 tablespoons butter or margarine	¼ cup red wine
1½ pounds flank steak, pounded thin for easy rolling	1 clove garlic, minced
2 green onions, chopped	2 tablespoons grated Parmesan cheese

1. Preheat oven to 350°F (175°C).
2. In a medium bowl, combine stuffing mix, water, and butter. Mix well and let stand for 5 minutes. Spoon the stuffing onto the steak, leaving a 1 inch border on all sides. Add the green onions and the red bell pepper over stuffing.
3. Roll up steak from the long end and secure with toothpicks. Place steak, seam side down, in a 9x13 inch baking dish.
4. In a small bowl, combine gravy, wine, garlic, and cheese. Mix well and pour over the steak.
5. Bake in the preheated oven for 1 hour. Remove from oven and let stand 10 minutes before slicing. **Yield:** 4 servings.

Per serving: About 496 calories, 26g protein, 29g carbohydrate, 29g fat, 4g fiber, 71mg cholesterol, 1129mg sodium

◄ **Out-of-the-Ordinary**

Prep Time: 10 minutes

Cook Time: 1 hour

Average Rating: ★★★★★

What other cooks have done:

"This was really a pleasant surprise! The sauce ingredients didn't sound appealing to me, but it was wonderful, and—oh, the aroma while it cooked! The only part my kids didn't like was the bell pepper, but I think it's a definite 'must' for flavor."

Teriyaki Steak *(pictured on page 151)*

Submitted by: **Deanna**

"Skirt steak comes from the short plate. It comes in a long, thin strip or 'skirt'. Sometimes it's hard to find, so if you don't see it out with the other meats, ask your butcher."

(pictured on page 151)

2	pounds beef skirt or flank steak	4	cloves garlic, minced
		2	cups teriyaki sauce

1. Score steak diagonally across the grain at 1-inch intervals. In a large heavy-duty, zip-top plastic bag, combine garlic and teriyaki sauce. Add steak to the sauce. Seal tightly, and refrigerate 8 hours or overnight to marinate.
2. Preheat grill for medium-high heat.
3. Remove meat from bag and discard remaining marinade. Place meat on the grill. Cook for about 5 minutes on each side or to desired doneness. Let stand 5 minutes. To serve, slice diagonally across the grain into thin slices. **Yield:** 4 servings.

Per serving: About 222 calories, 28g protein, 3g carbohydrate, 10g fat, 0g fiber, 67mg cholesterol, 635mg sodium

From the Grill ▶

Prep Time: 10 minutes

Marinate Time: 8 hours

Cook Time: 10 minutes

Average Rating: ★★★★★

What other cooks have done:

"The success of this recipe depends upon your teriyaki sauce. Next time I make it, I think I'll try a different cut of steak."

Broccoli Beef

Submitted by: **Sara**

"Round steak and broccoli are quickly cooked in a soy-ginger sauce. Serve hot over rice or noodles."

¼	cup all-purpose flour	¼	teaspoon chopped fresh ginger root
1	(10.5 ounce) can beef broth	1	clove garlic, minced
2	tablespoons white sugar	4	cups chopped fresh broccoli
2	tablespoons soy sauce		
1	pound boneless round steak, cut into bite size pieces		

1. In a small bowl, combine flour, broth, sugar, and soy sauce. Stir until sugar and flour are dissolved.
2. In a large skillet or wok over high heat, cook beef, stirring constantly, 2 to 4 minutes or until browned. Stir in broth mixture, ginger, garlic, and broccoli. Bring to a boil, then reduce heat. Simmer 5 to 10 minutes or until sauce thickens. **Yield:** 4 servings.

Per serving: About 173 calories, 19g protein, 18g carbohydrate, 3g fat, 3g fiber, 39mg cholesterol, 756mg sodium

Quick & Easy ▶

Prep Time: 15 minutes

Cook Time: 15 minutes

Average Rating: ★★★★☆

What other cooks have done:

"Here's a hint: Instead of slicing the beef, cut it into strips with kitchen shears. To save even more time, buy prepackaged stir-fry beef at the grocery store."

Slow-Cooked German Short Ribs

Submitted by: **Peggy**

"Dust off your slow cooker. This recipe is worth it. I love coming home to a waiting meal!"

1	teaspoon salt	3	tablespoons packed brown sugar
⅛	teaspoon ground black pepper	3	tablespoons white vinegar
2	tablespoons all-purpose flour	1	tablespoon Worcestershire sauce
3	pounds beef short ribs	½	teaspoon powdered mustard
2	tablespoons olive oil	½	teaspoon chili powder
1	onion, sliced	2	tablespoons all-purpose flour
½	cup dry red wine	¼	cup water
½	cup chili sauce		

1. In a small bowl, combine salt, pepper, and 2 tablespoons flour. Coat short ribs with flour mixture.

2. In a large skillet, heat olive oil over medium-high heat. Brown short ribs in olive oil.

3. In a slow cooker, combine onion, wine, chili sauce, brown sugar, vinegar, Worcestershire sauce, mustard, and chili powder. Mix thoroughly. Transfer the short ribs from the skillet to the slow cooker.

4. Cover and cook on High for 1 hour. Reduce heat to Low and cook for 5 hours.

5. Remove ribs and turn the slow cooker to High. Mix 2 tablespoons flour with ¼ cup water and stir into the sauce. Cook for 10 minutes or until slightly thickened. **Yield:** 6 servings.

Per serving: About 461 calories, 24g protein, 13g carbohydrate, 33g fat, 0g fiber, 84mg cholesterol, 486mg sodium

◄ Slow-Cooker Creation

Prep Time: 25 minutes

Cook Time: 6 hours 10 minutes

Average Rating: ★★★★★

What other cooks have done:

"This is a really good short rib recipe! I didn't have any red wine, so I substituted red wine vinegar and omitted the regular vinegar—it turned out fine. Short ribs are yummy and so is this recipe!"

Prep Time: 15 minutes

Cook Time: 30 minutes

Average Rating: ★★★★★

What other cooks have done:

"I cheated on this recipe to save time by substituting a package of taco seasoning and tomato sauce for the spices and taco sauce, and by stirring the beans in with the beef mixture before assembling. I usually fry chimichangas, but they were much less greasy this way. I will continue to bake rather than fry them. They were great and a lot less messy."

Beef and Bean Chimichangas *(pictured on facing page)*

Submitted by: **Nicole**

"Awesome recipe, if you like Mexican food! These tasty beef and bean treats are baked instead of fried."

1 pound lean ground beef	1 (16 ounce) can refried beans
¾ cup chopped onion	10 (9 inch) flour tortillas
¾ cup diced green bell pepper	1 (8 ounce) package shredded Monterey Jack cheese
1½ cups whole kernel corn, drained	1 tablespoon butter, melted
2 (8 ounce) bottles taco sauce	Toppings: shredded lettuce, diced tomato, sour cream
2 teaspoons chili powder	
1 teaspoon garlic salt	
1 teaspoon ground cumin	

1. Preheat the oven to 400°F (200°C).

2. Combine ground beef, onion, and bell pepper in a skillet over medium-high heat; cook until browned, stirring to crumble. Drain excess grease. Add corn and cook 1 to 2 minutes or until heated. Stir in taco sauce, chili powder, garlic salt, and cumin, stirring until blended. Cook until heated through, then remove from heat and set aside.

3. Spread a thin layer of beans evenly onto each of the tortillas. Spoon the beef mixture down the center of each tortilla and top with shredded cheese. Fold sides in and roll up, burrito-style, and place seam side down onto a lightly greased jellyroll pan. Brush the tortillas with melted butter.

4. Bake in the preheated oven for 15 to 20 minutes or until golden brown. Serve with desired toppings. **Yield:** 10 servings.

Per serving: About 444 calories, 21g protein, 39g carbohydrate, 20g fat, 4g fiber, 58mg cholesterol, 1058mg sodium

Beef and Bean Chimichangas,
facing page

Lamb Feta Peppers, page 122

Ground Beef Shepherd's Pie, page 118

Coconut Shrimp, page 158

Italian Chicken Marinade, page 139, and Goat Cheese and Arugula over Penne, page 200

Little Meat Loaves

Submitted by: **Ann Collins**
"These individual meat loaves are topped with a tangy-sweet sauce."

2	eggs, lightly beaten	1	teaspoon Worcestershire sauce
¾	cup crushed buttery round crackers	1	pound lean ground beef
½	cup milk	1	pound ground sausage
½	cup grated Parmesan cheese	1	cup ketchup
½	cup chopped onion	½	cup packed brown sugar
1	teaspoon dried Italian-style seasoning	1	tablespoon Worcestershire sauce
1	teaspoon garlic salt		

1. Preheat oven to 350°F (175°C). In a large bowl, combine eggs, cracker crumbs, milk, cheese, onion, Italian seasoning, garlic salt, 1 teaspoon Worcestershire sauce, ground beef, and ground sausage. Mix together; form into 6 individual loaves. Place in a 9x13 inch baking dish.
2. In a small bowl, combine ketchup, brown sugar, and 1 tablespoon Worcestershire sauce. Mix together and spoon evenly over each loaf.
3. Bake in the preheated oven for 45 to 60 minutes. **Yield:** 6 servings.

Per serving: About 837 calories, 33g protein, 51g carbohydrate, 56g fat, 1g fiber, 190mg cholesterol, 1925mg sodium

◀ Family Favorite

Prep Time: 30 minutes
Cook Time: 1 hour
Average Rating: ★★★★★
What other cooks have done:
"My kids just love these! Everybody is happy when these are on the menu. We love them for lunch the next day, sliced and made into sandwiches with some of the leftover barbecue sauce spread on the meat."

Cabbage Rolls II

Submitted by: **BJ**
"Cabbage leaves stuffed with ground beef, onion, and rice, covered in a sweet and tangy tomato sauce, and cooked in a slow cooker."

12	cabbage leaves	1¼	teaspoons ground black pepper
1	cup cooked white rice	1	(8 ounce) can tomato sauce
1	egg, lightly beaten	1	tablespoon brown sugar
¼	cup milk	1	tablespoon lemon juice
¼	cup minced onion	1	teaspoon Worcestershire sauce
1	pound extra-lean ground beef		
1¼	teaspoons salt		

1. In a large pot of boiling water, boil cabbage leaves 2 minutes; drain.
2. In a large bowl, combine rice, egg, milk, onion, ground beef, salt, and pepper. Place about ¼ cup of meat mixture in center of each cabbage leaf and roll up, tucking in ends. Place rolls in slow cooker.
3. In a small bowl, mix together tomato sauce, brown sugar, lemon juice, and Worcestershire sauce. Pour over cabbage rolls.
4. Cover and cook on High for 1 hour. Reduce heat to Low and cook for 6 to 8 hours. **Yield:** 6 servings.

Per serving: About 248 calories, 19g protein, 18g carbohydrate, 11g fat, 2g fiber, 88mg cholesterol, 778mg sodium

◀ Slow-Cooker Creation

Prep Time: 30 minutes
Cook Time: 9 hours
Average Rating: ★★★★★
What other cooks have done:
"The only problem I had with this recipe was that when I put the rolls in the slow cooker, there was not enough liquid, and they burned a little on the edges. Despite that, they were very good and got snatched right up at a church potluck. I think next time I'll double the sauce."

Ground Beef Shepherd's Pie (pictured on page 115)

Submitted by: **Ginger P.**

"Here's a quick, throw-together recipe for shepherd's pie. Browned meat smothered in rich mashed potatoes with your favorite vegetables. A quick and easy dinner to make for your family."

1	tablespoon vegetable oil	2	potatoes, cooked and mashed
1	onion, chopped		
1	pound lean ground beef	1	egg, lightly beaten
1	teaspoon dried basil	½	cup water
1	clove garlic, minced	1	teaspoon salt
1	cup green beans	¼	cup shredded Cheddar cheese (optional)
1	(14.5 ounce) can diced tomatoes, drained		

1. Preheat oven to 350°F (175°C).

2. Heat oil in a large skillet over medium heat. Cook onion in oil for 5 minutes, stirring frequently. Stir in ground beef and basil and cook for 5 more minutes, stirring frequently. Mix in the garlic, green beans, and tomatoes, and simmer for 5 minutes. Transfer beef mixture to a lightly greased 2 quart casserole dish.

3. In a bowl, mix together the mashed potatoes, egg, water, and salt. Spread evenly over meat mixture.

4. Bake in the preheated oven for 15 to 20 minutes or until potatoes start to brown on top. Sprinkle with cheese, if desired, and continue cooking for 5 minutes. **Yield:** 4 servings.

Per serving: About 371 calories, 27g protein, 18g carbohydrate, 21g fat, 3g fiber, 135mg cholesterol, 226mg sodium

---

One-Dish Meal ▶

Prep Time: 25 minutes

Cook Time: 35 minutes

Average Rating: ★★★★★

What other cooks have done:

"I added in some corn, fresh sliced mushrooms, and used diced plum tomatoes. I also used an additional large potato and stirred in a little low-fat milk when mashing. You can vary the flavor by stirring in different seasonings with the ground beef. Anything from seasoning salt to red wine or barbecue sauce tastes good."

Waikiki Meatballs

Submitted by: **Cathy**

"Beef meatballs flavored with ground ginger, simmered in a sweet pineapple sauce."

1½	pounds ground beef	2	tablespoons cornstarch
⅔	cup crushed saltine cracker crumbs	½	cup packed brown sugar
⅓	cup minced onion	1	(15 ounce) can pineapple chunks, drained and juice reserved
1	egg		
¼	cup milk	⅓	cup white vinegar
1½	teaspoons ground ginger	1	tablespoon soy sauce
½	teaspoon salt	⅓	cup chopped green bell pepper
1	tablespoon olive oil		

1. In a large bowl, combine ground beef, cracker crumbs, onion, egg, milk, ginger, and salt. Shape mixture by rounded tablespoonfuls into meatballs.

2. Heat olive oil in a large skillet over medium heat. Place meatballs in skillet and cook until evenly browned and meat is no longer pink. Drain excess fat.

3. In a small bowl, combine cornstarch, brown sugar, reserved pineapple juice, vinegar, and soy sauce. Mix until smooth, then pour into the skillet with meatballs. Cook, stirring constantly, until mixture thickens and boils, about 5 minutes. Stir in bell pepper and pineapple chunks. Heat through. **Yield:** 6 servings.

Per serving: About 442 calories, 22g protein, 40g carbohydrate, 22g fat, 1g fiber, 106mg cholesterol, 538mg sodium

◀ Out-of-the-Ordinary

Prep Time: 20 minutes

Cook Time: 25 minutes

Average Rating: ★★★★★

What other cooks have done:

"My family loves this. Here are a few tips to cut the prep time: Oven-bake the meatballs at 350°F (175°C) for 20 minutes on a foil lined broiler pan. The fat melts off and the meatballs stay firm instead of crumbling apart. It cuts down on calories and fat and improves the taste. Also, when making the sauce, just dump all the ingredients into a saucepan at the same time and whisk the heck out of it. No lumps and cuts down on dishes. Enjoy!"

Grilled Gyro Burgers

Submitted by: **Theresa**

"Creamy cucumber sauce tops off these grilled burgers inside a pita pocket shell."

2	(8 ounce) containers plain yogurt, divided	1½	pounds ground beef
1	(1 ounce) package Ranch-style dressing mix	¼	cup diced onion
		6	pita bread rounds
1	cucumber, peeled, seeded, and chopped	2	cups torn lettuce leaves
		1	tomato, seeded and diced

1. In a medium bowl, combine 1 container of yogurt with ranch dressing mix. Set aside half of mixture. Add remaining container of yogurt and diced cucumber; mix well. Cover and refrigerate. Lightly oil grill rack and preheat grill for medium heat.
2. Mix ground beef and onion into remaining half of yogurt mixture. Shape into 6 hamburger patties.
3. Grill patties on medium heat for 7 minutes on each side, turning patties once.
4. Cut ¼ end off pita pockets and fill each with torn lettuce, diced tomato, grilled burger, and cucumber sauce. **Yield:** 6 servings.

Per serving: About 590 calories, 29g protein, 44g carbohydrate, 32g fat, 2g fiber, 101mg cholesterol, 783mg sodium

Cajun-Style Burgers

Submitted by: **Gail**

"You can't beat spicy burgers cooked on the grill and topped with a hot barbecue sauce. Serve with hamburger rolls, lettuce, tomato, and red onion."

1	pound ground beef	1	tablespoon prepared mustard
3	tablespoons dry breadcrumbs	¼	cup barbecue sauce
1	egg	1	teaspoon Cajun seasoning
3	green onions, chopped	4	slices Cheddar cheese
1	tablespoon Cajun seasoning	4	hamburger buns

1. Lightly oil grill rack and preheat grill for high heat.
2. In a medium bowl, mix the ground beef, breadcrumbs, egg, green onions, 1 tablespoon Cajun seasoning, and mustard. Form into 4 patties.
3. In a bowl, blend barbecue sauce and 1 teaspoon Cajun seasoning.
4. Cook the patties on the prepared grill to desired doneness. Place a slice of cheese on each burger and allow to melt. Serve on hamburger buns with seasoned barbecue sauce. **Yield:** 4 servings.

Per serving: About 529 calories, 29g protein, 8g carbohydrate, 42g fat, 1g fiber, 179mg cholesterol, 958mg sodium

Emily's Famous Sloppy Joes

Submitted by: **Emily**

"This is a good old-fashioned Sloppy Joe recipe. Just slap some on a bun and enjoy!"

1½	pounds ground beef	1	teaspoon ground cumin
1	onion, chopped	1	teaspoon white vinegar
1	red bell pepper, chopped	3	tablespoons brown sugar
1	(6 ounce) can tomato paste	1	teaspoon dried oregano
1	cup water	½	teaspoon salt
3	cloves garlic, minced	½	teaspoon ground black
1	tablespoon chili powder		pepper
1	teaspoon paprika		

1. In a large skillet over medium-high heat, sauté the ground beef for 5 minutes. Add the onion and red bell pepper; sauté for 5 more minutes or until onion is tender and beef is browned. Drain.

2. Mix in tomato paste and water, stirring until paste is dissolved. Stir in garlic, chili powder, paprika, cumin, vinegar, brown sugar, oregano, salt, and pepper. Continue to heat for 5 to 10 minutes or until mixture is thick. **Yield:** 8 servings.

Per serving: About 204 calories, 16g protein, 13g carbohydrate, 10g fat, 2g fiber, 52mg cholesterol, 377mg sodium

◀ **Classic Comfort Food**

Prep Time: 10 minutes

Cook Time: 20 minutes

Average Rating: ★★★★★

What other cooks have done:

"I used ground turkey instead of beef and ¾ cup of beer instead of water. After simmering for 30 minutes or so, you get a great taste!"

Baked Lamb Chops

Submitted by: **Leslie W. Dobson**

"These are very tasty and make an easy main meal to prepare. Try serving them with mashed potatoes, peas, and pumpkin."

3	eggs	12	(5.5 ounce) lamb chops
1	tablespoon Worcestershire sauce	2	cups dry breadcrumbs

1. Preheat oven to 375°F (190°C).

2. In a medium bowl, combine eggs and Worcestershire sauce; stir well. Dip each lamb chop in egg mixture and lightly dredge in breadcrumbs. Arrange chops in a lightly greased 9x13 inch baking dish.

3. Bake in the preheated oven for 20 minutes. Turn chops over and bake for 20 more minutes or to desired doneness. **Yield:** 6 servings.

Per serving: About 740 calories, 52g protein, 27g carbohydrate, 45g fat, 1g fiber, 283mg cholesterol, 506mg sodium

◀ **Quick & Easy**

Prep Time: 10 minutes

Cook Time: 40 minutes

Average Rating: ★★★★★

What other cooks have done:

"The kids liked these chops and they were so easy to make! I didn't have any Worcestershire sauce so I substituted soy sauce, and it came out very good."

Prep Time: 15 minutes

Cook Time: 45 minutes

Average Rating: ★★★★★

What other cooks have done:

"These peppers made with lamb are more robust in flavor than an average stuffed pepper. I added a diced hot red pepper and more garlic to the filling and doubled the tomato sauce."

Lamb Feta Peppers *(pictured on page 114)*

Submitted by: **Taseia**

"Since I'm Greek, I've learned many good Greek recipes over the years! This is one of my favorites. It's a savory combination of lamb, rice, and feta cheese stuffed into sweet bell peppers and smothered with tomato sauce."

1	tablespoon olive oil	½	teaspoon ground black pepper
1	medium onion, chopped		
1	clove garlic, minced	1	cup cooked rice
8	ounces ground lamb	1	cup crumbled feta cheese
2	medium green bell peppers	1	(8 ounce) can tomato sauce
2	medium red bell peppers	½	cup cold water
2	medium yellow bell peppers	1	tablespoon fresh lemon juice
2	tablespoons chopped fresh dill		
¾	teaspoon salt	1	teaspoon white sugar
½	teaspoon ground allspice		Garnish: feta cheese

1. Preheat oven to 375°F (190°C).

2. Heat oil in a medium skillet over medium–high heat; add onion, garlic, and lamb, and cook for 5 minutes or until meat is browned.

3. Slice tops off peppers and remove seeds. Stand peppers upright in a lightly greased 9x13 inch baking dish.

4. In a large bowl, combine lamb mixture, dill, salt, allspice, and pepper. Mix in rice and fold in 1 cup feta cheese. Stuff peppers with mixture.

5. Mix tomato sauce with water, lemon juice, and sugar. Pour half of sauce over peppers, and half over bottom of dish. Cover with foil.

6. Bake in the preheated oven for 30 minutes. Uncover and continue baking 15 minutes or until heated through and peppers are tender, basting occasionally with sauce. Garnish, if desired. **Yield:** 6 servings.

Per serving: About 284 calories, 12g protein, 22g carbohydrate, 17g fat, 3g fiber, 50mg cholesterol, 945mg sodium

Tangy Slow-Cooker Pork Roast

Submitted by: **K**

"This recipe is a favorite with my husband. I usually serve it with buttered egg noodles and sugar snap peas."

1	large onion, sliced	1	tablespoon ketchup
2½	pounds boneless pork loin roast	½	teaspoon ground black pepper
1	cup hot water	½	teaspoon salt
¼	cup white sugar	¼	teaspoon garlic powder
3	tablespoons red wine vinegar		Dash hot pepper sauce or to taste
2	tablespoons soy sauce		

1. Arrange onion slices evenly in slow cooker; place the roast on top of the onion. In a bowl, mix together water, sugar, vinegar, soy sauce, ketchup, black pepper, salt, garlic powder, and hot sauce; pour over roast.
2. Cover and cook on High for 1 hour and Low for 4 to 6 hours, or on High for 3 to 4 hours. **Yield:** 8 servings.

Per serving: About 210 calories, 25g protein, 10g carbohydrate, 8g fat, 0g fiber, 66mg cholesterol, 487mg sodium

Vienna Schnitzel

Submitted by: **Frank Hasieber**

"Both my mother and father were from Vienna, Austria. This was my mother's recipe. Veal can also be used in place of pork."

1	quart vegetable oil	2	eggs, lightly beaten
6	(6 ounce) pork sirloin fillets	¼	cup milk
1	cup cake flour		Salt and ground black pepper to taste
2	cups dry breadcrumbs		

1. Heat oil in a deep fryer to 350°F (175°C).
2. Pound pork with a meat mallet to ⅛ to ¼ inch thickness.
3. Place flour and breadcrumbs in separate dishes. In a medium bowl, combine eggs, milk, and salt and pepper to taste.
4. Coat 1 fillet in flour, patting lightly by hand. Using a fork to hold the meat, dip into the egg mixture and drain slightly. Next, coat fillet with the breadcrumbs by lightly pressing the crumbs into the meat. When each piece of meat has been prepared, deep-fry in oil until golden brown. **Yield:** 6 servings.

Per serving: About 543 calories, 32g protein, 45g carbohydrate, 25g fat, 1g fiber, 139mg cholesterol, 379mg sodium

Pork Loin Stuffed with Spinach

Submitted by: **Mariah McGuinness**

"Pork loin stuffed with spinach, onion, garlic, and breadcrumbs, basted in a fabulous sweet sauce."

5	ounces chopped frozen spinach, thawed and pressed	⅓	cup dry breadcrumbs
3	tablespoons butter	3	pounds pork tenderloin
½	cup diced onion	2	tablespoons ketchup
1	clove garlic	¼	cup orange juice
		2	tablespoons teriyaki sauce
		½	teaspoon ground cumin

1. Preheat oven to 350°F (175°C).

2. Sauté spinach, butter, onion, and garlic over medium heat until soft. Add breadcrumbs. Cut tenderloin in half lengthwise. Stuff tenderloin with spinach mixture and secure with kitchen twine.

3. In a bowl, mix ketchup, orange juice, and teriyaki sauce. Baste tenderloin with half of mixture. Sprinkle pork with cumin. Place in a shallow roasting pan and bake, uncovered, in the preheated oven for 1 hour. Baste with reserved marinade and bake, covered, 1 more hour or until a meat thermometer inserted in thickest part registers 160°F (70°C). **Yield:** 5 servings.

Per serving: About 397 calories, 48g protein, 12g carbohydrate, 17g fat, 1g fiber, 127mg cholesterol, 596mg sodium

Tying Roasts ▼

There are many ways to tie a roast. Some methods are easier than others, and this method is the proven quickest! Roasts are tied for two reasons: 1) to keep the roast in an aesthetically pleasing round shape; and 2) to hold stuffing inside of the roast. We refer to a pork loin to highlight this method, however, most cuts of meat can be tied this way (even a deboned chicken thigh and stuffed fish).

1. To tie a roast, you'll need a long stretch of butcher's twine. If you're unclear how much twine will be necessary for tying the roast, use the entire ball or package of twine and cut the twine off only when you have finished tying the roast. Place the roast on a flat surface perpendicular to your body. Hold the twine taut by both ends and slide the twine underneath the roast until it reaches one end of the meat.

2. Pull the string very tightly around one end of the roast and make a square knot. If the knot is too loose, the muscle will relax and gravity will cause the roast to form an oval shape. If the knot is too tight, desirable juices may seep out of the meat. Make sure there is ample twine on one side of the knot.

3. Lay the string so that it rests along the length of the roast. Place your thumb on the string one inch from the first knot (or the last tie made). With your thumb holding the string firmly, wrap the string around the roast. Lift the corner you just created at your thumb and pass the end of string under the lifted piece. Pull the string upwards to tighten the hold.

4. Continue the process of wrapping and tying outlined in step 3 until the roast is completely tied. Once the entire roast is tied, it should be round in shape and feel very tight. If the roast isn't tight, tighten the entire roast by tightening each tie, beginning with the first tie made (excluding the knot). Once the roast feels secure, wrap the string around the roast lengthwise until the string reaches the original knot.

5. Pass the end of the string underneath the knot and pull tightly. Do not pull too tightly because pulling too tightly will cause the roast to form into a U shape. Only pull tight enough to keep the last loop on the roast from slipping. Tie another knot in the string to secure the work done.

6. The roast is ready for cooking! Note: If you're tying a stuffed roast, as you make and tighten the ties, some stuffing may ooze out. Push the stuffing back into the newly tightened area of the roast with your fingers and continue tying.

For more information, visit **Allrecipes.com**

Pork Tenderloin with Creamy Herb Sauce

Submitted by: **Carrie**

"A wonderfully elegant and easy pork tenderloin dish with a creamy herbed wine sauce. Very rich, without all of the fat and calories! Serve with garlic mashed potatoes. A wonderful dish."

1	tablespoon vegetable oil	½	teaspoon ground black pepper
½	cup minced carrots		
1½	pounds pork tenderloin medaillons	½	teaspoon beef bouillon granules
2	teaspoons all-purpose flour	⅔	cup half-and-half
1	tablespoon dried basil	¼	cup dry white wine
1	tablespoon dried parsley		

1. Heat oil in a skillet over medium heat; cook carrots in oil for 5 minutes, stirring often. Add pork and cook until lightly browned. Remove pork and keep warm.
2. In the skillet, stir together flour, basil, parsley, pepper, and beef granules. Whisk in half-and-half, stirring until thick. Stir in wine. Return pork to pan. Reduce heat to low and cover. Simmer for 20 minutes, stirring occasionally. **Yield:** 6 servings.

Per serving: About 225 calories, 21g protein, 3g carbohydrate, 13g fat, 1g fiber, 81mg cholesterol, 65mg sodium

◄ Party Food

Prep Time: 15 minutes
Cook Time: 30 minutes
Average Rating: ★★★★★
What other cooks have done:
"We've made this several times and everybody who has tried it has loved it. If you're not concerned about fat content, it's even better with heavy cream instead of light. It works nicely with red meat, too, if you substitute red wine for the white."

Burgundy Pork Tenderloin *(pictured on page 156)*

Submitted by: **Kathleen White**

"My husband doesn't care much for pork, but he loves this. It's very easy to fix and very rich tasting. Serve with baked potato."

2	pounds pork tenderloin	½	onion, thinly sliced
½	teaspoon salt	1	stalk celery, chopped
½	teaspoon ground black pepper	2	cups red wine
½	teaspoon garlic powder	1	(.75 ounce) package dry brown gravy mix

1. Preheat oven to 350°F (175°C).
2. Place pork in a 9x13 inch baking dish and sprinkle with salt, pepper, and garlic powder. Top with onion and celery and pour wine over all.
3. Bake in the preheated oven for 45 minutes or until a meat thermometer inserted in thickest part of tenderloin reaches 160°F (70°C).
4. Transfer meat to a serving platter, reserving juices in dish. Pour gravy mix into juices in baking dish and stir until thickened. To serve, slice meat and cover with gravy. **Yield:** 4 servings.

Per serving: About 421 calories, 48g protein, 7g carbohydrate, 13g fat, 1g fiber, 150mg cholesterol, 671mg sodium

◄ Company is Coming

Prep Time: 15 minutes
Cook Time: 45 minutes
Average Rating: ★★★★★
What other cooks have done:
"I'm only 13 and an aspiring chef, so I try to cook for my parents and sister. They're kind of like my recipe guinea pigs. So far I haven't found one person who didn't like this. Even my sister, who is extremely picky, liked it. I would definitely recommend this recipe to any- one with one tip: Make more red wine mix—the gravy-wine mixture is great with mashed potatoes."

Prep Time: 15 minutes

Marinate Time: 12 hours

Cook Time: 10 minutes

Average Rating: ★★★★☆

What other cooks have done:

"A very good recipe! After trying it the first time, I doubled the cayenne pepper for a really good flavor of Jamaican jerk spices, but I would recommend trying the recipe as written before adjusting the pepper."

Caribbean Jerk Pork Chops (*pictured on page 150*)

Submitted by: **Marvin**

"Hot and spicy Caribbean pork chops soaked in a killer 'jerk' marinade! This recipe will light your fire!"

¾	cup water	¾	teaspoon ground cinnamon
⅓	cup lemon juice	¾	teaspoon ground black pepper
⅓	cup chopped onion		
1	tablespoon packed brown sugar	½	teaspoon dried thyme, crushed
1	tablespoon chopped green onions	¼	teaspoon ground cayenne pepper
1	tablespoon canola oil	6	(½ inch thick) lean bone-in pork chops
¾	teaspoon salt		
¾	teaspoon ground allspice		

1. Place water, lemon juice, onion, brown sugar, green onions, oil, salt, allspice, cinnamon, black pepper, thyme, and cayenne pepper into a blender and puree until smooth. Pour ½ cup sauce in a small bowl to use for basting; cover and refrigerate.

2. Place pork in a shallow glass or plastic dish. Pour remaining marinade over pork. Cover and refrigerate at least 12 hours but no longer than 24 hours.

3. Preheat grill for medium-high heat.

4. Remove pork from marinade; discard marinade. Cover and grill pork. Turn pork frequently and brush with reserved marinade. Cook until a meat thermometer registers 160°F (70°C) or about 4 to 5 minutes on each side. **Yield:** 6 servings.

Per serving: About 140 calories, 16g protein, 5g carbohydrate, 6g fat, 1g fiber, 40mg cholesterol, 347mg sodium

Oven-Fried Pork Chops

Submitted by: **Rachel**

"This is a quick, simple, and above all, inexpensive way to make pork chops. I love it!"

2	tablespoons butter, melted	4	thick cut pork chops, trimmed
1	egg, lightly beaten	1	cup herb seasoned dry stuffing mix
2	tablespoons milk		
¼	teaspoon ground black pepper		

1. Preheat oven to 425°F (220°C). Pour butter into a 9x13 inch baking pan.

2. Stir together egg, milk, and pepper. Dip pork chops in egg mixture, coat with stuffing mix, and place in pan.

3. Bake in the preheated oven for 10 minutes. Turn chops and bake for 10 more minutes or until no pink remains in the meat and juices run clear. **Yield:** 4 servings.

Per serving: About 367 calories, 23g protein, 139g carbohydrate, 3g fat, 2g fiber, 109mg cholesterol, 905mg sodium

◀ Family Favorite

Prep Time: 10 minutes

Cook Time: 20 minutes

Average Rating: ★★★★☆

What other cooks have done:

"The stuffing crumbs really give the chops a nice flavor. I'll make these again, but I'll turn up the temperature toward the very end to brown the crumbs more and to make them crunchier. I really liked this recipe."

Orange Pork

Submitted by: **fireball2000**

"Quick, easy, and tasty. We double the sauce and pour it over baked potatoes and steamed broccoli."

1	tablespoon vegetable oil	1½	tablespoons white sugar
1	pound boneless pork chops	2	teaspoons water
⅔	cup orange juice	1	teaspoon cornstarch
¼	cup soy sauce		

1. Heat oil in a large, heavy skillet over medium heat. Cook pork chops until evenly browned on both sides; remove from skillet. Add orange juice, soy sauce, and sugar to skillet. Cook for 2 minutes, scraping the bottom of pan.

2. In a small bowl, mix together water and cornstarch and stir into sauce. Return pork to skillet and cook briefly until sauce is thickened and pork chops are heated through. **Yield:** 4 servings.

Per serving: About 288 calories, 24g protein, 11g carbohydrate, 16g fat, 0g fiber, 66mg cholesterol, 960mg sodium

◀ Quick & Easy

Prep Time: 10 minutes

Cook Time: 10 minutes

Average Rating: ★★★★☆

What other cooks have done:

"I cut boneless pork loin chops into small cubes and dredged them in flour before stir-frying for a yummy light coating. I substituted peanut oil for the vegetable oil, and brown sugar for the white. Also, I cut back a bit on the soy sauce and increased the orange juice accordingly. I let the pork simmer gently until it was tender. It was terrific served over Asian rice noodles with steamed broccoli."

Prep Time: 20 minutes

Cook Time: 25 minutes

Average Rating: ★★★★☆

What other cooks have done:

"This is one of those dishes that's easy, but makes others think you slaved. My husband loves it and so do I! The sauce is so yummy—you absolutely have to double it."

Caramel-Apple Pork Chops

Submitted by: **Karena**

"Warm, spicy, and sweet, this wonderful fall recipe is a guaranteed favorite for kids, and is great served with mashed potatoes and buttered green beans."

4 (¾ inch thick) pork chops	⅛ teaspoon ground nutmeg
1 teaspoon vegetable oil	2 tablespoons unsalted butter
2 tablespoons brown sugar	2 tart apples, peeled, cored,
Salt and ground black	and sliced
pepper to taste	3 tablespoons chopped pecans
⅛ teaspoon ground cinnamon	(optional)

1. Preheat oven to 175°F (80°C). Place a medium dish in the oven to warm.

2. Heat a large skillet over medium-high heat. Brush chops lightly with oil and place in hot skillet. Cook for 5 to 6 minutes, turning occasionally, or until done. Transfer to warm dish and keep warm in the preheated oven.

3. In a small bowl, combine brown sugar, salt and pepper to taste, cinnamon, and nutmeg. Add butter to skillet and stir in brown sugar mixture and apples. Cover and cook until apples are just tender. Remove apples with a slotted spoon and arrange on top of chops. Keep warm in the preheated oven.

4. Continue cooking remaining brown sugar mixture in skillet, uncovered, until sauce thickens slightly. Spoon sauce over apples and chops. Sprinkle with pecans, if desired. **Yield:** 4 servings.

Per serving: About 324 calories, 24g protein, 18g carbohydrate, 18g fat, 2g fiber, 74mg cholesterol, 51mg sodium

Kielbasa and Cabbage

Submitted by: **Katherine Denning**

"This smoked Polish sausage dish is great for company! It's easy and can be prepared ahead. Complete the meal with baked potato, fruit salad, and bread."

6	slices bacon	¼	teaspoon seasoning salt
¼	cup water	1	tablespoon caraway seeds
2	tablespoons white sugar	1	large head cabbage, cut into
1	onion, chopped		small wedges
2	teaspoons minced garlic	1	pound kielbasa
¼	teaspoon crushed red pepper flakes		

1. In a large skillet, fry bacon over medium-high heat until browned, turning once. Remove bacon, reserving drippings in pan; place bacon on paper towels.
2. Stir water, sugar, onion, garlic, red pepper flakes, seasoning salt, and caraway seeds into drippings. Add cabbage and gently stir. Cover and cook over medium heat for 10 to 15 minutes.
3. Add kielbasa to pan. Cook, covered, for 10 to 15 more minutes. Serve hot with bacon crumbled on top. **Yield:** 4 servings.

Per serving: About 570 calories, 26g protein, 29g carbohydrate, 41g fat, 8g fiber, 91mg cholesterol, 1331mg sodium

Sausage-Potato Casserole

Submitted by: **Sue Lauderbaugh**

"A family favorite combination of sausage, potatoes, and cheese that's my most requested recipe."

3	large baking potatoes, peeled and thinly sliced	1	pound kielbasa
	Ground black pepper to taste	½	teaspoon dried dill weed
		¼	teaspoon caraway seeds
1	cup shredded Cheddar cheese, divided	⅔	cup milk

1. Preheat oven to 375°F (190°C). Line a 9x13 inch pan with aluminum foil, allowing edges to hang outside pan.
2. Arrange sliced potatoes, overlapping slightly, in pan. Sprinkle with pepper to taste. Top with half of the cheese. Cut sausage in half crosswise and lengthwise and place cut side down over cheese layer. Top with dill weed, caraway seeds, milk, and remaining cheese. Seal edges of foil tightly over casserole.
3. Bake in the preheated oven for 1 hour. **Yield:** 6 servings.

Per serving: About 409 calories, 18g protein, 19g carbohydrate, 29g fat, 2g fiber, 75mg cholesterol, 800mg sodium

Chicken Pepper Steak

Submitted by: **Tiara**

"Chicken breasts simmered with onion, bell pepper, tomatoes, soy sauce, and spices to be served with a rich, pepper steak style gravy. If you like the taste of pepper steak but really don't enjoy red meat, now you can try it with chicken!"

1	tablespoon vegetable oil	1	large onion, cut into long slices
4	skinless, boneless chicken breast halves	2	tablespoons cornstarch
1	teaspoon seasoning salt	2½	cups water
½	teaspoon onion powder	1	green bell pepper, sliced
2	teaspoons minced garlic	4	roma (plum) tomatoes, seeded and chopped
½	cup soy sauce, divided		

1. Heat oil in a large skillet over medium heat. Season chicken with salt and onion powder and place in skillet. Cook for about 5 to 7 minutes. Add garlic, ¼ cup soy sauce, and half of the sliced onion. Cook until chicken is no longer pink and the juices run clear.
2. Dissolve cornstarch in water in a small bowl and blend into the chicken mixture. Stir in remaining ¼ cup soy sauce, bell pepper, tomatoes, and remaining onion. Simmer gravy to desired consistency. **Yield:** 4 servings.

Per serving: 250 calories, 30g protein, 16g carbohydrate, 8g fat, 2g fiber, 72mg cholesterol, 2126mg sodium

Spicy Grilled Chicken

Submitted by: **Jenn H.**

"This recipe is perfect for summer barbecues, but it can be broiled indoors."

⅓	cup vegetable oil	1	teaspoon salt
½	teaspoon grated lime zest	¼	teaspoon ground black pepper
2	tablespoons lime juice	6	skinless, boneless chicken breast halves
2	cloves garlic, crushed		
1½	teaspoons fresh oregano		
¼	teaspoon crushed red pepper flakes		

1. In a shallow bowl, combine oil, lime zest, lime juice, garlic, oregano, crushed red pepper, salt, and pepper. Mix all together. Add chicken and toss to coat. Cover and refrigerate for 1 hour to marinate, turning chicken occasionally.
2. Preheat grill for medium-high heat.
3. Remove chicken breasts from marinade, discarding marinade; grill chicken for 6 to 8 minutes on each side or until chicken is no longer pink and juices run clear. **Yield:** 6 servings.

Per serving: About 242 calories, 27g protein, 1g carbohydrate, 14g fat, 0g fiber, 68mg cholesterol, 465mg sodium

Mango Salsa Chicken

Submitted by: **Emma Brown–Beresford**

"Easy and refreshing chicken dinner—great in the summertime. Nice served with mashed potatoes and salad. The salsa is also yummy served with fish!"

1	ripe mango, chopped	4	skinless, boneless chicken
½	red onion, finely diced		breast halves
1	bunch cilantro, finely	1	egg
	chopped	¼	cup milk
½	green bell pepper, minced	1	cup dry breadcrumbs
1	red chile pepper, seeded	¼	cup olive oil
	and chopped		Garnish: fresh cilantro

1. In a small bowl, combine mango, onion, cilantro, green bell pepper, and red chile pepper. Set aside.

2. Lightly pound chicken breasts with a meat mallet to flatten. Beat egg and milk together. Coat chicken in the egg mixture, then dredge in breadcrumbs. Chill for 30 minutes.

3. Heat olive oil in a skillet. Sauté chicken in olive oil 5 minutes on each side or until chicken is no longer pink and juices run clear. Drain and serve with the mango salsa. Garnish, if desired. **Yield:** 4 servings.

Per serving: About 433 calories, 34g protein, 33g carbohydrate, 18g fat, 3g fiber, 123mg cholesterol, 342mg sodium

◄ **Around-the-World Cuisine**

Prep Time: 30 minutes

Cook Time: 15 minutes

Average Rating: ★★★★★

What other cooks have done:

"The salsa is even better if you make it a day ahead and let the flavors meld. I also took the suggestion to use it on fish, and it's excellent. I think it would also be good on grilled pork chops as well. I'll try that next. I wasn't too open-minded about the mango thing, but I'm a believer now!"

Braised Balsamic Chicken

Submitted by: **Beth**

"Good with either rice or pasta. Green beans make a nice side dish."

6	skinless, boneless chicken	1	(14.5 ounce) can diced
	breast halves		tomatoes, undrained
	Ground black pepper	½	cup balsamic vinegar
	to taste	1	teaspoon dried basil
1	teaspoon garlic salt	1	teaspoon dried oregano
2	tablespoons olive oil	1	teaspoon dried rosemary
1	onion, thinly sliced	½	teaspoon dried thyme

1. Season chicken breasts with ground black pepper and garlic salt. Heat olive oil in a medium skillet and brown the onion and seasoned chicken breasts.

2. Pour tomatoes and balsamic vinegar over chicken and add basil, oregano, rosemary, and thyme. Simmer until chicken is no longer pink and the juices run clear, about 15 minutes. **Yield:** 6 servings.

Per serving: About 206 calories, 28g protein, 8g carbohydrate, 6g fat, 1g fiber, 68mg cholesterol, 574mg sodium

◄ **Quick & Easy**

Prep Time: 10 minutes

Cook Time: 20 minutes

Average Rating: ★★★★★

What other cooks have done:

"Living in Tokyo, I have to make do with limited ingredients. I had everything for this recipe already in the cupboard. I used fresh tomatoes and served it with pasta, though rice would have been better to absorb some of the sauce. I didn't have any of the separate spices so I used an Italian seasoning blend instead. It makes a great quick weeknight meal."

Baked Lemon Chicken with Mushroom Sauce

Submitted by: **Joyce Sokoloff**

"A great chicken recipe that I've made for years. Serve with rice and a fresh veggie. Impressive!"

1	tablespoon olive oil	2	tablespoons all-purpose flour
6	skinless, boneless chicken breast halves	½	cup chicken broth
1	lemon	1	tablespoon chopped fresh parsley
¼	cup butter		
3	cups sliced fresh mushrooms		

1. Preheat oven to 400°F (200°C).

2. Pour olive oil into an 8x8 inch glass baking dish. Place the chicken breasts in the dish, coating each side with oil. Squeeze the juice of ½ lemon over all. Thinly slice the rest of the lemon and place a lemon slice on top of each chicken piece. Bake in the preheated oven for 30 to 40 minutes or until brown.

3. In a large skillet, melt ¼ cup butter. Add the sliced mushrooms. Sauté until mushrooms are brown and have released their juices, about 6 minutes. Add flour to skillet and blend. Add the chicken broth, stirring to make a medium-thick sauce. Allow to reduce, adjusting with a little more broth to make a creamy sauce. Add fresh parsley at the last minute. Spoon sauce over baked chicken breasts.

Yield: 6 servings.

Per serving: About 369 calories, 45g protein, 18g carbohydrate, 8g fat, 2g fiber, 134mg cholesterol, 432mg sodium

Anniversary Chicken

Submitted by: **Vicki Frew**

"I made this chicken for 100 people at my in-laws' 50th wedding anniversary party. Boy, was it a hit!"

2	tablespoons vegetable oil	1	cup shredded Cheddar cheese
6	skinless, boneless chicken breast halves	3	green onions, chopped
½	cup teriyaki sauce	½	(3 ounce) can bacon bits
½	cup Ranch-style salad dressing		Garnish: chopped fresh parsley

1. Preheat oven to 350°F (175°C).
2. In a large skillet, heat oil over medium-high heat. Add chicken breasts and sauté 4 to 5 minutes on each side or until lightly browned.
3. Place browned chicken breasts in a 9x13 inch baking dish. Brush with teriyaki sauce and cover with salad dressing. Sprinkle with cheese, green onions, and bacon bits.
4. Bake in the preheated oven for 25 to 35 minutes or until chicken is no longer pink and juices run clear. Garnish, if desired. **Yield:** 6 servings.

Per serving: About 528 calories, 63g protein, 7g carbohydrate, 26g fat, 0g fiber, 167mg cholesterol, 898mg sodium

Aimee's Quick Chicken

Submitted by: **Aimee Woolwine**

"This recipe came about by accident when I had only a few minutes. My husband declared it, 'The best chicken ever!'"

4	skinless, boneless chicken breast halves	¼	cup teriyaki sauce
		¼	cup bacon bits
4	ounces prepared Dijon-style mustard	½	cup grated Parmesan cheese

1. Preheat oven to 400°F (200°C).
2. Place chicken in a 9x13 inch baking dish. Spread mustard evenly over chicken and pour teriyaki sauce evenly over all. Sprinkle with bacon bits and cover with cheese.
3. Bake in the preheated oven for 30 minutes. **Yield:** 4 servings.

Per serving: About 260 calories, 38g protein, 7g carbohydrate, 9g fat, 0g fiber, 83mg cholesterol, 1902mg sodium

Almond Crusted Chicken with Tomato-Citrus Sauce

Submitted by: **Justin Parrott**

"Chicken breasts coated in an almond seasoned flour and sautéed, then topped with a tomato/orange/herb sauce that could be citrus heaven! Elegant and unique enough for guests, tasty enough for down home cookin'!"

¼	cup olive oil	1	cup ground almonds
2	cloves garlic, chopped	¼	cup all-purpose flour
2	cups roma (plum) tomatoes, diced	⅛	teaspoon ground cumin
1	cup diced orange wedges	⅛	teaspoon curry powder
¼	cup chopped fresh rosemary	⅛	teaspoon ground turmeric
¼	cup chopped fresh thyme	6	skinless, boneless chicken breast halves
¼	teaspoon salt, divided	¼	cup olive oil
¼	teaspoon ground black pepper, divided	¼	cup clarified butter

1. Heat ¼ cup olive oil in a large saucepan over medium heat. Sauté garlic for 2 minutes, then add tomato, orange, rosemary, thyme, ⅛ teaspoon salt, and ⅛ teaspoon pepper. Cover and cook over medium heat for 15 minutes; uncover and let sauce reduce for 15 more minutes. Set aside and keep warm.

2. In a shallow dish or bowl, mix together the almonds, flour, cumin, curry powder, turmeric, ⅛ teaspoon salt, and ⅛ teaspoon pepper. Coat chicken breasts in flour mixture and fry in a large skillet with ¼ cup oil and clarified butter for about 5 to 7 minutes on each side or until golden brown and juices run clear.

3. When ready to serve, place chicken on a platter and top with warm sauce just before serving. **Yield:** 6 servings.

Per serving: About 578 calories, 35g protein, 17g carbohydrate, 43g fat, 5g fiber, 90mg cholesterol, 180mg sodium

Cashew-Crusted Chicken

Submitted by: **Brennan**

"Guaranteed to satisfy anyone! These chicken breasts are dipped in an apricot-mustard sauce, then rolled in chopped cashew nuts for a wonderfully tangy, crunchy, and easy baked chicken dish."

1 (12 ounce) jar apricot preserves	1 cup coarsely chopped cashews
¼ cup prepared Dijon-style mustard	4 skinless, boneless chicken breast halves
1 teaspoon curry powder	

1. Preheat oven to 375°F (190°C). Lightly grease a 9x13 inch baking dish.
2. Combine preserves, mustard, and curry powder in a large skillet and cook over low heat, stirring constantly, until preserves are completely melted and smooth.
3. Place cashews in a shallow dish or bowl. Dip chicken breasts in sauce; roll in nuts to coat and place in prepared baking dish.
4. Bake in the preheated oven for 20 to 30 minutes. Boil any remaining sauce and serve with the baked chicken. **Yield:** 4 servings.

Per serving: About 610 calories, 33g protein, 66g carbohydrate, 26g fat, 3g fiber, 67mg cholesterol, 761mg sodium

◀ Family Favorite

Prep Time: 20 minutes

Cook Time: 30 minutes

Average Rating: ★★★★★

What other cooks have done:

"I cut the chicken into bite-sized pieces, which cut the baking time to 25 to 30 minutes. I also added dried Thai chile peppers to add 'zing' and to make it more Asian. It was easy and quite delicious!"

Chicken and Red Wine Sauce

Submitted by: **Robin**

"A simple red wine sauce with brown sugar, garlic, paprika, salt, and pepper makes this dish simply yummy! Braised chicken breasts, brazenly good taste."

1 tablespoon olive oil	1 cup packed brown sugar
1 tablespoon minced garlic	1 cup red wine
3 pounds skinless, boneless chicken breast halves	Salt and ground black pepper to taste
1 tablespoon paprika	

1. Heat oil in a large skillet over medium-high heat. Cook garlic in oil until tender. Place chicken in the skillet and cook for about 10 minutes on each side or until no longer pink and juices run clear.
2. Drain oil from skillet. Sprinkle chicken with paprika and brown sugar. Pour red wine around chicken. Cover and simmer for 15 to 20 minutes; lightly baste chicken with wine sauce while cooking. Season with salt and pepper to taste. **Yield:** 6 servings.

Per serving: About 421 calories, 44g protein, 37g carbohydrate, 7g fat, 0g fiber, 117mg cholesterol, 500mg sodium

◀ Party Food

Prep Time: 10 minutes

Cook Time: 45 minutes

Average Rating: ★★★★☆

What other cooks have done:

"I adjusted this recipe slightly. It must have worked because my husband, who belongs to 'picky-eaters anonymous,' asked for seconds! This recipe makes the best chicken I have ever tasted. The adjustments I made were to decrease the paprika and brown sugar by half, only use ¾ cup wine, and leave the lid off so it thickens better. Try it, you'll love it!"

Prep Time: 30 minutes

Cook Time: 40 minutes

Average Rating: ★★★★★

What other cooks have done:

"Very, very, very tasty. I substituted white wine for the water. I also found it easier to cube the chicken. I didn't have celery seeds or powdered mustard on hand but it still was very tasty. Next time, I may make more sauce."

Chicken Breasts Pierre

Submitted by: **Nancy**

"One of my husband's favorites. I've been making this for over 15 years, and he's not sick of it yet! Serve with pan sauces, crusty French bread, and a tossed green salad."

¼	cup all-purpose flour	2	tablespoons white vinegar
½	teaspoon salt	2	tablespoons Worcestershire
	Pinch ground black pepper		sauce
6	skinless, boneless chicken	1	teaspoon salt
	breast halves	2	teaspoons chili powder
3	tablespoons butter	1	teaspoon powdered mustard
1	(14.5 ounce) can stewed	½	teaspoon celery seeds
	tomatoes, undrained	1	clove garlic, minced
½	cup water	⅛	teaspoon hot pepper sauce
2	tablespoons brown sugar		

1. In a shallow dish or bowl, combine flour, ½ teaspoon salt, and ground black pepper. Coat chicken breasts with flour mixture. Melt butter in a large skillet over medium heat and brown chicken on all sides. Remove chicken from skillet and drain on paper towels.

2. In the same skillet, combine tomatoes, water, brown sugar, vinegar, and Worcestershire sauce. Season with 1 teaspoon salt, chili powder, powdered mustard, celery seeds, garlic, and hot sauce. Bring to a boil; reduce heat and return chicken to skillet. Cover and simmer for 35 to 40 minutes or until chicken is no longer pink and juices run clear.

Yield: 6 servings.

Per serving: About 247 calories, 29g protein, 15g carbohydrate, 8g fat, 1g fiber, 84mg cholesterol, 934mg sodium

Green Olive Chicken II (pictured on page 152)

Submitted by: **Michelle**
"The green olives in this dish really make the flavors soar!"

3	tablespoons butter	½	cup chopped green bell pepper
½	cup chopped onion	1	tablespoon chopped fresh parsley
1	(8 ounce) package sliced fresh mushrooms	1	teaspoon paprika
4	skinless, boneless chicken breast halves	½	teaspoon salt
1	(14.5 ounce) can diced tomatoes, drained	¼	teaspoon ground black pepper
1	cup water	1	cup uncooked long-grain white rice
½	cup sliced green olives		

1. Melt butter in a large skillet over medium-high heat. Add onion and mushrooms and sauté until lightly browned, about 5 minutes. Arrange chicken in skillet; stir in tomatoes, water, olives, bell pepper, parsley, paprika, salt, pepper, and rice. Cover and bring to a boil.
2. Reduce heat to medium-low and simmer for 45 minutes. (If chicken is cooked through but rice is unfinished, remove chicken and let rice finish cooking.) To serve, slice chicken and serve over rice.
Yield: 4 servings.

Per serving: About 443 calories, 33g protein, 47g carbohydrate, 14g fat, 4g fiber, 92mg cholesterol, 2711mg sodium

◄ **One-Dish Meal**

Prep Time: 10 minutes

Cook Time: 1 hour

Average Rating: ★★★★★

What other cooks have done:

"Great-tasting one-dish chicken recipe! I cut way back on the salt, used fresh tomatoes instead of canned, and added an additional half cup of water to help cook the rice. My husband and I both loved it."

Thai Coconut Chicken (pictured on page 3)

Submitted by: **Abart**
"This dish is super easy!"

2	cups uncooked jasmine rice	1	cup snow peas, sliced
1½	pounds skinless, boneless chicken breast halves, cubed	½	cup shredded carrots
		1	cup chopped green onions
1	tablespoon curry powder	1	(14 ounce) can coconut milk
2	cups chopped asparagus (cut into ½ inch pieces)		

1. Cook rice according to package directions. Set aside; keep warm.
2. In a medium bowl, combine chicken and curry powder; toss to coat.
3. Spray a large nonstick skillet with cooking spray. Sauté chicken over medium-high heat for 4 minutes. Add asparagus, snow peas, carrots, and green onions; cook for 3 minutes. Add coconut milk; heat through, approximately 3 minutes. Serve over the rice. **Yield:** 4 servings.

Per serving: About 765 calories, 50g protein, 88g carbohydrate, 24g fat, 7g fiber, 99mg cholesterol, 135mg sodium

◄ **Around-the-World Cuisine**

Prep Time: 15 minutes

Cook Time: 30 minutes

Average Rating: ★★★★☆

What other cooks have done:

"We made a couple of minor changes. We steamed the veggies to make them more tender and we julienned the snow peas, and it was great."

Prep Time: 20 minutes

Cook Time: 20 minutes

Average Rating: ★★★★☆

What other cooks have done:

"I followed the recipe exactly and it turned out perfect. I served it on a bed of angel hair pasta. In addition to tasting great, the combination of chicken, tomatoes, and spinach looks beautiful on a plate. I'm planning on serving this at my next dinner party."

Cousin Cosmo's Greek Chicken *(pictured on page 155)*

Submitted by: **Orisha**

"My son requests this every year for his birthday. It's a favorite."

2	tablespoons all–purpose flour, divided	6	skinless, boneless chicken breast halves
½	teaspoon salt	2	tablespoons olive oil
¼	teaspoon ground black pepper	1½	cups water
¼	pound feta cheese, crumbled	1	chicken bouillon cube, crumbled
1	tablespoon fresh lemon juice	2	cups loosely packed fresh baby spinach leaves
1	teaspoon dried oregano	1	ripe tomato, chopped
			Hot cooked couscous

1. On a large plate, combine 1 tablespoon flour, salt, and pepper. Set aside. In a small bowl, combine cheese, lemon juice, and oregano. Set aside.

2. With a meat mallet, pound each chicken breast to ½ inch thickness. Spread cheese mixture on each chicken breast, leaving ½ inch border. Fold chicken breasts in half; secure each with a toothpick. Coat chicken breasts with flour mixture.

3. In a large skillet, heat oil over medium heat. Cook chicken breasts for 4 to 5 minutes on each side or until golden. In a small bowl, whisk together 1½ cups water, chicken bouillon cube, and remaining flour; pour over chicken breasts in skillet and bring to a boil. Cover, reduce heat to low, and simmer for 7 minutes. Stir in spinach and tomato and simmer for 3 minutes or until spinach is wilted and chicken is no longer pink. Discard toothpicks before serving. Serve over couscous. **Yield:** 6 servings.

Per serving: About 240 calories, 31g protein, 5g carbohydrate, 10g fat, 1g fiber, 85mg cholesterol, 689mg sodium

Italian Chicken Marinade *(pictured on page 116)*

Submitted by: **Steve Harrity**
"Try this simple and delicious way of marinating chicken."

1	(16 ounce) bottle Italian-style salad dressing	1	teaspoon salt
1	teaspoon garlic powder	4	skinless, boneless chicken breast halves

1. Combine salad dressing, garlic powder, and salt. Add chicken and marinate for at least 4 hours or overnight in the refrigerator.
2. Preheat grill for medium heat.
3. Grill chicken 8 to 10 minutes per side or until chicken is no longer pink and juices run clear. **Yield:** 4 servings.

Per serving: About 649 calories, 28g protein, 12g carbohydrate, 55g fat, 0g fiber, 68mg cholesterol, 1529mg sodium

Spicy Garlic Lime Chicken

Submitted by: **C. Perez**
"A delightful chicken dish with a little spicy kick. Serve with rice and your favorite vegetable."

¾	teaspoon salt	⅛	teaspoon onion powder
¼	teaspoon ground black pepper	4	skinless, boneless chicken breast halves
¼	teaspoon cayenne pepper	2	tablespoons butter
¼	teaspoon garlic powder	1	tablespoon olive oil
¼	teaspoon dried thyme	2	teaspoons garlic powder
¼	teaspoon dried parsley	3	tablespoons lime juice
⅛	teaspoon paprika		

1. In a small bowl, mix together salt, black pepper, cayenne pepper, ¼ teaspoon garlic powder, thyme, parsley, paprika, and onion powder. Sprinkle spice mixture generously on both sides of chicken breasts.
2. Heat butter and olive oil in a large, heavy skillet over medium heat. Sauté chicken until golden brown, about 6 minutes on each side. Sprinkle with 2 teaspoons garlic powder and lime juice. Cook 5 minutes, stirring frequently to coat chicken evenly with sauce.
Yield: 4 servings.

Per serving: About 220 calories, 28g protein, 3g carbohydrate, 11g fat, 0g fiber, 8mg cholesterol, 572mg sodium

Easier Chicken Marsala

Submitted by: **D. Alexander**

"Here's a lighter version of one of my favorite chicken dishes. For my family, this one's a keeper!"

¼	cup all-purpose flour	1	tablespoon olive oil
½	teaspoon garlic salt	1	tablespoon butter
½	teaspoon dried oregano	1	cup sliced fresh mushrooms
¼	teaspoon ground black pepper	½	cup Marsala wine
4	skinless, boneless chicken breast halves		

1. In a medium bowl, stir together the flour, garlic salt, oregano, and pepper. Dredge chicken in the mixture to lightly coat.

2. Heat olive oil and butter in a large skillet over medium heat. Fry chicken in skillet for 2 minutes or until lightly browned on 1 side. Turn chicken over; add mushrooms. Cook about 2 minutes or until other side of chicken is lightly browned. Stir mushrooms so that they cook evenly.

3. Pour Marsala wine over the chicken. Cover skillet and reduce heat to low. Simmer for 10 minutes or until chicken is no longer pink and juices run clear. **Yield:** 4 servings.

Per serving: About 284 calories, 28g protein, 11g carbohydrate, 10g fat, 1g fiber, 80mg cholesterol, 322mg sodium

Simply Parmesan Chicken *(pictured on cover)*

Submitted by: **Jenny**

"This is a favorite around our house; it's quick, easy, and tastes great! The measurements can be varied depending on your taste. You really can't mess it up as long as you use this recipe as a foundation."

½	cup dried breadcrumbs	1	egg, lightly beaten
½	cup grated Parmesan cheese	4	skinless, boneless chicken breast halves
2	teaspoons Italian seasoning		

1. Preheat oven to 350°F (175°C). Line a jellyroll pan with aluminum foil and lightly spray with cooking spray.

2. In a medium bowl, mix together the breadcrumbs, grated Parmesan cheese, and Italian seasoning. Dip chicken breasts in egg, then in breadcrumb mixture to coat. Place coated chicken on prepared pan and bake in the preheated oven for 30 to 35 minutes or until juices run clear, turning chicken 5 minutes before removing from oven. **Yield:** 4 servings.

Per serving: About 235 calories, 34g protein, 9g carbohydrate, 6g fat, 1g fiber, 119mg cholesterol, 369mg sodium

---

Restaurant Fare ▶

Prep Time: 10 minutes

Cook Time: 14 minutes

Average Rating: ★★★★★

What other cooks have done:

"I cheated and used dry white wine, and I still loved the taste. I pounded the breasts a little before flouring to make more even pieces. It was quick and easy, but tasted like it took a lot of time to prepare."

Family Favorite ▶

Prep Time: 10 minutes

Cook Time: 35 minutes

Average Rating: ★★★★☆

What other cooks have done:

"I used Italian breadcrumbs and Italian seasoning. I was worried it might be overwhelming, but it was absolutely delicious. So easy to make and full of flavor! This will definitely become a regular dish."

Garlic Chicken and Grapes

Submitted by: **Christine Johnson**

"Grapes and sesame seeds are baked with the chicken in this unusual recipe. Served with a mustard sauce."

3 tablespoons prepared Dijon-style mustard	2 cloves garlic, minced
3 tablespoons soy sauce	2 tablespoons vegetable oil
2 tablespoons honey	3 pounds skinless, boneless chicken breast halves
2 tablespoons white wine vinegar	1 tablespoon sesame seeds
	2 cups seedless green grapes

1. Combine mustard, soy sauce, honey, and vinegar. Set sauce aside.
2. Preheat oven to 400°F (200°C).
3. In a 9x13 inch pan, combine garlic and oil. Place chicken in pan.
4. Bake, covered, in the preheated oven for 10 minutes. Uncover and turn chicken pieces over. Sprinkle with sesame seeds. Bake about 15 to 20 minutes or until no longer pink in center. Sprinkle grapes over chicken; bake 5 more minutes. Remove from oven and arrange chicken and grapes on a serving platter. Serve with sauce. **Yield:** 4 servings.

Per serving: About 561 calories, 81g protein, 26g carbohydrate, 14g fat, 1g fiber, 198mg cholesterol, 1211mg sodium

Feta Chicken

Submitted by: **Debbie**

"Chicken wrapped around tomato-basil feta cheese—simple, succulent, and sensational."

6 skinless, boneless chicken breast halves	¼ cup Italian-style dry breadcrumbs, divided
6 ounces tomato-basil feta cheese, crumbled	

1. Preheat oven to 350°F (175°C). Lightly grease a 9x13 inch baking dish.
2. Place chicken breasts between 2 pieces of wax paper. Gently pound chicken with flat side of a meat mallet or rolling pin to ¼ inch thickness; remove wax paper. Place feta cheese evenly in the center of each chicken breast and fold chicken breast in half.
3. Spread 2 tablespoons breadcrumbs in the prepared baking dish. Arrange chicken in dish and top with the remaining breadcrumbs.
4. Bake in the preheated oven for 25 to 30 minutes or until chicken is no longer pink and juices run clear. **Yield:** 6 servings.

Per serving: About 223 calories, 32g protein, 5g carbohydrate, 8g fat, 0g fiber, 94mg cholesterol, 526mg sodium

Famous Chicken Française

Submitted by: **Paula Tomlinson**

"Chicken with lemon juice, egg, butter, and garlic. C'est magnifique!"

1	egg, lightly beaten	2	tablespoons butter
½	lemon, juiced	1	(14.5 ounce) can chicken broth
1	cup all-purpose flour		
	Pinch garlic powder	1	lemon, juiced
	Pinch paprika		Garnishes: lemon slices, parsley sprigs
6	skinless, boneless chicken breast halves		

1. In a shallow dish or bowl, mix together the egg and juice of ½ lemon. In another shallow dish or bowl, mix together the flour, garlic powder, and paprika. Dip chicken breasts in egg mixture, then flour mixture. Heat butter in a large skillet over medium heat. Add chicken breasts and sauté until golden on each side.

2. In a medium bowl, mix together broth and juice of 1 lemon; pour mixture over chicken in skillet. Reduce heat to medium–low and simmer for about 8 minutes. Place on a serving platter and garnish, if desired. **Yield:** 6 servings.

Per serving: About 273 calories, 32g protein, 21g carbohydrate, 7g fat, 3g fiber, 114mg cholesterol, 425mg sodium

Pecan Dijon Chicken

Submitted by: **Brian Corbin**

"A delicious chicken dish with an unusual sauce that's sure to please. Serve over rice."

6	tablespoons prepared Dijon-style mustard	¼	teaspoon salt
¼	cup honey		Dash ground black pepper
¼	cup orange juice	¼	teaspoon powdered mustard (optional)
2	tablespoons milk	½	cup chopped pecans
2	tablespoons butter	6	skinless, boneless chicken breast halves
2	teaspoons lemon juice		

1. Preheat oven to 350°F (175°C).

2. In a medium saucepan over medium heat, blend Dijon-style mustard, honey, orange juice, milk, butter, and lemon juice. Season with salt, pepper, and powdered mustard, if desired. Stir in pecans.

3. Arrange chicken in a lightly greased 9x13 inch baking dish and bake in the preheated oven for 10 minutes. Cover with mustard mixture and continue baking for 20 minutes or until chicken is no longer pink and juices run clear. **Yield:** 6 servings.

Per serving: About 304 calories, 27g protein, 16g carbohydrate, 15g fat, 1g fiber, 78mg cholesterol, 598mg sodium

RamJam Chicken

Submitted by: **Laura Ramanjooloo**

"What a marinade! This is my absolute favorite for chicken. I could eat this every night! The longer you let it marinate, the more intense the flavor. I usually let it sit overnight in the refrigerator, but a few hours will do."

¼ cup soy sauce
3 tablespoons dry white wine
2 tablespoons lemon juice
2 tablespoons vegetable oil
¾ teaspoon dried Italian-style seasoning
1 teaspoon grated fresh ginger root
1 clove garlic, crushed
¼ teaspoon onion powder
  Pinch ground black pepper
8 skinless, boneless chicken breast halves, cut into strips

1. In a heavy-duty, zip-top plastic bag, combine soy sauce, wine, lemon juice, oil, Italian-style seasoning, ginger, garlic, onion powder, and ground black pepper. Place chicken in bag. Seal and marinate in the refrigerator for at least 3 hours or overnight.
2. Lightly oil cold grill rack and preheat grill for medium-high heat.
3. Thread chicken onto skewers and set aside. Pour marinade into a small saucepan and bring to a boil over high heat for 1 minute. Remove from heat and set aside.
4. Cook chicken on the preheated grill for approximately 5 minutes per side, basting with sauce several times. Chicken is done when no longer pink and juices run clear. **Yield:** 8 servings.

Per serving: About 302 calories, 50g protein, 1g carbohydrate, 9g fat, 0g fiber, 134mg cholesterol, 573mg sodium

◄ **Crowd-Pleaser**

Prep Time: 20 minutes

Marinate Time: 3 hours

Cook Time: 10 minutes

Average Rating: ★★★★

What other cooks have done:

"I made kabobs with chicken tenders, cherry tomatoes, mushrooms, and sliced corn cobs. I marinated it for about 4 hours and then basted it on the grill. I could see using this marinade for lots of things."

Chicken Scampi II

Submitted by: **Cyndee Horn**

"All the flavor and taste of shrimp scampi! Serve over rice or with spaghetti. Do not forget to serve with crusty rolls or bread to sop up the sauce! Enjoy!"

1. In a large skillet, heat the butter and oil over medium-high heat until the butter melts. Add parsley, basil, oregano, garlic, and salt; mix together in the skillet. Stir in lemon juice.

2. Add chicken to skillet; sauté for about 3 minutes or until no longer pink. Lower heat and cook for 10 to 15 more minutes or until the juices run clear. **Yield:** 4 servings.

Per serving: 458 calories, 28g protein, 1g carbohydrate, 38g fat, 0g fiber, 131mg cholesterol, 748mg sodium

A Jerky Chicken

Submitted by: **Rikk**

"A great Jamaican-style dish. A spicy blend of herbs, vinegar, and habanero pepper makes this chicken dish unforgettable. Serve with rice—yum!"

<table>
<tr><td>1</td><td>teaspoon finely chopped onion</td><td>1</td><td>teaspoon sesame oil</td></tr>
<tr><td>3</td><td>tablespoons brown sugar</td><td>3</td><td>cloves garlic, chopped</td></tr>
<tr><td>¼</td><td>cup soy sauce</td><td>½</td><td>teaspoon ground allspice</td></tr>
<tr><td>¼</td><td>cup red wine vinegar</td><td>1</td><td>habanero pepper, sliced</td></tr>
<tr><td>2</td><td>teaspoons chopped fresh thyme</td><td>4</td><td>skinless, boneless chicken breast halves, cut into 1 inch strips</td></tr>
</table>

1. Combine onion, brown sugar, soy sauce, vinegar, thyme, sesame oil, garlic, allspice, and habanero pepper in a food processor or blender. Process until smooth. Place chicken in a large heavy-duty, zip-top plastic bag and pour in three-fourths of the sauce. Squeeze out excess air and seal. Marinate in the refrigerator for at least 1 hour.

2. Preheat broiler.

3. Remove chicken from bag and discard marinade. Broil chicken for 10 to 15 minutes, turning once to ensure even cooking. Heat remaining sauce in a small pan and serve over chicken. **Yield:** 4 servings.

Per serving: About 197 calories, 28g protein, 14g carbohydrate, 3g fat, 0g fiber, 68mg cholesterol, 996mg sodium

---

Family Favorite ▶

Prep Time: 10 minutes

Cook Time: 18 minutes

Average Rating: ★★★★★

What other cooks have done:

"I added about a half cup of white wine to the sauce while the chicken was cooking and cut up a tomato for some color."

Hot & Spicy ▶

Prep Time: 1 hour

Marinate Time: 1 hour

Cook Time: 15 minutes

Average Rating: ★★★★★

What other cooks have done:

"Terrific! It was a little hot (I will use only a small pepper or half of a pepper next time) but very good. I let it marinate for 1 hour and served it with white rice. I will make this again!"

Wild Rice and Asparagus Chicken Breasts

Submitted by: **Geezer Gourmet**
"Stir-fried chicken breast with asparagus served over wild or long grain rice."

½	pound fresh asparagus	1	whole skinless, boneless
3	tablespoons hoisin sauce		chicken breast, cubed
1	tablespoon brown sugar	2	cups hot cooked wild rice
3	tablespoons peanut oil		

1. Cut asparagus into ¾ to 1 inch pieces, discarding tough bottoms of spears. In a small bowl, mix together hoisin sauce and brown sugar; set aside.
2. Heat wok over medium-high heat. When hot, drizzle 1 tablespoon oil around the rim. Stir-fry asparagus for approximately 2 minutes. Remove from the wok and keep warm.
3. Heat wok to high heat. Add 2 tablespoons of oil and chicken pieces. Stir-fry until chicken is no longer pink. Add sauce and reserved asparagus and stir-fry until pieces are coated with sauce. Serve over hot rice. **Yield:** 2 servings.

Per serving: About 639 calories, 37g protein, 57g carbohydrate, 30g fat, 6g fiber, 69mg cholesterol, 474mg sodium

◀ **Quick & Easy**

Prep Time: 20 minutes

Cook Time: 10 minutes

Average Rating: ★★★★★

What other cooks have done:
"Quick and easy. Clear instructions and it tasted great. I made it two times in one week already. Really nice. I used string beans and asparagus one time and string beans and carrots the next. Also, I substituted honey for the sugar—turned out great."

Chili-Lime Chicken Kabobs

Submitted by: **Simmi Gupta**
"I invented this recipe for a quick dinner. I marinated the chicken for only 1 hour, but I'm sure if you marinate longer, it would taste even better."

3	tablespoons olive oil		Pinch ground cayenne
1½	tablespoons red wine		pepper
	vinegar		Salt and ground black
1	lime, juiced		pepper to taste
1	teaspoon chili powder	1	pound skinless, boneless
½	teaspoon paprika		chicken breast halves,
½	teaspoon onion powder		cut into 1½ inch pieces
½	teaspoon garlic powder		

1. In a large bowl, combine the olive oil, vinegar, and lime juice. Add chili powder, paprika, onion powder, garlic powder, cayenne pepper, and salt and pepper to taste. Whisk until oil and vinegar are blended.
2. Add chicken to the bowl. Cover and marinate in refrigerator for 1 to 2 hours.
3. Preheat grill for medium-high heat.
4. Thread chicken onto skewers. Grill chicken for about 10 minutes or until the juices run clear. **Yield:** 4 servings.

Per serving: About 227 calories, 24g protein, 3g carbohydrate, 13g fat, 1g fiber, 65mg cholesterol, 64mg sodium

◀ **From the Grill**

Prep Time: 15 minutes

Marinate Time: 1 hour

Cook Time: 10 minutes

Average Rating: ★★★★★

What other cooks have done:
"I was surprised how good this tasted. I sautéed the chicken in a skillet because we don't have a grill, and served it over rice with a little Cheddar cheese sprinkled on top. Even my picky husband liked it!"

Haddock Bubbly Bake

Submitted by: **Susan**
"Great served with mashed potatoes and peas or veggie of your choice. It's a favorite of Nova Scotia, Canada."

2	pounds haddock fillets	1	(10.75 ounce) can cream of
	Salt and ground black		mushroom soup
	pepper to taste	1	cup shredded mild Cheddar
1	onion, thinly sliced		cheese

1. Preheat the oven to 350°F (175°C). Lightly butter a 2 quart casserole dish.
2. Arrange fish fillets in the prepared casserole dish and sprinkle with salt and pepper to taste. Layer onion slices over fish. Spread cream of mushroom soup over all and top with shredded cheese.
3. Bake in the preheated oven for about 40 minutes or until bubbly and fish flakes easily with a fork. **Yield:** 6 servings.

Per serving: About 266 calories, 34g protein, 6g carbohydrate, 11g fat, 1g fiber, 106mg cholesterol, 561mg sodium

Barbecue Halibut Steak

Submitted by: **Duane Glende**
"A simple recipe for barbecued halibut. Soy sauce and brown sugar add a special zip that's delicious."

2	tablespoons butter	2	teaspoons soy sauce
2	tablespoons brown sugar	½	teaspoon ground black
2	cloves garlic, minced		pepper
1	tablespoon lemon juice	1	(1 pound) halibut steak

1. Lightly oil grill rack and preheat grill for medium-high heat.
2. Combine butter, brown sugar, garlic, lemon juice, soy sauce, and pepper in a small saucepan. Cook over medium heat until the sugar dissolves.
3. Coat halibut with sauce and place on the grill. Grill for 5 minutes on each side, basting frequently or until fish flakes easily with a fork. **Yield:** 2 servings.

Per serving: About 412 calories, 48g protein, 16g carbohydrate, 17g fat, 0g fiber, 104mg cholesterol, 549mg sodium

Ginger-Glazed Mahi Mahi *(pictured on page 154)*

Submitted by: **Diana Fairbanks**

"This Ginger-Glazed Mahi Mahi is bursting with flavor and combines both sweet and sour taste sensations. It's a snap to make and so delicious. You'll love it!"

3	tablespoons honey	1	clove garlic, chopped
3	tablespoons soy sauce	2	teaspoons olive oil
3	tablespoons balsamic vinegar	4	(6 ounce) mahi mahi fillets
1	teaspoon grated fresh ginger root		Salt and ground black pepper to taste
		1	tablespoon vegetable oil

1. In a shallow glass dish, stir together the honey, soy sauce, balsamic vinegar, ginger, garlic, and olive oil. Season fish fillets with salt and pepper to taste and place them in the dish. If the fillets have skin on them, place them skin side down. Cover and refrigerate for 20 minutes to marinate.

2. Heat vegetable oil in a large skillet over medium–high heat. Remove fish from the dish and reserve marinade. Fry fish for 4 to 6 minutes on each side, turning only once, until fish flakes easily with a fork. Remove fillets to a serving platter and keep warm.

3. Pour reserved marinade into the skillet and heat over medium heat 1 minute or until the mixture reduces to a glaze consistency. Spoon glaze over fish and serve immediately. **Yield:** 4 servings.

Per serving: About 259 calories, 32g protein, 16g carbohydrate, 7g fat, 0g fiber, 124mg cholesterol, 839mg sodium

◄ Healthy

Prep Time: 5 minutes

Marinate Time: 20 minutes

Cook Time: 15 minutes

Average Rating: ★★★★★

What other cooks have done:

"Superb glaze—works well over chicken, pork, or steamed veggies. I'm still thinking about the flavor!"

Fresh Fish ▼

The freshness of fish is very important. Obtaining the freshest fish possible can make all the difference between a family who adores fish and one that detests the mere mention of it.

The Retailer

Choosing a good fishmonger can make your life a lot easier. While you will want to inspect every fish you buy, knowing that your retailer is reliable can take much of the guesswork out of the job. Look for clean, well drained ice; whole fish should be stored directly on the ice. There should be no staining or greying areas, indicating that the ice is not changed at frequent intervals. Nor should there be any pools of unidentifiable liquids. If the fish is prepackaged, look for clean, dry materials. Most important, there should not be a strong fishy smell. Fresh fish should smell like a sea breeze.

Spend a little extra time talking to the fishmonger. Ask if the fish has been previously frozen. Flash freezing techniques have improved to such an extent that texture is hardly affected, if at all, by freezing, but previously frozen and thawed fish shouldn't be refrozen. It must be used on the day of purchase.

Whole Fish

The skin of fresh fish should be bright and shiny with close fitting scales. Dry, dull flesh is a sign of age, as are loose scales. The eyes should be clear and bulging; if the fish has sunken or cloudy eyes look for a fresher specimen. Gills should be reddish and damp, not sticky. The flesh should be firm and elastic: When you press it, the flesh should bounce back, leaving no indentation.

Steaks and Fillets

There are many good reasons to buy steaks and fillets. The cleaning is done for you, it's possible to buy just the right amount for your needs, and mealtime preparation is shortened. However, the freshness of the fish is harder to discern. Again, the flesh should be firm. It should appear moist; a whitish film on the surface indicates dehydration. In addition, the coloring should be even.

- Sydney Carter

For more information, visit **Allrecipes.com**

Red Snapper Livornese (pictured on facing page)

Submitted by: **Ro**

"A tangy, easy recipe for almost any firm-fleshed fish fillets: red snapper, sea bass, grouper. Adaptable for sole, flounder, tilapia, and other thin fillets by adjusting cooking time. Serve with white rice or orzo and a salad or steamed broccoli."

2	tablespoons olive oil	¼	teaspoon crushed red pepper flakes
½	small onion, diced	½	tablespoon chopped fresh parsley
2	cloves garlic, minced	1	pound red snapper fillets
1	(14.5 ounce) can whole tomatoes, drained and chopped	1	tablespoon fresh lemon juice
2	tablespoons capers, chopped		
1	(2.25 ounce) can sliced black olives, drained		

1. Preheat oven to 400°F (200°C).

2. In a medium skillet, heat olive oil and sauté onion until tender, about 5 minutes. Add garlic and sauté for 1 minute. Stir in tomatoes, capers, black olives, red pepper flakes, and parsley. Bring to a boil, reduce heat, and simmer sauce for 10 minutes.

3. Spread ½ cup sauce in a lightly greased 7x11 inch baking dish and arrange snapper fillets in a single layer in the dish. Drizzle lemon juice over the fillets and then pour the remaining sauce over all.

4. Bake in the preheated oven for 15 minutes for ½ inch thick fillets or 30 minutes for 1 inch thick fillets or until fish flakes easily with a fork. Baste once with the sauce while baking. **Yield:** 4 servings.

Per serving: About 228 calories, 25g protein, 9g carbohydrate, 10g fat, 2g fiber, 42mg cholesterol, 561mg sodium

---

Restaurant Fare ▶

Prep Time: 20 minutes

Cook Time: 46 minutes

Average Rating: ★★★★★

What other cooks have done:

"This recipe had a good flavor. I would make this again with grouper or flounder, and I would add more tomato juice to make more sauce."

Red Snapper Livornese, facing page

Caribbean Jerk Pork Chops, page 126, and Caribbean Sweet Potato Salad, page 241

Teriyaki Steak, page 110, and Eastern Rice Salad, page 240

Brown Rice, Broccoli, Cheese, and Walnut Surprise, page 166

Green Olive Chicken II, page 137

Seared Scallops with Spicy
Papaya Sauce, page 162

Zucchini Patties, page 164

Ginger-Glazed Mahi Mahi,
page 147

Cousin Cosmo's Greek Chicken, page 138

Burgundy Pork Tenderloin,
page 125

Broiled Tilapia Parmesan

Submitted by: **Phoebe**

"Flavorful recipe for this farm raised fish that's easy and done in minutes! The fish is broiled with a creamy cheese coating for an impressive flavor and texture."

½	cup grated Parmesan cheese	¼	teaspoon dried basil
¼	cup butter, softened	¼	teaspoon ground black pepper
3	tablespoons mayonnaise	⅛	teaspoon onion powder
2	tablespoons fresh lemon juice	⅛	teaspoon celery salt
		2	pounds tilapia fillets

1. Preheat broiler. Grease a broiling pan or line with aluminum foil.

2. In a small bowl, mix together Parmesan cheese, butter, mayonnaise, and lemon juice. Add basil, pepper, onion powder, and celery salt. Mix well and set aside.

3. Arrange fillets in a single layer on the prepared pan. Broil a few inches from heat for 2 to 3 minutes. Turn fillets and broil for 2 more minutes. Remove from oven and pour Parmesan cheese mixture over fillets. Broil for 2 more minutes or until topping is browned and fish flakes easily with a fork. Be careful not to overcook. **Yield:** 8 servings.

Per serving: About 231 calories, 26g protein, 1g carbohydrate, 13g fat, 0g fiber, 66mg cholesterol, 300mg sodium

Baked Salmon Fillets Dijon

Submitted by: **Christine Johnson**

"Delicious baked salmon coated with Dijon-style mustard and seasoned breadcrumbs and topped with butter."

4	(4 ounce) salmon fillets	¼	cup Italian-style dry breadcrumbs
3	tablespoons prepared Dijon-style mustard	¼	cup butter, melted
	Salt and ground black pepper to taste		

1. Preheat oven to 400°F (200°C). Line a shallow baking pan with aluminum foil.

2. Place salmon, skin side down, on foil. Spread a thin layer of mustard over each fillet and season with salt and pepper to taste. Top with breadcrumbs and drizzle with melted butter.

3. Bake in the preheated oven for 15 minutes or until salmon flakes easily with a fork. **Yield:** 4 servings.

Per serving: About 333 calories, 26g protein, 7g carbohydrate, 22g fat, 1g fiber, 107mg cholesterol, 674mg sodium

Coconut Shrimp *(pictured on page 115)*

Submitted by: **Linda Vergura**

"These crispy shrimp are rolled in a coconut beer batter before frying. For dipping sauce, I use orange marmalade, mustard, and horseradish mixed to taste."

Prep Time: 10 minutes

Cook Time: 20 minutes

Average Rating: ★★★★★

What other cooks have done:

"I cannot believe how great these turned out. They're as good or better than the restaurant versions I've tried. I think the secret to success is chilling the shrimp and making sure the oil is hot."

1	egg	1½	pounds uncooked large
½	cup all-purpose flour		shrimp, peeled and
⅔	cup beer		deveined with tails
1½	teaspoons baking powder		attached
¼	cup all-purpose flour	3	cups vegetable oil for frying
2	cups flaked coconut		

1. In a medium bowl, combine egg, ½ cup flour, beer, and baking powder. Place ¼ cup flour and coconut in 2 separate bowls.
2. Hold shrimp by tail and dredge in flour, shaking off excess flour. Dip in batter; allow excess to drip off. Roll shrimp in coconut and place on a baking sheet lined with wax paper. Refrigerate for 30 minutes. Heat oil to 350°F (175°C) in a deep fryer.
3. Fry shrimp in batches. Cook for 2 to 3 minutes or until golden brown, turning once. Using tongs, remove shrimp to paper towels to drain. Serve warm with your favorite dipping sauce. **Yield:** 6 servings.

Per serving: About 321 calories, 8g protein, 25g carbohydrate, 20g fat, 2g fiber, 72mg cholesterol, 233mg sodium

Note: Serve Coconut Shrimp with a simple dipping sauce. Mix together ¾ cup orange marmalade, ¼ cup prepared Dijon-style mustard, 2 tablespoons prepared horseradish, and ¼ cup honey.

Buffalo Shrimp

Submitted by: **Janet Roetzel**

"This is the best . . . you can adjust the intensity of the buffalo sauce to your liking. We like it hot!!"

2 cups all-purpose flour
2 tablespoons Creole-style seasoning
1 tablespoon garlic powder
1 tablespoon cayenne pepper
1 teaspoon onion powder
1 teaspoon freshly ground black pepper
1 pound uncooked large shrimp, peeled and deveined with tails attached

4 cloves garlic, minced
2½ tablespoons butter
6 ounces hot pepper sauce
1 teaspoon ground cayenne pepper
4 cups vegetable oil for frying

1. In a large heavy-duty, zip-top plastic bag, combine the flour, Creole-style seasoning, garlic powder, 1 tablespoon cayenne pepper, onion powder, and ground black pepper. Seal bag and shake to combine the ingredients well.
2. Rinse shrimp under cold water and place in plastic bag. Seal bag and shake to coat shrimp well with the flour mixture.
3. Place shrimp on a baking sheet and refrigerate for 15 to 20 minutes. Save remaining flour mixture in the bag.
4. In a bowl, whisk together garlic, butter, hot pepper sauce, and 1 teaspoon cayenne pepper; set sauce aside. In a pot, heat oil to 375°F (190°C).
5. Remove shrimp from refrigerator and shake a second time in flour mixture.
6. Fry shrimp in hot oil for about 2 to 3 minutes or until shrimp turn pink. Immediately coat with buffalo sauce. **Yield:** 4 servings.

Per serving: About 605 calories, 27g protein, 54g carbohydrate, 32g fat, 4g fiber, 194mg cholesterol, 2098mg sodium

◀ **Party Food**

Prep Time: 15 minutes

Cook Time: 20 minutes

Average Rating: ★★★★★

What other cooks have done:

"An easy dinner to prepare. I served it with rice and garlic bread for a complete meal. For the coating, I left the shrimp in the bag for the 15 minutes, then shook them. My suggestion is to remove the tails, for simpler eating."

Louisiana Shrimp Creole II

Submitted by: **Katrina Berry**

"Tomatoes and shrimp cooked up with garlic and onions—this Gulf Coast tradition will have you dreaming of the bayou. This recipe can either be a main dish or a side dish. You can make it as hot as you want, just add more chili powder and hot sauce. Serve over hot cooked rice."

Prep Time: 20 minutes

Cook Time: 25 minutes

Average Rating: ★★★★★

What other cooks have done:

"I added cayenne pepper and extra hot sauce. I used fresh tomatoes and chopped them in my food processor. I also like adding kielbasa and precooked frozen shrimp at the end."

3	tablespoons butter
½	cup finely diced onion
½	cup chopped green bell pepper
½	cup chopped celery
2	cloves garlic, minced
2	tablespoons cornstarch
1	(14.5 ounce) can stewed tomatoes
1	(8 ounce) can tomato sauce
1	tablespoon Worcestershire sauce
1	teaspoon chili powder
	Dash hot pepper sauce
1	pound uncooked medium shrimp, peeled and deveined

1. In a 2 quart saucepan, melt butter over medium heat. Add onion, bell pepper, celery, and garlic; cook until tender.

2. Mix in cornstarch. Stir in stewed tomatoes, tomato sauce, Worcestershire sauce, chili powder, and pepper sauce. Bring to a boil, stirring frequently. Stir in shrimp and cook for 3 to 5 minutes or until shrimp turn pink. **Yield:** 5 servings.

Per serving: About 197 calories, 17g protein, 16g carbohydrate, 8g fat, 2g fiber, 157mg cholesterol, 735mg sodium

Cajun or Creole? ▼

The two major cultures that have grown out of Louisiana are Creole and Cajun. We often hear these two words used, but many people outside of Louisiana are not sure what the difference is. Originally, Creoles were descended from the wealthy French and Spanish colonists who settled in southern Louisiana. Often the term Creole also includes the African and Caribbean heritage that eventually became mingled with the French and Spanish—through sharing cooking techniques and ingredients, and also through marriage. Creole cuisine was born in upper-class households and still carries the reputation of being more refined and of using more expensive ingredients.

Cajuns, on the other hand, are the descendents of French colonists who settled in Acadia (modern-day Nova Scotia).

The Acadians were driven out of Canada in the 1750s and some of them fled to southern Louisiana. There, they managed to survive with the help of the native Choctaw Indians who taught them how to hunt and fish and forage. Eventually their name was shortened from "Acadians" to "Cajuns" and the culture developed a strong foothold in the bayous of Louisiana. The food of Cajuns is the food of hardy people accustomed to extreme hardship and making do with whatever they could grow or hunt. Traditional Cajun dishes are cooked in one pot—a throwback to when the settlers had no stoves and did their cooking over open fires.

- Jennifer Anderson

For more information, visit **Allrecipes.com**

Seafood Enchiladas

Submitted by: **Cathy**

"These crab and shrimp stuffed enchiladas taste like the ones served at a popular Mexican restaurant in my area. My husband just loves them. After sprinkling the cheese over the enchiladas before baking, you can also garnish with tomatoes, cilantro, olive slices, or whatever other garnish you enjoy."

1	onion, chopped	6	(10 inch) flour tortillas
1	tablespoon butter, melted	1	cup half-and-half
½	pound fresh crabmeat	½	cup sour cream
¼	pound cooked shrimp, peeled, deveined, and coarsely chopped	¼	cup butter, melted
		1½	teaspoons dried parsley
2	cups shredded Colby cheese	½	teaspoon garlic salt

1. Preheat oven to 350°F (175°C).

2. In a large skillet over medium heat, sauté onions in 1 tablespoon butter until transparent. Remove skillet from heat and stir in crabmeat and shrimp. Mix in 1 cup shredded cheese. Place a large spoonful of the mixture into each tortilla. Roll up and arrange in a 9x13 inch baking dish.

3. In a saucepan, combine half-and-half, sour cream, ¼ cup butter, parsley, and garlic salt. Stir until mixture is lukewarm and blended. Pour sauce over the enchiladas and sprinkle with remaining cheese.

4. Bake in the preheated oven for 30 minutes. **Yield:** 6 servings.

Per serving: About 616 calories, 27g protein, 46g carbohydrate, 36g fat, 3g fiber, 136mg cholesterol, 994mg sodium

◄ Restaurant Fare

Prep Time: 15 minutes

Cook Time: 40 minutes

Average Rating: ★★★★★

What other cooks have done:

"I added some garlic and cayenne pepper and a few other seasonings to give it more flavor. I also added some sour cream to the seafood mixture to moisten it a bit."

Seared Scallops with Spicy Papaya Sauce *(pictured on page 153)*

Submitted by: **Carla Waltersdorf**
"I made this for my husband's birthday, and it was a hit. We both oohed and ahed throughout dinner."

Out-of-the-Ordinary ▶

Prep Time: 20 minutes

Cook Time: 14 minutes

Average Rating: ★★★★☆

What other cooks have done:

"I wouldn't call it a sauce as much as a salsa. I think there's no need to flour the scallops. They're better with just a pinch of salt and seared over high heat for a few minutes."

1	small papaya, peeled, seeded, and chopped	1	teaspoon salt, divided
1	red bell pepper, chopped	2	tablespoons all-purpose flour
1	teaspoon minced jalapeño pepper	⅛	teaspoon ground black pepper
½	red onion, chopped	1	pound sea scallops
2	tablespoons fresh lime juice	1	tablespoon olive oil
1	tablespoon chopped fresh cilantro		

1. In a medium bowl, combine papaya, bell pepper, jalapeño, red onion, lime juice, cilantro, and ¼ teaspoon salt. Refrigerate sauce until ready to use.
2. In a large heavy-duty, zip-top plastic bag, combine flour, black pepper, and remaining ¾ teaspoon salt. Add scallops and shake to coat.
3. In a large skillet, heat oil over high heat. Add scallops; cook 2 minutes on each side or until golden. Serve papaya sauce over scallops.
Yield: 2 servings.

Per serving: About 349 calories, 40g protein, 27g carbohydrate, 9g fat, 3g fiber, 75mg cholesterol, 1534mg sodium

Baked Scallops

Submitted by: **John Bragg**
"Bay scallops are the little ones, and they tend to be sweeter than sea scallops."

Restaurant Fare ▶

Prep Time: 30 minutes

Cook Time: 20 minutes

Average Rating: ★★★★☆

What other cooks have done:

"Reminded me of an Italian dish I used to eat back in Rhode Island. I would suggest only sautéing the garlic with the butter rather than adding to the breadcrumbs (it clumps up). Thanks for the great recipe."

4	tablespoons butter, melted	1	teaspoon garlic powder
1½	pounds bay scallops, rinsed and drained	½	teaspoon paprika
½	cup seasoned dry breadcrumbs	½	teaspoon dried parsley
		3	cloves garlic, minced
1	teaspoon onion powder	¼	cup grated Parmesan cheese

1. Preheat oven to 400°F (200°C).
2. Pour melted butter into a 2 quart casserole dish. Place scallops evenly in dish.
3. Combine breadcrumbs, onion powder, garlic powder, paprika, parsley, minced garlic, and Parmesan cheese. Sprinkle over scallops.
4. Bake in the preheated oven 20 minutes or until scallops are opaque. **Yield:** 4 servings.

Per serving: About 370 calories, 32g protein, 16g carbohydrate, 19g fat, 1g fiber, 89mg cholesterol, 658mg sodium

Addictive Sweet Potato Burritos

Submitted by: **Karena**

"Once you've had one, you'll want another. The recipe is a little different from most burrito recipes, but I've had many, many requests for it. Serve these with sour cream, chopped green onions, and salsa. For vegetarian burritos, omit the cheese and sour cream. These can be made ahead, individually frozen, then heated. For an interesting variation, try deep-frying these tasty burritos."

1	tablespoon vegetable oil		Pinch cayenne pepper
1	onion, chopped	3	tablespoons soy sauce
4	cloves garlic, minced	12	(10 inch) flour tortillas, warmed
6	cups canned kidney beans, drained	4	cups cooked and mashed sweet potatoes
2	cups water	8	ounces shredded Cheddar cheese
3	tablespoons chili powder		
2	teaspoons ground cumin		
4	teaspoons prepared mustard		

1. Preheat oven to 350°F (175°C).

2. Heat oil in a medium skillet and sauté onion and garlic until soft. Stir in beans and mash. Gradually stir in water and heat until warm. Remove from heat and stir in chili powder, cumin, mustard, cayenne pepper, and soy sauce.

3. Divide bean mixture evenly among the warm flour tortillas. Spread sweet potatoes evenly over bean layer and top with cheese. Roll up tortillas, burrito-style, and place in a single layer on a lightly greased baking sheet.

4. Bake in the preheated oven for 12 minutes and serve. **Yield:** 12 servings.

Per serving: About 513 calories, 20g protein, 79g carbohydrate, 8g fat, 14g fiber, 20mg cholesterol, 1174mg sodium

◀ Out-of-the-Ordinary

Prep Time: 25 minutes

Cook Time: 12 minutes

Average Rating: ★★★★★

What other cooks have done:

"These burritos are awesome, but I use refried beans to avoid the hassle of mashing the kidney beans. Heat the refried beans in the microwave to streamline the recipe even more."

Zucchini Patties *(pictured on page 154)*

Submitted by: **Sherlie A. Magaret**

"Cheesy zucchini patties are an excellent way to use up that abundance of zucchini from the garden. Serve with a bit of tomato sauce or sour cream dabbed on top."

2 cups grated zucchini	½ cup shredded mozzarella cheese
2 eggs, lightly beaten	½ teaspoon salt
¼ cup chopped onion	2 tablespoons vegetable oil
½ cup all-purpose flour	Freshly grated Parmesan
½ cup grated Parmesan cheese	cheese (optional)

1. In a medium bowl, combine the zucchini, eggs, onion, flour, Parmesan cheese, mozzarella cheese, and salt. Stir well.
2. Heat a small amount of oil in a skillet over medium-high heat. Drop zucchini mixture by ⅓ cup and cook 2 to 3 minutes on each side or until golden. Sprinkle with Parmesan cheese, if desired. **Yield:** 6 patties (2 patties per serving).

Per serving: About 294 calories, 18g protein, 16g carbohydrate, 18g fat, 1g fiber, 132mg cholesterol, 397mg sodium

Spaghetti Squash

Submitted by: **James**

"The flesh of spaghetti squash comes out in long strands that resemble spaghetti. In this recipe, the 'noodles' are tossed with vegetables and feta cheese."

1 spaghetti squash, halved lengthwise and seeded	¾ cup crumbled feta cheese
2 tablespoons vegetable oil	3 tablespoons sliced black olives
1 onion, chopped	2 tablespoons chopped fresh basil
1 clove garlic, minced	
1½ cups chopped tomatoes	

1. Preheat oven to 350°F (175°C). Lightly grease a baking sheet.
2. Place spaghetti squash, cut sides down, on the prepared baking sheet and bake in the preheated oven 30 minutes or until a sharp knife can be inserted with only a little resistance. Remove squash from oven and set aside to cool enough to be handled easily.
3. Heat oil in a skillet over medium heat. Sauté onion in oil until tender. Add garlic and sauté for 2 to 3 minutes. Stir in tomatoes and cook only until tomatoes are warm.
4. Use a large spoon to scoop the stringy pulp from the squash and place in a medium bowl. Toss with the sautéed vegetables, feta cheese, olives, and basil. Serve warm. **Yield:** 6 servings.

Per serving: About 148 calories, 4g protein, 13g carbohydrate, 10g fat, 3g fiber, 17mg cholesterol, 270mg sodium

Aunt Mary's Eggplant Balls

Submitted by: **Lynette**

"These hearty, delicious eggplant morsels can be used as a replacement for meatballs, or they can be fried into patties and eaten like burgers."

3	tablespoons olive oil	½	cup grated Parmesan cheese
3	cloves garlic, minced	1	cup chopped fresh parsley
4	cups cubed eggplant, with peel	2	eggs, lightly beaten
1	tablespoon water	¾	cup dry breadcrumbs

1. Preheat oven to 350°F (175°C). Grease a baking sheet.

2. Heat olive oil in a medium skillet over medium heat. Sauté garlic just until lightly browned. Stir in eggplant and water. Reduce heat to low and cover skillet. Allow eggplant to steam until soft, about 20 minutes. Place eggplant in a large bowl and allow to cool slightly.

3. Mix cheese, parsley, eggs, and breadcrumbs into eggplant. Stir with a wooden spoon or mix with your hands until ingredients are thoroughly combined and mixture can be rolled into balls. Add more breadcrumbs as needed to make mixture workable. Refrigerate mixture for 15 minutes and roll into balls or form into patties.

4. Place eggplant balls on prepared baking sheet. Bake in the preheated oven for 30 minutes. Serve immediately. **Yield:** 6 servings.

Per serving: About 199 calories, 8g protein, 15g carbohydrate, 12g fat, 2g fiber, 65mg cholesterol, 326mg sodium

◄ Make-Ahead

Prep Time: 30 minutes

Cook Time: 30 minutes

Average Rating: ★★★★☆

What other cooks have done:

"I'm not always a big eggplant fan, but I couldn't get enough of these. We served them with spaghetti. I prepared the mixture and froze them in balls before baking. I took them out when I needed them and baked them. They were very good."

Baked Spinach

Submitted by: **Joanna Wallbillich**

"This spinach casserole makes a good family meal."

1¼	pounds fresh spinach	¾	cup shredded Cheddar cheese
¼	cup all-purpose flour		
3	eggs, lightly beaten	½	cup dried breadcrumbs
¼	cup butter, melted	2	tablespoons chopped fresh parsley (optional)
1	cup milk		
½	teaspoon salt		
⅛	teaspoon ground black pepper		

1. Preheat oven to 350°F (175°C). Lightly grease a 2 quart baking dish.

2. Clean spinach thoroughly. Remove all excess water. Chop spinach. Place spinach in dish. Whisk together flour, eggs, butter, milk, salt, and pepper until smooth; pour over spinach.

3. Combine cheese and breadcrumbs. Mix in parsley, if desired. Sprinkle over spinach. Bake in the preheated oven for 50 minutes to 1 hour. **Yield:** 8 servings.

Per serving: About 194 calories, 9g protein, 12g carbohydrate, 12g fat, 2g fiber, 109mg cholesterol, 423mg sodium

◄ Restaurant Fare

Prep Time: 15 minutes

Cook Time: 1 hour

Average Rating: ★★★★☆

What other cooks have done:

"I loved it! My boyfriend enjoyed it so much, he asked again and again for more. I thought it was interesting that the pie turned out like spanakopita, the Greek spinach pie (except that it uses feta cheese). We will definitely serve this again in the future."

Prep Time: 15 minutes

Cook Time: 25 minutes

Average Rating: ★★★★☆

What other cooks have done:

"I'll try any recipe with brown rice. I really liked this one. I steamed the broccoli first. Then I put all the ingredients in a casserole dish and baked it at 350°F (175°C) for 25 minutes, and it was all gooey and good. I recommend using reduced-fat cheese to keep it yummy and gooey but not greasy."

Brown Rice, Broccoli, Cheese, and Walnut Surprise *(pictured on page 151)*

Submitted by: **Candice**

"This recipe was born one night when I didn't have too much to do. I guess the only surprise about it is that it tastes so good!"

½ cup chopped walnuts	1 pound fresh broccoli florets
1 tablespoon butter	½ teaspoon salt
1 onion, chopped	⅛ teaspoon ground black pepper
½ teaspoon minced garlic	
1 cup uncooked instant brown rice	1 cup shredded Cheddar cheese
1 cup vegetable broth	

1. Preheat oven to 350°F (175°C). Place walnuts on a small baking sheet and bake for 6 to 8 minutes or until toasted. Remove from oven and set aside.

2. Melt butter in a medium saucepan over medium heat. Cook onion and garlic in melted butter for 3 minutes, stirring frequently. Stir in rice and add broth; bring to a boil. Reduce heat to medium-low. Cover and simmer until liquid is absorbed, about 7 to 8 minutes.

3. Place broccoli in a microwave-safe casserole dish and sprinkle with salt and pepper. Cover and microwave 3 to 4 minutes or until tender but still firm.

4. Spoon rice onto a serving platter and top with broccoli. Sprinkle walnuts and cheese on top. **Yield:** 4 servings.

Per serving: About 360 calories, 16g protein, 28g carbohydrate, 23g fat, 6g fiber, 37mg cholesterol, 780mg sodium

Coconut Curry Tofu

Submitted by: **Kathy Collins**

"My vegetarian daughter-in-law gave me this recipe for a creamy coconut milk, spicy curry, and ginger tofu dish! I serve it over rice."

2 bunches green onions
1 (14 ounce) can light coconut milk
¼ cup soy sauce, divided
½ teaspoon brown sugar
1½ teaspoons curry powder
1 teaspoon minced fresh ginger root
2 teaspoons chile paste
1 pound firm tofu, cut into ¾ inch cubes

4 roma (plum) tomatoes, chopped
1 yellow bell pepper, thinly sliced
4 ounces fresh mushrooms, chopped
¼ cup chopped fresh basil
4 cups chopped bok choy
Salt to taste

1. Finely chop white parts of green onions. Slice green parts into 2 inch pieces.

2. In a large, heavy skillet over medium heat, mix coconut milk, 3 tablespoons soy sauce, brown sugar, curry powder, ginger, and chile paste. Bring to a boil.

3. Stir tofu, tomatoes, bell pepper, mushrooms, and finely chopped green onions into the skillet. Cover and cook 5 minutes, stirring occasionally. Mix in basil and bok choy. Season with salt and remaining soy sauce. Cook 5 more minutes or until vegetables are tender–crisp. Top with remaining green onions. **Yield:** 6 servings.

Per serving: About 234 calories, 16g protein, 18g carbohydrate, 13g fat, 5g fiber, 0mg cholesterol, 687mg sodium

◄ **Around-the-World Cuisine**

Prep Time: 25 minutes
Cook Time: 15 minutes
Average Rating: ★★★★★
What other cooks have done:
"Frying or searing the tofu beforehand helps it keep its shape. Avoid overcooking the veggies—they provide a great crunchy texture."

What to Do with Tofu ▼

Soy is brimming with health benefits, but do you still skitter nervously away from the tofu shelf? Once you've had a basic tofu initiation, you'll be ready to sup on soy with the best of them!

Talented Tofu
While you can eat tofu just as it is, right out of the package, it's not awfully tasty that way. It's pretty bland stuff, but that's one of its attributes! One major talent of tofu is its ability to take on the flavor of whatever marinade it's soaked in or whatever sauce it's simmered in. This means that tofu is about the most versatile protein source you could possibly imagine.

Choices, Choices
The kind of tofu you should buy depends on what you want to use it for. Firm and extra-firm tofu is chewier and more substantial. It absorbs marinades well because it's not as saturated with moisture to begin with. Tofu will stay together and

absorb marinades even better if you drain it before using it. To do this, place a few layers of paper towels on a plate, set the block of tofu on top of it, then set another plate on top of the tofu, weighting down the plate with a can or a heavy bowl. (The weight should be heavy enough that the sides of the tofu bulge, but don't split.) Drain for 15 to 30 minutes. Once drained, you can slice, dice, marinate, and cook the tofu just as you would meat. Firm tofu varieties are best for deep-frying, stir-frying, and grilling because they're more sturdy. You can also freeze firm tofu to make the texture chewy and hearty—similar to that of ground beef.

Silken tofu has a texture similar to that of custard. While firm tofu is usually found in a refrigerated case, silken tofu often comes in aseptic packaging (like a juice box) and doesn't need refrigeration. It's best for eating raw or putting in soup at the last minute, or for pureeing to use as a dairy alternative in smoothies, dips, spreads, and desserts.

For more information, visit **Allrecipes.com**

Seven-Layer Tortilla Pie

Submitted by: **Karen C. Greenlee**

"Looks like a pie, cuts like a pie, and tastes like a little bit of Southwestern heaven. This casserole is made from pinto and black beans layered with tortillas and cheese. Picante sauce gives it just the right kick. You can replace the Cheddar cheese with Monterey Jack, if you like."

Prep Time: 15 minutes

Cook Time: 40 minutes

Average Rating: ★★★★★

What other cooks have done:

"I have a two-year-old and another child on the way, so I developed a speed method for this great recipe! I substituted refried beans for the mashed pintos and swapped a can of Mexican-style tomatoes with green chiles (plus a tablespoon of taco seasoning for an extra kick) for the chopped tomatoes. I also added a can of drained corn to the black bean mixture and I had more than enough for a five-layer pie! My family loved it!"

2	(15 ounce) cans pinto beans, rinsed and drained	½	cup chopped tomatoes
1	cup salsa	7	(8 inch) flour tortillas
2	cloves garlic, minced	2	cups shredded reduced-fat Cheddar cheese, divided
2	tablespoons chopped fresh cilantro	1	cup salsa
1	(15 ounce) can black beans, rinsed and drained	½	cup sour cream

1. Preheat oven to 400°F (200°C).

2. In a large bowl, mash pinto beans. Stir in ¾ cup salsa and garlic.

3. In a separate bowl, mix together ¼ cup salsa, cilantro, black beans, and tomatoes.

4. Place 1 tortilla in a 9 inch pie plate or tart dish. Spread ¾ cup pinto bean mixture over tortilla to within ½ inch of edge. Top with ¼ cup cheese and cover with another tortilla. Spread with ⅔ cup black bean mixture and top with ¼ cup cheese. Repeat layering twice. Cover with remaining tortilla and spread with remaining pinto bean mixture and cheese.

5. Cover pie with foil and bake in the preheated oven for about 40 minutes. Cut into wedges and serve with 1 cup salsa and sour cream.

Yield: 6 servings.

Per serving: About 501 calories, 27g protein, 70g carbohydrate, 13g fat, 14g fiber, 16mg cholesterol, 1518mg sodium

Pizza, Pasta & More

Exquisite Pizza Sauce

Submitted by: **Angie Zayac**

"Sauce is wonderfully flavorful and is worth adding in the numerous ingredients."

1	(6 ounce) can tomato paste	¼	teaspoon dried oregano
¾	cup warm water	¼	teaspoon dried marjoram
3	tablespoons grated Parmesan cheese	¼	teaspoon dried basil
1	teaspoon minced garlic	¼	teaspoon ground black pepper
2	tablespoons honey	⅛	teaspoon cayenne pepper
1	teaspoon anchovy paste (optional)	⅛	teaspoon crushed red pepper flakes
¾	teaspoon onion powder		Salt to taste

1. In a small bowl, combine all ingredients, breaking up any clumps of cheese.

2. Sauce should stand for 30 minutes to blend flavors; spread over pizza dough and prepare pizza as desired. **Yield:** 4 servings.

Per serving: About 90 calories, 4g protein, 18g carbohydrate, 1g fat, 2g fiber, 4mg cholesterol, 564mg sodium

Whole Wheat and Honey Pizza Dough

Submitted by: **Brookes**

"You can top this quick homemade pizza dough any way that you like. This makes a thin crust, but it can be doubled for a thick crust."

1	(.25 ounce) package active dry yeast	2	cups whole wheat flour
1	cup warm water (110°F/45°C)	¼	cup wheat germ
		1	teaspoon salt
		1	tablespoon honey

1. Preheat oven to 350°F (175°C).

2. In a small bowl, dissolve yeast in warm water. Let stand until creamy, about 10 minutes.

3. In a large bowl, combine flour, wheat germ, and salt. Make a well in the middle and add honey and yeast mixture. Stir well to combine. Cover and set in a warm place to rise for a few minutes.

4. Roll dough on a floured pizza pan and poke a few holes in it with a fork.

5. Bake in the preheated oven for 5 to 10 minutes or to desired crispness. **Yield:** 12 servings.

Per serving: About 83 calories, 4g protein, 17g carbohydrate, 1g fat, 3g fiber, 0mg cholesterol, 196mg sodium

Summer Squash Pizza Crust

Submitted by: **Dawn Davis**

"Enjoy this frittata-type crust made with summer squash. Smother it with your favorite pizza toppings: tomato sauce or pesto and vegetables galore! Enjoy and be creative! Try sprinkling feta cheese or adding artichoke hearts for a Mediterranean flair."

1	teaspoon salt	½	cup shredded mozzarella cheese
4	cups finely shredded yellow summer squash or zucchini	2	eggs, lightly beaten
¾	cup all-purpose flour	½	teaspoon ground black pepper
¾	cup grated Parmesan cheese		Olive oil

1. Preheat oven to 350°F (175°C).

2. Sprinkle salt over shredded squash or zucchini; transfer to a strainer. Let stand 15 to 30 minutes and press all remaining liquid out of squash.

3. In a medium bowl, combine squash, flour, Parmesan cheese, mozzarella cheese, eggs, and pepper. Mix well.

4. Spread the mixture into a greased and floured jellyroll pan. Bake in the preheated oven for 25 minutes.

5. Remove the pan from the oven and increase the oven temperature to Broil. Brush the top of the crust with oil and broil the crust for 3 to 5 minutes or until the top is lightly browned.

6. Allow the crust to cool slightly and slide spatula underneath all edges and under the middle. Place a large baking sheet over the top of the crust and gently flip the crust over so that the bottom of the crust is now facing upwards. (Cut the crust in half to facilitate flipping, if needed.)

7. Brush the top of the crust with oil and broil for another 3 to 5 minutes or until the top is browned. Cover with toppings as desired.

Yield: 4 servings.

Per serving: About 264 calories, 17g protein, 23g carbohydrate, 12g fat, 2g fiber, 132mg cholesterol, 437mg sodium

◀ **Out-of-the-Ordinary**

Prep Time: 30 minutes

Cook Time: 35 minutes

Average Rating: ★★★★★

What other cooks have done:

"I sprinkled a little feta cheese on top and couldn't stop eating it! We ate it as a side dish or appetizer rather than as a main-dish pizza."

Brie, Cranberry, and Chicken Pizza

Submitted by: **Gill**
"A simple pizza using an exotic mixture of chicken, cranberry, and Brie."

2	skinless, boneless chicken breast halves	6	ounces Brie cheese, chopped
1	tablespoon vegetable oil	8	ounces shredded mozzarella cheese
1½	cups cranberry sauce		
1	(12 inch) prepared pizza crust		

1. Preheat oven to 350°F (175°C).
2. Chop chicken breasts into bite-size pieces. Heat oil in a medium skillet until hot. Add chicken and sauté until browned and almost cooked through.
3. Spread cranberry sauce over the pizza crust. Top with chicken, Brie, and mozzarella.
4. Bake in the preheated oven for 20 minutes. **Yield:** 2 servings.

Per serving: About 1707 calories, 95g protein, 184g carbohydrate, 69g fat, 6g fiber, 262mg cholesterol, 2255mg sodium

Holiday Fare ▶

Prep Time: 20 minutes
Cook Time: 20 minutes
Average Rating: ★★★★☆
What other cooks have done:

"I prebake the pizza crust for 10 minutes or so before adding the cranberries and other toppings to prevent having a soggy crust. I suggest trying it with whole berry cranberry sauce to vary the texture a little."

Buffalo-Style Chicken Pizza

Submitted by: **Brown**
"Pizza with a little kick of buffalo wing flavor! Have your pizza and wings together!"

3	skinless, boneless chicken breast halves, cooked and cubed	1	(16 inch) prepared pizza crust
2	tablespoons butter, melted	1	(8 ounce) package shredded mozzarella cheese
1	(2 ounce) bottle hot sauce		
1	(16 ounce) bottle blue cheese salad dressing		

1. Preheat oven to 425°F (220°C).
2. In a medium bowl, combine the cubed chicken, melted butter, and hot sauce. Mix well. Spread salad dressing over crust and top with chicken mixture; sprinkle with shredded cheese.
3. Bake in the preheated oven for 5 to 10 minutes or until crust is golden brown and cheese is bubbly. Let stand a few minutes before slicing. **Yield:** 6 servings.

Per serving: About 997 calories, 38g protein, 69g carbohydrate, 62g fat, 2g fiber, 93mg cholesterol, 2143mg sodium

Party Food ▶

Prep Time: 30 minutes
Cook Time: 10 minutes
Average Rating: ★★★★★
What other cooks have done:

"I found that spreading just enough blue cheese dressing to cover the crust was better than using the whole bottle. Also, instead of using regular hot sauce, I used a bottled buffalo wing sauce. It gave the chicken a nice kick and a more authentic buffalo wing taste. This recipe will be used in my home often."

Teriyaki Chicken Pizza

Submitted by: **Renee**

"A family favorite. This slightly sweet chicken pizza has been a requested meal with my family since coming up with the recipe some years ago. The different flavors work so well together."

1   (15 ounce) can pineapple chunks, drained with juice reserved
2   skinless, boneless chicken breast halves, cut into bite-size pieces
1   teaspoon minced garlic
2   (10 ounce) cans refrigerated pizza crust dough
1   cup teriyaki sauce
1   small sweet onion, thinly sliced
1   cup shredded Cheddar cheese
1   cup crumbled feta cheese

1. Combine reserved pineapple juice, chicken, and garlic in a small baking dish. Cover and refrigerate for 1 hour.
2. Preheat oven to 400°F (200°C).
3. Remove chicken from pineapple juice mixture. Sauté chicken and garlic in a skillet over medium-high heat 8 minutes or until chicken browns slightly.
4. Roll out pizza dough on a 16 inch pizza pan. Bake dough in the preheated oven for 7 minutes and remove from oven. Brush dough with a thin layer of teriyaki sauce; top with a layer of onion and Cheddar cheese. Then top with chicken, reserved pineapple chunks, and feta cheese. Bake for 15 more minutes or until cheese is bubbly and slightly browned. **Yield:** 8 servings.

Per serving: About 423 calories, 23g protein, 50g carbohydrate, 14g fat, 2g fiber, 60mg cholesterol, 2306mg sodium

◀ **Crowd-Pleaser**

Prep Time: 30 minutes

Chill Time: 1 hour

Cook Time: 30 minutes

Average Rating: ★★★★★

What other cooks have done:

"I used a little more chicken than called for and I cooked it in teriyaki sauce and shredded it. The crust didn't need to be cooked as long as suggested, but by pre-cooking the chicken, I was able to bake the crust to perfection, without worrying about the chicken being undercooked."

Cheesy Cheeseburger Pizzas

Submitted by: **Nicole**

"If you don't want to spend hours in the kitchen, try this recipe—you won't be disappointed! Very kid-friendly and delicious. I serve it with a fresh green salad."

½	pound lean ground beef	1	(10 ounce) can refrigerated biscuit dough
½	cup diced pepperoni		
1¼	cups pizza sauce	1	egg yolk
1	cup crumbled feta cheese	¼	teaspoon water
½	teaspoon Worcestershire sauce	1	cup shredded mozzarella cheese
½	teaspoon hot pepper sauce		
	Salt and ground black pepper to taste		

1. Preheat oven to 375°F (190°C). Place ground beef in a large, deep skillet. Cook over medium–high heat until evenly browned. Reduce heat to medium. Drain excess fat. Stir in pepperoni, pizza sauce, and feta cheese. Season with Worcestershire sauce, hot pepper sauce, salt, and pepper. Continue cooking for 1 minute, stirring constantly.

2. Lightly coat a baking sheet with cooking spray. Separate biscuits and place on prepared baking sheet at least 3 inches apart. With bottom of a glass, press each biscuit to form a 4 inch round biscuit with ½ inch rim around the outside edge. Beat together egg yolk and ¼ teaspoon water. Brush sides and edges of biscuits with egg mixture.

3. Spoon about ¼ cup beef mixture into each biscuit cup. Sprinkle with mozzarella cheese.

4. Bake in the preheated oven for 15 to 20 minutes or until biscuits are golden brown and cheese is bubbly. Allow to cool for 2 minutes before serving. **Yield:** 8 servings.

Per serving: About 349 calories, 17g protein, 21g carbohydrate, 22g fat, 1g fiber, 80mg cholesterol, 1178mg sodium

Pesto Pizza

Submitted by: **SKWms**

"A great alternative to your regular pizza."

½	cup pesto	1	(2 ounce) can chopped black olives, drained
1	(12 inch) prebaked pizza crust	½	small red onion, chopped
1	tomato, chopped	1	(4 ounce) can artichoke hearts, drained and sliced
½	cup green bell pepper, chopped	1	cup crumbled feta cheese

1. Preheat oven to 450°F (230°C).
2. Spread pesto on pizza crust. Top with tomato, bell pepper, olives, red onion, artichoke hearts, and feta cheese.
3. Bake in the preheated oven for 8 to 10 minutes or until cheese is melted and browned. **Yield:** 6 servings.

Per serving: About 394 calories, 17g protein, 39g carbohydrate, 20g fat, 3g fiber, 36mg cholesterol, 937mg sodium

◀ **Quick & Easy**

Prep Time: 10 minutes
Cook Time: 10 minutes
Average Rating: ★★★★★
What other cooks have done:

"Quick, easy, and a nice twist on 'same-ol' boring pizza.' Pesto gives a wonderful gourmet flavor."

Pita Pizza *(pictured on page 191)*

Submitted by: **Mindy Pretner**

"Pita Pizza is a quick, healthy snack or meal that can be customized to your likings!"

1	teaspoon olive oil	½	cup shredded mozzarella cheese
1	pita		
3	tablespoons pizza sauce	⅛	teaspoon garlic salt
¼	cup sliced cremini mushrooms		

1. Lightly oil grill rack; preheat grill for medium-high heat.
2. Spread olive oil on pita. Add sauce, mushrooms, and cheese. Sprinkle on garlic salt.
3. Place pizza on grill and cook until cheese completely melts, about 5 minutes. **Yield:** 1 serving.

Per serving: About 395 calories, 18g protein, 40g carbohydrate, 18g fat, 3g fiber, 44mg cholesterol, 1014mg sodium

◀ **From the Grill**

Prep Time: 5 minutes
Cook Time: 5 minutes
Average Rating: ★★★★★
What other cooks have done:

"Cool! This is a great, easy dinner that can be cooked without heating up your kitchen. I set out some additional toppings—chopped peppers, onions, pepperoni, and others—and let the kids fix their own. Everybody was happy and all I had to do was toss the pizzas on the grill (and keep an eye on the pitas to avoid overcooking). Nobody can complain when they fix it themselves!"

Pizza on the Grill

Submitted by: **Doug**

"Even with a baking stone, a conventional oven is no match for a professional oven when it comes to making pizza. At home, the grill is the way to go. The heat of a hot grill is perfect and makes it possible to make incredible pizza at home. Use your favorite toppings, but keep in mind not to overload the pizza. Keep it light. Try it—everything is better on the grill!"

Prep Time: 45 minutes

Rise Time: 30 minutes

Cook Time: 15 minutes

Average Rating: ★★★★★

What other cooks have done:

"The wonderful 'outdoors' taste that the grill imparts to the pizza truly elevates it to the next level! It cooks very quickly, though. I pulled mine off the grill and onto a baking sheet while adding the toppings. Make sure you knock your coals down so it cooks evenly on a lower heat."

1	(.25 ounce) package active dry yeast	1	teaspoon minced garlic
1	cup warm water (110°F/45°C)	¼	cup tomato sauce, divided
¼	teaspoon white sugar	1	cup chopped tomatoes, divided
2	teaspoons kosher salt	¼	cup sliced black olives, divided
1	tablespoon olive oil		
2	cloves garlic, minced	¼	cup roasted red peppers, divided
1	tablespoon chopped fresh basil	2	cups shredded mozzarella cheese, divided
3⅓	cups all-purpose flour	¼	cup chopped fresh basil, divided
½	cup olive oil		

1. In a large bowl, dissolve yeast in warm water and add sugar. Let stand for 10 minutes or until frothy. Add salt, 1 tablespoon olive oil, 2 cloves garlic, 1 tablespoon basil, and flour; mix until dough pulls away from the sides of the bowl. Turn onto a lightly floured surface. Knead until smooth, about 6 to 8 minutes. Place dough in a well oiled bowl and cover with a damp cloth. Set aside to rise until doubled, about 30 minutes.

2. Heat ½ cup olive oil with 1 teaspoon minced garlic for 30 seconds in the microwave. Set aside.

3. Brush grill rack with garlic flavored olive oil; preheat the grill for high heat.

4. Punch dough down and divide in half. On baking sheets, form into 2 (½-inch-thick) ovals.

5. Carefully place dough on hot grill. The dough will begin to puff almost immediately. When the bottom crust has lightly browned, turn the dough over using 2 spatulas. Working quickly, brush warm oil and 2 tablespoons tomato sauce over each crust. Arrange ½ cup chopped tomatoes, ⅛ cup sliced black olives, and ⅛ cup roasted red peppers over crust. Sprinkle with 1 cup cheese and 2 tablespoons basil. Close the lid and cook 3 to 5 minutes or until the cheese melts. Remove from grill and set aside to cool. Repeat procedure for second pizza using remaining warm oil, tomato sauce, chopped tomatoes, black olives, roasted peppers, cheese, and basil. **Yield:** 16 servings.

Per serving: About 210 calories, 6g protein, 22g carbohydrate, 11g fat, 1g fiber, 11mg cholesterol, 362mg sodium

Potato Pizza

Submitted by: **Paul Suto**

"Vegetables rest atop a crisp potato crust with a smattering of tomato sauce and cheese."

4	potatoes, shredded	6	ounces firm tofu, crumbled
1	medium onion, grated	2	tablespoons olive oil
2	eggs, beaten	½	cup tomato sauce
¼	cup all-purpose flour	2	tablespoons chopped fresh
1	zucchini, thinly sliced		basil
1	yellow squash, thinly sliced	2	tomatoes, sliced
1	green bell pepper, chopped	1	cup shredded fat-free
1	onion, thinly sliced		mozzarella cheese
2	cloves garlic, minced		

1. Preheat oven to 425°F (220°C).

2. In a large bowl, combine the potatoes, grated onion, eggs, and flour. Mix well and press into a lightly greased 12 inch pizza pan or a baking sheet.

3. Bake in the preheated oven for 15 minutes. Spray top of crust with cooking spray and bake for 10 more minutes. Set oven to Broil and broil for 3 minutes or until golden and crisp. Remove crust from oven. Reduce oven temperature to 425°F (220°C).

4. In a large bowl, combine the zucchini, squash, green pepper, thinly sliced onion, garlic, and tofu. Toss to combine.

5. In a large nonstick skillet, sauté tofu mixture in hot oil until vegetables are tender-crisp.

6. Combine the tomato sauce and basil. Spread half of the sauce over the top to the potato crust. Top with the sautéed vegetables and sliced tomatoes. Pour the remaining sauce evenly over all. Top with the cheese.

7. Bake in the preheated oven for 7 minutes or until cheese melts.

Yield: 4 servings.

Per serving: About 398 calories, 25g protein, 48g carbohydrate, 14g fat, 9g fiber, 112mg cholesterol, 548mg sodium

◀ **Out-of-the-Ordinary**

Prep Time: 40 minutes

Cook Time: 35 minutes

Average Rating: ★★★★★

What other cooks have done:

"I recommend squeezing some of the liquid out of the potatoes to keep the crust from being mushy. Also, use the potatoes right away so they don't discolor."

Pear and Gorgonzola Cheese Pizza

(pictured on page 1)

Submitted by: **Brian Golden**

"A very interesting pizza. Sounds strange, but everyone will love the unique combination of fragrant pears and distinctive Gorgonzola."

1	(10 ounce) can refrigerated pizza crust dough	2	ounces chopped walnuts
4	ounces sliced provolone cheese	2½	ounces Gorgonzola cheese, crumbled
1	Bosc or Red Bartlett pear, thinly sliced	2	tablespoons chopped fresh chives

1. Preheat oven to 450°F (230°C).

2. Place pizza dough on a lightly greased medium baking sheet. Top with provolone cheese and pear slices. Sprinkle with walnuts and Gorgonzola cheese.

3. Bake in the preheated oven for 8 to 10 minutes or until cheese is melted and crust is lightly browned. Top with chives and slice to serve. **Yield:** 8 servings.

Per serving: About 286 calories, 12g protein, 31g carbohydrate, 13g fat, 2g fiber, 19mg cholesterol, 585mg sodium

Restaurant Fare ▶

Prep Time: 10 minutes

Cook Time: 10 minutes

Average Rating: ★★★★★

What other cooks have done:

"I served this at a party and it was a big hit. I also thought it was easy to put together. People who don't normally like Gorgonzola loved it combined with pears—and I even used a little more Gorgonzola than called for!"

Pizza for All Occasions ▼

With a yeasty crust, zesty tomato sauce, gooey cheese, and any meat and veggie combination you can possibly dream up, pizza is a simple but universally loved concoction that charms the pickiest of eaters and the most discriminating of palates the whole world over.

The Food Pyramid in One Delicious Package

Pizza is an explosion of flavors and textures. Part of its appeal is that it can be customized to suit any palate, any diet, and any season. You can make the crust thin and crispy or thick and chewy, and you can pile on the toppings according to your tastes. If you've banished pizza because you're worried about calories, then use a thin crust, go easy on the cheese, and load up on the produce and lean meats. It will still be delicious, and, here's the bonus: It has all the food groups and can be very healthy indeed! When you realize all the possibilities, you'll want to welcome pizza back to your regular menu with open arms.

Pizza Party!

When you want to have a fun and relaxing get-together, consider one of our favorite party ideas for people of all ages: a pizza-making extravaganza! Tell your guests you'll provide the crust if they'll provide their favorite pizza toppings! Make sure that somebody brings sauce and cheese (or you can supply these yourself), but after that, the sky's the limit!

In case your guests need a few suggestions, here are some pizza toppings we love:

Vegetables and Fruit: fresh or roasted red, green, orange, or yellow bell peppers; fresh or sun-dried tomatoes; white, portobello, or marinated mushrooms; black, green, or kalamata olives; raw or caramelized onions; corn; spinach; arugula; roasted garlic; fresh basil; very thinly sliced red potatoes; green onions; thinly sliced eggplant; fresh or roasted poblano, Anaheim, or jalapeño peppers; artichoke hearts; zucchini; pineapple; pears; or apples.

Meat: sausage, pepperoni, salami, prosciutto, ham, Canadian-style bacon, barbecued chicken or ground beef.

Cheeses: mozzarella, fresh mozzarella, Gorgonzola, blue cheese, Parmesan, Romano, ricotta, fontina, cotija, feta, Cheddar, Brie, provolone, or goat cheese.

Miscellaneous delights: tuna, anchovies, smoked salmon, pine nuts, walnuts, almonds, hazelnuts, raisins, capers, or an egg. (Crack a raw egg or two over the top; it will be cooked through by the time the pizza's done.)

Tomato Sauce Alternatives: pesto, cranberry sauce, herbed cream cheese, Alfredo sauce, barbecue sauce, or chopped herbs and extravirgin olive oil. *- Jennifer Anderson*

For more information, visit **Allrecipes.com**

Personal Portobello Pizza

Submitted by: **KJONES27**

"This recipe substitutes a portobello mushroom for a pizza crust. Try using pesto sauce instead of spaghetti sauce and experiment with your favorite toppings."

1	large portobello mushroom, stem removed	½	tablespoon sliced black olives
1	tablespoon spaghetti sauce	4	slices pepperoni
½	cup shredded mozzarella cheese	1	clove garlic, chopped

1. Preheat the oven to 375°F (190°C).

2. Place the mushroom on a baking sheet and bake in the preheated oven for 5 minutes. Remove from oven and spread spaghetti sauce in the cup of the cap. Top with cheese, olives, pepperoni, and garlic.

3. Bake for 20 more minutes or until cheese is melted and golden. **Yield:** 1 serving.

Per serving: About 372 calories, 32g protein, 12g carbohydrate, 22g fat, 2g fiber, 71mg cholesterol, 793mg sodium

Bubble Pizza

Submitted by: **Ginny**

"You can't miss with this. It's my granddaughter's most requested meal when she comes to visit. It's a meal in itself, but a salad would go nicely with it."

1	pound ground beef	1	(4.5 ounce) can sliced mushrooms
¼	pound sliced pepperoni	1½	cups shredded mozzarella cheese
1	(14 ounce) can pizza sauce		
2	(12 ounce) cans refrigerated buttermilk biscuits	1	cup shredded Cheddar cheese
½	onion, sliced and separated into rings		
1	(10 ounce) can sliced black olives		

1. Preheat oven to 400°F (200°C). Place ground beef in a large, deep skillet. Cook over medium-high heat until evenly browned. Stir in pepperoni and cook until browned. Drain excess fat. Stir in pizza sauce. Remove from heat and set aside.

2. Cut biscuits into quarters and place in a lightly greased 9x13 inch baking dish. Spread meat mixture evenly over the biscuits. Sprinkle with onion, olives, and mushrooms.

3. Bake, uncovered, in the preheated oven for 20 to 25 minutes. Sprinkle top with mozzarella and Cheddar cheeses. Bake 5 to 10 more minutes or until cheese is melted. Let stand 10 minutes before serving. **Yield:** 8 servings.

Per serving: About 694 calories, 28g protein, 46g carbohydrate, 45g fat, 4g fiber, 87mg cholesterol, 2080mg sodium

Bread Machine Calzone

Submitted by: **Kevin K**.

"For this tasty Italian specialty, the dough is prepared in the bread machine and then it's filled with Italian sausage, pizza sauce, and mozzarella cheese."

1. Place water, yeast, sugar, flour, salt, and powdered milk in the pan of the bread machine in the order suggested by the manufacturer. Select Dough setting and press Start. After cycle is completed, roll out dough on a lightly floured surface.

2. Meanwhile, brown sausage for about 8 to 10 minutes in a large skillet over medium heat. Drain excess fat and reserve.

3. Preheat oven to 350°F (175°C).

4. Shape dough into a 10x16 inch rectangle. Transfer to a lightly greased baking sheet and spoon pizza sauce lengthwise down the center of the dough, followed by the browned sausage and the cheese. Make diagonal cuts 1½ inches apart down each long side of the dough, cutting to within ½ inch of the filling. Criss-cross cut strips of dough over the filling and seal edges with water. Brush top of calzone with melted butter.

5. Bake in the preheated oven for 35 to 45 minutes or until golden brown. Remove from oven and cool for 5 minutes before serving.

Yield: 4 servings.

Per serving: About 741 calories, 37g protein, 87g carbohydrate, 26g fat, 4g fiber, 79mg cholesterol, 1488mg sodium

---

Classic Comfort Food ▶

Prep Time: 30 minutes

Cook Time: 55 minutes

Average Rating: ★★★★★

What other cooks have done:

"I use this recipe not just to make calzones, but for pizzas, too. The crust is fantastic!"

Broccoli and Four-Cheese Calzones

Submitted by: **Holly**

"Calzones are a fun variation for pizza lovers! Try substituting frozen chopped spinach for the broccoli. All-purpose flour will work if you do not have bread flour handy!"

1⅓	cups warm water (110°F/45°C)	¼	teaspoon garlic powder
2	tablespoons olive oil	2	tablespoons olive oil
½	teaspoon salt	½	cup shredded provolone cheese
½	teaspoon dried oregano	½	cup grated Parmesan cheese
4	cups bread flour	½	cup shredded mozzarella cheese
1	(.25 ounce) package active dry yeast	½	cup ricotta cheese
1	(10 ounce) package frozen chopped broccoli, thawed	1	tablespoon olive oil

1. Place the water, 2 tablespoons olive oil, salt, oregano, bread flour, and yeast in the bread machine pan in the order recommended by the manufacturer. Select Dough setting and press Start.

2. Meanwhile, squeeze out excess liquid from broccoli. In a large skillet, sauté the broccoli and garlic powder in 2 tablespoons olive oil. Stir in the provolone cheese, grated Parmesan cheese, mozzarella cheese, and ricotta cheese.

3. Once bread cycle has finished, remove dough from machine and roll into 6 (8 inch) circles. Spread filling on one half of each circle, leaving a border around it for closing. Close the calzones and crimp the edges closed with your fingers or a fork. Place on a lightly greased baking sheet. Let rise in a draft-free area for 30 minutes. Preheat the oven to 500°F (260°C).

4. Brush tops lightly with 1 tablespoon olive oil. Bake in the preheated oven for 20 to 30 minutes or until golden brown. **Yield:** 6 servings.

Per serving: About 581 calories, 24g protein, 71g carbohydrate, 22g fat, 4g fiber, 27mg cholesterol, 622mg sodium

◄ **Meatless Main Dish**

Prep Time: 40 minutes

Rise Time: 30 minutes

Cook Time: 30 minutes

Average Rating: ★★★★★

What other cooks have done:

"I added grilled chicken to mine and thought the whole recipe was great!"

Stromboli

Submitted by: **Jessica**

"The stromboli that I make uses premade pizza dough, but bread dough can be used as well. Kids and adults love the pizza creation. Also, I always have mixture left over, which I use the following day with spaghetti."

½	pound lean ground beef	1	(10 ounce) can refrigerated pizza crust dough
1	cup cooked ham, diced		
1	green bell pepper, chopped	1	(8 ounce) package sliced pepperoni
1	red onion, finely chopped		
1	(14 ounce) jar pizza sauce	1	cup shredded mozzarella cheese
1	(4.5 ounce) can mushrooms, drained		
		¼	cup butter, melted

1. Preheat oven to 400°F (200°C).

2. In a skillet over medium heat, cook the ground beef until evenly browned; drain. Mix in the ham, bell pepper, onion, pizza sauce, and mushrooms.

3. Lay pizza dough flat on a baking sheet. Distribute pepperoni slices over dough. Place a heaping pile of the sauce mixture on 1 side of dough (some may be left over). Sprinkle with mozzarella cheese. Fold dough over and pinch ends and sides together. Poke holes in the top and brush melted butter over dough.

4. Cook in the preheated oven for 30 minutes or until golden brown. Slice into individual sections to serve. **Yield:** 4 servings.

Per serving: About 875 calories, 45g protein, 43g carbohydrate, 57g fat, 3g fiber, 158mg cholesterol, 2089mg sodium

Alla Checca

Submitted by: **Star Pooley**

"A wonderful recipe for an uncooked sauce made with fresh garden tomatoes, and you don't have to cook a thing except the pasta!"

5 tomatoes, seeded and diced	1 (16 ounce) package
4 cloves garlic, minced	uncooked angel hair pasta
½ cup chopped fresh basil	2 tablespoons grated
½ cup olive oil	Parmesan cheese
Salt to taste	

1. Combine tomatoes, garlic, basil, and olive oil in a nonmetal bowl. Stir in salt. Cover with plastic wrap. Allow to stand at room temperature at least 2 hours or as long as 10 hours.

2. Bring a large pot of lightly salted water to a boil. Add pasta and cook in boiling water for 8 to 10 minutes or until al dente; drain. Pour uncooked sauce over hot pasta and toss. Sprinkle with grated Parmesan cheese. **Yield:** 4 servings.

Per serving: About 615 calories, 16g protein, 71g carbohydrate, 31g fat, 6g fiber, 85mg cholesterol, 91mg sodium

The Perfecto Pot of Pasta ▼

Pasta is the one dish a lot of people claim to be able to cook. It's true, pasta is relatively simple to prepare. After all, anyone can boil water, right? Even so, there're a few simple tricks to making this most pedestrian of dinnertime staples soar.

- Don't scrimp on the boiling water! Pasta likes to have "breathing" room, with plenty of space for moving around. If possible, use an 8-quart pot with 5 to 6 quarts of water for a pound of pasta.
- It's not necessary to add oil to the water—just use plenty of water and stir occasionally to prevent sticking. Gently stir pasta immediately after adding to water.
- Salt the water to add flavor and help pasta absorb the sauce, about 1 to 2 tablespoons salt to 6 quarts water.
- Add pasta slowly to water, scattering the smaller shapes, and gradually pushing in the long strand types. Don't break pasta in half.
- Don't combine two types or sizes of pasta in the same pot of water. One kind will probably be ready before the other.
- One of the biggest no-no's in pasta preparation is over-cooking. Don't do it! Take a cue from the Italians and boil your pasta only "al dente," which means "to the tooth." In other words, it should be tender but slightly firm to the bite. The longer you cook pasta, the mushier it gets. Don't rely on the clock to evaluate doneness. Use those teeth!

- Save cooking water after pasta is done to add to your sauce. Starch in water binds the sauce, helping it adhere to the pasta.
- Do not rinse pasta unless you're using it for a cold pasta salad. Otherwise, you'll rinse off the starch.

A Noodle for Every Occasion

It's all well and good to know how to cook pasta, but the truly important question now is, what kind of pasta will it be? You're going to have to choose from a dizzying array of shapes, sizes, colors, and types. But before you panic, read on. The endless variations can be contained within just a few basic forms:

- long, round pasta (e.g., spaghetti, capellini, vermicelli)
- long, flat pasta (e.g., lasagna, fettuccine, linguine)
- short, shaped pasta (e.g., penne, conchiglie or shells, fusilli)
- stuffed pasta (e.g., ravioli, tortellini, cannelloni)

A wide range of flours and other ingredients provides even more variety: Try pasta made with semolina, whole grains, rice, mung beans (cellophane noodles), or buckwheat. Spinach, tomato, saffron, green tea, or beets can be added to pasta dough for color and flavor. And all this is even before you think about what kind of sauce to use!   - Emilie Coulter

For more information, visit **Allrecipes.com**

Pasta Pomodoro

Submitted by: **Dinah**

"Easy and light pasta with tomatoes and garlic. Cooked chicken breast chunks or shrimp can also be added to the sauce for a great main dish!"

2   (8 ounce) packages angel hair pasta
¼   cup olive oil
½   onion, chopped
4   cloves garlic, minced
2   cups roma (plum) tomatoes, diced
2   tablespoons balsamic vinegar
1   (10.75 ounce) can low-sodium chicken broth
    Crushed red pepper flakes to taste
    Freshly ground black pepper to taste
2   tablespoons chopped fresh basil
¼   cup grated Parmesan cheese

1. Bring a large pot of lightly salted water to a boil. Add pasta and cook in boiling water for 8 minutes or until al dente; drain.
2. Pour olive oil in a large, deep skillet over high heat. Sauté onion and garlic until lightly browned. Reduce heat to medium-high and add the tomatoes, vinegar, and chicken broth; simmer for about 8 minutes.
3. Stir in red pepper, black pepper, basil, and cooked pasta, tossing thoroughly with sauce. Simmer for about 5 more minutes and serve topped with grated cheese. **Yield:** 4 servings.

Per serving: About 515 calories, 17g protein, 71g carbohydrate, 19g fat, 5g fiber, 6mg cholesterol, 401mg sodium

Beef Parmesan with Garlic Angel Hair Pasta

Submitted by: **Lorrie**

"This is a great, inexpensive alternative to veal Parmesan!"

1½ pounds beef cube steak
1 cup Italian-seasoned breadcrumbs
½ cup grated Parmesan cheese
2 tablespoons olive oil
2 teaspoons minced garlic, divided
1 onion, sliced into thin rings
1 green bell pepper, sliced into rings

1 (16 ounce) jar spaghetti sauce
½ cup shredded mozzarella cheese
12 ounces uncooked angel hair pasta
¼ cup butter
Grated Parmesan cheese
Chopped fresh parsley (optional)

1. Preheat oven to 350°F (175°C).
2. Cut cube steak into serving size pieces. Coat meat with the breadcrumbs and ½ cup Parmesan cheese. Heat olive oil in a large skillet and sauté 1 teaspoon of the garlic for 3 minutes. Add beef steaks and brown quickly on both sides. Place meat in a lightly greased 9x13 inch baking dish, slightly overlapping edges. Place onion rings and peppers on meat and pour spaghetti sauce over all.
3. Bake in the preheated oven for 30 to 45 minutes, depending on the thickness of the meat. Sprinkle mozzarella over meat and bake until bubbly.
4. Bring a large pot of lightly salted water to a boil. Add pasta and cook in boiling water 4 to 5 minutes or until al dente; drain. Add butter and remaining 1 teaspoon minced garlic. Top with grated Parmesan and parsley, if desired. Serve meat and sauce over pasta.
Yield: 4 servings.

Per serving: About 989 calories, 60g protein, 82g carbohydrate, 46g fat, 7g fiber, 156mg cholesterol, 1916mg sodium

◀ **Family Favorite**

Prep Time: 15 minutes

Cook Time: 50 minutes

Average Rating: ★★★★★

What other cooks have done:

"My fiancé and I loved this dish. I chopped up the veggies because we don't like big pieces of pepper. I also used New York strip steak cubes, so it was very tender. Next time, I'll definitely put more meat in because we were fighting each other over the last few pieces of steak."

Fabulous Cilantro Pesto

Submitted by: **Gena Urias**

"A delicious version of the classic with a little more zip! You can substitute lime juice, lemon juice, or Italian salad dressing for the vinegar."

Out-of-the-Ordinary ▶

Prep Time: 15 minutes

Cook Time: 15 minutes

Average Rating: ★★★★☆

What other cooks have done:

"What a difference! I would have never thought to make pesto out of cilantro because I've had only the basil-based kind, but this was fantastic and much cheaper than using fresh basil. I brushed mine over some sea bass steaks, which I then broiled a few minutes. It was really delicious. I can't wait to try it over pasta."

1	(16 ounce) package farfalle (bow tie) pasta	¼	cup grated Parmesan cheese
1	bunch fresh cilantro	½	teaspoon cayenne pepper
5	cloves garlic, minced	½	cup walnuts or pecans
1	tablespoon white wine vinegar		Salt to taste
		½	cup olive oil

1. Bring a large pot of lightly salted water to a boil. Cook pasta in boiling water for 8 to 10 minutes or until al dente; drain.

2. In a food processor or blender, place cilantro, garlic, vinegar, Parmesan cheese, cayenne pepper, nuts, and salt. Add ¼ cup of the olive oil and blend. Add more olive oil until desired consistency.

3. Pour pesto in a small saucepan and simmer over low heat, stirring constantly. Pour over cooked pasta and toss. **Yield:** 4 servings.

Per serving: About 776 calories, 20g protein, 86g carbohydrate, 41g fat, 5g fiber, 5mg cholesterol, 130mg sodium

Bow Ties with Sausage, Tomatoes, and Cream

Submitted by: **Linda Caroline**

"A friend gave this recipe to me a few years back, and my family can't seem to get enough of it. The cream enhances the flavor and texture."

Classic Comfort Food ▶

Prep Time: 15 minutes

Cook Time: 30 minutes

Average Rating: ★★★★★

What other cooks have done:

"I used half-and-half instead of heavy cream to cut the calories and fat, and it tasted great. I also think it's a good idea to drain the grease after cooking the sausage."

1	(12 ounce) package farfalle (bow tie) pasta	3	cloves garlic, minced
2	tablespoons olive oil	1	(28 ounce) can Italian-style plum tomatoes, drained and coarsely chopped
1	pound sweet Italian sausage, casings removed and crumbled	1½	cups heavy whipping cream
½	teaspoon crushed red pepper flakes	½	teaspoon salt
½	cup diced onion	3	tablespoons minced fresh parsley

1. Bring a large pot of lightly salted water to a boil. Add pasta and cook in boiling water for 8 to 10 minutes or until al dente; drain.

2. Heat oil in a large, deep skillet over medium heat. Cook sausage and pepper flakes until sausage is evenly browned. Stir in onion and garlic and cook until onion is tender. Stir in tomatoes, cream, and salt. Simmer until mixture thickens, about 8 to 10 minutes.

3. Stir cooked pasta into sauce and heat through. Sprinkle with parsley. **Yield:** 6 servings.

Per serving: About 645 calories, 21g protein, 49g carbohydrate, 41g fat, 3g fiber, 122mg cholesterol, 940mg sodium

Blackened Shrimp Stroganoff (pictured on page 190)

Submitted by: **Linda Johnson**

"A definite winner! I've gotten many bravos for this recipe. I hope your family and friends enjoy this recipe as much as mine do. I've subbed frozen green peas for the roasted red bell peppers."

1	pound uncooked fresh shrimp, peeled and deveined		1	tablespoon chopped shallot
			⅔	cup chicken broth
			½	cup sour cream
1	tablespoon olive oil		1	tablespoon cornstarch
1	tablespoon Cajun seasoning		1	cup chicken broth
6	ounces uncooked fettuccine		1	(7 ounce) jar roasted red bell peppers
1	tablespoon butter		1	tablespoon drained capers
3	cups sliced fresh mushrooms			Salt and pepper to taste

1. Combine peeled shrimp, oil, and Cajun seasoning in a medium bowl. Set aside.

2. Bring a large pot of lightly salted water to a boil. Add pasta and cook in boiling water for 8 to 10 minutes or until al dente; drain.

3. Meanwhile, melt butter over medium heat in a large skillet. Cook and stir mushrooms and shallot in butter until tender. Remove from skillet. Add shrimp; cook until shrimp turn pink, about 2 to 3 minutes. Remove from skillet. Add ⅔ cup chicken broth to pan and bring to a boil. Cook, uncovered, until reduced to ¼ cup, about 2 to 3 minutes.

4. In a small bowl, stir together sour cream and cornstarch; mix in 1 cup chicken broth. Stir into reduced chicken broth in skillet. Cook and stir until thick and bubbly. Cook 1 more minute. Stir in shrimp, mushroom mixture, roasted red peppers, and capers. Heat through and season with salt and pepper to taste. Serve over pasta. **Yield:** 4 servings.

Per serving: About 449 calories, 33g protein, 42g carbohydrate, 17g fat, 3g fiber, 193mg cholesterol, 1232mg sodium

---

◀ Company is Coming

Prep Time: 30 minutes

Cook Time: 30 minutes

Average Rating: ★★★★★

What other cooks have done:

"This recipe does dirty a few dishes, but it's worth it. I used the individually frozen shrimp, which added liquid when thawed and heated, leaving my sauce a little runny. If you use the same type of shrimp, drain the liquid after cooking the shrimp. Sourdough bread is a must-have with this dish to sop up every last bit of the delicious sauce."

Alfredo Blue

Submitted by: **Melanie**

"This is the best Alfredo sauce I have ever come up with, and any kind of meat or vegetable can be added to it."

1 (16 ounce) package fettuccine	¼ cup grated Parmesan cheese
1 tablespoon olive oil	2 cups heavy whipping cream
1 clove garlic, sliced	1 tablespoon Italian seasoning
4 ounces blue cheese, crumbled	Salt and ground black pepper to taste

1. Bring a large pot of lightly salted water to a boil. Cook pasta in boiling water for 8 to 10 minutes or until al dente; drain.
2. Heat olive oil in a small skillet over medium heat. Sauté garlic in olive oil until golden. Discard garlic and reserve oil.
3. In a medium saucepan over medium-low heat, combine blue cheese, Parmesan cheese, and cream. Stir until cheeses are melted. Stir in the reserved oil. Season with Italian seasoning, salt, and pepper.
4. Toss hot pasta with sauce and let stand 5 minutes before serving.
Yield: 8 servings.

Per serving: About 490 calories, 13g protein, 44g carbohydrate, 30g fat, 2g fiber, 95mg cholesterol, 281mg sodium

Ham and Asparagus Fettuccine

Submitted by: **Stephanie Moon**

"I love fettuccine and, when made with a bit of leftover ham, it takes on a heartiness and richness so filling there isn't room for dessert!"

12 ounces uncooked fettuccine	¾ cup grated Parmesan cheese
8 ounces fresh asparagus, cut into 2 inch pieces	¼ teaspoon garlic powder
½ cup butter	¼ teaspoon ground black pepper
2 cups heavy whipping cream	Pinch cayenne pepper
	½ pound cooked ham, diced

1. Bring a large pot of lightly salted water to a boil. Add pasta and cook for 8 to 10 minutes or until al dente. Stir asparagus into pot in the last 5 minutes of cooking; drain.
2. While pasta is cooking, heat butter and cream in a medium saucepan over medium heat. When mixture begins to bubble, stir in Parmesan cheese, garlic powder, pepper, and cayenne. Continue cooking until mixture thickens, stirring occasionally. Stir in ham; heat through.
3. Toss pasta and asparagus with sauce and serve immediately. **Yield:** 4 servings.

Per serving: About 1168 calories, 38g protein, 68g carbohydrate, 85g fat, 4g fiber, 293mg cholesterol, 672mg sodium

Chicken and Broccoli Pasta,
page 200

Blackened Shrimp Stroganoff, page 187

Greek Chicken Pasta, page 199

Pita Pizza, page 175

Italian Spaghetti Sauce with Meatballs, page 204

Hearty Vegetable Lasagna

Submitted by: **Sue**

"This hearty vegetable lasagna is the only lasagna my husband will eat. We love it! Hope you all enjoy it as much as we do."

6 uncooked lasagna noodles
1 pound fresh mushrooms, sliced
¾ cup chopped green bell pepper
¾ cup chopped onion
3 cloves garlic, minced
2 tablespoons vegetable oil
1 (26 ounce) jar pasta sauce
1 teaspoon dried basil
1 (15 ounce) container part-skim ricotta cheese
4 cups shredded mozzarella cheese, divided
2 eggs
½ cup grated Parmesan cheese, divided

1. Bring a large pot of lightly salted water to a boil. Cook lasagna noodles in boiling water for 8 to 10 minutes or until al dente; drain.
2. In a large saucepan, cook and stir mushrooms, green pepper, onion, and garlic in oil. Stir in pasta sauce and basil; bring to a boil. Reduce heat and simmer 15 minutes.
3. Mix together ricotta, 2 cups mozzarella cheese, and eggs.
4. Preheat oven to 350°F (175°C). Spread 1 cup tomato sauce in a greased 9x13 inch baking dish. Layer half each of lasagna noodles, ricotta mixture, sauce, and Parmesan cheese. Repeat layering and top with remaining 2 cups mozzarella cheese.
5. Bake, uncovered, in the preheated oven for 40 minutes. Let stand 15 minutes before serving. **Yield:** 12 servings.

Per serving: About 426 calories, 22g protein, 43g carbohydrate, 19g fat, 4g fiber, 79mg cholesterol, 776mg sodium

◄ **Crowd-Pleaser**

Prep Time: 25 minutes

Cook Time: 1 hour

Average Rating: ★★★★

What other cooks have done:

"Finally! A veggie lasagna I like. I added thawed and drained frozen spinach to the ricotta mixture. (After all, what is lasagna without spinach?) I also added about ¾ cup each of shredded carrot, chopped broccoli, and zucchini."

Black Bean Lasagna

Submitted by: **Carol**

"A yummy meatless pasta dish."

"Excellent lasagna! I live in a dorm and find that the leftovers are as good as, if not better than, the first time! I add cumin and chili powder to the sauce as well as extra onion and green pepper to give it a southwestern flair. I highly recommend this as a great alternative to standard lasagna!"

9	uncooked lasagna noodles	2	cloves garlic, minced
1	(15 ounce) container part-skim ricotta cheese	2	(16 ounce) cans black beans
1	egg	1	(15 ounce) can tomato sauce
½	cup chopped onion	8	ounces shredded mozzarella cheese, divided
½	cup chopped green bell pepper		

1. Bring a large pot of lightly salted water to a boil. Cook the lasagna noodles in boiling water for 8 to 10 minutes or until al dente; drain.
2. In a bowl, blend the ricotta cheese and egg; set aside. Preheat oven to 350°F (175°C).
3. Spray a large skillet with cooking spray and sauté the onion, green bell pepper, and garlic until tender. Mash 1 can of black beans. Stir mashed black beans, whole black beans, and tomato sauce into skillet and cook until heated through.
4. Arrange 3 lasagna noodles in a lightly greased 9x13 inch baking dish; layer with ⅓ each of the ricotta mixture, black bean mixture, and mozzarella cheese. Repeat twice.
5. Bake in the preheated oven for 40 to 45 minutes. Let stand 10 minutes before serving. **Yield:** 8 servings.

Per serving: About 419 calories, 28g protein, 52g carbohydrate, 12g fat, 10g fiber, 65mg cholesterol, 985mg sodium

Linguine with Broccoli and Red Peppers

Submitted by: **Chris Catley**

"You get lots of mileage out of this recipe. It's a wonderful side dish, but on many occasions we make this our whole meal, along with a salad and bread!"

1 (16 ounce) package linguine pasta	1 tablespoon butter
1 pound fresh broccoli, chopped	3 cloves garlic, minced
3 tablespoons extra virgin olive oil	1 red bell pepper, thinly sliced
	Pinch garlic salt
	¼ cup grated Parmesan cheese

1. Bring a large pot of lightly salted water to a boil. Add pasta and cook in boiling water for 8 to 10 minutes or until al dente; drain.
2. Steam broccoli with 2 tablespoons water in a covered casserole dish in microwave on high for 6 to 7 minutes.
3. In a medium skillet, heat olive oil and butter over low heat and sauté garlic and red pepper slices.
4. Drain broccoli and add to skillet. Sprinkle lightly with garlic salt and sauté broccoli and peppers until soft. Toss vegetable mixture with hot pasta. Sprinkle with Parmesan cheese. **Yield:** 6 servings.

Per serving: About 399 calories, 14g protein, 61g carbohydrate, 12g fat, 5g fiber, 8mg cholesterol, 177mg sodium

◄ **Family Favorite**

Prep Time: 5 minutes
Cook Time: 15 minutes
Average Rating: ★★★★☆

What other cooks have done:
"I cut the fat a little by omitting the butter and using less oil and substituting reduced-fat chicken broth. I would also recommend either doubling the veggies or cutting the pasta amount in half for a better balance."

Broccoli Wears the Crown ▼

If there was an awards ceremony for vegetables, broccoli would win the category for Most Health Benefits, stalks down! In addition to being tasty, broccoli is a nutritional power-house! It has been proven to help protect against cataracts, stroke, and many kinds of cancer. A one-cup serving has 200 percent of your recommended daily allowance of vitamin C, in addition to having a good dose of vitamin A, riboflavin, calcium, and fiber. All this great stuff, and only 40 calories!

Pick the Perfect Broccoli

It's available fresh year-round, though it thrives in the cold weather, so its peak season runs from late autumn to early spring. The fresh broccoli you select from your grocery store should have dark green tops with lighter green stems. The tops are actually bunches of tiny flower buds—the buds should be tightly closed, with no mushy spots or signs of yellowing. The stalks should feel firm and crisp, never limp or wobbly. You can buy packages of precut broccoli florets at most stores, too. Look at them carefully before buying to ensure that they are bright green and firm. Once you get the broccoli home, it will stay fresh up to two weeks if you refrigerate it, unwashed, dry, and tightly wrapped in a plastic bag. Keep in mind, though, that broccoli's nutritional value depletes the longer you store it, so you're best off using it as soon as possible after you bring it home. If you'd like to keep broccoli on hand all the time, buy a bag or two of frozen broccoli; freezing does a great job of preserving nutrients, and you can use as much or as little from the bag as you like!

Cook the Perfect Broccoli

When you cook broccoli, it's important not to overdo it. Perfectly cooked broccoli is an appetizing bright green with a mild, pleasant flavor and a tender but firm texture you can really sink your teeth into. Overcooked broccoli, however, becomes a pile of gray-green mush with a somewhat sulfurous aroma and an off-flavor. To avoid overcooking broccoli, don't leave it covered up once it's done! Uncover it and either serve it right away or plunge it into a bowl of ice water to stop the cooking and preserve the color, flavor, and vitamins.

Try broccoli lightly steamed or just raw as a snack, battered and fried, simmered in soup, seared in a stir-fry, baked in a casserole or quiche, tossed in a salad, sprinkled on pizza, or mixed into your favorite pasta. And don't throw away that stalk! Try shredding it and substituting it for its cousin, cabbage, in your favorite coleslaw recipe. Broccoli is a fabulous addition to all kinds of savory dishes and a great way to pack nutrition in your diet.
- Jennifer Anderson

For more information, visit **Allrecipes.com**

Fra Diavolo Sauce with Pasta

Submitted by: **Holly**

"This sauce includes shrimp and scallops and is best served with linguine."

Company is Coming ▶

Prep Time: 20 minutes

Cook Time: 40 minutes

Average Rating: ★★★★★

What other cooks have done:

"Next time I prepare this dish, I'll omit the salt; the seafood adds enough salt for my taste. I tried this recipe adding ½ pound mussels. I cooked them with the shrimp and scallops until they opened. My husband had three helpings!"

4	tablespoons olive oil, divided	1	(16 ounce) package linguine pasta
6	cloves garlic, crushed	½	pound small uncooked shrimp, peeled and deveined
3	cups whole peeled tomatoes with liquid, chopped	½	pound bay scallops
1½	teaspoons salt	1	tablespoon chopped fresh parsley
1	teaspoon crushed red pepper flakes		

1. In a large saucepan, heat 2 tablespoons olive oil and the garlic over medium heat. When the garlic starts to sizzle, pour in the tomatoes. Season with salt and red pepper. Bring to a boil. Lower the heat and simmer for 30 minutes, stirring occasionally.

2. Meanwhile, bring a large pot of lightly salted water to a boil. Cook pasta in boiling water for 8 to 10 minutes or until al dente; drain.

3. In a large skillet, heat the remaining 2 tablespoons olive oil over high heat. Add the shrimp and scallops. Cook for about 2 minutes, stirring frequently, or until the shrimp turn pink. Add shrimp and scallops to the tomato mixture and stir in the parsley. Cook for 3 to 4 minutes or just until the sauce begins to bubble. Serve sauce over pasta. **Yield:** 8 servings.

Per serving: About 336 calories, 19g protein, 47g carbohydrate, 9g fat, 3g fiber, 52mg cholesterol, 659mg sodium

The Best Clam Sauce

Submitted by: **Jodie B.**

"You won't find a better clam sauce than this—not even in a restaurant. My boyfriend begs me to make this! Serve this dish with fresh garlic bread and a nice white wine."

1	(16 ounce) package linguine pasta	4	(6.5 ounce) cans minced clams
1	onion, chopped	½	cup butter
6	cloves garlic, chopped		Salt and pepper to taste
3	tablespoons olive oil	2	tablespoons dry white wine

1. Bring a large pot of lightly salted water to a boil. Add linguine and cook in boiling water for 8 to 10 minutes or until al dente; drain.
2. In a large skillet, sauté the onion and garlic in olive oil until the onions are translucent. Drain the cans of minced clams, reserving half of the juice.
3. Stir the clams, reserved juice, butter, salt, pepper, and wine into the onion mixture. Simmer the mixture for 20 minutes or until the sauce has reduced by one-third and has thickened.
4. Spoon the sauce over the linguine and serve. **Yield:** 4 servings.

Per serving: About 905 calories, 61g protein, 74g carbohydrate, 39g fat, 4g fiber, 186mg cholesterol, 665mg sodium

---

◄ **Classic Comfort Food**

Prep Time: 5 minutes
Cook Time: 40 minutes
Average Rating: ★★★★★

What other cooks have done:
"The only improvements I can suggest for this great sauce are to add mushrooms and to wait until the end to add the clams and simmer them for just about 1 to 2 minutes. This way, you avoid having chewy clams."

Shrimp Linguine Alfredo

Submitted by: **Tina**

"Elegant but simple, fast, and very impressive!"

1	(12 ounce) package linguine pasta	1	cup half-and-half
¼	cup butter, melted	2	teaspoons ground black pepper
¼	cup diced onion	6	tablespoons grated Parmesan cheese
1	tablespoon minced garlic		Garnishes: fresh parsley sprigs, lemon slices
40	small uncooked shrimp, peeled and deveined		

1. Bring a large pot of lightly salted water to a boil. Add pasta and cook in boiling water for 8 to 10 minutes or until al dente; drain.
2. Meanwhile, melt butter in a large saucepan. Sauté onion and garlic over medium heat until tender. Add shrimp; sauté over high heat for 1 minute, stirring constantly. Stir in half-and-half. Cook, stirring constantly, until sauce thickens.
3. Place pasta in a serving dish; cover with shrimp sauce. Sprinkle with black pepper and Parmesan cheese. Garnish, if desired. **Yield:** 4 servings.

Per serving: About 592 calories, 28g protein, 70g carbohydrate, 24g fat, 5g fiber, 135mg cholesterol, 377mg sodium

---

◄ **Restaurant Fare**

Prep Time: 10 minutes
Cook Time: 25 minutes
Average Rating: ★★★★★

What other cooks have done:
"I recommend removing the shrimp from the pan once it's cooked through; then add the half-and-half to the pan to thicken. Otherwise, the shrimp can become overcooked and tough. Just add the shrimp back to the sauce once it's thickened. For some color, stir in some steamed broccoli."

Classic Comfort Food ▶

Prep Time: 10 minutes

Cook Time: 45 minutes

Average Rating: ★★★★☆

What other cooks have done:

"Really enjoyed this recipe. It makes a slightly different style of mac and cheese, so it's nice for a change of pace. I have used cracker crumbs, cornflake crumbs, and even potato chip crumbs as a topping, and they are all good."

Restaurant Fare ▶

Prep Time: 20 minutes

Cook Time: 1 hour

Average Rating: ★★★★☆

What other cooks have done:

"I used ricotta instead of cottage cheese. I put the filling in a zip-top plastic bag and snipped off one corner. Then, using it like a pastry bag, I piped the filling into the shells. I sprinkled the remaining mozzarella on top during the last 5 minutes of baking."

Chuck's Favorite Mac and Cheese

Submitted by: **Carla**

"Cottage cheese and sour cream are the unique elements in this macaroni and cheese recipe. Easily doubles for a potluck."

1	(8 ounce) package elbow macaroni	1	(8 ounce) container sour cream
1	(8 ounce) package shredded sharp Cheddar cheese	¼	cup grated Parmesan cheese
1	(12 ounce) container small curd cottage cheese		Salt and pepper to taste
		1	cup dry breadcrumbs
		¼	cup butter, melted

1. Preheat oven to 350°F (175°C). Bring a large pot of lightly salted water to a boil. Add pasta and cook in boiling water for 8 to 10 minutes or until al dente; drain.

2. In a 9x13 inch baking dish, stir together macaroni, shredded Cheddar cheese, cottage cheese, sour cream, Parmesan cheese, salt, and pepper. In a small bowl, mix together breadcrumbs and melted butter. Sprinkle topping over macaroni mixture.

3. Bake in the preheated oven for 30 to 35 minutes or until top is golden. **Yield:** 6 servings.

Per serving: About 579 calories, 26g protein, 43g carbohydrate, 33g fat, 2g fiber, 88mg cholesterol, 794mg sodium

Meat-Filled Manicotti

Submitted by: **Steph**

"This tasty and filling dish pairs nicely with a green salad, if desired."

1	(8 ounce) package manicotti pasta	½	cup grated Parmesan cheese
1	pound lean ground beef	2	egg whites, lightly beaten
1½	cups cottage cheese	½	teaspoon dried oregano
2	cups shredded mozzarella cheese, divided	1	(32 ounce) jar spaghetti sauce

1. Bring a large pot of lightly salted water to a boil. Add pasta; cook in boiling water for 8 to 10 minutes or until al dente. Drain and reserve.

2. Meanwhile, in a large skillet, cook beef over medium heat until browned. Drain and cool.

3. Preheat oven to 350°F (175°C).

4. Combine beef, cottage cheese, 1 cup mozzarella cheese, Parmesan cheese, egg whites, and oregano. Mix well. Stuff shells with mixture.

5. Lightly grease a 9x13 inch baking dish. Pour enough spaghetti sauce in dish to cover the bottom. Place stuffed shells in the dish. Cover with sauce and top with the remaining 1 cup mozzarella cheese. Bake in the preheated oven for 50 minutes. **Yield:** 6 servings.

Per serving: About 625 calories, 39g protein, 42g carbohydrate, 33g fat, 4g fiber, 101mg cholesterol, 1210mg sodium

Greek Chicken Pasta *(pictured on page 190)*

Submitted by: **Lalena**

"Chicken with a Greek accent! This pasta dish makes a wonderfully complete and satisfying meal. For extra flavor, toss in a few kalamata olives."

1	pound uncooked penne pasta	1	large tomato, chopped
1	tablespoon olive oil	½	cup crumbled feta cheese
2	cloves garlic, crushed	3	tablespoons chopped fresh parsley
½	cup chopped red onion	2	tablespoons lemon juice
1	pound skinless, boneless chicken breasts, cut into bite-size pieces	2	teaspoons dried oregano
			Salt and pepper to taste
1	(12 ounce) can marinated artichoke hearts, drained and chopped		Garnish: lemon wedges

1. Bring a large pot of lightly salted water to a boil. Cook pasta in boiling water for 8 to 10 minutes or until al dente; drain.

2. Meanwhile, heat olive oil in a large skillet over medium-high heat. Add garlic and onion; sauté for 2 minutes. Stir in the chicken. Cook, stirring occasionally, until chicken is no longer pink and the juices run clear, about 5 to 6 minutes.

3. Reduce heat to medium-low and add the artichoke hearts, tomato, feta cheese, parsley, lemon juice, oregano, and cooked pasta. Stir until heated through, about 2 to 3 minutes. Remove from heat, season to taste with salt and pepper, and garnish, if desired. **Yield:** 6 servings.

Per serving: About 438 calories, 31g protein, 57g carbohydrate, 11g fat, 8g fiber, 110mg cholesterol, 460mg sodium

◀ **Quick & Easy**

Prep Time: 15 minutes

Cook Time: 15 minutes

Average Rating: ★★★★★

What other cooks have done:

"I cut the amount of pasta in half, resulting in a terrific chicken to veggie to pasta ratio. I prefer the consistency of feta cheese that's not melted, so I just sprinkled it on top along with some olives instead of mixing it into the dish."

Chicken and Broccoli Pasta *(pictured on page 189)*

Submitted by: **Gloria McShane**
"Boneless chicken and broccoli make a delicious, low-fat pairing in a tomato-garlic sauce. Use your favorite shaped pasta—penne and shells work well."

3	tablespoons olive oil	2	cups fresh broccoli florets
1	pound skinless, boneless chicken breast halves, cut into 1 inch pieces		Salt and pepper to taste Pinch dried oregano
1	tablespoon chopped onion	18	ounces uncooked pasta
2	cloves garlic, chopped	¼	cup fresh basil leaves, cut into thin strips
2	(14.5 ounce) cans diced tomatoes	2	tablespoons grated Parmesan cheese

1. In a large skillet over medium heat, warm oil and add chicken; cook until slightly brown. Add onion and garlic and cook for about 5 minutes or until garlic is golden and onions are translucent.
2. Add tomatoes, broccoli, salt, pepper, and oregano; stir well and bring to a boil. Cover and reduce heat to medium-low to simmer for about 10 minutes.
3. Meanwhile, bring a large pot of lightly salted water to a boil. Add pasta and cook in boiling water for 8 to 10 minutes or until al dente; drain and add back to pot. Pour chicken sauce into pot and mix well.
4. Add basil and toss well; top with Parmesan cheese. Serve. **Yield:** 8 servings.

Per serving: About 323 calories, 23g protein, 40g carbohydrate, 8g fat, 4g fiber, 80mg cholesterol, 367mg sodium

Goat Cheese and Arugula over Penne *(pictured on page 116)*

Submitted by: **Christine L.**
"This is a quick, easy, and elegant dish. Serve as a main course with a good loaf of bread or as a side dish."

8	ounces uncooked penne pasta	¼	cup olive oil
5½	ounces goat cheese	2	teaspoons minced garlic
2	cups arugula, stems included	½	teaspoon salt
1	cup halved cherry tomatoes	½	teaspoon ground black pepper

1. Bring a large pot of lightly salted water to a boil. Add pasta and cook in boiling water for 8 to 10 minutes or until al dente; drain.
2. Crumble goat cheese into a large serving bowl. Add arugula, cherry tomatoes, olive oil, garlic, salt, and pepper.
3. Toss pasta with goat cheese mixture. **Yield:** 6 servings.

Per serving: About 317 calories, 11g protein, 30g carbohydrate, 18g fat, 2g fiber, 21mg cholesterol, 334mg sodium

---

Healthy ▶

Prep Time: 10 minutes

Cook Time: 15 minutes

Average Rating: ★★★★☆

What other cooks have done:

"I changed a few things to speed up cooking time. I cut up the chicken and browned it, then added chicken broth and frozen mixed veggies instead of fresh. It was easy and still tasted great."

Company is Coming ▶

Prep Time: 15 minutes

Cook Time: 10 minutes

Average Rating: ★★★★★

What other cooks have done:

"Terrific and fast dinner recipe. I couldn't find any arugula so I used mixed salad greens, which has some arugula in the mix. I loved the end result."

Penne with Spicy Vodka Tomato Cream Sauce

Submitted by: **Star Pooley**

"A nice change from your typical tomato sauce! If you're worried about the alcohol, don't be! It cooks off and cannot be tasted! It simply helps to enhance the flavors."

1 (16 ounce) package penne pasta	1 (28 ounce) can crushed tomatoes
¼ cup extra virgin olive oil	¾ teaspoon salt
2 (3.5 ounce) links sweet Italian sausage	2 tablespoons vodka
4 cloves garlic, minced	½ cup heavy whipping cream
½ teaspoon crushed red pepper flakes	¼ cup chopped fresh parsley

1. Bring a large pot of lightly salted water to a boil. Add pasta and cook in boiling water for 8 to 10 minutes or until al dente; drain.

2. Meanwhile, in a large skillet, heat oil over medium heat. Remove casings from sausage. Cook sausage, breaking up the meat, until browned. Add garlic and red pepper and cook, stirring until garlic is golden brown.

3. Add tomatoes and salt; bring to a boil. Reduce heat and simmer 15 minutes.

4. Add vodka and cream and bring to a boil. Reduce heat to low and add pasta; toss for 1 minute. Stir in fresh parsley and serve. **Yield:** 4 servings.

Per serving: About 878 calories, 26g protein, 99g carbohydrate, 43g fat, 8g fiber, 75mg cholesterol, 1047mg sodium

---

◀ Out-of-the-Ordinary

Prep Time: 10 minutes

Cook Time: 25 minutes

Average Rating: ★★★★★

What other cooks have done:

"I liked the addition of sausage to this vodka sauce, and the dish actually tasted better the next day. The only changes I felt it needed were reducing the oil and omitting the salt. I did, and they weren't missed."

Cheese Ravioli with Three-Pepper Topping

Submitted by: **Amanda**

"Try this for a change from tomato sauces. I cooked this one day for myself, and my family ate all of it before I had a chance. It's that good."

1	(16 ounce) package uncooked cheese ravioli	½	yellow bell pepper, thinly sliced
3	tablespoons olive oil	2	cups chicken broth, divided
1	small onion, diced	¼	teaspoon crushed red pepper flakes
1	green bell pepper, thinly sliced		
½	red bell pepper, thinly sliced		

1. Bring a large pot of lightly salted water to a boil. Cook ravioli in boiling water for 8 to 10 minutes or until al dente; drain.
2. Heat olive oil in a large skillet over medium heat. Sauté onion and bell peppers until tender. Add 1 cup of the broth, season with pepper flakes, and simmer 5 minutes. Stir in remaining broth and cook until most of broth has evaporated. Spoon pepper mixture over ravioli.
Yield: 6 servings.

Per serving: About 265 calories, 10g protein, 28g carbohydrate, 13g fat, 3g fiber, 30mg cholesterol, 461mg sodium

Country Pasta with Mozzarella

Submitted by: **Jennifer**

"A hearty pasta dish versatile enough to serve as the main dish or as a side."

8	ounces uncooked rigatoni pasta	2	cups shredded mozzarella cheese
8	slices bacon, cut into 1 inch pieces	¼	cup grated Parmesan cheese
2	cups broccoli florets	⅛	teaspoon cayenne pepper
2	cloves garlic, minced	¼	cup chopped fresh parsley

1. Bring a large pot of lightly salted water to a boil. Add pasta and cook in boiling water for 8 to 10 minutes or until al dente; drain.
2. In a 10 inch skillet, cook the bacon over medium heat, stirring occasionally, until the bacon is browned. Add the broccoli and garlic. Cook, stirring occasionally, until the broccoli is slightly tender, about 4 to 5 minutes.
3. Stir in the cooked rigatoni, mozzarella cheese, Parmesan cheese, and cayenne pepper. Cook, stirring occasionally, until the cheese is melted. Sprinkle with the fresh chopped parsley. **Yield:** 6 servings.

Per serving: About 476 calories, 18g protein, 30g carbohydrate, 32g fat, 2g fiber, 57mg cholesterol, 501mg sodium

Tacos in Pasta Shells

Submitted by: **grannycancook**

"Pasta with a Mexican flavor that's tasty and easy to make. It's great any-time; kids and adults will love it. Garnish with green onions, sliced tomatoes, lettuce, and black olives, if desired."

1¼ pounds lean ground beef
1 (3 ounce) package cream cheese
1 teaspoon salt
1 teaspoon chili powder
18 jumbo pasta shells
2 tablespoons butter, melted
1 cup taco sauce

1 cup shredded Cheddar cheese
1 cup shredded Monterey Jack cheese
1½ cups crushed tortilla chips
1 (8 ounce) container sour cream

1. In a large skillet, cook beef over medium heat until browned; drain. Add cream cheese, salt, and chili powder; mix and simmer for 5 minutes.

2. Meanwhile, bring a large pot of lightly salted water to a boil. Add pasta and cook in boiling water for 8 to 10 minutes or until al dente; drain. Toss cooked shells in butter.

3. Preheat oven to 350°F (175°C).

4. Fill shells with beef mixture and arrange in a 9x13 inch baking dish; pour taco sauce over shells. Cover with foil and bake in the pre-heated oven for 15 minutes.

5. Remove dish from oven and top with Cheddar cheese, Monterey Jack cheese, and tortilla chips; return dish to oven and cook for 15 more minutes.

6. Top with sour cream and serve. **Yield:** 6 servings.

Per serving: About 682 calories, 33g protein, 27g carbohydrate, 47g fat, 1g fiber, 144mg cholesterol, 982mg sodium

◀ **Kid-Friendly**

Prep Time: 30 minutes

Cook Time: 35 minutes

Average Rating: ★★★★★

What other cooks have done:

"This is the perfect recipe for using the crumbs at the bottom of the bag of chips. My bag was about half full, but I tipped it to the side and got the crumbs out of the bottom so I didn't have to crush any of the 'good' chips."

Prep Time: 20 minutes

Cook Time: 2 hours 7 minutes

Average Rating: ★★★★★

What other cooks have done:

"I like to make the sauce ahead of time and keep it on hand for dinner. Then all I have to do is make the meatballs, brown them, and simmer with the sauce. A sprinkling of Parmesan cheese over the top makes it perfect!"

Italian Spaghetti Sauce with Meatballs *(pictured on page 192)*

Submitted by: **Jeremy**

"My mother gave me this recipe years ago. It's great."

1 pound lean ground beef	¼ cup olive oil
1 cup fresh breadcrumbs	2 (28 ounce) cans whole peeled tomatoes, undrained
1 tablespoon dried parsley	
1 tablespoon grated Parmesan cheese	2 teaspoons salt
¼ teaspoon ground black pepper	1 teaspoon white sugar
	1 bay leaf
⅛ teaspoon garlic powder	1 (6 ounce) can tomato paste
1 egg, lightly beaten	¾ teaspoon dried basil
2 tablespoons olive oil	½ teaspoon ground black pepper
¾ cup chopped onion	
5 cloves garlic, minced	

1. To make the meatballs, in a large bowl, combine ground beef, breadcrumbs, parsley, Parmesan, ¼ teaspoon black pepper, garlic powder, and egg. Mix well and form into 30 balls. In a large skillet, cook meatballs in 2 tablespoons hot oil over medium-high heat 7 minutes or until browned; remove from skillet and drain.

2. To make sauce, sauté onion and garlic in ¼ cup olive oil until onion is translucent. Stir in tomatoes, salt, sugar, and bay leaf. Cover, reduce heat to medium-low, and simmer 1 hour 30 minutes. Stir in tomato paste, basil, ½ teaspoon pepper, and meatballs and simmer 30 more minutes. Discard bay leaf. **Yield:** 6 servings.

Per serving: About 356 calories, 19g protein, 25g carbohydrate, 21g fat, 5g fiber, 82mg cholesterol, 1496mg sodium

Vegetable Lo Mein

Submitted by: **Angela Creighton**

"A great accompaniment with any Asian meal. Try adding cooked chicken for variety."

8	ounces uncooked spaghetti	1	tablespoon cornstarch
¼	cup vegetable oil	1	cup chicken broth
2	cups sliced fresh mushrooms	¼	cup hoisin sauce
1	cup shredded carrots	2	tablespoons honey
½	cup sliced red bell pepper	1	tablespoon soy sauce
1	onion, chopped	1	teaspoon grated fresh ginger
2	cloves garlic, minced	¼	teaspoon cayenne pepper
2	cups fresh bean sprouts	¼	teaspoon curry powder
½	cup chopped green onions		

1. Bring a large pot of lightly salted water to a boil. Add pasta and cook in boiling water for 8 to 10 minutes or until al dente; drain.
2. Heat oil in a large wok or sauté pan. Stir-fry mushrooms, carrots, pepper, onion, and garlic until tender. Stir in bean sprouts and green onions; cook 1 minute. Stir cornstarch into chicken broth; add to stir-fry. Stir in hoisin sauce, honey, soy sauce, ginger, cayenne pepper, and curry powder. Cook and stir until thickened and bubbly.
3. Add cooked spaghetti and toss. Serve immediately. **Yield:** 4 servings.

Note: Hoisin sauce, also called Peking sauce, is a thick, reddish-brown sauce that's sweet and spicy and widely used in Asian cooking. It's a mixture of soybeans, garlic, chile peppers, and various spices. It can be found in Asian markets and many large supermarkets in the Asian or ethnic section. If this item isn't available at your local store, ask your grocer to order it for you.

Per serving: About 470 calories, 12g protein, 72g carbohydrate, 16g fat, 5g fiber, 1mg cholesterol, 757mg sodium

Pasta with Kielbasa and Sauerkraut

Submitted by: **Gail**
"Fast, easy, and something a little different."

12	ounces ziti pasta
3	tablespoons olive oil
1	onion, chopped
1	red bell pepper, chopped
2	cloves garlic, minced
1	pound kielbasa sausage, sliced into ½ inch pieces
12	ounces sauerkraut, drained and rinsed
2	tablespoons prepared Dijon-style mustard
	Pinch cayenne pepper
¼	cup white wine
2	tablespoons chopped fresh parsley

1. Bring a large pot of lightly salted water to a boil. Add pasta and cook in boiling water for 8 to 10 minutes or until al dente; drain.
2. Heat olive oil in a large skillet over medium heat. Cook onion and bell pepper in oil, stirring frequently, until onion is tender. Stir in garlic and kielbasa and cook until kielbasa begins to brown, about 8 minutes. Stir in sauerkraut, mustard, and cayenne pepper; cook about 4 more minutes. Stir in wine and parsley and heat through.
3. Toss ziti with kielbasa and sauerkraut and serve immediately.
Yield: 6 servings.

Per serving: About 542 calories, 19g protein, 50g carbohydrate, 29g fat, 4g fiber, 51mg cholesterol, 1324mg sodium

Take a Wok on the Wild Side ▼

The genius behind wok cooking is that the stir-fry technique can cook a gigantic variety of foods quickly and efficiently. In addition to cooking quickly, stir-frying also yields deliciously vibrant colored dishes! Another excellent thing about stir-frying is that even the most inexperienced cook will have great results.

What Type of Wok Should I Buy?

Woks are generally made of carbon steel or aluminum because of its excellent heat conductivity. A good wok should be heavy and last for years. The new nonstick woks made of these materials are worth checking out since cleaning them is so simple! Electric woks are less desirable than stovetop woks because they are often too shallow and will not achieve the high degree of heat that's necessary for successful stir-fry cooking.

How Do I Season My Wok?

A well-seasoned wok is imperative if you intend to make out-of-this-world stir-fries! Once you have bought a wok, wash it well, then apply a thin layer of vegetable oil to the bottom and sides of the wok. Place the wok over medium-high heat for about 15 seconds. Remove your wok from the heat and wipe it gently with a paper towel.

How Do I Wash It?

Wash your wok in water with a mild detergent, but don't scour it because scouring will ruin the wok's protective coating. After cleaning and drying your wok, place a few drops of oil on the surface of the wok, to further protect it before putting it away.

Get Cooking!

Chop and dice all of your ingredients into identical or similar-sized chunks. Using a sharp knife or a Chinese cleaver, take your time and cut the vegetables into as uniform a shape as you can so that they will cook evenly in the wok. I recommend you place foods, once cut, into small bowls and place them near your cooking surface to allow you to continue chopping. Once everything is chopped, prepare any sauce you may be cooking with, and get cooking.

Think about color when making a stir-fry. Strips of bright orange carrots or bold red peppers offset stir-fried mushrooms. Also consider bold flavors for your sauces. Although you can prepare a stir-fry without a sauce, sauce can transform a stir-fry into something really delicious.
- *Robyn Webb*

For more information, visit **Allrecipes.com**

House-Fried Rice

Submitted by: **Lynda**

"Loaded with shrimp, ham, chicken, and veggies, just like in your favorite Chinese restaurant. This 'House' Fried Rice is delicious and an excellent use of leftovers! Feel free to substitute ingredients, depending on what you have on hand."

1½	cups uncooked white rice	1	cup chopped cooked chicken
3	tablespoons sesame oil	2	stalks celery, chopped
1	small onion, chopped	2	carrots, peeled and diced
1	clove garlic, chopped	1	green bell pepper, chopped
1	cup uncooked small shrimp, peeled and deveined	½	cup green peas
		1	egg, lightly beaten
½	cup cooked diced ham	¼	cup soy sauce

1. Cook rice according to package directions. While rice is cooking, heat a wok or large skillet over medium-high heat. Pour in sesame oil and stir in onion. Fry until golden. Add garlic and cook until lightly browned. Mix in shrimp, ham, and chicken. Fry until shrimp turn pink.

2. Reduce heat to medium and stir in celery, carrot, green pepper, and peas. Fry until vegetables are crisp-tender. Stir in beaten egg and cook just until egg is scrambled and firm.

3. When rice is done, mix thoroughly with vegetables and stir in soy sauce. Adjust seasoning to your preference and serve immediately.

Yield: 8 servings.

Per serving: About 240 calories, 13g protein, 26g carbohydrate, 9g fat, 2g fiber, 63mg cholesterol, 618mg sodium

◄ **Restaurant Fare**

Prep Time: 10 minutes

Cook Time: 30 minutes

Average Rating: ★★★★★

What other cooks have done:

"I love how flexible this recipe is. One night I had only shrimp, the next time chicken. I make a big batch every two weeks and freeze individual portions to eat for lunch. To reheat, just add a teaspoon of water to the rice to ensure it doesn't dry out in the microwave. It reheats very well and goes with many of my favorite lunches!"

Spanish Rice Bake

Submitted by: **Melodie Keaunui**

"Ground beef, fresh onion, green bell pepper, tomatoes, and rice are simmered in a sweet-hot sauce of chili sauce, brown sugar, cumin, and Worcestershire. This savory rice dish is then baked with Cheddar and garnished with fresh cilantro."

Prep Time: 15 minutes

Cook Time: 45 minutes

Average Rating: ★★★★★

What other cooks have done:

"I stirred in a can of tomatoes with mild green chiles for a little extra oomph. I didn't have time to put it in the oven so I just put the cheese on top of the rice mixture in the skillet and covered it until it melted. It saved not only prep time but also cleanup time because I had one less pan to clean!"

1	pound lean ground beef	1	teaspoon salt
½	cup finely chopped onion	1	teaspoon brown sugar
¼	cup chopped green bell pepper	½	teaspoon ground cumin
1	(14.5 ounce) can tomatoes, undrained	½	teaspoon Worcestershire sauce
1	cup water		Pinch ground black pepper
¾	cup uncooked long grain rice	½	cup shredded Cheddar cheese
½	cup chili sauce	2	tablespoons chopped fresh cilantro

1. Preheat oven to 375°F (190°C).

2. Cook the ground beef in a large skillet over medium-high heat until browned. Drain excess fat and transfer beef to a large pot over medium-low heat. Stir in the onion, bell pepper, tomatoes, water, rice, chili sauce, salt, brown sugar, cumin, Worcestershire sauce, and ground black pepper.

3. Let simmer for about 30 minutes, stirring occasionally; transfer to a 2 quart casserole dish. Press down firmly and sprinkle with shredded Cheddar cheese.

4. Bake in the preheated oven for 10 to 15 minutes or until cheese is melted and bubbly. Sprinkle with chopped fresh cilantro. **Yield:** 4 servings.

Per serving: About 527 calories, 28g protein, 38g carbohydrate, 29g fat, 2g fiber, 100mg cholesterol, 910mg sodium

Easy Red Beans and Rice

Submitted by: **Paula**

"Enjoy this easy and delicious take on a Louisiana classic that you can prepare and cook in 40 minutes! I use turkey kielbasa to cut down on the fat, but not the flavor. Season with hot pepper sauce, if you like."

2 cups water	2 (15 ounce) cans kidney beans, drained
1 cup uncooked rice	
1 (16 ounce) package turkey kielbasa, cut diagonally into ¼ inch slices	1 (16 ounce) can whole peeled tomatoes, undrained and chopped
1 onion, chopped	½ teaspoon dried oregano
1 green bell pepper, chopped	Salt to taste
1 clove garlic, chopped	½ teaspoon pepper

1. In a saucepan, bring water to a boil. Add rice and stir. Reduce heat, cover, and simmer for 20 minutes.

2. In a large skillet over low heat, cook sausage for 5 minutes. Stir in onion, bell pepper, and garlic; sauté until tender. Pour in beans and tomatoes with juice. Season with oregano, salt, and pepper. Simmer, uncovered, for 20 minutes. Serve over rice. **Yield:** 8 servings.

Per serving: About 281 calories, 17g protein, 42g carbohydrate, 5g fat, 8g fiber, 37mg cholesterol, 938mg sodium

Coconut Rice

Submitted by: **Sara K.**

"Delicious, simple coconut rice adds an exotic touch to any meal! Especially great with fish such as salmon."

2 cups uncooked long grain rice	¾ cup water
¼ cup diced onion	2 slices fresh ginger root
1½ cups coconut milk	2 teaspoons curry powder
	½ teaspoon salt

1. In a medium saucepan, combine rice, onion, coconut milk, water, ginger, curry powder, and salt. Cover and bring to a boil. Reduce heat and simmer for 20 to 30 minutes or until rice is tender and liquid is absorbed. **Yield:** 8 servings.

Per serving: About 256 calories, 4g protein, 39g carbohydrate, 9g fat, 1g fiber, 0mg cholesterol, 154mg sodium

Prep Time: 5 minutes

Cook Time: 1 hour

Average Rating: ★★★★★

What other cooks have done:

"I cut down on fat by using less butter. I didn't use basil this time and didn't miss it at all. The broth and soup make it taste great anyway, especially with the can of sliced mushrooms that I love to add."

Prep Time: 10 minutes

Cook Time: 40 minutes

Average Rating: ★★★★★

What other cooks have done:

"Impressive! I made this for a dinner party, and it makes way more than four servings! All of it was eaten, though, and everyone thought I was magic or something. I did use skim milk and fat-free half-and-half instead of whole milk and heavy cream, and it was plenty rich and creamy. It's definitely worth the effort if you want to impress a date or dinner guests."

Brown Rice

Submitted by: **Monica**

"Easy enough for people who can't make rice at all, and everyone will love it!"

1½	cups uncooked long-grain white rice	
1	(14 ounce) can beef broth	
1	(10.5 ounce) can condensed French onion soup	
¼	cup butter, melted	
1	tablespoon Worcestershire sauce	
1	tablespoon dried basil	

1. Preheat oven to 350°F (175°C).
2. In a 2 quart casserole dish, combine rice, broth, soup, butter, Worcestershire sauce, and basil.
3. Bake, covered, in the preheated oven for 1 hour, stirring once after 30 minutes. **Yield:** 5 servings.

Per serving: About 340 calories, 7g protein, 53g carbohydrate, 11g fat, 1g fiber, 27mg cholesterol, 901mg sodium

Mushroom Risotto

Submitted by: **Sarah**

"Delicious mushroom risotto made with vegetable broth, cream, and a variety of fresh vegetables. Serve as a side dish or as a filling main course."

1	tablespoon olive oil	1½	cups sliced fresh mushrooms
3	small onions, finely chopped	1	cup whole milk
1	clove garlic, crushed	¼	cup heavy cream
1	teaspoon minced fresh parsley	1	cup uncooked Arborio rice
1	teaspoon minced celery	5	cups vegetable broth
	Salt and pepper to taste	1	teaspoon butter
		1	cup grated Parmesan cheese

1. Heat olive oil in a large skillet over medium-high heat. Sauté the onions and garlic in the olive oil until onion is tender and garlic is lightly browned. Remove garlic and stir in the parsley, celery, salt, and pepper. Cook until celery is tender; add the mushrooms. Reduce heat to low and continue cooking until the mushrooms are soft.
2. Pour the milk and cream into the skillet and stir in the rice. Heat to a simmer. Stir the broth into the rice, 1 cup at a time, until absorbed, about 25 to 30 minutes.
3. When the rice is cooked, stir in the butter and Parmesan cheese and remove from heat. Serve hot. **Yield:** 4 servings.

Per serving: About 445 calories, 18g protein, 49g carbohydrate, 20g fat, 2g fiber, 48mg cholesterol, 859mg sodium

Wild Rice Casserole

Submitted by: **Kathleen Burton**
"Pork sausage, chicken breast, wild rice, and mushrooms flavor this jam-packed meat and rice casserole."

1	pound ground pork sausage
2	skinless, boneless chicken breast halves, chopped
1	onion, chopped
3	cloves garlic, crushed
1	cup chopped celery
3	cups chicken broth
1	(10.75 ounce) can condensed cream of mushroom soup
1	(10.75 ounce) can condensed cream of chicken soup
1	(6 ounce) can sliced mushrooms, drained
1	(6 ounce) package long grain and wild rice mixture
1	(3 ounce) package sliced almonds

1. In a large skillet, combine the sausage, chicken, onion, garlic, and celery. Sauté over medium heat until sausage and chicken are browned and vegetables are tender. Crumble sausage, drain fat from skillet, and return sausage to skillet.
2. Preheat oven to 350°F (175°C).
3. Stir in the chicken broth, cream of mushroom soup, cream of chicken soup, mushrooms, and rice. Mix well and spoon mixture into a lightly greased 9x13 inch baking dish. Sprinkle with almonds.
4. Cover and bake in the preheated oven for 1½ hours or until cooked through. **Yield:** 8 servings.

Per serving: About 508 calories, 21g protein, 28g carbohydrate, 35g fat, 3g fiber, 59mg cholesterol, 1748mg sodium

◄ **Holiday Fare**

Prep Time: 30 minutes

Cook Time: 1 hour 30 minutes

Average Rating: ★★★★★

What other cooks have done:
"I used ground pork instead of sausage because that's what I had on hand, and I used 2 packages of wild rice. Other than those two changes, I left all the same. I stirred occasionally while baking. It turned out great and was very filling. I'll make this again!"

Italian Summer Squash Polenta Bake

Submitted by: **Melissa McGee**

"Fresh summer vegetables paired with creamy polenta baked in an Italian sauce and topped with cheese—delicioso! I recommend serving it with crusty garlic bread."

3	carrots, sliced		Ground black pepper to taste
1	large zucchini, sliced	1	cup spaghetti sauce
1	large yellow squash, sliced	1	(18 ounce) package prepared polenta
1	red onion, chopped		
1	red bell pepper, chopped	1½	cups shredded mozzarella cheese
4	tablespoons olive oil, divided		
	Garlic salt to taste	½	cup grated Parmesan cheese

1. Preheat oven to 350°F (175°C).

2. In a large saucepan, sauté carrots, zucchini, squash, onion, and bell pepper with 2 tablespoons olive oil. Season with garlic salt and pepper. Sauté vegetables 5 minutes; pour in spaghetti sauce. Stir, cover, and simmer until vegetables are slightly tender.

3. Slice polenta into ½ inch circles and season with garlic salt and black pepper. Heat remaining 2 tablespoons oil in a medium skillet. Pan-fry seasoned polenta in hot oil, about 3 minutes per side. Remove from oil and layer the slices in a lightly greased 9x13 inch baking dish. Spoon the vegetable mixture over the polenta and sprinkle with mozzarella and Parmesan cheeses.

4. Bake in the preheated oven for 30 minutes. Remove from oven and let cool for 5 minutes before serving. **Yield:** 6 servings.

Per serving: About 266 calories, 12g protein, 15g carbohydrate, 19g fat, 4g fiber, 28mg cholesterol, 502mg sodium

Soups, Sandwiches & Salads

Apricot Lentil Soup

Submitted by: **Karena**

"Lentil soup with a sweet-tangy twist. This is great with a piece of warm black bread slathered with butter."

Out-of-the-Ordinary ▶

Prep Time: 15 minutes

Cook Time: 50 minutes

Average Rating: ★★★★★

What other cooks have done:

"Wonderful soup—much more interesting than run-of-the-mill lentil soup. I doubled the amount of cumin and added some ancho chili powder to make it a little spicier."

3	tablespoons olive oil	½	teaspoon ground cumin
1	onion, chopped	½	teaspoon dried thyme
2	cloves garlic, minced		Salt and ground black
⅓	cup dried apricots		pepper to taste
1½	cups red lentils	2	tablespoons fresh lemon
5	cups chicken broth		juice
3	roma (plum) tomatoes, peeled, seeded, and chopped		

1. Heat olive oil in a Dutch oven. Sauté onion, garlic, and apricots. Add lentils and broth. Bring to a boil; reduce heat and simmer 30 minutes.

2. Stir in tomatoes, cumin, thyme, and salt and pepper to taste. Simmer for 10 minutes.

3. Stir in lemon juice. Puree half of the soup in a blender, then return to Dutch oven and heat through. **Yield:** 6 servings.

Per serving: About 281 calories, 16g protein, 37g carbohydrate, 9g fat, 16g fiber, 0mg cholesterol, 843mg sodium

Bachelor's Creamy Pumpkin Soup

Submitted by: **Katherine1971**

"Pumpkin a pain? This scrumptious and hearty soup is perfect for those reluctant to tackle cumbersome fresh pumpkin."

Holiday Fare ▶

Prep Time: 5 minutes

Cook Time: 20 minutes

Average Rating: ★★★★☆

What other cooks have done:

"Made a sample batch before serving for Thanksgiving dinner. I liked it and added it to my Thanksgiving Day menu. Thoroughly enjoyed by all, even those who do not like pumpkin. Will surely make it again, even just for my husband and myself."

1	(10.75 ounce) can condensed cream of potato soup	1	teaspoon salt
		¼	teaspoon ground black pepper
1¼	cups water	½	teaspoon garlic powder
1	(15 ounce) can pumpkin	½	teaspoon ground ginger
2	tablespoons butter		Garnishes: paprika, seasoned
1	cup whipping cream		croutons

1. In a saucepan over medium heat, combine soup, water, pumpkin, butter, and cream. Season with salt, pepper, garlic powder, and ginger. Stir until blended and bring to a simmer. Reduce heat to low and simmer for 15 minutes.

2. Remove from heat and pour into a tureen. Garnish, if desired. **Yield:** 6 servings.

Per serving: About 268 calories, 3g protein, 18g carbohydrate, 22g fat, 3g fiber, 69mg cholesterol, 1081mg sodium

Cream of Cauliflower Soup II

Submitted by: **Vivien**

"I always make some modifications—like add or substitute other vegetables such as broccoli and spinach. But this is a great 'basic' recipe."

2	tablespoons butter	1	cup milk
1	large onion, chopped	1	teaspoon salt
4	cloves garlic, minced	½	teaspoon ground black pepper
2	large potatoes, peeled and cubed	⅛	teaspoon ground nutmeg
2	carrots, chopped	1	tablespoon dry sherry
2	(14.5 ounce) cans chicken broth	1	tablespoon chopped fresh parsley
1	head cauliflower, chopped		

1. In a large pot over medium heat, melt butter. Stir in onion and garlic and cook until onion is translucent, about 5 minutes. Stir in potatoes and carrots and cook 5 more minutes. Add chicken broth and bring to a boil. Stir in cauliflower. Cover, reduce heat, and simmer until vegetables are tender, 10 to 20 minutes. Remove from heat.
2. Puree in batches in a blender or food processor, or in the pot using an immersion blender. Return to low heat and stir in milk, salt, pepper, nutmeg, and sherry. Heat through. Sprinkle with parsley.
Yield: 6 servings.

Per serving: About 165 calories, 6g protein, 23g carbohydrate, 6g fat, 4g fiber, 14mg cholesterol, 1076mg sodium

Red Pepper Soup

Submitted by: **Judi**

"This light and creamy soup will surprise those who didn't realize they were pepper lovers at heart. Serve with a dollop of sour cream, if desired."

2	tablespoons butter	3	cups chicken broth
4	red bell peppers, chopped	½	cup whipping cream
1	onion, chopped	⅛	teaspoon ground black pepper
4	cloves garlic, minced		

1. Melt the butter in a large saucepan over medium heat. Place the bell peppers, onion, and garlic in the saucepan and sauté for 5 to 10 minutes or until tender.
2. Pour in the chicken broth, stirring well; reduce heat to low and simmer for 30 minutes. Transfer to a blender and puree until smooth.
3. Strain soup and return the liquid to the saucepan over medium-low heat; discard solids. Stir in the whipping cream and the ground black pepper and heat through, about 5 to 10 minutes. **Yield:** 5 servings.

Per serving: About 184 calories, 5g protein, 10g carbohydrate, 15g fat, 2g fiber, 45mg cholesterol, 517mg sodium

Apple-Bacon-Tomato Soup

Submitted by: **Jennifer Fey**

"Warm and soothing in the winter. By the second day the apples have infused the soup—so tasty! Wonderful with mozzarella cheese on top."

5	slices bacon	2	stalks celery, chopped
1	tablespoon olive oil	1	bay leaf
½	onion, chopped	1	medium apple, thinly sliced
2	teaspoons minced garlic	½	cup red wine
2	cups beef stock		Salt and ground black
1	(15.5 ounce) can pinto beans		pepper to taste
1	(14.5 ounce) can Italian-style stewed tomatoes		

1. Place bacon in a large, deep skillet. Cook over medium–high heat until evenly browned. Drain, coarsely chop, and set aside.
2. Heat olive oil in a large saucepan over medium heat and sauté onion and garlic 3 to 5 minutes or until tender. Stir in beef stock, pinto beans, tomatoes, celery, and bay leaf. Bring the mixture to a boil. Reduce heat and simmer for 5 minutes.
3. In a small saucepan over medium heat, cook apple in red wine until soft, stirring constantly.
4. Mix reserved bacon, apple, and red wine into the soup mixture. Season with salt and pepper to taste. Continue to simmer, stirring occasionally, until well blended. Discard bay leaf. **Yield:** 8 servings.

Per serving: About 211 calories, 6g protein, 17g carbohydrate, 13g fat, 4g fiber, 12mg cholesterol, 429mg sodium

Catherine's Spicy Chicken Soup

Submitted by: **Catherine**

"The longer this soup simmers, the better. Top with tortilla chips and cheese."

2	quarts water	2	(14.5 ounce) cans peeled, diced tomatoes
8	skinless, boneless chicken breast halves	1	(14.5 ounce) can whole, peeled tomatoes
½	teaspoon salt	1	(10.75 ounce) can condensed tomato soup
1	teaspoon ground black pepper		
1	teaspoon garlic powder	3	tablespoons chili powder
2	tablespoons dried parsley	1	(15 ounce) can whole kernel corn, drained
1	tablespoon onion powder		
5	chicken bouillon cubes	2	(16 ounce) cans chili beans, undrained
3	tablespoons olive oil		
1	onion, chopped	1	(8 ounce) container sour cream
3	cloves garlic, chopped		
1	(16 ounce) jar chunky salsa		

1. In a large pot over medium heat, combine water, chicken, salt, pepper, garlic powder, parsley, onion powder, and bouillon cubes. Bring to a boil, then reduce heat and simmer 1 hour or until chicken is done and juices run clear. Remove chicken, reserving broth. Shred chicken.

2. Heat olive oil in a large pot over medium heat and cook onion and garlic in olive oil until slightly browned. Stir in salsa, diced tomatoes, whole tomatoes, tomato soup, chili powder, corn, chili beans, sour cream, shredded chicken, and 5 cups reserved broth. Simmer 30 minutes. **Yield:** 8 servings.

Per serving: About 474 calories, 40g protein, 50g carbohydrate, 15g fat, 10g fiber, 82mg cholesterol, 2302mg sodium

Avocado Soup with Chicken and Lime

Submitted by: **Michelle**
"Thin strips of chicken breast are simmered in broth with jalapeños, onion, garlic, and lime and then combined with avocado and topped with crisp corn tortilla strips in this spicy soup."

4	(6 inch) corn tortillas, julienned
1½	tablespoons olive oil
1	onion, thinly sliced
8	cloves garlic, thinly sliced
4	jalapeño peppers, sliced
8	ounces skinless, boneless chicken breast halves, cut into thin strips
1	quart chicken broth
¼	cup fresh lime juice
1	tomato, seeded and diced
	Salt and ground black pepper to taste
1	avocado, peeled, pitted, and diced
¼	cup chopped fresh cilantro

1. Preheat oven to 400°F (200°C).
2. Arrange tortilla strips on a baking sheet and bake in the preheated oven 3 to 5 minutes or until lightly browned.
3. Heat olive oil in a large saucepan over medium heat; cook onion, garlic, and jalapeños in olive oil 4 to 5 minutes or until lightly browned. Stir in chicken, chicken broth, lime juice, tomato, and salt and pepper to taste. Gently simmer until chicken is cooked, 3 to 5 minutes. Stir in avocado and cilantro and heat through.
4. To serve, ladle soup into bowls and sprinkle with tortilla strips.
Yield: 4 servings.

Per serving: About 312 calories, 19g protein, 25g carbohydrate, 16g fat, 5g fiber, 33mg cholesterol, 1084mg sodium

◀ Hot & Spicy

Prep Time: 10 minutes

Cook Time: 20 minutes

Average Rating: ★★★★☆

What other cooks have done:
"Fantastic! I loved the lime juice in this soup—it gave it a nice tang. It was very filling, but light so you can have it any day of the week. I like more avocado so I used 2 instead of 1½. I also added a dollop of sour cream at the end, and it gave the soup a rich flavor. Will definitely make this again."

Black Bean Vegetable Soup

Submitted by: **DeeDee**

"Half of the black beans in this spicy soup are pureed with tomatoes, the other half are simmered with the carrots, onion, and corn."

1	tablespoon vegetable oil	¼	teaspoon ground black pepper
1	onion, chopped		
1	clove garlic, minced	2	(15 ounce) cans black beans, rinsed and drained
2	carrots, chopped		
2	teaspoons chili powder	1	(14.5 ounce) can stewed tomatoes, undrained
1	teaspoon ground cumin		
4	cups vegetable broth		
1	(8.75 ounce) can whole kernel corn		

1. In large saucepan, heat oil over medium heat; cook onion, garlic, and carrots, stirring occasionally, for 5 minutes or until onion is softened. Add chili powder and cumin; cook, stirring, for 1 minute. Add broth, corn, pepper, and 1 can of the beans; bring to a boil.

2. In a food processor or blender, puree tomatoes and remaining can of beans; add to pot. Reduce heat, cover, and simmer for 10 to 15 minutes or until carrots are tender. **Yield:** 8 servings.

Per serving: About 166 calories, 8g protein, 27g carbohydrate, 3g fat, 8g fiber, 0mg cholesterol, 651mg sodium

Absolutely Ultimate Potato Soup *(pictured on page 228)*

Submitted by: **Karena**

"I've made this for many who have given it the title. This takes a bit of effort but is well worth it. For those who do not wish to use bacon, substitute ¼ cup melted butter for the bacon grease and continue with the recipe. I generally serve this soup as a special treat because it's not recommended for people counting calories."

1	pound bacon, chopped	¼	cup all-purpose flour
2	stalks celery, diced	1	cup whipping cream
1	onion, chopped	1	teaspoon dried tarragon
3	cloves garlic, minced	¾	teaspoon salt
8	potatoes, peeled and cubed	½	teaspoon ground black pepper
4	cups chicken broth or enough to cover potatoes	1	tablespoon chopped fresh cilantro
3	tablespoons butter		

1. In a Dutch oven, cook bacon over medium heat until done. Remove bacon from pan; crumble ½ cup bacon, and set aside. Drain bacon drippings, reserving ¼ cup drippings in Dutch oven.

Prep Time: 15 minutes

Cook Time: 35 minutes

Average Rating: ★★★★★

What other cooks have done:

"Really good recipe that turns out well. I thought that the recipe could use a bit more 'oomph,' so I used more chili powder and cumin, but this is a great comfort food recipe. Also, I find that cooking it a bit longer makes it thicker, which I like."

Prep Time: 10 minutes

Cook Time: 30 minutes

Average Rating: ★★★★★

What other cooks have done:

"This is the best potato soup I've ever had. I used 6 inch sourdough rolls as bread bowls. There's just something awesome about eating the bowl."

2. In drippings in the pan, sauté the celery and onion until onion begins to turn clear. Add garlic and continue cooking for 1 to 2 minutes. Add cubed potatoes and toss to coat. Sauté for 3 to 4 minutes. Crumble remaining bacon and add to pan along with enough chicken broth to just cover the potatoes. Cover and simmer until potatoes are tender.

3. In a separate saucepan, melt butter over medium heat. Whisk in flour and cook, stirring constantly, for 1 to 2 minutes. Whisk in cream and tarragon. Bring the cream mixture to a boil and cook, stirring constantly, until thickened. Stir the cream mixture into the potato mixture. Puree about half of soup and return to the pan. Add salt, pepper, and cilantro. Sprinkle with crumbled ½ cup bacon. **Yield:** 8 servings.

Per serving: About 582 calories, 9g protein, 28g carbohydrate, 48g fat, 4g fiber, 91mg cholesterol, 830mg sodium

Avgolemono

Submitted by: **Michelle Chen**

"The most popular of Greek soups. The name means 'egg and lemon,' the two most important ingredients in the soup. Orzo is a rice-shaped pasta, but you can use any small shape. Do not let soup boil once the eggs have been added or it will curdle!"

7	cups chicken broth	1	tablespoon cold water
½	cup uncooked orzo pasta		Salt and ground black
3	eggs		pepper to taste
1	lemon, juiced		Garnish: lemon slices

1. Pour chicken broth into a large saucepan and bring to a boil. Add pasta and cook for 5 minutes.

2. Beat eggs until frothy, then add lemon juice and cold water. Slowly stir in a ladleful of the hot chicken stock, then stir in another ¼ cup of hot stock, being careful not to scramble the eggs.

3. Return mixture to the pan. Immediately remove pan from heat and stir well. Season soup with salt and pepper to taste and serve at once. Garnish, if desired. **Yield:** 4 servings.

Per serving: About 204 calories, 12g protein, 24g carbohydrate, 8g fat, 2g fiber, 159mg cholesterol, 1788mg sodium

◀ **Around-the-World Cuisine**

Prep Time: 10 minutes

Cook Time: 15 minutes

Average Rating: ★★★★☆

What other cooks have done:

"I love this soup, being Greek, and I've eaten it since I was a child. In Greece, we usually use rice instead of pasta. My family likes to sprinkle a bit of cinnamon on top, which gives it a nice taste."

Prep Time: 15 minutes

Cook Time: 25 minutes

Average Rating: ★★★★★

What other cooks have done:

"Fabulous soup and so quick and easy to make! I did, however, add a bit too much hot pepper sauce so it was very spicy. I would say 4 or 5 dashes would be plenty, and let people season it after that as they please. Also, I omitted the salt altogether because there's plenty in the tomato and clam juices."

Prep Time: 10 minutes

Cook Time: 25 minutes

Average Rating: ★★★★★

What other cooks have done:

"Yummy! We really liked this soup. We didn't have any cheese, and we replaced the half-and-half with non-fat plain yogurt. Still tasted great and without all the calories and fat!"

Big Ed's Cajun Shrimp Soup

Submitted by: **Eddie**
"This is an excellent recipe that's quick and easy, and it tastes great, too!"

1	tablespoon butter	¼	teaspoon dried basil
½	cup chopped green bell pepper	¼	teaspoon red pepper flakes
¼	cup sliced green onions	1	bay leaf
1	clove garlic, minced	½	teaspoon salt
3	cups tomato-vegetable juice cocktail	½	cup uncooked long-grain white rice
1	(8 ounce) bottle clam juice	¾	pound uncooked fresh shrimp, peeled and deveined
½	cup water		
¼	teaspoon dried thyme		Hot pepper sauce to taste

1. Melt butter in a large pot over medium heat. Sauté green pepper, onions, and garlic until tender. Stir in vegetable juice, clam juice, and water. Season with thyme, basil, red pepper, bay leaf, and salt. Bring to a boil and stir in rice. Reduce heat, cover, and simmer 15 minutes or until rice is tender.
2. Stir in shrimp and cook 3 to 5 minutes or until shrimp turn pink. Discard bay leaf and season soup with hot sauce. **Yield:** 6 servings.

Per serving: About 163 calories, 14g protein, 20g carbohydrate, 3g fat, 1g fiber, 93mg cholesterol, 728mg sodium

Colorful Corn Chowder

Submitted by: **Margo Collins**
"Was rated delicious by my children, ages 6 to 11! Plus this is an easy meal."

2	tablespoons butter	¼	teaspoon ground black pepper
1	large onion, chopped		
1	green bell pepper, chopped	¼	teaspoon ground cayenne pepper
1	red bell pepper, chopped		
2	carrots, chopped	3	cups water
2	(10 ounce) packages frozen corn kernels, thawed	2	cups milk
		1	cup half-and-half
1½	cups dry potato flakes	½	cup shredded Cheddar cheese
2	teaspoons salt		

1. In a large saucepan over medium-high heat, melt butter. Cook onion, bell peppers, and carrots until tender.
2. Stir in corn, potato flakes, salt, black pepper, cayenne pepper, and water. Bring to a boil. Reduce heat, cover, and simmer for 10 minutes.
3. Stir in milk and half-and-half. Warm through, being careful not to boil. Sprinkle with Cheddar cheese before serving. **Yield:** 10 servings.

Per serving: About 192 calories, 7g protein, 25g carbohydrate, 9g fat, 3g fiber, 25mg cholesterol, 575mg sodium

Newport Clam Chowder

Submitted by: **Dee**

"Outstanding! This won a chowder cook-off in Newport, Rhode Island, a few years ago. Try it; I guarantee it gets rave reviews!"

½	cup butter	3	cups half-and-half
1½	large onions, chopped		Salt and ground black pepper to taste
¾	cup all-purpose flour		
1	quart shucked clams, with liquid	½	teaspoon chopped fresh dill weed
6	(8 ounce) bottles clam juice		
1	pound potatoes, peeled and chopped		

1. Melt butter in a large skillet over medium heat. Add onions and sauté until translucent. Stir in flour and cook over low heat, stirring frequently, for 2 to 4 minutes. Set aside to cool.

2. In a medium pot, bring clams and clam juice to a boil. Reduce heat and simmer for 15 minutes.

3. In a small saucepan, cover potatoes with water. Bring to a boil and cook until potatoes are tender, about 15 minutes. Drain and set aside.

4. Slowly pour hot clam stock into flour mixture, stirring constantly. Continue stirring and slowly bring to a boil. Reduce heat and add cooked potatoes. Mix in half-and-half, salt and pepper to taste, and chopped dill. Heat through but do not boil. **Yield:** 8 servings.

Per serving: About 337 calories, 9g protein, 26g carbohydrate, 22g fat, 2g fiber, 79mg cholesterol, 662mg sodium

◄ **Blue Ribbon Winner**

Prep Time: 30 minutes

Cook Time: 40 minutes

Average Rating: ★★★★★

What other cooks have done:

"I've tried making clam chowder using many different recipes, but this is the best recipe I've ever used. From now on, it's the only recipe for clam chowder I'll use. I substituted fat-free half-and-half, and it was still wonderful."

Chicken Stew with Pepper and Pineapple

Submitted by: **Corwynn Darkholme**

"A sweet and savory stew that's best served over mounds of hot cooked rice— try basmati rice for best results."

1	skinless, boneless chicken breast half, cut into cubes	2	tablespoons soy sauce
4	cups carrots, cut into 1 inch pieces	½	teaspoon ground allspice
½	cup chicken broth	½	teaspoon hot pepper sauce
1	tablespoon minced fresh ginger root	1	tablespoon cornstarch
1	tablespoon packed brown sugar	1	(8 ounce) can pineapple chunks, juice reserved
		1	red bell pepper, diced

1. Mix chicken, carrots, broth, ginger root, brown sugar, soy sauce, allspice, and pepper sauce in a 1½ to 4 quart slow cooker. Cover and cook on High for 1 hour and Low for 5 to 7 hours or until vegetables are tender.

2. Mix cornstarch and reserved pineapple juice; gradually stir into chicken mixture. Stir in pineapple and bell pepper. Cover and cook on High for about 15 minutes or until slightly thickened and bubbly. **Yield:** 4 servings.

Per serving: About 158 calories, 10g protein, 29g carbohydrate, 1g fat, 5g fiber, 17mg cholesterol, 633mg sodium

Jamaican Me Crazy Chili

Submitted by: **Marianne**

"A Caribbean twist to a great wintertime dish! This can be prepared without meat—just omit the steps with ground beef. Serve the chili by itself or over basmati rice."

1½	pounds ground round	2	(14.5 ounce) cans stewed tomatoes
1	teaspoon olive oil	1	(15 ounce) can kidney beans, drained
1½	cups chopped onion		
2	cloves garlic, crushed	1	(15 ounce) can black beans, drained
2½	cups chopped yellow bell pepper	1	(15 ounce) can cannellini beans
1	tablespoon ground cumin		
1	tablespoon hot paprika	1	(6 ounce) can tomato paste
1	tablespoon chili powder	2	tablespoons balsamic vinegar
2	teaspoons white sugar		
½	teaspoon salt	⅓	cup chopped fresh cilantro
¼	teaspoon ground cloves		

1. Cook ground round in a large, deep skillet over medium-high heat until evenly browned. Drain and set aside. Coat a large Dutch oven with cooking spray and place over medium-high heat. When pan is hot, add the olive oil and sauté the onion and garlic until the onion is tender. Add bell pepper and cook until tender. Season with cumin, paprika, chili powder, sugar, salt, and cloves. Stir in the stewed tomatoes, kidney beans, black beans, and cannellini beans. Add water to cover. Bring to a boil and stir in ground round and tomato paste. Bring to a boil and simmer for 30 minutes.

2. Remove from heat and stir in the vinegar. Serve chili hot, topped with fresh cilantro. **Yield:** 12 servings.

Per serving: About 259 calories, 18g protein, 29g carbohydrate, 8g fat, 8g fiber, 40mg cholesterol, 730mg sodium

Michelle's Blonde Chicken Chili

Submitted by: **Marshmom**

"People who have tasted this thick mix of beans, spices, and chicken say: 'So good it'll make you perky and stupid!' I've placed in the annual Halloween chili cook-off at work for the last three years. Looks strange but tastes great! Serve with shredded Monterey Jack cheese and warm flour tortillas."

1	tablespoon vegetable oil	1	tablespoon garlic powder
3	pounds skinless, boneless chicken breasts, cubed	1	tablespoon ground cumin
1	cup chopped onion	1	tablespoon dried oregano
2	cups chicken broth	2	teaspoons chopped fresh cilantro
2	(4.5 ounce) cans chopped green chiles	1	teaspoon crushed red pepper flakes
5	(14.5 ounce) cans great Northern beans, undrained and divided		

1. In a large skillet over medium-high heat, heat the vegetable oil. Cook chicken, stirring occasionally, until all pieces are evenly browned. Stir in onion and cook until translucent. Drain mixture and set aside.

2. In a large saucepan over medium heat, bring the chicken broth and green chiles to a boil. Stir in 3 cans great Northern beans, garlic powder, cumin, oregano, cilantro, and crushed red pepper. Stir in the chicken and onion mixture and reduce heat. Simmer 30 minutes, adding more beans from the remaining 2 cans for desired consistency. **Yield:** 10 servings.

Per serving: About 418 calories, 48g protein, 47g carbohydrate, 5g fat, 11g fiber, 79mg cholesterol, 561mg sodium

◀ Out-of-the-Ordinary

Prep Time: 30 minutes

Cook Time: 35 minutes

Average Rating: ★★★★★

What other cooks have done:

"This is great chicken chili! I added two cans of white corn (drained), and it was even better. Highly recommended!"

Basil Pesto Sunshine Sandwich

Submitted by: **Erin Rowland**
"You'll never forget this sandwich. Two kinds of pesto are spread on focaccia, which is then piled high with roasted red peppers, feta cheese, and basil."

2 tablespoons mayonnaise	½ cup roasted red peppers
4 teaspoons basil pesto	1 cup crumbled feta cheese
2 slices focaccia bread, cut in half horizontally	1 cup fresh basil leaves
¼ cup sun-dried tomato pesto	

1. In a small bowl, mix together mayonnaise and basil pesto; spread on top halves of bread. Spread sun-dried tomato pesto on bottom halves of bread. Arrange roasted red peppers on bottom halves. Cover with feta cheese, then fresh basil. Top with top halves of bread. **Yield:** 2 servings.

Per serving: About 751 calories, 28g protein, 38g carbohydrate, 52g fat, 4g fiber, 126mg cholesterol, 2272mg sodium

Eggplant and Pepper Parmesan Sandwiches

Submitted by: **Marlena**
"Smoky grilled veggies, rich tapenade, and tangy goat cheese make these sandwiches hearty and satisfying."

1 eggplant, seeded and cut lengthwise into ¼ inch slices	1 French baguette
1 red bell pepper, sliced into thin strips	2 ounces soft goat cheese
Salt and ground black pepper to taste	¼ cup tapenade
	¼ cup grated Parmesan cheese

1. Preheat the broiler.
2. Place eggplant and red bell pepper on a baking sheet and season with salt and pepper to taste. Broil 5 to 10 minutes or until tender and slightly browned.
3. Cut baguette in half lengthwise. Spread bottom half with goat cheese, then with tapenade. Layer with eggplant and red pepper, then sprinkle with Parmesan cheese. Cover with top half of baguette. Cut into 4 pieces. Serve warm or cold. **Yield:** 4 servings.

Per serving: About 447 calories, 17g protein, 70g carbohydrate, 11g fat, 7g fiber, 12mg cholesterol, 1090mg sodium

Bulgur Chickpea Salad,
page 240

Reuben Sandwich II, page 234

California Grilled Veggie Sandwich, page 229

Summer Corn Salad, page 236

Absolutely Ultimate Potato Soup, page 218,
and Mama's Best Broiled Tomato Sandwich, page 230

California Grilled Veggie Sandwich *(pictured on page 227)*

Submitted by: **Heather Johnson**
"The first time I made this, my meat-lover friends raved!"

¼ cup mayonnaise	1 red onion, sliced
3 cloves garlic, minced	1 small yellow squash, cut into ½ inch thick strips
1 tablespoon lemon juice	
2 tablespoons olive oil	1 (1 pound) loaf focaccia bread
1 cup sliced red bell pepper	
1 small zucchini, sliced	½ cup crumbled feta cheese

1. Combine mayonnaise, minced garlic, and lemon juice. Chill.
2. Lightly oil grill rack and preheat grill for high heat.
3. Brush vegetables with olive oil. Place bell pepper and zucchini pieces closest to the middle of the grill and surround with onion and squash pieces. Cook for about 3 minutes on each side. Set aside.
4. Cut focaccia in half horizontally. Spread bottom half with mayonnaise mixture. Layer with grilled vegetables and sprinkle with feta. Top with other focaccia half. Grill 2 minutes or until feta is slightly melted. Cut into 4 wedges and serve warm. **Yield:** 4 servings.

Per serving: About 546 calories, 14g protein, 65g carbohydrate, 26g fat, 5g fiber, 25mg cholesterol, 953mg sodium

---

◄ From the Grill

Prep Time: 30 minutes
Cook Time: 8 minutes
Average Rating: ★★★★★
What other cooks have done:
"Absolutely delicious! One serving filled me up. We grilled the veggies on an aluminum foil platter sprayed with olive oil and it worked great. We grilled them for 7 minutes on each side to make sure the onions were soft and a bit caramelized."

Mediterranean Vegetable Sandwich

Submitted by: **Chris M.**
"Roasted vegetables taste delicious in this sandwich. It's great for picnics!"

1 eggplant, sliced into strips	3 cloves garlic, crushed
2 red bell peppers	¼ cup mayonnaise
2 tablespoons olive oil, divided	1 (1 pound) loaf focaccia bread
2 portobello mushrooms, sliced	

1. Preheat oven to 400°F (200°C).
2. Brush eggplant and red bell peppers with 1 tablespoon olive oil. Place on a baking sheet and roast in preheated oven about 25 minutes or until eggplant is tender and peppers blacken. Set aside.
3. Heat remaining 1 tablespoon olive oil and sauté mushrooms until tender. Stir crushed garlic into mayonnaise. Slice focaccia in half lengthwise. Spread mayonnaise mixture on 1 or both halves.
4. Peel, core, and slice peppers. Arrange eggplant, peppers, and mushrooms on focaccia. Wrap sandwich in plastic wrap; place a cutting board on top of sandwich and weight board down. Allow sandwich to stand for 2 hours before slicing and serving. **Yield:** 6 servings.

Per serving: About 356 calories, 9g protein, 48g carbohydrate, 15g fat, 6g fiber, 5mg cholesterol, 500mg sodium

---

◄ Make-Ahead

Prep Time: 20 minutes
Cook Time: 30 minutes
Stand Time: 2 hours
Average Rating: ★★★★★
What other cooks have done:
"This sandwich was worth every minute it took to prepare it. My husband especially loved it. The only change I would make would be to add fresh spinach leaves between the vegetables and the bread so that the bread doesn't get soggy. I intend to try this with feta cheese next time and perhaps add some grilled red onion. This is a wonderful sandwich for a picnic."

(pictured on page 228)

Mama's Best Broiled Tomato Sandwich

(pictured on page 228)

Submitted by: **Kat**
"A broiled sandwich made with in-season tomatoes with an Italian accent. A perfect match for soup."

2 tablespoons olive oil	¼ teaspoon dried oregano
2 tablespoons balsamic vinegar	¼ teaspoon ground black pepper
4 ripe tomatoes, sliced	3 tablespoons grated Parmesan cheese
3 tablespoons mayonnaise	4 slices bread, lightly toasted
½ teaspoon dried parsley	

1. Preheat the broiler.
2. In a shallow bowl, whisk together olive oil and vinegar. Marinate tomatoes in the mixture for at least 10 minutes, stirring occasionally.
3. In a small bowl, combine mayonnaise, parsley, oregano, pepper, and half the Parmesan cheese. Spread mixture on each slice of toasted bread. Divide marinated tomatoes evenly between 2 slices and sprinkle with remaining Parmesan cheese.
4. Place on a baking sheet and broil for 5 minutes or until cheese turns golden brown. Serve immediately, open faced or closed. **Yield:** 2 servings.

Per serving: About 512 calories, 10g protein, 43g carbohydrate, 35g fat, 5g fiber, 19mg cholesterol, 559mg sodium

Real N'awlins Muffuletta

Submitted by: **Boo**
"The spicy, tangy olive salad is what really sets this meat and cheese sandwich apart. Consider doubling the recipe so you'll have extra olive salad waiting around for when you get another muffuletta craving."

1 cup pimento-stuffed green olives, crushed	¾ teaspoon ground black pepper
½ cup kalamata olives, drained and crushed	¼ cup red wine vinegar
2 cloves garlic, minced	½ cup olive oil
¼ cup pickled cauliflower florets, roughly chopped	¼ cup canola oil
2 tablespoons capers	2 (1 pound) loaves Italian bread
1 tablespoon chopped celery	8 ounces thinly sliced Genoa salami
1 tablespoon chopped carrot	8 ounces thinly sliced cooked ham
½ cup pepperoncini, drained	
¼ cup cocktail onions	8 ounces sliced mortadella
½ teaspoon celery seed	8 ounces sliced mozzarella
1 teaspoon dried oregano	8 ounces sliced provolone
1 teaspoon dried basil	

Quick & Easy ▶

Prep Time: 20 minutes

Cook Time: 5 minutes

Average Rating: ★★★★

What other cooks have done:

"Delicious! The mayo sauce added a great touch and the vinegar/olive oil mixture on the tomatoes was fantastic. I added a bit of mozzarella cheese on top before grilling and it was very nice. I'll make this again."

Restaurant Fare ▶

Prep Time: 40 minutes

Average Rating: ★★★★

What other cooks have done:

"Great muffuletta. I used red onion instead of the pickled onions and omitted the vegetable oil. I used only olive oil. It turned out great! Totally authentic. You'll think you're in the Big Easy!"

1. In a medium bowl, combine green olives, kalamata olives, garlic, cauliflower, capers, celery, carrot, pepperoncini, cocktail onions, celery seed, oregano, basil, black pepper, vinegar, olive oil, and canola oil. Mix together and transfer mixture to a glass jar. If needed, pour in more oil to cover. Cover jar or container and refrigerate olive salad at least 8 hours or overnight.

2. Cut loaves of bread in half horizontally; hollow out some of the excess bread to make room for filling. Layer bottom half of each loaf with equal amounts of olive salad, including oil. Top each loaf with half each of the salami, ham, mortadella, mozzarella, and provolone. Replace top half on each loaf and cut each sandwich into quarters.

3. Serve immediately or wrap tightly and refrigerate for a few hours. **Yield:** 8 servings.

Per serving: About 1020 calories, 44g protein, 63g carbohydrate, 65g fat, 4g fiber, 100mg cholesterol, 3127mg sodium

Italian Grilled Cheese Sandwiches

Submitted by: **NYCDAVE**

"I came up with this recipe for my niece. I combined grilled cheese sandwiches with garlic bread. It's tasty, quick, and the perfect appetizer for friends, family, and unexpected guests. Use a firm white bread for best results."

12 slices white bread	1 teaspoon dried oregano
1 (8 ounce) package shredded mozzarella cheese	1 (24 ounce) jar marinara sauce
¼ cup unsalted butter	
⅛ teaspoon garlic powder (optional)	

1. Preheat the broiler.

2. Place 6 slices of bread on a baking sheet. Spread a small handful of mozzarella cheese over each slice. Top with the remaining 6 slices of bread. Mix together butter and garlic powder, if desired, and brush half of butter mixture over the tops of the sandwiches. Sprinkle with dried oregano.

3. Broil sandwiches for 2 to 3 minutes or until golden brown. Remove from oven, flip sandwiches, and brush the other sides with butter mixture; sprinkle with oregano. Return to the broiler and cook until golden, about 2 minutes.

4. Cut sandwiches in half diagonally and serve immediately with marinara sauce for dipping. **Yield:** 6 servings.

Per serving: About 361 calories, 15g protein, 35g carbohydrate, 18g fat, 3g fiber, 43mg cholesterol, 906mg sodium

◀ **Family Favorite**

Prep Time: 8 minutes

Cook Time: 5 minutes

Average Rating: ★★★★★

What other cooks have done:

"Marinara dipping sauce! What a great idea. Bet'cha can't eat just one. Just for fun, I tucked in thinly sliced onion rings and tomatoes between slices of bread (in addition to the cheese, of course). Everyone loved it."

Darra's Famous Tuna Waldorf Salad Sandwich Filling

Submitted by: **Darra Mangahas**
"Tired of boring tuna salad? You'll love this one!"

½	cup mayonnaise	1	Granny Smith apple, cored and diced
1	tablespoon prepared Dijon-style mustard	¼	cup chopped walnuts
¼	teaspoon curry powder	½	cup diced celery
	Salt and ground black pepper to taste	1	teaspoon sweet pickle relish
1	(6 ounce) can oil-packed tuna, drained	4	large croissants
		4	leaves lettuce
1	shallot, finely chopped	4	slices Swiss cheese

1. In a medium bowl, whisk together mayonnaise, mustard, curry powder, and salt and pepper to taste. Add tuna, shallot, apple, walnuts, celery, and pickle relish and toss until all ingredients are coated with dressing.
2. Lightly toast the croissants. Split in half, place a lettuce leaf on the bottom halves of croissants, and fill with tuna salad. Top with a slice of Swiss cheese and the top halves of croissants. **Yield:** 4 servings.

Per serving: About 737 calories, 27g protein, 42g carbohydrate, 52g fat, 4g fiber, 100mg cholesterol, 1021mg sodium

Pita Chicken

Submitted by: **Kim Fliehmann**
"Kinda like a fajita sandwich. Great with a green salad. Enjoy!"

2	skinless, boneless chicken breasts	¼	teaspoon cayenne pepper
1	tablespoon olive oil	¼	cup salsa
¼	teaspoon garlic powder	2	pita bread rounds
¼	teaspoon onion powder	8	ounces diced tomato
¼	teaspoon salt	1	cup shredded lettuce
¼	teaspoon ground black pepper	½	cup sliced avocado
		1	(8 ounce) container low-fat sour cream

1. Cut chicken into strips. In a skillet, sauté chicken in hot oil until almost done. Sprinkle garlic powder, onion powder, salt, pepper, and cayenne pepper over chicken. Add salsa and simmer until chicken is done, about 5 minutes.
2. Split pitas in half, fill with chicken, and top with tomato, lettuce, avocado, and sour cream. **Yield:** 2 servings.

Per serving: About 607 calories, 38g protein, 50g carbohydrate, 29g fat, 5g fiber, 112mg cholesterol, 886mg sodium

Philly Steak Sandwich

Submitted by: **Wendy L.**
"I buy steak that has been sliced for making stir-fry, which takes a little less time, but achieves the same results."

½ teaspoon salt
½ teaspoon ground black pepper
½ teaspoon paprika
½ teaspoon chili powder
½ teaspoon onion powder
½ teaspoon garlic powder
½ teaspoon dried thyme
½ teaspoon dried marjoram
½ teaspoon dried basil

1 pound beef sirloin, thinly sliced into 2 inch strips
3 tablespoons vegetable oil, divided
1 onion, sliced
1 green bell pepper, julienned
4 hoagie rolls, split lengthwise
3 ounces Swiss cheese, thinly sliced

1. In a small bowl, mix together salt, pepper, paprika, chili powder, onion powder, garlic powder, thyme, marjoram, and basil. Sprinkle over beef.
2. Heat 1½ tablespoons oil in a skillet over medium-high heat. Sauté beef to desired doneness and remove from pan. Heat the remaining oil in the skillet and sauté onion and green pepper.
3. Preheat broiler.
4. Divide the meat among the bottoms of 4 rolls, layer with onion and green pepper, then top with sliced cheese. Place on a baking sheet and broil until cheese is melted. Cover with tops of rolls and serve. **Yield:** 4 servings.

Per serving: About 642 calories, 36g protein, 39g carbohydrate, 38g fat, 3g fiber, 96mg cholesterol, 751mg sodium

◄ **Family Favorite**

Prep Time: 15 minutes
Cook Time: 25 minutes
Average Rating:★★★★★

What other cooks have done:
"You can't get much closer to a real Philly sandwich than this. I used provolone instead of Swiss the second time I made it. That makes a big difference, so I stick to provolone. Don't let all the spices keep you from trying it because it's well worth it. Here's a tip for buying spices: Look in the Mexican food section in grocery stores for little packages of all the spices needed. They're a lot less expensive than some other brands."

Prep Time: 10 minutes

Cook Time: 10 minutes

Average Rating: ★★★★☆

What other cooks have done:

"'Yum' pretty much sums it up. There aren't too many recipes that give you options for using up leftover pork loin— and this one is a winner! If you can shred the pork, the sauce will penetrate the meat better. Great flavor!"

Prep Time: 15 minutes

Cook Time: 15 minutes

Average Rating: ★★★★★

What other cooks have done:

"Just 'built' a couple of these and they're great! The kids don't like the sauerkraut or corned beef, so this is a 'grown-up' sandwich in my house! The sandwiches took only 5 minutes per side. I weighted down the sandwich with a heavy pan. Very delicious!"

Tangy Sliced Pork Sandwiches

Submitted by: **Holly**

"Hot pork bun sandwiches, great for small or big kids on a chilly afternoon. Serve with additional sauce on the side, if desired."

¼	cup butter	⅛	teaspoon salt
¼	cup Worcestershire sauce	⅛	teaspoon cayenne pepper
2	tablespoons lemon juice	½	pound boneless pork,
2	tablespoons white sugar		cooked and cubed
¼	teaspoon paprika	4	hamburger buns

1. Melt butter in a large saucepan over medium heat. Add the Worcestershire sauce, lemon juice, sugar, paprika, salt, and cayenne pepper. Mix together and bring mixture to a boil, stirring often. Add cooked pork and let simmer just until pork is heated through. Divide the meat among the bottoms of 4 buns. Cover with tops of buns. **Yield:** 4 servings.

Per serving: About 382 calories, 15g protein, 32g carbohydrate, 22g fat, 1g fiber, 65mg cholesterol, 621mg sodium

Reuben Sandwich II *(pictured on page 226)*

Submitted by: **Colette Gerow**

"These sandwiches are really delicious and easy to make. They're one of my family's fix-it-quick favorites. I like to serve them with big bowls of steaming vegetable soup and dill pickles on the side. Enjoy!"

2	tablespoons butter, softened	8	slices deli sliced corned beef
8	slices rye bread		
½	cup Thousand Island dressing	2	cups sauerkraut, drained
		8	slices Swiss cheese

1. Preheat a large skillet or griddle on medium heat.

2. Lightly butter 1 side of bread slices. Spread nonbuttered sides with dressing. On each of 4 bread slices, layer 2 slices corned beef, ½ cup sauerkraut, and 2 slices of Swiss cheese. Top with remaining bread slices, buttered sides out.

3. Cook sandwiches in the preheated skillet until both sides are golden brown, about 6 minutes per side. Serve warm. **Yield:** 4 servings.

Per serving: About 655 calories, 33g protein, 42g carbohydrate, 40g fat, 5g fiber, 115mg cholesterol, 1987mg sodium

Lettuce with Hot Bacon Dressing *(pictured on page 2)*

Submitted by: **Vera**

"Here's something a little different for a salad. A friend gave me this years ago. Hope you like it."

2	eggs	½	teaspoon salt
6	slices bacon	8	cups leaf lettuce, rinsed, dried, and torn into bite-size pieces
½	cup sliced onion		
¼	cup white wine vinegar		
¼	cup water	8	radishes, thinly sliced
4	teaspoons white sugar		

1. Place eggs in a saucepan and cover with cold water. Bring water to a boil; cover, remove from heat, and let stand for 10 to 12 minutes. Remove eggs and cool; peel and chop eggs.
2. Cook bacon in a large, deep skillet over medium-high heat until evenly browned. Crumble bacon and set aside, reserving drippings in pan.
3. Add onion to skillet with reserved drippings and cook until tender. Add bacon, vinegar, water, sugar, and salt. Stir and bring to a boil.
4. Place lettuce in a large bowl. Pour hot dressing over lettuce and toss well. Top with chopped eggs and radishes. Serve immediately.
Yield: 6 servings.

Per serving: About 198 calories, 5g protein, 7g carbohydrate, 17g fat, 2g fiber, 54mg cholesterol, 420mg sodium

◄ **Family Favorite**

Prep Time: 15 minutes

Cook Time: 20 minutes

Average Rating: ★★★★★

What other cooks have done:

"Awesome salad! We enjoyed it with red leaf lettuce, red onion, and 2 eggs. I left off the radish garnish only because we don't care for the radish flavor. The dressing is to die for. Everyone at my luncheon loved this salad. Many asked for the dressing recipe."

Garlicky Beet Delight

Submitted by: **Meredyth Levering**

"A simple but elegant dish of beets tossed with a tangy garlic vinaigrette dressing. Feel free to use more than the two cloves of garlic—I do!"

6	medium beets	2	cloves garlic, crushed
3	tablespoons olive oil		Salt to taste
2	tablespoons red wine vinegar		

1. Wash beets and boil in water to cover until tender, about 45 minutes. Remove the skins by running cold water over the boiled beets and then slipping off their skins. Combine olive oil, vinegar, garlic, and salt to taste. Slice the beets and toss with dressing. **Yield:** 4 servings.

Per serving: About 141 calories, 2g protein, 12g carbohydrate, 10g fat, 2g fiber, 0mg cholesterol, 222mg sodium

◄ **Company is Coming**

Prep Time: 10 minutes

Cook Time: 45 minutes

Average Rating: ★★★★☆

What other cooks have done:

"These even go over well with non-beet people. Savory and sweet at the same time. Makes good use of a somewhat neglected veggie."

Spinach and Orzo Salad

Submitted by: **Christine R.**
"A light, easy to make salad that's pleasing to the palate."

1	(16 ounce) package uncooked orzo pasta	¾	cup pine nuts
1	(10 ounce) package baby spinach leaves, finely chopped	½	teaspoon dried basil
		¼	teaspoon ground white pepper
½	pound crumbled feta cheese	½	cup olive oil
½	red onion, finely chopped	½	cup balsamic vinegar

1. Bring a large pot of lightly salted water to a boil. Add orzo and cook in boiling water for 8 minutes or until al dente; drain and rinse with cold water. Transfer to a large bowl and stir in spinach, feta, onion, pine nuts, basil, and white pepper. Toss with olive oil and balsamic vinegar. Refrigerate and serve cold. **Yield:** 8 servings.

Per serving: About 491 calories, 16g protein, 49g carbohydrate, 27g fat, 3g fiber, 25mg cholesterol, 349mg sodium

Summer Corn Salad *(pictured on page 227)*

Submitted by: **Eileen**
"This fresh and flavorful salad features buttery yellow corn tossed with chunks of tomato and onion with a fresh basil vinaigrette."

6	ears corn, husked and cleaned	¼	cup olive oil
3	large tomatoes, diced	2	tablespoons white vinegar
1	large onion, diced	1	teaspoon salt
¼	cup chopped fresh basil	½	teaspoon ground black pepper

1. Bring a large pot of lightly salted water to a boil. Add corn and cook for 7 to 10 minutes or to desired tenderness. Drain, cool, and cut kernels off the cob with a sharp knife.
2. In a large bowl, toss together the corn, tomatoes, onion, basil, oil, vinegar, salt, and pepper. Chill until ready to serve. **Yield:** 4 servings.

Per serving: About 309 calories, 6g protein, 44g carbohydrate, 16g fat, 6g fiber, 0mg cholesterol, 36mg sodium

---

Party Food ▶

Prep Time: 20 minutes
Cook Time: 8 minutes
Average Rating: ★★★★★
What other cooks have done:
"A great recipe, very easy to make, and tastes wonderful. The only changes I've made are to use frozen spinach that has been defrosted and squeezed dry, then shredded. Try using the flavored feta cheeses, like garlic and cumin. Also, use fresh basil. I've used a gourmet basil that has a hint of lemon to it."

Out-of-the-Ordinary ▶

Prep Time: 25 minutes
Cook Time: 10 minutes
Average Rating: ★★★★★
What other cooks have done:
"I used green onions because I like the milder flavor, and balsamic vinegar in place of the white vinegar."

Outrageous Caesar Salad

Submitted by: **Jeff Winett**

"I've gleaned the best qualities of Caesar salad recipes from various restaurants. Then I put them all together to create my ultimate version!"

2	cloves garlic, crushed		1	French baguette, cut into ½ inch cubes
6	tablespoons corn oil		¼	cup melted butter
¼	cup egg substitute		1	teaspoon Italian seasoning
¾	teaspoon salt		½	teaspoon Worcestershire sauce
¼	teaspoon powdered mustard		1	tablespoon grated Parmigiano-Reggiano cheese
¼	teaspoon ground black pepper		1	large head romaine lettuce, rinsed, dried, and torn into bite-size pieces
1½	teaspoons Worcestershire sauce		½	cup grated Parmigiano-Reggiano cheese
⅛	teaspoon cayenne pepper			
2	tablespoons fresh lemon juice			
1	(2 ounce) can anchovy fillets			

1. Preheat oven to 275°F (135°C).

2. Prepare dressing by combining the garlic, oil, egg substitute, salt, mustard, pepper, Worcestershire sauce, cayenne pepper, and lemon juice in a glass jar. Rinse anchovy fillets under warm water, pat dry on paper towels, and coarsely chop. Place anchovy in jar with other ingredients. Cover jar with a tight fitting lid and shake to mix.

3. Combine bread cubes, melted butter, Italian seasoning, ½ teaspoon Worcestershire sauce, and 1 tablespoon grated cheese. Toss well to coat bread, then place in a single layer on a 10x15 inch jellyroll pan; bake in the preheated oven for 30 minutes.

4. In a large bowl, combine romaine, ½ cup grated cheese, dressing, and croutons to taste. Toss well to coat and serve. **Yield:** 4 servings.

Per serving: About 722 calories, 22g protein, 64g carbohydrate, 42g fat, 5g fiber, 104mg cholesterol, 1984mg sodium

◄ Restaurant Fare

Prep Time: 15 minutes

Cook Time: 35 minutes

Average Rating: ★★★★★

What other cooks have done:

"An amazing dressing with intense flavors! I love this dressing because you don't have to use much to get a great Caesar taste. I make this whenever I start feeling blah about eating one more salad—works like a charm!"

Strawberry Romaine Salad

Submitted by: **Mary J Wright**

"For my wedding shower everyone brought a few recipes and this is one of my favorites. It's refreshing and pretty. This salad also travels well. Just save the dressing and use it just before serving."

1	head romaine lettuce, rinsed, dried, and chopped	1	Bermuda onion, sliced
2	bunches fresh spinach, rinsed, dried, and chopped	½	cup mayonnaise
		2	tablespoons white wine vinegar
1	pint fresh strawberries, sliced	⅓	cup white sugar
		¼	cup milk
		2	tablespoons poppy seeds

1. In a large salad bowl, combine the romaine, spinach, strawberries, and sliced onion.
2. In a jar with a tight fitting lid, combine mayonnaise, vinegar, sugar, milk, and poppy seeds. Shake well and pour the dressing over salad. Toss until evenly coated. **Yield:** 6 servings.

Per serving: About 252 calories, 6g protein, 24g carbohydrate, 17g fat, 6g fiber, 12mg cholesterol, 206mg sodium

Holiday Fare ▶

Prep Time: 15 minutes

Average Rating: ★★★★★

What other cooks have done:

"Delicious and so refreshing! And I'm not normally a fan of really sweet salads, but this was so light! It was perfect. I just left out the onions (don't like 'em). I made it for a family dinner—it was a perfect accompaniment with a cheesy pasta—and exceedingly easy to throw together."

Tomato, Cucumber, and Red Onion Salad with Mint

Submitted by: **Alison**

"Refreshing light summer salad."

2	large cucumbers, halved lengthwise, seeded, and sliced	⅔	cup coarsely chopped red onion
⅓	cup red wine vinegar	½	cup chopped fresh mint leaves
1	tablespoon white sugar	3	tablespoons olive oil
1	teaspoon salt		Salt and ground black pepper to taste
3	large tomatoes, seeded and coarsely chopped		

1. In a large bowl, toss together cucumber, vinegar, sugar, and salt. Let stand at room temperature for 1 hour, stirring occasionally.
2. Add tomatoes, onion, mint, and oil to cucumbers and toss to blend. Season with salt and pepper to taste. **Yield:** 6 servings.

Per serving: About 116 calories, 2g protein, 12g carbohydrate, 7g fat, 2g fiber, 0mg cholesterol, 399mg sodium

Quick & Easy ▶

Prep Time: 15 minutes

Stand Time: 1 hour

Average Rating: ★★★★☆

What other cooks have done:

"The mint is an enjoyable change from basil or oregano, which is typically used in salads of this type. Great salad!"

Greek Pasta Salad with Roasted Vegetables and Feta *(pictured on cover)*

Submitted by: **Cypress**

"This salad is wonderful served warm or at room temperature with some French bread."

1   red bell pepper, cut into 1 inch pieces
1   yellow bell pepper, cut into 1 inch pieces
1   medium eggplant, cut into 1½ inch pieces
3   small yellow squash, cut into ½ inch slices
¼   teaspoon salt
½   teaspoon ground black pepper
6   tablespoons extra virgin olive oil, divided
1   (12 ounce) package farfalle pasta (bow tie)
1½ ounces sun-dried tomatoes, soaked in ½ cup boiling water
½   cup arugula leaves
½   cup fresh basil leaves
2   tablespoons balsamic vinegar
1   tablespoon minced garlic
4   ounces crumbled feta cheese
    Salt and ground black pepper to taste
    Garnish: fresh basil leaves

1. Preheat oven to 450°F (230°C). Line a baking sheet with lightly greased foil.
2. In a medium bowl, toss red bell pepper, yellow bell pepper, eggplant, and squash with salt, pepper, and 2 tablespoons olive oil. Arrange on prepared baking sheet.
3. Bake vegetables in the preheated oven for 15 to 20 minutes, tossing occasionally, or until lightly browned.
4. Bring a large pot of lightly salted water to a boil. Add pasta and cook 8 to 10 minutes or until al dente; rinse with cold water and drain.
5. Drain the softened sun-dried tomatoes, reserving water. In a large bowl, toss together the roasted vegetables, cooked pasta, sun-dried tomatoes, arugula, and basil. Mix in remaining 4 tablespoons olive oil, reserved water from tomatoes, balsamic vinegar, garlic, and feta cheese; toss to coat. Season with salt and pepper to taste. Serve immediately or refrigerate until chilled. Garnish, if desired. **Yield:** 6 servings.

Per serving: About 450 calories, 13g protein, 57g carbohydrate, 20g fat, 7g fiber, 17mg cholesterol, 324mg sodium

◀ **Family Favorite**

Prep Time: 20 minutes

Cook Time: 35 minutes

Average Rating: ★★★★★

What other cooks have done:

"Instead of farfalle, I used orzo. The vegetables taste so good and the sun-dried tomatoes make it authentic. A brilliant addition to any summer cookout."

Eastern Rice Salad *(pictured on page 151)*

Submitted by: **Teri**
"A fresh Eastern-style rice salad with lots of vegetables!"

¾	cup long-grain white rice	½	pound fresh bean sprouts
1	cup sliced fresh mushrooms	1	cup fresh spinach
½	cup chopped green bell pepper	3	stalks celery, chopped
½	cup chopped red bell pepper	½	cup vegetable oil
1	cup salted cashew pieces	¼	cup soy sauce
1	cup chopped green onions	1	teaspoon chopped fresh parsley
		½	teaspoon crushed garlic

1. In a saucepan, bring 1½ cups salted water to a boil. Add ¾ cup rice; reduce heat, cover, and simmer for 20 minutes. Refrigerate rice until chilled.
2. Combine the chilled rice, mushrooms, bell peppers, cashews, green onions, bean sprouts, spinach, and celery in a large bowl.
3. In a bowl, blend the vegetable oil, soy sauce, parsley, and garlic.
4. Pour the dressing over the salad 1 hour before serving and toss well. **Yield:** 10 servings.

Per serving: About 249 calories, 5g protein, 20g carbohydrate, 18g fat, 2g fiber, 0mg cholesterol, 472mg sodium

Bulgur Chickpea Salad *(pictured on page 225)*

Submitted by: **Leah Perez**
"This tabbouleh salad variation is a meal in itself."

2	cups boiling water	1	cup chopped green onions
1	cup bulgur	1	(15 ounce) can chickpeas, drained
½	cup vegetable oil		
½	cup fresh lemon juice	1	cup chopped fresh parsley
½	teaspoon salt	1	cup grated carrots
¼	teaspoon ground black pepper		

1. In a heatproof bowl, pour boiling water over bulgur. Let stand 1 hour at room temperature.
2. In a small bowl, beat together oil, lemon juice, salt, and pepper. Pour over bulgur, and mix with a fork.
3. Place bulgur in a glass serving bowl. Layer green onions, chickpeas, parsley, and carrots. Cover and refrigerate. Toss salad just before serving. **Yield:** 7 servings.

Per serving: About 299 calories, 6g protein, 34g carbohydrate, 17g fat, 8g fiber, 0mg cholesterol, 200mg sodium

---

Caribbean Sweet Potato Salad *(pictured on page 150)*

Submitted by: **Jessica**

"A new and improved, redone, much better potato salad. Not only does it have a sweet potato in addition to a russet potato, but it also contains corn, cucumber, and peanuts! Corn oil will do if you don't have canola."

1	large russet potato, peeled and quartered
1	large sweet potato, peeled and quartered
1	cup frozen whole kernel corn
1	teaspoon prepared Dijon-style mustard
2	tablespoons fresh lime juice
3	tablespoons chopped fresh cilantro
1	clove garlic, minced
3	tablespoons canola oil
½	teaspoon salt
¼	teaspoon ground black pepper
1	cucumber, halved lengthwise and chopped
½	cup chopped red onion
¼	cup finely chopped peanuts

1. Place the russet potato pieces in a large saucepan and cover with salted water. Bring to a boil, reduce heat, and simmer for 10 minutes. Add the sweet potato and cook about 15 minutes. Once the potatoes are tender, add corn; cook 30 seconds. Drain and cool. Cover and chill 8 hours or overnight.

2. In a large bowl, whisk together mustard, lime juice, cilantro, and garlic. Slowly whisk in oil. Mix in salt and pepper.

3. Cut potatoes into 1 inch cubes and add to dressing along with cucumber and red onion. Toss well. Serve at room temperature or chilled. Sprinkle with peanuts just before serving. **Yield:** 5 servings.

Per serving: About 187 calories, 4g protein, 17g carbohydrate, 13g fat, 3g fiber, 0mg cholesterol, 332mg sodium

◄ **Out-of-the-Ordinary**

Prep Time: 30 minutes

Cook Time: 30 minutes

Chill Time: 8 hours

Average Rating: ★★★★★

What other cooks have done:

"Excellent! I used a little less oil to cut down on the fat, and it was fantastic. Served this with jerk chicken and mango salsa. Will make this potato salad again!"

Around-the-World Cuisine ▶

Prep Time: 30 minutes

Cook Time: 12 minutes

Chill Time: 3 hours

Average Rating: ★★★★☆

What other cooks have done:

"I go to a small Thai restaurant that serves beef salad hot with rice. Sounds crazy—salad over rice—but I wouldn't eat it any other way."

Crowd-Pleaser ▶

Prep Time: 10 minutes

Cook Time: 10 minutes

Average Rating: ★★★★☆

What other cooks have done:

"Great recipe. I made it during the week on one of those nights when you feel like ordering out instead of cooking! It was easy and a huge hit with my 3-year-old son. He gobbled up a whole plateful. I added sour cream after serving. My son liked his with Ranch dressing."

Thai Beef Salad

Submitted by: **Mick**
"A colorful, tangy salad that brings out the best in Thai cuisine and spices."

2	green onions, chopped	½	cup white sugar
1	stack lemon grass, cut into 1 inch pieces	1½	pounds (1 inch thick) steak fillet
1	cup chopped fresh cilantro	1	head leaf lettuce, rinsed, dried, and torn into bite-size pieces
1	cup chopped fresh mint		
1	cup lime juice		
⅓	cup fish sauce	½	English cucumber, diced
1	tablespoon sweet chili sauce	1	pint cherry tomatoes

1. Preheat grill for high heat.
2. In a large bowl, stir together green onions, lemon grass, cilantro, mint, lime juice, fish sauce, chili sauce, and sugar until well combined and sugar is dissolved. Set aside.
3. Grill steak over high heat for approximately 4 to 6 minutes on each side or until cooked medium. Remove from heat and slice into thin strips. Add the meat and its juices to the sauce and refrigerate, tightly covered, for at least 3 hours.
4. Place the lettuce in a large bowl. Arrange the cucumber over lettuce and then pour the meat and sauce over cucumber. Top with cherry tomatoes. **Yield:** 6 servings.

Per serving: About 233 calories, 16g protein, 29g carbohydrate, 7g fat, 2g fiber, 34mg cholesterol, 1056mg sodium

Lazy Katie's Taco Salad

Submitted by: **Victoria Jones**
"My daughter's absolute favorite recipe. It's so quick and easy. Try adding sour cream for even more flavor."

1	pound ground beef	2	tomatoes, diced
1	(8 ounce) bag corn tortilla chips	2	cups shredded Cheddar cheese
½	head romaine lettuce, rinsed, dried, and chopped	½	cup chopped onion
		¾	cup taco sauce

1. In a large skillet over medium-high heat, cook ground beef for 5 to 10 minutes or until well browned. Drain excess fat.
2. Crumble tortilla chips on a large plate. Layer with beef, lettuce, tomatoes, cheese, onion, and taco sauce. **Yield:** 8 servings.

Per serving: About 452 calories, 19g protein, 22g carbohydrate, 32g fat, 2g fiber, 79mg cholesterol, 531mg sodium

Crab Salad III

Submitted by: **Joyce DeFaye**

"This creamy and colorful salad is inexpensive and flavorful. Seashell macaroni and crabmeat are dotted with a delicious blend of herbs, green pepper, olives, radishes, tomato, and celery. If you don't have celery on hand, just substitute some celery seed."

1½	cups seashell pasta	1	(12 ounce) package imitation crabmeat
¾	cup mayonnaise		
1	tablespoon white vinegar	1	small green bell pepper, diced
1	teaspoon lemon juice		
½	packet artificial sweetener	1	sweet onion, diced
½	teaspoon garlic powder	½	cup diced black olives
½	teaspoon dried dill weed	5	radishes, diced
½	teaspoon dried basil	1	tomato, seeded and diced
½	teaspoon dried oregano	½	cup diagonally sliced celery

1. Bring a large pot of lightly salted water to a boil. Add pasta and cook in boiling water for 8 to 10 minutes or until al dente; rinse with cold water and drain.

2. In a large bowl, whisk together the mayonnaise, vinegar, lemon juice, artificial sweetener, garlic powder, dill, basil, and oregano.

3. Add dressing to pasta and toss to coat. Add crab, bell pepper, onion, olives, radishes, tomato, and celery and gently fold into the salad mixture. Cover and refrigerate until ready to serve. **Yield:** 8 servings.

Per serving: About 291 calories, 9g protein, 24g carbohydrate, 19g fat, 2g fiber, 21mg cholesterol, 559mg sodium

◀ **Make-Ahead**

Prep Time: 25 minutes

Cook Time: 8 minutes

Average Rating: ★★★★★

What other cooks have done:

"My family and friends loved this recipe! It was well worth the time spent chopping the ingredients. I took it to a cookout at a friend's house and everyone loved it. I left out the radishes and substituted julienned carrots. I also used sugar instead of the artificial sweetener. I placed a bowl of croutons on the table for an optional topping and they added even more crunch! This will be a regular in my house!"

Enjoying Your Salad Days ▼

Craving the refreshing, crisp feel of raw vegetables between your teeth? We all know how to make a salad, of course: All you have to do is toss your favorite greens with your favorite veggies. Your family probably has one or two favorite salad dressings that have taken up permanent residence in the door of your refrigerator, but you can put a brand new spin on the same old salad by trying out different kinds of homemade dressings!

Dressing Up

Does making your own salad dressing sound too time-consuming? It's not! Most salad dressings take only a few minutes to whip together. There are two general categories of salad dressings: creamy and vinaigrette. Creamy dressings, which include Ranch, blue cheese, and Thousand Island, have a base of sour cream, mayonnaise, buttermilk, heavy cream, yogurt, or a combination of all these ingredients. Creamy dressings are very simple to make: All you need to do is stir!

Vinaigrettes have a base of oil and vinegar. Like creamy dressings, they can be accented with ingredients such as herbs, spices, garlic, and shallots. From the simple combination of oil and vinegar, there are countless variations on the theme. The secret to astonishing vinaigrettes is to use high-quality ingredients—they will make your greens sing!

- Jennifer Anderson

For more information, visit **Allrecipes.com**

Grandma's Salad Dressing

Submitted by: **Mary Ann Benzon**

"A real family favorite! This dressing recipe has been in our family for four generations. We keep passing it on because it's so good, and we pass it on to our guests who want it as well."

1	cup vegetable oil	½	teaspoon salt
¾	cup white wine vinegar	2	teaspoons Worcestershire
1	cup white sugar		sauce
½	cup ketchup	1	onion, chopped

1. Pour oil, wine vinegar, sugar, ketchup, salt, Worcestershire sauce, and onion in a large jar with a tight fitting lid. Shake until the sugar is dissolved. Refrigerate dressing and shake well before using. **Yield:** 28 servings.

Per serving: About 103 calories, 0g protein, 9g carbohydrate, 8g fat, 0g fiber, 0mg cholesterol, 97mg sodium

Magical Dressing

Submitted by: **Laura**

"Perfect for any green salad, especially cucumber!"

½	cup olive oil	2	tablespoons brown sugar
½	cup balsamic vinegar	1	tablespoon lemon juice
5	dashes lemon pepper		

1. Whisk together oil, vinegar, lemon pepper, sugar, and lemon juice. Pour into a clean bottle with a tight fitting lid. Shake bottle before using and pour over favorite green salad. **Yield:** 8 servings.

Per serving: About 144 calories, 0g protein, 6g carbohydrate, 14g fat, 0g fiber, 0mg cholesterol, 149mg sodium

Raspberry Vinaigrette Dressing

Submitted by: **Jan**

"A winner! This dressing has a mild raspberry flavor. I usually prepare it with canola oil."

½	cup vegetable oil	¼	teaspoon dried oregano
½	cup raspberry wine vinegar	¼	teaspoon ground black
½	cup white sugar		pepper
2	teaspoons prepared Dijon-style mustard		

1. In a jar with a tight fitting lid, combine oil, vinegar, sugar, mustard, oregano, and pepper. Shake well. **Yield:** 12 servings.

Per serving: About 118 calories, 0g protein, 10g carbohydrate, 9g fat, 0g fiber, 0mg cholesterol, 23mg sodium

Mustard Vinaigrette

Submitted by: **Sara**

"This spicy honey-mustard vinaigrette does double duty as a salad dressing and as a marinade for chicken."

½	cup white vinegar	2	teaspoons salt
1	tablespoon honey	2	teaspoons minced garlic
1	tablespoon prepared Dijon-style mustard	1	cup vegetable oil
½	teaspoon ground black pepper	4	drops hot sauce

1. In a small bowl, whisk together vinegar, honey, mustard, pepper, salt, garlic, oil, and hot sauce until thoroughly combined. Chill until ready to serve. **Yield:** 12 servings.

Per serving: About 169 calories, 0g protein, 2g carbohydrate, 18g fat, 0g fiber, 0mg cholesterol, 423mg sodium

Avocado Salsa

Submitted by: **Barbara Vinson**

"This appetizer takes some time putting together but it's worth the work!"

1 (16 ounce) package frozen corn kernels, thawed	¼ cup lemon juice
2 (2.25 ounce) cans sliced black olives, drained	3 tablespoons cider vinegar
1 red bell pepper, chopped	1 tablespoon fresh oregano
1 small onion, chopped	½ teaspoon salt
5 cloves garlic, minced	½ teaspoon ground black pepper
⅓ cup olive oil	4 avocados, peeled, pitted, and diced

1. In a large bowl, mix corn, olives, red bell pepper, and onion.
2. In a small bowl, mix garlic, olive oil, lemon juice, cider vinegar, oregano, salt, and pepper. Pour on corn mixture and toss to coat. Cover and chill 8 hours or overnight.
3. Stir avocados into mixture before serving. **Yield:** 32 servings.

Per serving: About 81 calories, 1g protein, 6g carbohydrate, 7g fat, 2g fiber, 0mg cholesterol, 74mg sodium

Watermelon Fire and Ice Salsa

Submitted by: **Dawn**

"Juicy watermelon replaces tomatoes in this salsa that's simultaneously cool and spicy hot—perfect for a summer cookout. Serve it with tortilla chips or use it as a topping for grilled chicken or fish."

3 cups seeded and chopped watermelon	1 tablespoon chopped green onions
½ cup chopped green bell pepper	1 tablespoon chopped jalapeño pepper
2 tablespoons lime juice	½ teaspoon garlic salt
2 tablespoons chopped fresh cilantro	

1. In a large bowl, combine the watermelon, green bell pepper, lime juice, cilantro, green onions, jalapeño, and garlic salt. Mix well and serve. **Yield:** 32 servings (about 4 cups).

Per serving: About 6 calories, 0g protein, 1g carbohydrate, 0g fat, 0g fiber, 0mg cholesterol, 29mg sodium

Simple Sides

Grilled Peaches *(pictured on page 262)*

Submitted by: **Karen**

"This is a very simple, yet delicious, end to a grilled meal. Peaches are grilled with a balsamic glaze, then served up with crumbled blue cheese. Perfect for summer entertaining!"

3	tablespoons white sugar	2	large fresh peaches with peel, halved and pitted
1	cup balsamic vinegar		
2	teaspoons freshly ground black pepper	2½	ounces blue cheese, crumbled

1. Lightly oil cold grill rack and preheat grill to medium-high heat.

2. In a saucepan over medium heat, stir together the white sugar, balsamic vinegar, and pepper. Simmer until liquid is reduced by half. Remove from heat and set aside.

3. Place peaches, cut side down, onto the grill and cook for 4 to 5 minutes or until the flesh is browned. Turn peaches over. Brush the top sides with the balsamic glaze and cook for another 2 to 3 minutes.

4. Transfer the peach halves to individual serving dishes and drizzle with remaining glaze. Sprinkle with crumbled blue cheese. **Yield:** 4 servings.

Per serving: About 177 calories, 5g protein, 29g carbohydrate, 5g fat, 2g fiber, 13mg cholesterol, 264mg sodium

From the Grill ▶

Prep Time: 20 minutes

Cook Time: 10 minutes

Average Rating: ★★★★★

What other cooks have done:

"Check the sugar content of the peaches you use. You may need to add more sugar if your peaches are tart."

Pineapple Cheese Casserole

Submitted by: **Kerri**

"A divinely delicious pineapple and cheese bake."

3	(15 ounce) cans pineapple chunks, ½ cup juice reserved	½	cup all-purpose flour
		1	cup white sugar
2½	cups shredded Cheddar cheese	30	buttery round crackers, crushed
		½	cup butter, sliced

1. Preheat oven to 350°F (175°C).

2. In a large bowl, combine pineapple chunks, reserved ½ cup pineapple juice, cheese, flour, and sugar. Spoon into a 9x13 inch baking dish. Top with crushed crackers and butter slices.

3. Bake in the preheated oven for 30 minutes. **Yield:** 12 servings.

Per serving: About 360 calories, 8g protein, 44g carbohydrate, 18g fat, 1g fiber, 45mg cholesterol, 306mg sodium

Classic Comfort Food ▶

Prep Time: 10 minutes

Cook Time: 30 minutes

Average Rating: ★★★★★

What other cooks have done:

"Everyone liked this recipe. It also works well as a dessert, served warm and topped with vanilla ice cream."

Puerto Rican Tostones (Fried Plantains)

Submitted by: **Lymari**

"Try frying plantains for a crispy and exotic side dish."

1 green plantain, peeled	3 cups cold water
5 tablespoons vegetable oil	Salt to taste

1. Cut lengthwise slits in plantain skin and peel off.
2. Heat the oil in a large skillet. Fry the plantain in the oil about 3 to 4 minutes on each side.
3. Remove the plantain from the pan and flatten by placing a plate over the fried plantain and pressing down.
4. Dip the plantain in water and return to the hot oil; fry 1 minute on each side. Sprinkle with salt to taste and serve immediately.
Yield: 2 servings.

Per serving: About 413 calories, 1g protein, 29g carbohydrate, 35g fat, 2g fiber, 0mg cholesterol, 14mg sodium

◄ **Around-the-World Cuisine**

Prep Time: 5 minutes
Cook Time: 10 minutes
Average Rating: ★★★★★
What other cooks have done:
"These are exactly like they are in the Dominican Republic. I loved them when I lived there. In the Dominican, they're more commonly called platino fritos. They're great for dinner. I make one tostone per person accompanied with fried salami, which is another Dominican favorite. I'm in heaven now that I can have my platino fritos!"

Zesty Marinated Asparagus

Submitted by: **J. Carter Lebshier**

"Tender asparagus is marinated in a balsamic vinaigrette and sprinkled with tangy lemon zest and fresh parsley. This is a quick and easy side dish."

2 pounds fresh asparagus, trimmed and cut into 2½ inch pieces	¼ cup chopped fresh parsley
1½ cups balsamic vinaigrette salad dressing	½ teaspoon kosher salt
2 teaspoons grated lemon zest	½ teaspoon freshly ground black pepper

1. Bring a large pot of salted water to a boil. Blanch asparagus just until tender, about 1 minute. Plunge into a bowl of cold water to cool. Drain asparagus and place in a large resealable plastic bag. Pour in vinaigrette and seal bag. Refrigerate at least 3 hours, turning bag occasionally.
2. Just before serving, drain asparagus, reserving vinaigrette. Arrange on a serving platter and sprinkle with lemon zest, parsley, salt, and pepper. Serve reserved vinaigrette in a small dish on the side. **Yield:** 4 servings.

Per serving: About 163 calories, 5g protein, 35g carbohydrate, 1g fat, 5g fiber, 0mg cholesterol, 2194mg sodium

◄ **Company is Coming**

Prep Time: 15 minutes
Cook Time: 5 minutes
Chill Time: 3 hours
Average Rating: ★★★★☆
What other cooks have done:
"This was simple to make and looked absolutely beautiful on the platter with the lemon zest on top. For the prettiest results, sprinkle lemon zest on after the parsley, salt, and pepper."

Sesame Green Beans

Submitted by: **Rhonda**

"I had always been indifferent to green beans until a friend gave me this recipe. For such a simple dish, you'll be surprised at how much flavor this has! Broccoli is equally delicious prepared this way."

1 tablespoon olive oil	¼ cup chicken broth
1 tablespoon sesame seeds	¼ teaspoon salt
1 pound fresh green beans, cut into 2 inch pieces	Freshly ground black pepper to taste

1. Heat oil in a large skillet or wok over medium heat. Add sesame seeds. When seeds start to darken, stir in green beans. Cook, stirring, until the beans turn bright green.

2. Pour in chicken broth, salt, and pepper. Cover and cook until beans are tender-crisp, about 10 minutes. Uncover and cook until liquid evaporates. **Yield:** 4 servings.

Per serving: About 80 calories, 3g protein, 9g carbohydrate, 5g fat, 4g fiber, 0mg cholesterol, 215mg sodium

Tasty Green Beans

Submitted by: **Carol**

"An easy, yet delicious, way to prepare green beans. Slightly crispy and bursting with flavor!"

2 pounds fresh green beans, rinsed and trimmed	½ cup soy sauce
½ cup butter	2 tablespoons beef bouillon granules
½ onion, chopped	¼ cup water
1 tablespoon minced garlic	Salt and pepper to taste

1. Bring a large pot of water to a boil. Add green beans and cook for 5 minutes. Drain and rinse with cold water.

2. Melt butter in a large saucepan over high heat. Mixing well, add green beans, onion, and garlic. Stir in soy sauce. While stirring, add bouillon and ¼ cup water. Reduce heat to low and simmer, stirring occasionally, for 20 minutes. Season with salt and pepper to taste. **Yield:** 8 servings.

Per serving: About 149 calories, 3g protein, 11g carbohydrate, 12g fat, 4g fiber, 0mg cholesterol, 1070mg sodium

Green Beans with Breadcrumbs

Submitted by: **Marie Kenney**

"My mom gave me this recipe, which has been in our family for years. It's a sure way to get kids to eat green beans. You can easily double this recipe."

1	pound fresh green beans, rinsed and trimmed		Salt and pepper to taste
½	cup water	¼	teaspoon garlic powder
¼	cup Italian-seasoned breadcrumbs	¼	teaspoon dried oregano
¼	cup olive oil	¼	teaspoon dried basil
		¼	cup grated Parmesan cheese

1. Combine green beans and ½ cup water in a medium pot. Cover and bring to a boil. Reduce heat to medium and cook beans for 10 minutes or until tender. Drain well.

2. Place beans in a medium serving bowl and mix in breadcrumbs, olive oil, salt, pepper, garlic powder, oregano, and basil. Toss mixture until the beans are coated. Sprinkle with Parmesan cheese and serve. **Yield:** 4 servings.

Per serving: About 212 calories, 6g protein, 14g carbohydrate, 16g fat, 4g fiber, 5mg cholesterol, 232mg sodium

◄ **Quick & Easy**

Prep Time: 15 minutes

Cook Time: 10 minutes

Average Rating: ★★★★☆

What other cooks have done:

"This is a great side dish that's even better with slivered almonds on top."

Calico Beans

Submitted by: **Bea**

"These hearty beans full of ground beef and bacon are great for a picnic."

½	pound bacon	1	(15 ounce) can pork and beans, undrained
1	pound lean ground beef		
1	onion, chopped	2	tablespoons powdered mustard
1	(15 ounce) can lima beans, drained		
1	(15 ounce) can kidney beans, undrained	½	cup packed brown sugar
			Salt and pepper to taste

1. Preheat oven to 350°F (175°C).

2. Place bacon in a large, deep skillet. Cook over medium-high heat until evenly browned. Drain, crumble, and set aside. In the same skillet, crumble ground beef and cook over medium-high heat 2 minutes. Mix in onion and continue to sauté until beef is browned and onion is golden. Drain drippings, if desired.

3. In a lightly greased 4-quart casserole, mix together bacon, beef, onion, lima beans, kidney beans, pork and beans, mustard, brown sugar, salt, and pepper. Cover and bake in the preheated oven for 45 minutes or until bubbly. **Yield:** 8 servings.

Per serving: About 495 calories, 34g protein, 62g carbohydrate, 14g fat, 19g fiber, 49mg cholesterol, 850mg sodium

◄ **Family Favorite**

Prep Time: 20 minutes

Cook Time: 45 minutes

Average Rating: ★★★★★

What other cooks have done:

"Really easy to prepare. I added both chorizo and kielbasa to the recipe. It turned out great. This is a wonderful recipe to take to a potluck."

Pat's Baked Beans

Submitted by: **Kelly**

"My stepmom gave me this tasty recipe when I was lamenting over what to bring to a barbecue. I've taken this dish to several parties, and there's never been any left over!"

6	slices bacon	¾	cup ketchup
1	cup chopped onion	½	cup molasses
1	clove garlic, minced	¼	cup packed brown sugar
1	(16 ounce) can pinto beans	2	tablespoons Worcestershire sauce
1	(16 ounce) can great Northern beans, drained	1	tablespoon prepared yellow mustard
1	(16 ounce) can baked beans	½	teaspoon pepper
1	(16 ounce) can red kidney beans, drained		
1	(15 ounce) can garbanzo beans, drained		

1. Preheat oven to 375°F (190°C).

2. Place bacon in a large, deep skillet. Cook over medium–high heat until evenly browned. Drain, reserving 2 tablespoons drippings; crumble bacon and set aside in a large bowl. Cook the onion and garlic in the reserved drippings until onion is tender; drain excess drippings and transfer to the bowl with the bacon.

3. To the bacon and onions, add pinto beans, great Northern beans, baked beans, kidney beans, and garbanzo beans. Stir in ketchup, molasses, brown sugar, Worcestershire sauce, mustard, and pepper. Mix well and transfer to a lightly greased 9x13 inch baking dish.

4. Cover and bake in preheated oven for 1 hour. **Yield:** 10 servings.

Per serving: About 429 calories, 14g protein, 70g carbohydrate, 11g fat, 11g fiber, 12mg cholesterol, 1014mg sodium

---

Covered-Dish Favorite ▶

Prep Time: 15 minutes

Cook Time: 1 hour 15 minutes

Average Rating: ★★★★★

What other cooks have done:

"It couldn't have been easier. I liked that there are different types of beans. I had some ground turkey meat, which I substituted for the bacon. That was great! It's perfect for a big cookout crowd."

Side Dishes That Travel ▼

When tasked with making a side dish to take to someone else's home, be sure to make a dish that travels well. Spare yourself embarrassment and unnecessary hassles by preparing only these types of side dishes that make the best travelers:

- Dishes that need no reheating
- Prebaked casseroles held together with cheese or eggs
- Slow-cooked dishes
- Salads with separate dressing to be tossed just before serving
- Pasta salads
- Savory pies and tarts
- Dishes frozen ahead of time to be defrosted and/or baked at the destination

Wrap 'em Up, Move 'em Out

Choose the most appropriate container for your dish and consider how it needs to be padded, heated, cooled, or otherwise altered to be safe, clean, and efficient.

- Wrap the dish so that it fits securely in the container. Use plastic wrap and aluminum foil generously to ensure that the dish is airtight.
- Label the dish with your name, the name of the dish, and any directions for serving it. It's possible that others will be bringing side dishes also, so if yours is well labeled, you can avoid any confusion and complications.
- Bring a serving utensil and any condiments that you want to serve with the dish. Label serving items with your name so that they can be returned easily to you. - *Tammy Weisberger*

For more information, visit **Allrecipes.com**

Fat-Free Refried Beans

Submitted by: **Lisa Bromfield**

"These fat-free refried beans are great to use in enchiladas, tacos, or even as a spread."

2	cups canned black beans, rinsed, drained, and divided	1	teaspoon salt
½	cup water	1	teaspoon pepper
2	cloves garlic, minced	1	teaspoon liquid smoke
		¾	cup diced onion

1. In a small bowl, mash ⅔ cup beans to a smooth paste.

2. In a medium saucepan over medium heat, combine the remaining beans with the water. When heated through, stir in garlic, salt, pepper, and liquid smoke.

3. Stir the bean paste into the whole beans and mix well. Stir in the onion and cook for 10 minutes or until onions are slightly cooked. **Yield:** 4 servings.

Per serving: About 134 calories, 8g protein, 23g carbohydrate, 2g fat, 9g fiber, 0mg cholesterol, 1044mg sodium

Broccoli and Cauliflower Casserole

Submitted by: **Bridget**

"This is a favorite family recipe that I ate quite a bit of when I was pregnant. It's one of those things that you just can't get enough of!"

1	cup water	1	pound processed cheese food, cubed
½	cup uncooked white rice	1	(10.75 ounce) can condensed cream of chicken soup
1	(16 ounce) package broccoli florets		
1	(16 ounce) package cauliflower florets	¾	cup milk
½	cup butter	1½	cups crushed buttery round crackers
1	onion, chopped		

1. Preheat oven to 350°F (175°C).

2. In a saucepan, bring 1 cup water to a boil. Add rice and stir. Reduce heat, cover, and simmer for 20 minutes. Drain and set aside.

3. Simmer broccoli and cauliflower florets in water for 10 minutes.

4. In a large saucepan, melt butter and sauté onion. Stir cauliflower, broccoli, and rice into the saucepan. Once the vegetables and rice are coated, stir in the cheese, chicken soup, and milk. Transfer mixture to a 9x13 inch baking dish and sprinkle crushed crackers on top.

5. Bake in the preheated oven for 30 minutes. **Yield:** 7 servings.

Per serving: About 543 calories, 21g protein, 30g carbohydrate, 39g fat, 3g fiber, 101mg cholesterol, 1546mg sodium

Broccoli-Potato Bake

Submitted by: **Sally**

"Excellent for a potluck, company dish, or a heart-warming family dinner. This casserole is a scrumptious blend of cheese, potatoes, and broccoli."

2	tablespoons butter	⅓	cup shredded Swiss cheese
2	tablespoons all-purpose flour	1	(12 ounce) package frozen hash brown potatoes
1	teaspoon salt	1	(10 ounce) package frozen chopped broccoli
2	cups milk	½	cup breadcrumbs
1	(3 ounce) package cream cheese, diced	1	tablespoon butter, melted

1. Preheat oven to 350°F (175°C).

2. In a large saucepan, melt 2 tablespoons butter. Stir in flour and salt. Add milk and stir until bubbly. Add cheeses and stir until melted. Stir in potatoes and heat thoroughly.

3. Pour half of the potato mixture into a lightly greased 7x11 inch baking dish.

4. Cook broccoli according to package directions; drain well. Layer broccoli over the potatoes in the baking dish. Pour the remaining potato mixture over the broccoli. Sprinkle the breadcrumbs and 1 tablespoon melted butter over the casserole.

5. Bake in the preheated oven for 20 to 30 minutes or until bubbly and lightly browned. **Yield:** 8 servings.

Per serving: About 202 calories, 7g protein, 19g carbohydrate, 11g fat, 2g fiber, 32mg cholesterol, 486mg sodium

---

Fried Cabbage II

Submitted by: **Jen**

"Cabbage and onions are sautéed in bacon drippings and served with a splash of vinegar for a tangy, hearty dish that will surprise you."

3	slices bacon, chopped	2	tablespoons water
¼	cup chopped onion		Pinch white sugar
6	cups cabbage, cut into thin wedges		Salt and pepper to taste
		1	tablespoon cider vinegar

1. Place bacon in a large, deep skillet. Cook over medium-high heat until browned. Remove bacon, reserving drippings in pan.

2. Cook onion in the hot drippings until tender. Add cabbage and stir in water, sugar, salt, and pepper. Cook until cabbage wilts, about 15 minutes. Stir in bacon. Splash with vinegar before serving. **Yield:** 6 servings.

Per serving: About 48 calories, 2g protein, 5g carbohydrate, 3g fat, 2g fiber, 4mg cholesterol, 81mg sodium

---

Baked Zesty Carrots

Submitted by: **Doreen**

"Always a hit. Don't let the horseradish fool you! Everyone who eats this requests the recipe."

1	(16 ounce) package frozen, chopped carrots	1	cup mayonnaise
½	cup whipping cream	1	teaspoon salt
3½	tablespoons prepared horseradish	¼	teaspoon black pepper
1	tablespoon grated onion	¼	cup melted butter
		½	cup crushed corn flakes cereal

1. Preheat oven to 350°F (175°C). Place carrots in a 9x13 inch baking dish.
2. In a medium bowl, combine cream, horseradish, onion, mayonnaise, salt, and pepper. Pour mixture over carrots.
3. Combine melted butter and corn flakes; sprinkle over carrots.
4. Bake in the preheated oven for 15 to 20 minutes or until heated through. **Yield:** 8 servings.

Per serving: About 325 calories, 2g protein, 12g carbohydrate, 31g fat, 2g fiber, 42mg cholesterol, 593mg sodium

◄ **Out-of-the-Ordinary**

Prep Time: 10 minutes

Cook Time: 20 minutes

Average Rating: ★★★★★

What other cooks have done:

"I use fresh veggies rather than frozen. I do steam them for about 5 to 7 minutes and then continue with the recipe. My 2-year-old loved this!"

Honey Ginger Carrots

Submitted by: **Linda**

"Carrots sweetened with honey and lemon make a delicate side dish. A hint of ginger adds a peppery-sweet kick."

1	pound carrots, sliced		Pinch ground ginger
¼	cup butter	1	tablespoon lemon juice, or to taste
2½	tablespoons honey		

1. Bring a pot of water to a boil. Add carrots and cook until tender but still firm, about 5 minutes. Drain.
2. In a large skillet over low heat, melt butter with honey. Stir in ground ginger and lemon juice. Stir in carrots and simmer until heated through. **Yield:** 6 servings.

Per serving: About 130 calories, 1g protein, 16g carbohydrate, 8g fat, 3g fiber, 21mg cholesterol, 128mg sodium

◄ **Holiday Fare**

Prep Time: 20 minutes

Cook Time: 10 minutes

Average Rating: ★★★★★

What other cooks have done:

"I grated a little fresh ginger root to use instead of ground ginger and added a pinch of grated lemon rind along with the lemon juice. It was delicious. I served the carrots with fish, and it was light and flavorful (a tough combination to find for carrots)."

Cafeteria Carrot Soufflé

Submitted by: **Tammy**
"This carrot casserole is a classic."

2 pounds carrots, chopped	1 teaspoon baking powder
½ cup melted butter	1 teaspoon vanilla extract
1 cup white sugar	3 eggs, beaten
3 tablespoons all-purpose flour	2 tablespoons confectioners' sugar, divided

1. Preheat oven to 350°F (175°C).
2. Bring a large pot of salted water to a boil. Add carrots and cook until tender, about 15 minutes. Drain and mash. To the carrots add melted butter, white sugar, flour, baking powder, vanilla, and eggs. Mix well and transfer to an ungreased 2 quart baking dish. Sprinkle with 1 tablespoon confectioners' sugar.
3. Bake in the preheated oven for 30 minutes. Dust with remaining confectioners' sugar. **Yield:** 8 servings.

Per serving: About 291 calories, 4g protein, 40g carbohydrate, 14g fat, 4g fiber, 111mg cholesterol, 247mg sodium

Cauliflower Casserole

Submitted by: **Betty Houston**
"A quick, delightful dish that's easy to make and sure to please! Even those who say they hate cauliflower always enjoy this dish."

1 large head cauliflower, broken into small florets	Pinch salt
½ cup butter, melted	1 teaspoon crushed red pepper flakes
¼ cup grated Parmesan cheese	1 cup shredded Cheddar cheese
⅔ cup Italian-seasoned breadcrumbs	

1. Preheat oven to 350°F (175°C).
2. Bring 2 inches of water to a boil in a medium saucepan. Add cauliflower, cover, and cook for about 10 minutes. Drain and place in a lightly greased 2 quart baking dish.
3. In a small bowl, mix together butter, Parmesan cheese, breadcrumbs, salt, and red pepper flakes. Sprinkle mixture over cauliflower and top with Cheddar cheese.
4. Bake in the preheated oven for 20 minutes or until cheese is melted and bubbly. **Yield:** 6 servings.

Per serving: About 308 calories, 11g protein, 15g carbohydrate, 24g fat, 4g fiber, 64mg cholesterol, 624mg sodium

Southern Collard Greens

Submitted by: **Tina V. Hare**
"A must-eat dish on New Year's Day."

1½	quarts water	½	teaspoon crushed red
1½	pounds ham hocks		pepper flakes
4	pounds collard greens,	¼	cup vegetable oil
	rinsed and trimmed		Salt and pepper to taste

1. Place the water and ham hocks in a large pot with a tight-fitting lid. Bring to a boil. Reduce heat to low and simmer, covered, for 30 minutes.
2. Add the collards and red pepper flakes to the pot. Simmer, covered, for about 2 hours, stirring occasionally.
3. Add the vegetable oil, salt, and pepper, and simmer, covered, for 30 minutes. **Yield:** 6 servings.

Per serving: About 471 calories, 27g protein, 17g carbohydrate, 34g fat, 11g fiber, 77mg cholesterol, 130mg sodium

Daddy's Fried Corn and Onions

Submitted by: **Michelle Lewis**
"By combining my two favorites, fried onions and fresh corn, my husband came up with this very simple, delicious side dish."

4	ears fresh corn	1	small sweet onion, diced
2	tablespoons butter		Salt and pepper to taste

1. Cut corn kernels from cob. Melt butter in a medium skillet over medium heat. Sauté corn kernels just until tender and mix in onion. Continue to sauté until onion is just beginning to brown. Season with salt and pepper. Serve warm or cold. **Yield:** 4 servings.

Per serving: About 161 calories, 4g protein, 26g carbohydrate, 7g fat, 3g fiber, 16mg cholesterol, 384mg sodium

Zesty Hominy and Cheese

Submitted by: **Jeanie Bean**

"Here's a different side dish using hominy, sour cream, cheese, and green chiles. Friends who say they don't like hominy eat it and ask for more. It's fast and tasty. Adjust chile peppers to taste."

3	(15 ounce) cans white hominy, drained	1	(4.5 ounce) can chopped green chiles
1	(8 ounce) container sour cream		Pinch cayenne pepper (optional)
2	cups shredded Cheddar cheese		

1. Preheat oven to 350°F (175°C).

2. In a lightly greased 2 quart baking dish, mix together hominy, sour cream, Cheddar cheese, and chiles. Add cayenne pepper, if desired.

3. Bake in the preheated oven for 25 minutes or until heated through. **Yield:** 6 servings.

Per serving: About 421 calories, 16g protein, 33g carbohydrate, 25g fat, 6g fiber, 65mg cholesterol, 965mg sodium

Sautéed Portobellos and Spinach

Submitted by: **Leslie**

"Tender portobello mushrooms and spinach are simmered with Parmesan cheese, wine, and seasoning for a unique, easy, and extremely flavorful side dish! Excellent with a steak and baked potato dinner."

3	tablespoons butter	¼	teaspoon salt
2	large portobello mushrooms, sliced	¼	teaspoon ground black pepper
1	(10 ounce) package frozen chopped spinach, thawed and drained	1	clove garlic, chopped
		2	tablespoons dry red wine
¼	teaspoon dried basil	¼	cup grated Parmesan cheese

1. Melt butter in a large skillet over medium heat. Sauté mushrooms, spinach, basil, salt, pepper, and garlic until the mushrooms are tender and spinach is heated through.

2. Pour in wine and reduce heat to low; simmer 1 minute. Stir in Parmesan cheese and serve. **Yield:** 4 servings.

Per serving: About 143 calories, 6g protein, 6g carbohydrate, 11g fat, 3g fiber, 28mg cholesterol, 406mg sodium

Grilled Portobello Mushrooms

Submitted by: **Barry Follick**

"Portobello mushrooms are the steaks of the mushroom family. Here, they're marinated and grilled—yummy!"

3	portobello mushrooms	4	cloves garlic, minced
¼	cup canola oil	¼	cup balsamic vinegar
3	tablespoons chopped onion		

1. Preheat the grill for high heat.
2. Clean mushrooms and remove stems. Place caps on a plate with the gills up.
3. In a small bowl, combine the oil, onion, garlic, and vinegar. Pour mixture evenly over the mushroom caps and let stand for 1 hour.
4. Grill mushrooms for 10 minutes. Serve immediately. **Yield:** 3 servings.

Per serving: About 218 calories, 3g protein, 11g carbohydrate, 19g fat, 2g fiber, 0mg cholesterol, 13mg sodium

◄ **From the Grill**

Prep Time: 10 minutes

Cook Time: 10 minutes

Average Rating: ★★★★★

What other cooks have done:

"Good, easy recipe for tasty grilled mushrooms. I grilled them and made sandwiches with mozzarella cheese, mayo, and roasted red peppers on a toasted whole wheat roll. I used 3 tablespoons balsamic vinegar and that was definitely enough. Yum!"

Grilled Garlic Potatoes

Submitted by: **Kelly Cetnarski**

"This grilled potato recipe is so moist and delicious. It goes great with any meal, but I love to serve it with steak. The cheese tops it off perfectly. Add mushrooms and carrots for an excellent variation. Delicious with sour cream on the side."

6	medium baking potatoes, peeled and thinly sliced	1	teaspoon chopped fresh parsley
1	large onion, sliced		Salt and pepper to taste
3	tablespoons butter	1	cup shredded Cheddar cheese
3	cloves garlic, minced		

1. Preheat the grill for high heat.
2. Place potato slices on a large piece of heavy-duty aluminum foil and toss with onion and butter. Top with garlic and season with parsley, salt, and pepper.
3. Tightly seal vegetables in the foil packet and grill 20 minutes or until potatoes are tender, turning once.
4. Sprinkle potatoes with Cheddar cheese, reseal foil, and continue grilling 5 more minutes or until cheese is melted. **Yield:** 4 servings.

Per serving: About 377 calories, 13g protein, 37g carbohydrate, 20g fat, 5g fiber, 59mg cholesterol, 316mg sodium

◄ **Party Fare**

Prep Time: 15 minutes

Cook Time: 25 minutes

Average Rating: ★★★★★

What other cooks have done:

"I have one word for this dish— yummy! I've tried this with fresh chopped cilantro instead of the parsley and liked it even better. We've started making this every time we fire up the grill."

Prep Time: 15 minutes

Cook Time: 1 hour 5 minutes

Average Rating: ★★★★★

What other cooks have done:

"I made this for Easter dinner with leg of lamb. We stuffed leftovers into corn tortillas, deep-fried them, and topped them with shredded lettuce and hot sauce for some awesome potato tacos."

Au Gratin Potatoes II

Submitted by: **Kerie Kelly**

"This was a favorite recipe of mine when I was growing up. My mom made it for Thanksgiving every year. I have served it with chicken and beef."

1	(8 ounce) container sour cream	2	cups shredded Cheddar cheese
1	(10.75 ounce) can condensed cream of celery soup	½	cup chopped green onions
		½	cup unsalted butter, melted
4½	cups peeled and shredded potatoes	1	cup corn flakes cereal
		1	tablespoon chopped fresh parsley (optional)

1. Preheat oven to 350°F (175°C). Spray an 8x8 inch baking dish with vegetable cooking spray.

2. In a large bowl, stir together the sour cream and soup. Add potatoes, cheese, and onions. Mix well and pour into the prepared baking dish. Cover the dish with aluminum foil.

3. Bake in the preheated oven for 45 minutes. In a small bowl, mix together the melted butter and corn flakes. Sprinkle over the potatoes and return to the oven.

4. Bake, uncovered, for 20 more minutes or until bubbly and corn flakes are golden brown. Remove from the oven and sprinkle with chopped parsley, if desired. **Yield:** 6 servings.

Per serving: About 518 calories, 14g protein, 31g carbohydrate, 38g fat, 4g fiber, 103mg cholesterol, 701mg sodium

Calico Squash Casserole, page 271

Potato Rosemary Rolls, page 98

Grilled Peaches, page 248

Mini Parmesan Scones, page 274

Cranberry Upside-Down Coffee Cake,
page 286

Cream Cheese Ranch Potatoes

Submitted by: **Sarah**

"This is an absolutely divine spin on standard mashed potatoes. Everyone who has tried them has asked me for the recipe. A great addition to any type of meat, and it works well with leftovers."

8	baking potatoes, peeled and quartered	1	(8 ounce) container sour cream
1	(8 ounce) package cream cheese, softened	½	cup butter, softened
1	(1 ounce) package dry Ranch-style salad dressing		

1. Bring a large pot of salted water to a boil. Add potatoes and cook until tender, about 25 minutes. Drain and mash.

2. In a large bowl, beat the cream cheese and salad dressing until smooth. Stir in mashed potatoes, sour cream, and butter; beat to desired consistency. **Yield:** 8 servings.

Per serving: About 364 calories, 5g protein, 26g carbohydrate, 27g fat, 2g fiber, 75mg cholesterol, 466mg sodium

◀ Kid-Friendly

Prep Time: 20 minutes

Cook Time: 25 minutes

Average Rating: ★★★★☆

What other cooks have done:

"I cut the potatoes into small cubes instead of mashing, and browned them under the broiler for a few minutes. I will definitely make these again!"

Garlic Red Potatoes

Submitted by: **Laura**

"Simple, savory, and very flavorful variation on red potatoes. Excellent side dish!"

2	pounds red potatoes, quartered	1	teaspoon salt
¼	cup butter, melted	1	lemon, juiced
2	teaspoons minced garlic	1	tablespoon grated Parmesan cheese

1. Preheat oven to 350°F (175°C).

2. Place potatoes in an 8x8 inch baking dish.

3. In a small bowl, combine melted butter, garlic, salt, and lemon juice; pour over potatoes and stir to coat. Sprinkle Parmesan cheese over potatoes.

4. Bake, covered, in the preheated oven for 30 minutes. Uncover and bake 10 more minutes or until golden brown. **Yield:** 4 servings.

Per serving: About 279 calories, 5g protein, 40g carbohydrate, 12g fat, 5g fiber, 32mg cholesterol, 738mg sodium

◀ Company is Coming

Prep Time: 10 minutes

Cook Time: 40 minutes

Average Rating: ★★★★★

What other cooks have done:

"Oh my goodness, these potatoes are so good! My aunt made them for Christmas dinner this year, and I ate a ton of them! She needed to get them done quickly and cooked them in the microwave for about 15 minutes total."

Oven-Roasted Red Potatoes

Submitted by: **Donna Lasater**
"These roasted red potatoes are very easy to prepare and taste excellent!"

1	(1 ounce) envelope dry onion soup mix	2	pounds red potatoes, halved
		⅓	cup olive oil

1. Preheat oven to 450°F (230°C).
2. In a large heavy-duty, zip-top resealable bag, combine the soup mix, red potatoes, and olive oil. Seal bag and shake until potatoes are fully coated.
3. Pour potatoes into a medium baking dish; bake in the preheated oven 40 minutes, stirring occasionally. **Yield:** 8 servings.

Per serving: About 171 calories, 2g protein, 20g carbohydrate, 9g fat, 2g fiber, 0mg cholesterol, 317mg sodium

Rosemary Mashed Potatoes and Yams

Submitted by: **Ibby**
"A twist on the traditional mashed potatoes."

8	cloves garlic	½	cup milk
3	tablespoons olive oil	¼	cup butter
1½	pounds baking potatoes, peeled and cubed	½	teaspoon dried rosemary
1½	pounds yams, peeled and cubed	½	cup grated Parmesan cheese, divided
			Salt and pepper to taste

1. Preheat oven to 350°F (175°C). Lightly grease an 8x8 inch baking dish.
2. Place garlic in a small ovenproof bowl and drizzle with olive oil. Bake in the preheated oven for 30 minutes or until very soft. Cool and peel the garlic and reserve the oil.
3. Boil potatoes and yams in a large pot of salted water until tender, about 20 minutes. Drain, reserving 1 cup liquid.
4. Place potatoes and yams in a large bowl with milk, butter, rosemary, garlic, and reserved olive oil. Mash to desired consistency, adding reserved cooking liquid as needed. Mix in ¼ cup cheese. Season with salt and pepper to taste. Transfer to the prepared baking dish. Sprinkle with remaining cheese.
5. Bake until heated through and golden on top, about 45 minutes. **Yield:** 10 servings.

Per serving: About 243 calories, 5g protein, 33g carbohydrate, 11g fat, 5g fiber, 17mg cholesterol, 157mg sodium

Grilled Potatoes and Onion

Submitted by: **Bob Cody**

"Always cook up a package of potatoes and onions with the rest of your grilled meal! Start early because it takes about a half hour to cook."

4	potatoes, sliced	1	teaspoon ground black
1	red onion, sliced		pepper
1	teaspoon salt	¼	cup butter

1. Preheat the grill for medium heat.
2. Measure out 2 sheets of aluminum foil large enough to easily wrap half each of the vegetables. Layer potatoes and onion in the center of 1 sheet, sprinkle with salt and pepper, and dot with butter. Wrap into a flattened square and seal the edges. Repeat procedure with remaining sheet of foil.
3. Place packages on grill. Cover and cook about 30 minutes, turning once. **Yield:** 4 servings.

Per serving: About 210 calories, 3g protein, 25g carbohydrate, 12g fat, 4g fiber, 31mg cholesterol, 708mg sodium

◀ From the Grill

Prep Time: 15 minutes

Cook Time: 30 minutes

Average Rating: ★★★★★

What other cooks have done:

"Here's what I did: Prepare the foil sheets and dot with butter before putting the veggies inside to prevent burning and sticking. Slice the potatoes and onion and mix together in a large bowl with olive oil, salt, and pepper. Place on foil, wrap tightly, flatten, and grill for 30 minutes, turning after 15 minutes."

Cheese and Bacon Potato Rounds

Submitted by: **Michele O'Sullivan**

"Potatoes, cheese, and bacon—a great combination! Serve with sour cream, if you desire."

4	baking potatoes, cut into ½ inch slices	8	ounces shredded Cheddar cheese
¼	cup melted butter	½	cup chopped green onions
8	slices bacon, cooked and crumbled		

1. Preheat oven to 400°F (200°C).
2. Brush both sides of potato slices with butter; place them on an ungreased baking sheet. Bake in the preheated oven for 30 to 40 minutes or until lightly browned on both sides, turning once.
3. Top potatoes with bacon, cheese, and green onions; continue baking until the cheese is melted. **Yield:** 4 servings.

Per serving: About 742 calories, 22g protein, 24g carbohydrate, 63g fat, 3g fiber, 128mg cholesterol, 888mg sodium

◀ Kid-Friendly

Prep Time: 20 minutes

Cook Time: 40 minutes

Average Rating: ★★★★★

What other cooks have done:

"Awesome. I sprinkled the potatoes with a little salt and pepper while baking and added parsley flakes and garlic powder to the toppings."

Baked French Fries

Submitted by: **Ashlee**
"A great side dish for burgers."

1 large baking potato	½ teaspoon garlic powder
1 tablespoon olive oil	½ teaspoon chili powder
½ teaspoon paprika	½ teaspoon onion powder

1. Preheat oven to 450°F (230°C).
2. Cut potato into wedges. Mix olive oil, paprika, garlic powder, chili powder, and onion powder together. Coat potatoes with oil/spice mixture and place on a baking sheet.
3. Bake in the preheated oven for 45 minutes. **Yield:** 1 serving.

Per serving: About 246 calories, 3g protein, 29g carbohydrate, 14g fat, 3g fiber, 0mg cholesterol, 21mg sodium

---

Family Favorite ▶

Prep Time: 5 minutes

Cook Time: 45 minutes

Average Rating: ★★★★☆

What other cooks have done:

"The fries tasted great—moist inside with a crunch outside. However, the next time I make this recipe, I'm going to coat the potatoes with oil and then season with spices afterward for even more flavor."

Emily's Famous Fried Potatoes

Submitted by: **Emily B.**
"This is a very tasty potato recipe that's also great for using up leftover baked potatoes. The vinegar gives the spinach a sweet flavor. I like to crumble feta cheese over the potatoes, too!"

6 medium red potatoes, diced	1 teaspoon chopped fresh oregano
2 tablespoons light olive oil	
½ red onion, chopped	1 bunch fresh spinach, rinsed and stems removed
4 cloves garlic, minced	
1 tablespoon chopped fresh basil	2 tablespoons red wine vinegar
1 teaspoon chopped fresh rosemary	Salt and ground black pepper to taste

1. Place potatoes in a large saucepan over medium heat and cover with water. Bring to a boil and cook until tender, about 15 to 20 minutes. Drain and set aside.
2. Heat oil in a large, heavy skillet over medium heat. Sauté the onion and garlic with the basil, rosemary, and oregano until onion is just tender. Add the potatoes and sauté until lightly browned. Cover with spinach and sprinkle with vinegar. Cover and cook on low until the spinach is tender.
3. Remove from heat and stir the mixture together. Season with salt and pepper. **Yield:** 6 servings.

Per serving: About 149 calories, 4g protein, 23g carbohydrate, 5g fat, 4g fiber, 0mg cholesterol, 150mg sodium

---

Classic Comfort Food ▶

Prep Time: 20 minutes

Cook Time: 20 minutes

Average Rating: ★★★★★

What other cooks have done:

"I made this for a Mother's Day brunch, and it was a hit! I used sherry vinegar and green onions, and the flavor was incredible. It's easy to prepare in no time. The spinach was so tasty, too."

Gourmet Sweet Potato Classic

Submitted by: **Heather**

"Once you taste this, you won't ever go back to the marshmallow-topped variety! I peeled the potatoes and cooked them in the microwave, and I've also boiled them. They taste the same no matter how you cook them, so use the technique that works best for you."

5	sweet potatoes	¼	cup butter, softened
¼	teaspoon salt	3	tablespoons all-purpose flour
¼	cup butter	¾	cup packed light brown sugar
2	eggs	½	cup chopped pecans
1	teaspoon vanilla extract		
½	teaspoon ground cinnamon		
½	cup white sugar		
2	tablespoons heavy whipping cream		

1. Preheat the oven to 350°F (175°C). Lightly grease a 9x13 inch baking dish.

2. Bake sweet potatoes in the preheated oven for 35 minutes or until they begin to soften. Cool slightly, peel, and mash.

3. In a large bowl, mix the mashed sweet potatoes, salt, ¼ cup butter, eggs, vanilla, cinnamon, white sugar, and cream. Transfer to the prepared baking dish.

4. In a medium bowl, combine ¼ cup butter, flour, brown sugar, and chopped pecans. Mix with a pastry blender or your fingers to the consistency of coarse meal. Sprinkle over the sweet potato mixture.

5. Bake in the preheated oven for 30 minutes or until topping is crisp and lightly browned. **Yield:** 8 servings.

Per serving: About 408 calories, 4g protein, 56g carbohydrate, 20g fat, 2g fiber, 89mg cholesterol, 226mg sodium

◄ **Holiday Fare**

Prep Time: 20 minutes

Cook Time: 1 hour 5 minutes

Average Rating: ★★★★★

What other cooks have done:

"I made this a day ahead for Thanksgiving. Overall, the recipe was good, but we felt that it was a bit sweet. Next time, I'll reduce the sugar amounts a bit. Otherwise, easy, tasty, and a crowd-pleaser. The chopped nuts added a nice texture. Didn't miss the marshmallows a bit. They would have added to the sweetness."

Brandied Candied Sweet Potatoes

Submitted by: **Kathy Bennett**

"This has been a Thanksgiving favorite of ours for many years because it's different from the many mashed sweet potato recipes."

2	pounds sweet potatoes, peeled and diced	½	cup packed brown sugar
½	cup butter	½	cup brandy
		½	teaspoon salt

1. Place sweet potatoes in a large saucepan with enough water to cover. Bring to a boil. Cook 15 minutes or until tender but firm. Drain and set aside.

2. In a large skillet over low heat, melt the butter. Stir in the brown sugar, brandy, and salt. Add the sweet potatoes and stir to coat. Cook, stirring gently, until sweet potatoes are heated through and well glazed. **Yield:** 8 servings.

Per serving: About 316 calories, 2g protein, 41g carbohydrate, 12g fat, 3g fiber, 31mg cholesterol, 283mg sodium

Company is Coming ▶

Prep Time: 15 minutes

Cook Time: 30 minutes

Average Rating: ★★★★★

What other cooks have done:

"Fabulous! I cut the recipe in half, but I shouldn't have because there were no leftovers. I baked the sweet potatoes at 350°F (175°C) for about 1 hour instead of cooking them on the stovetop. They came out perfect."

Amazing Butternut Squash

Submitted by: **Hope**

"I got this recipe from a relative years ago. Delicious, colorful squash is baked with a crunchy Parmesan cheese topping. It's excellent!"

1	butternut squash, peeled, seeded, and cubed		Salt and pepper to taste
½	cup mayonnaise	¼	cup crushed saltine crackers
½	cup finely chopped onion	2	tablespoons grated Parmesan cheese
1	egg, lightly beaten	1	tablespoon butter, melted
1	teaspoon brown sugar		

1. Preheat oven to 350°F (175°C).

2. Place squash in a large pot with enough water to cover. Bring to a boil; reduce to a simmer and cook until squash is soft.

3. In a large bowl, mash the softened squash. Mix in the mayonnaise, onion, egg, brown sugar, salt, and pepper. Pour the mixture into a lightly greased 2 quart baking dish.

4. In a medium bowl, mix together crackers, Parmesan cheese, and butter. Sprinkle over the squash mixture.

5. Bake, uncovered, in the preheated oven for 35 to 45 minutes or until the topping is lightly browned. **Yield:** 6 servings.

Per serving: About 283 calories, 5g protein, 29g carbohydrate, 18g fat, 7g fiber, 53mg cholesterol, 212mg sodium

Family Favorite ▶

Prep Time: 20 minutes

Cook Time: 45 minutes

Average Rating: ★★★★☆

What other cooks have done:

"We all really enjoyed this recipe. I used vanilla yogurt in place of the mayo and cooked the ½ cup of onions a little before adding. I also added more crunchy topping. We'll definitely try this one again!"

Calico Squash Casserole (pictured on page 261)

Submitted by: **Meli**

"My great-aunt made this for a family gathering, and it's been a hit ever since, even with the kids! The water chestnuts add a different texture, and my husband has even used whole baby carrots instead of shredded carrots. Easy and fast to make and a good way to use up all that squash from the garden."

2 cups sliced yellow squash	1 (8 ounce) can sliced water chestnuts, drained
1 cup sliced zucchini	
1 onion, chopped	1 large carrot, shredded
¼ cup sliced green onions	½ cup mayonnaise
1 cup water	½ (4 ounce) jar diced pimentos, drained
1 teaspoon salt, divided	
2 cups crushed buttery round crackers	1 teaspoon ground sage
	½ teaspoon ground white pepper
½ cup melted butter	
1 (10.75 ounce) can condensed cream of mushroom soup	1 cup shredded sharp Cheddar cheese

1. Preheat oven to 350°F (175°C).

2. In a large saucepan, combine yellow squash, zucchini, onion, green onions, water, and ½ teaspoon salt. Cover and cook over medium heat about 6 minutes. Drain well and set aside.

3. In a medium bowl, combine the cracker crumbs and butter. Mix well and spread half of the mixture into a lightly greased 9x13 inch baking dish.

4. In a large bowl, combine soup, water chestnuts, carrot, mayonnaise, pimentos, sage, pepper, and remaining ½ teaspoon salt. Fold in squash mixture and spoon over crumb crust. Sprinkle with cheese and the remaining cracker crumbs.

5. Bake in the preheated oven for 20 to 30 minutes or until firm and heated through. **Yield:** 8 servings.

Per serving: About 409 calories, 6g protein, 21g carbohydrate, 34g fat, 3g fiber, 54mg cholesterol, 1139mg sodium

◄ **Classic Comfort Food**

Prep Time: 10 minutes

Cook Time: 40 minutes

Average Rating: ★★★★★

What other cooks have done:

"Very good recipe. I used almonds instead of water chestnuts but left everything else the same. It does take awhile to prepare, but it's so worth it."

Grilled Zucchini and Squash

Submitted by: **Jay Peaslee**
"Sautéed squash and zucchini on the grill, wrapped in a foil pack. Great served with steak."

2	zucchini	2	teaspoons ground black
1	yellow squash		pepper
¼	cup butter	2	teaspoons garlic powder
1	teaspoon salt		

1. Lightly oil the grill rack and preheat grill for medium–high heat.
2. Cut the zucchini and squash into ¼ inch slices and cut those slices in half.
3. Place the zucchini, squash, butter, salt, pepper, and garlic powder onto a sheet of aluminum foil large enough to fold into a sealed package.
4. Place the foil package on the preheated grill and cook for 20 minutes. Remove and serve. **Yield:** 3 servings.

Per serving: About 175 calories, 3g protein, 9g carbohydrate, 16g fat, 3g fiber, 41mg cholesterol, 943mg sodium

From the Grill ▶

Prep Time: 20 minutes

Cook Time: 20 minutes

Average Rating: ★★★★★

What other cooks have done:

"Great recipe! I used yellow squash and zucchini, added sliced onions, and decreased the amount of butter. Made the package early in the day, put it in the refrigerator, and onto the grill for dinner."

Lemon Pepper Zucchini

Submitted by: **JJ**
"Quick and easy. Everyone will love it!"

2	zucchini, cut into ½ inch slices	3	tablespoons butter, melted
		2	tablespoons lemon pepper

1. Preheat oven to 400°F (200°C).
2. Place zucchini slices on a baking sheet and brush with melted butter. Sprinkle with lemon pepper.
3. Bake in the preheated oven for 20 to 25 minutes or until tender. **Yield:** 4 servings.

Per serving: About 94 calories, 1g protein, 4g carbohydrate, 9g fat, 1g fiber, 23mg cholesterol, 784mg sodium

Quick & Easy ▶

Prep Time: 10 minutes

Cook Time: 25 minutes

Average Rating: ★★★★☆

What other cooks have done:

"This deserves a try. The 2 tablespoons of lemon pepper is a lot. I used less than a teaspoon probably—just sprinkled it on without measuring. I paired it with spaghetti and pesto sauce, and it was a great combo. Decrease the time if you want firmer zucchini."

Fuss-Free Breads

Mini Parmesan Scones *(pictured on page 263)*

Submitted by: **Karla**

"A winner! This was my first scone recipe, and I have loved it ever since my mom taught me how to make it. It has a light cheese flavor. It reminds me of fast food biscuits, but with cheese."

Prep Time: 25 minutes

Cook Time: 12 minutes

Average Rating: ★★★★★

What other cooks have done:

"Wow! These are darn good. It's such a simple recipe that I actually doubted it at first, but they're so yummy and cheesy. I added more Parmesan and some Romano as well. These can also become herb cheese scones, too. More people need to discover these!"

¼	cup butter	½	teaspoon ground cayenne pepper
2	cups self-rising flour		
½	cup freshly grated Parmesan cheese	2	tablespoons freshly grated Parmesan cheese
¾	cup milk		

1. Preheat oven to 425°F (220°C). Lightly grease a large baking sheet.

2. In a small saucepan, melt butter over low heat. In a large bowl, combine flour and ½ cup Parmesan cheese. Make a well in the center of the flour mixture and add the butter and milk; stir gently to combine until dough pulls together.

3. Turn dough out onto a lightly floured surface and knead 4 or 5 times; press out to ½ inch thickness. Cut dough into rounds with a floured 1½ inch cookie or biscuit cutter. Place rounds on prepared baking sheet and sprinkle evenly with cayenne pepper and 2 tablespoons Parmesan cheese.

4. Bake in the preheated oven for 10 to 12 minutes. **Yield:** 2 dozen scones.

Per serving: About 115 calories, 4g protein, 16g carbohydrate, 4g fat, 1g fiber, 9mg cholesterol, 658mg sodium

English Royalty Chocolate Chip Scones

Submitted by: **Holly**

"Tallyho! These scrumptious scones will make you feel like you're queen for a day! The chocolate chips make them yummy, and the orange juice makes them special. Make sure the butter is well chilled to produce the flakiest texture possible. Serve with clotted cream or lemon curd."

1¾ cups all-purpose flour	½ cup miniature semisweet chocolate chips
⅓ cup white sugar	3 tablespoons orange juice
2 teaspoons baking powder	
½ teaspoon salt	
5 tablespoons unsalted butter, chilled and cut into pieces	

1. Preheat oven to 400°F (200°C). Lightly grease a baking sheet.

2. In a large bowl, whisk together flour, sugar, baking powder, and salt. With a pastry blender or a large fork, cut in the butter until mixture resembles coarse crumbs. Stir in the chocolate chips. Mix in the orange juice to form a dough.

3. Turn dough out on a floured surface. Pat into a 9 inch circle about ½ inch thick. With a 2½ inch fluted biscuit cutter, cut out 12 scones, rerolling scraps, if necessary. Transfer the scones to the prepared baking sheet.

4. Bake in the preheated oven about 12 minutes or until golden brown. Transfer to a wire rack to cool. **Yield:** 1 dozen scones.

Per scone: About 172 calories, 2g protein, 25g carbohydrate, 8g fat, 1g fiber, 13mg cholesterol, 180mg sodium

◀ Party Food

Prep Time: 15 minutes

Cook Time: 12 minutes

Average Rating: ★★★★★

What other cooks have done:

"Light, moist, and delicious! My kids went crazy for these. I increased the amount of butter to 7 tablespoons and I used ½ cup of orange juice. We'll make these again."

The Scoop on Scones ▼

This Scottish wheat bread was originally made with oats and baked on a griddle. Modern versions of scones are usually made with flour and baked in the oven. They are sweet, rich, and much like biscuits, although their texture is flakier than traditional biscuits. The dough should be "shaggy" or rough; don't strive for a smooth dough here. Work quickly with cold butter and do very little mixing for a flaky product. And pat rather than roll the dough into shape. You can cut your scones into rounds, squares, triangles, or diamond shapes.

Enjoy scones as a snack or serve them at teatime. During afternoon tea, a light meal or refreshments can be served; this might include bread and butter, cucumber or other delicate sandwiches, cookies, your favorite scones, and clotted cream.

Clotted cream is a thick cream made from unpasteurized milk gently heated until a semisolid layer of cream forms on top. After cooling, the thickened cream can be spread on scones or bread or served over fresh fruit.

Last but not least, the classic accompaniment—tea. When brewing tea, start with cold water; hot water has lost most of its oxygen and will make tea taste flat and stale. Bring water to a full boil and add tea immediately, putting the lid on your teapot and leaving it to steep about 5 minutes. If the water isn't hot enough, tea won't fully steep. If you boil the water too long, it'll become flat and lose its freshness. After steeping, remove the tea bag immediately. And don't judge the strength of tea by its color—taste it!

Brunch Scones

Submitted by: **Bianca Elshafei**

"I enjoy scones with morning tea or just as an afternoon snack. Serve warm with clotted cream and strawberry jam."

1¾	cups all-purpose flour	⅔	cup whole milk
4	teaspoons baking powder	½	cup currants
5	tablespoons unsalted butter	1	egg yolk, lightly beaten
5	tablespoons white sugar		

1. Preheat oven to 400°F (200°C). Lightly grease a baking sheet or line with parchment paper.

2. Sift flour and baking powder into a medium bowl. Using a pastry blender, cut butter and sugar into flour until crumbly. Make a well in center and add milk and currants. Knead gently, being careful not to overmix. Dough will be sticky.

3. On a well floured surface, roll out dough to ¾ inch thickness. Cut out 8 rounds with a 2½ inch cutter. Transfer to prepared baking sheet and brush tops with egg yolk. Allow to stand for 15 minutes.

4. Bake in the preheated oven for 12 to 15 minutes or until lightly golden. Remove immediately to a wire rack to cool. **Yield:** 8 scones.

Per serving: About 240 calories, 4g protein, 37g carbohydrate, 9g fat, 1g fiber, 49mg cholesterol, 137mg sodium

Holiday Fare ▶

Prep Time: 20 minutes

Cook Time: 15 minutes

Average Rating: ★★★★★

What other cooks have done:

"These were really good and not too sweet. I doubled the recipe and made 12 nice sized scones. I added blueberries to half of them and made a sugar glaze. When I doubled this recipe, I didn't double the milk or the baking powder. Worked great!"

Best-Ever Muffins

Submitted by: **Lori**

"Start with this basic recipe and add one of several different ingredients for a variety of different muffins. Add 1 cup fresh blueberries, or 1 cup finely chopped raisins, or 1 cup grated sharp Cheddar cheese."

2	cups all-purpose flour	1	egg, lightly beaten
¾	cup white sugar	1	cup milk
1	tablespoon baking powder	¼	cup vegetable oil
½	teaspoon salt		

1. Preheat oven to 400°F (200°C). Line muffin pan with paper cups.

2. Stir together flour, sugar, baking powder, and salt in a large bowl. Make a well in the center. In a small bowl, stir together egg, milk, and oil. Pour into the well in flour mixture. Mix quickly and lightly with a fork just until moistened, but do not beat. The batter will be lumpy. Pour the batter into muffin pan.

3. Bake in the preheated oven for 25 minutes or until golden. Remove from pan immediately and cool on a wire rack. **Yield:** 1 dozen muffins.

Per serving: About 182 calories, 3g protein 30g carbohydrate, 6g fat, 1g fiber, 19mg cholesterol, 235mg sodium

Quick & Easy ▶

Prep Time: 10 minutes

Cook Time: 25 minutes

Average Rating: ★★★★★

What other cooks have done:

"What a terrific basic muffin recipe! I made a double batch and then split the batter into four bowls and made the following variations: strawberry with almond extract and nutmeg, banana with cinnamon, banana with chocolate chips and pecans, and blueberry. They were all fantastic! Fluffy and not brick-like (like some other recipes I've tried)."

Autumn Muffins

Submitted by: **Jack Dickson**
"Lots of fruit, lots of spices, and lots of goodness. Perfect on cold fall mornings."

¾	cup packed brown sugar	½	teaspoon ground nutmeg
¾	cup white sugar	1	cup butter, melted
3	cups all-purpose flour	1¼	cups milk
1	tablespoon baking powder	2	eggs, lightly beaten
½	teaspoon baking soda	1	cup chopped cranberries
½	teaspoon salt	1	cup chopped, peeled apple
2	teaspoons ground cinnamon	½	cup chopped dried figs
1	teaspoon ground ginger	¾	cup chopped toasted hazelnuts

1. Preheat oven to 375°F (190°C). Line muffin pans with paper cups.
2. Combine brown sugar, white sugar, flour, baking powder, baking soda, salt, cinnamon, ginger, and nutmeg. Make a well in the center and add melted butter, milk, and eggs; mix well. Stir in cranberries, apple, figs, and hazelnuts. Spoon batter into muffin pans, filling ¾ full.
3. Bake in the preheated oven for 15 to 20 minutes or until a toothpick inserted in the center of a muffin comes out clean. Remove from pans immediately and cool on wire racks. **Yield:** 18 muffins.

Per serving: About 304 calories, 4g protein, 41g carbohydrate, 15g fat, 2g fiber, 53mg cholesterol, 299mg sodium

Banana Oat Muffins

Submitted by: **Karen Resciniti**
"A healthy and delicious morning treat!"

1½	cups all-purpose flour	1	egg, lightly beaten
1	cup rolled oats	¾	cup milk
½	cup white sugar	⅓	cup vegetable oil
2	teaspoons baking powder	½	teaspoon vanilla extract
1	teaspoon baking soda	1	cup mashed bananas
½	teaspoon salt		

1. Preheat oven to 400°F (200°C). Line muffin pan with paper cups.
2. Combine flour, oats, sugar, baking powder, baking soda, and salt.
3. In a large bowl, stir together egg, milk, oil, and vanilla extract. Add mashed banana and combine thoroughly. Stir flour mixture into banana mixture until just combined. Pour batter into muffin pan.
4. Bake in the preheated oven for 18 to 20 minutes. Remove from pan immediately and cool on a wire rack. **Yield:** 1 dozen muffins.

Per serving: About 201 calories, 4g protein, 30g carbohydrate, 8g fat, 2g fiber, 19mg cholesterol, 297mg sodium

Prep Time: 15 minutes

Cook Time: 20 minutes

Average Rating: ★★★★★

What other cooks have done:

"This is a hearty wholesome muffin. For those with a food processor, I highly recommend using a fine shredding blade for the carrots and apple. I took these to work and they were a hit—a nice change from overly sweet dessertlike muffins."

Prep Time: 15 minutes

Cook Time: 1 hour

Average Rating: ★★★★★

What other cooks have done:

"Great banana flavor and moist texture that I like in banana bread. I added 1 teaspoon each of vanilla extract and ground cinnamon and ½ teaspoon of ground nutmeg."

Bran Flax Muffins

Submitted by: **Jane Massey**

"These oatmeal muffins are low in fat, have lots of fiber, and are delicious."

1½	cups all-purpose flour	¾	cup skim milk
¾	cup ground flax seed	2	tablespoons vegetable oil
¾	cup oat bran	2	eggs, lightly beaten
1	cup packed brown sugar	1	teaspoon vanilla extract
2	teaspoons baking soda	2	cups shredded carrots
1	teaspoon baking powder	½	cup raisins
1	teaspoon salt	2	apples, peeled and shredded
2	teaspoons ground cinnamon	1	cup chopped mixed nuts

1. Preheat oven to 350°F (175°C). Lightly grease muffin pans or line with paper cups.

2. In a large bowl, mix together flour, flax seed, oat bran, brown sugar, baking soda, baking powder, salt, and cinnamon. Add milk, oil, eggs, and vanilla; mix until just blended. Stir in carrots, raisins, apples, and nuts. Spoon batter into prepared muffin pans, filling ⅔ full.

3. Bake in the preheated oven for 15 to 20 minutes or until a toothpick inserted in the center of a muffin comes out clean. **Yield:** 15 muffins.

Per serving: About 270 calories, 7g protein, 42g carbohydrate, 10g fat, 5g fiber, 29mg cholesterol, 446mg sodium

Banana Bread II

Submitted by: **Carol**

"I've made this recipe that belonged to my mother since I was a teenager."

1¾	cups all-purpose flour	⅓	cup butter, softened
2	teaspoons baking powder	2	eggs
¼	teaspoon baking soda	½	cup chopped walnuts
½	teaspoon salt	1	cup mashed banana
⅔	cup white sugar		

1. Preheat the oven to 350°F (175°C). Lightly grease a 4x8 inch loaf pan.

2. In a large mixing bowl, sift together flour, baking powder, baking soda, salt, and sugar. Add butter, eggs, nuts, and mashed banana. Beat just until blended. Pour batter into prepared pan.

3. Bake in the preheated oven about 1 hour or until a toothpick inserted in the center of the loaf comes out clean. **Yield:** 1 (4x8 inch) loaf (12 servings).

Per serving: About 217 calories, 4g protein, 30g carbohydrate, 10g fat, 1g fiber, 49mg cholesterol, 268mg sodium

Lemon Poppy Seed Bread

Submitted by: **Margie**

"Delicious and easy poppy seed bread made from scratch."

3	cups all-purpose flour	3	eggs
1½	teaspoons salt	1½	cups milk
1½	teaspoons baking powder	1½	teaspoons vanilla extract
1½	tablespoons poppy seeds	1½	teaspoons lemon extract
2½	cups white sugar	¼	cup orange juice
1	cup plus 2 tablespoons	¾	cup white sugar
	vegetable oil	½	teaspoon lemon extract

1. Preheat the oven to 350°F (175°C). Lightly grease 3 (4x8) inch loaf pans.

2. Stir together flour, salt, baking powder, poppy seeds, and 2½ cups sugar. Add oil, eggs, milk, vanilla, and 1½ teaspoons lemon extract; mix until smooth, about 1 minute. Pour batter evenly into prepared pans.

3. Bake in the preheated oven for 50 to 55 minutes or until a toothpick inserted in the center of the loaves comes out clean. Cool in pans for 10 minutes.

4. Combine orange juice, ¾ cup sugar, and ½ teaspoon lemon extract; stir well. Pour over loaf while still hot. Allow loaf to cool completely before serving. **Yield:** 3 (4x8 inch) loaves (36 servings).

Per serving: About 169 calories, 2g protein, 22g carbohydrate, 8g fat, 0g fiber, 19mg cholesterol, 125mg sodium

◄ **Crowd-Pleaser**

Prep Time: 20 minutes

Cook Time: 55 minutes

Average Rating: ★★★★★

What other cooks have done:

"Wonderful bread! Made it last night and didn't use the glaze because I was freezing two of the three loaves for the holidays. It was still great! Wish I had made only two loaves. My three are not as high as I would like."

Sophie's Zucchini Bread

Submitted by: **Laura Stotko**

"Dense with zucchini, this loaf has the classic pairing of cinnamon and nuts."

3	cups all-purpose flour	2	cups white sugar
1	teaspoon salt	3	teaspoons vanilla extract
1	teaspoon baking soda	1	cup vegetable oil
1	tablespoon ground cinnamon	3	cups grated zucchini
¼	teaspoon baking powder	1	cup chopped walnuts (optional)
3	eggs, lightly beaten		

1. Preheat oven to 350°F (175°C).

2. Sift together flour, salt, baking soda, cinnamon, and baking powder.

3. Mix together eggs, sugar, vanilla, and oil. Stir zucchini into egg mixture. Add dry ingredients, mixing well. Stir in nuts, if desired. Pour into 2 (5x9 inch) loaf pans.

4. Bake in the preheated oven for 1 hour. **Yield:** 2 (5x9 inch) loaves (24 servings).

Per serving: About 249 calories, 3g protein, 30g carbohydrate, 13g fat, 1g fiber, 27mg cholesterol, 163mg sodium

◄ **Kid-Friendly**

Prep Time: 10 minutes

Cook Time: 1 hour

Average Rating: ★★★★★

What other cooks have done:

"Seriously, this bread is so good. It's moist and sweet and comes out perfect every time. My nephew and nieces love it and have no idea we're sneaking in veggies on them."

Pumpkin Swirl Bread

Submitted by: **Ellen Warfield**

"For more flavor, this pumpkin bread has cream cheese in the middle. I generally double it and make three 4x8 inch loaves. They freeze well."

1	(8 ounce) package cream cheese, softened	½	teaspoon salt
¼	cup white sugar	1	teaspoon ground cinnamon
1	egg, lightly beaten	¼	teaspoon ground nutmeg
1¾	cups all-purpose flour	1	cup canned pumpkin
1½	cups white sugar	½	cup butter, melted
1	teaspoon baking soda	1	egg, lightly beaten
		⅓	cup water

1. Preheat oven to 350°F (175°C). Lightly grease and flour a 5x9 inch loaf pan.

2. Blend cream cheese, ¼ cup sugar, and 1 egg. Set aside.

3. Combine flour, 1½ cups white sugar, baking soda, salt, cinnamon, and nutmeg. Set aside.

4. Combine pumpkin, butter, egg, and water. Add flour mixture to pumpkin mixture, mixing just until moistened. Reserve 2 cups of the batter. Pour the remaining batter into prepared loaf pan. Pour cream cheese mixture over pumpkin batter and top with reserved pumpkin batter. Run a knife through batter to create a swirl.

5. Bake in the preheated oven for 70 minutes or until a toothpick inserted in the center of the pan comes out clean. Cool in the pan for 10 minutes and then remove from pan to a wire rack to cool completely. **Yield:** 1 (5x9 inch) loaf (12 servings).

Per serving: About 318 calories, 4g protein, 44g carbohydrate, 14g fat, 1g fiber, 41mg cholesterol, 346mg sodium

Boston Brown Bread

Submitted by: **Sarah**

"This is an excellent whole wheat raisin bread recipe that needs only several ingredients."

1	cup all-purpose flour	1	cup molasses
2	cups whole wheat flour	1½	cups buttermilk
1	teaspoon baking soda	⅔	cup raisins
¼	teaspoon salt		

1. Preheat oven to 375°F (190°C). Lightly grease a 5x9 inch loaf pan.
2. In a large bowl, stir together flours, baking soda, and salt. Mix in molasses and buttermilk. Stir in raisins. Pour batter into prepared pan.
3. Bake in the preheated oven for 1 hour or until a toothpick inserted in the center of the loaf comes out clean. **Yield:** 1 (5x9 inch) loaf (12 servings).

Per serving: About 215 calories, 5g protein, 49g carbohydrate, 1g fat, 3g fiber, 1mg cholesterol, 198mg sodium

Cranberry Nut Bread

Submitted by: **Karin Christian**

"A moist quick bread with a hint of orange flavor and the tang of cranberries."

2	cups all-purpose flour	½	cup chopped walnuts
¾	cup white sugar	1	egg
¾	teaspoon salt	2	tablespoons vegetable oil
1½	teaspoons baking powder	1	tablespoon grated orange zest
½	teaspoon baking soda		
1	cup chopped cranberries	¾	cup orange juice

1. Preheat oven to 350°F (175°C). Grease a 5x9 inch loaf pan.
2. Combine flour, sugar, salt, baking powder, and baking soda. Add cranberries and walnuts; stir to coat with flour.
3. Combine the egg, oil, orange zest, and orange juice. Add the egg mixture to the flour mixture and stir until just combined. Spoon batter into prepared pan.
4. Bake in the preheated oven for 50 minutes or until a toothpick inserted in the center of the pan comes out clean. Cool in pan for 10 minutes and then remove from the pan and cool completely on a wire rack. **Yield:** 1 (5x9 inch) loaf (12 servings).

Per serving: About 196 calories, 4g protein, 32g carbohydrate, 6g fat, 1g fiber, 18mg cholesterol, 265mg sodium

Strawberry Bread

Submitted by: **Ellen Rainey**

"Wonderful hot or cold, for breakfast or dessert. A definite family favorite."

2	cups fresh strawberries	1	teaspoon salt
2	teaspoons white sugar	1	teaspoon baking soda
3	cups plus 2 tablespoons all-purpose flour	1¼	cups vegetable oil
2	cups white sugar	4	eggs, lightly beaten
1	tablespoon ground cinnamon	1¼	cups chopped pecans

1. Preheat the oven to 350°F (175°C). Lightly grease 2 (5x9 inch) loaf pans.
2. Slice strawberries and place in a medium bowl. Sprinkle with 2 teaspoons sugar, and set aside.
3. Combine flour, 2 cups sugar, cinnamon, salt, and baking soda in a large bowl; mix well. Blend oil and eggs into strawberries. Add strawberry mixture to flour mixture, blending until dry ingredients are just moistened. Stir in pecans. Divide batter into pans.
4. Bake in the preheated oven for 55 to 60 minutes or until a toothpick inserted in the center of the loaf comes out clean. Let cool in pans on a wire rack for 10 minutes. Remove from pans and cool completely. **Yield**: 2 (5x9 inch) loaves (24 servings).

Per serving: About 285 calories, 3g protein, 31g carbohydrate, 17g fat, 2g fiber, 35mg cholesterol, 161mg sodium

Golden Sweet Cornbread

Submitted by: **Lori White**

"If you like sweet cornbread, this is the recipe for you!"

1	cup all-purpose flour	3½	teaspoons baking powder
1	cup yellow cornmeal	1	egg
⅔	cup white sugar	1	cup milk
1	teaspoon salt	⅓	cup vegetable oil

1. Preheat the oven to 400°F (200°C). Lightly grease a 9 inch round cake pan.
2. In a large bowl, combine flour, cornmeal, sugar, salt, and baking powder. Stir in egg, milk, and vegetable oil until well combined. Pour batter into prepared pan.
3. Bake in the preheated oven for 20 to 25 minutes or until a toothpick inserted in the center of the loaf comes out clean. **Yield:** 1 (9 inch) round (12 servings).

Per serving: About 189 calories, 3g protein, 28g carbohydrate, 7g fat, 1g fiber, 19mg cholesterol, 355mg sodium

Overnight Blueberry French Toast

Submitted by: **Karan Cox**

"A unique breakfast dish good for any holiday breakfast or brunch. It's filled with the fresh taste of blueberries and covered with a rich blueberry sauce."

12	slices day-old bread, cut into 1 inch cubes	1	teaspoon vanilla extract
2	(8 ounce) packages cream cheese, cut into 1 inch cubes	⅓	cup maple syrup
		1	cup white sugar
1	cup fresh blueberries	2	tablespoons cornstarch
12	eggs, lightly beaten	1	cup water
2	cups milk	1	cup fresh blueberries
		1	tablespoon butter

1. Lightly grease a 9x13 inch baking dish.

2. Arrange half of bread cubes in prepared dish and top with cream cheese cubes. Sprinkle 1 cup blueberries over cream cheese and top with remaining bread cubes.

3. In a large bowl, mix eggs, milk, vanilla, and syrup. Pour over bread cubes. Cover and refrigerate overnight.

4. Remove bread cube mixture from the refrigerator about 30 minutes before baking. Preheat the oven to 350°F (175°C).

5. Cover and bake in the preheated oven for 30 minutes. Uncover and bake 25 to 30 minutes more or until center is firm and surface is lightly browned.

6. In a medium saucepan, mix sugar, cornstarch, and water. Bring to a boil and cook, stirring constantly, 3 to 4 minutes. Mix in 1 cup blueberries. Reduce heat and simmer 10 minutes or until blueberries burst. Stir in butter and pour over baked French toast. **Yield:** 10 servings.

Per serving: About 489 calories, 15g protein, 52g carbohydrate, 25g fat, 2g fiber, 312mg cholesterol, 410mg sodium

◄ **Crowd-Pleaser**

Prep Time: 15 minutes

Cook Time: 1 hour 15 minutes

Average Rating: ★★★★☆

What other cooks have done:

"This is scrumptious! I use only about half of an 8 ounce package of cream cheese. I cut it into small pieces and distribute it evenly over all. Don't skip the blueberry syrup—it's a must!"

Buttermilk Pancakes II

Submitted by: **Lebury**

"Buttermilk's the secret to these light and fluffy pancakes—it's the best I've ever made!"

3	cups all-purpose flour	3	cups buttermilk
3	tablespoons white sugar	½	cup milk
1	tablespoon baking powder	3	eggs
1½	teaspoons baking soda	⅓	cup butter, melted
¾	teaspoon salt		

1. In a large bowl, combine flour, sugar, baking powder, baking soda, and salt. In a separate bowl, beat together buttermilk, milk, eggs, and melted butter.

2. Heat a lightly oiled griddle or frying pan over medium-high heat.

3. Pour buttermilk mixture into flour mixture, using a wooden spoon or fork to blend. Stir just until blended. Do not overstir. Pour or scoop ½ cupfuls of batter onto the griddle. Cook until pancakes are golden brown on both sides; serve hot. **Yield:** 12 servings.

Per serving: About 220 calories, 7g protein, 31g carbohydrate, 7g fat, 1g fiber, 70mg cholesterol, 502mg sodium

Banana Pancakes

Submitted by: **Andrea**

"Crowd-pleasing banana pancakes made from scratch. A fun twist on ordinary pancakes."

1	cup all-purpose flour	1	egg, lightly beaten
1	tablespoon white sugar	1	cup milk
2	teaspoons baking powder	2	tablespoons vegetable oil
¼	teaspoon salt	2	ripe bananas, mashed

1. Combine flour, white sugar, baking powder, and salt. In a separate bowl, mix together egg, milk, vegetable oil, and bananas.

2. Stir flour mixture into banana mixture; batter will be slightly lumpy.

3. Heat a lightly oiled griddle or frying pan over medium-high heat. Pour or scoop ¼ cupfuls of batter onto the griddle. Cook until pancakes are golden brown on both sides; serve hot. **Yield:** 6 servings.

Per serving: About 195 calories, 5g protein, 30g carbohydrate, 7g fat, 2g fiber, 39mg cholesterol, 211mg sodium

---

Family Favorite ▶

Prep Time: 15 minutes

Cook Time: 10 minutes

Average Rating: ★★★★★

What other cooks have done:

"Very good, but the batter made too much for myself and my daughter, and we're fairly big eaters. We refrigerated the leftovers and had another meal a few days later. Scale down the recipe if you want just one meal."

Quick & Easy ▶

Prep Time: 5 minutes

Cook Time: 10 minutes

Average Rating: ★★★★☆

What other cooks have done:

"My 4-year-old daughter devoured her portion, which says a lot because she's not much of a pancake fan. To jazz up the final presentation, I served them with maple syrup and real whipped cream enhanced with a bit of brandy extract."

Emma's Belgian Waffles

Submitted by: **Emma**

"These waffles taste wonderful and are simple to make; they include self-rising flour instead of yeast."

2	egg yolks, lightly beaten	1	teaspoon salt
5	tablespoons white sugar	2¾	cups self-rising flour
1½	teaspoons vanilla extract	2	cups warm milk
½	cup butter, melted	2	egg whites

1. In a large bowl, mix together egg yolks and sugar. Beat in vanilla, butter, and salt. Alternately mix in flour and milk until well blended.
2. In a separate bowl, beat egg whites until they form soft peaks. Fold egg whites into batter and let stand for 40 minutes.
3. Spray waffle iron with cooking spray. Pour batter, in batches, onto hot waffle iron. Cook until golden brown and fluffy. **Yield**: 6 servings.

Per serving: About 448 calories, 11g protein, 57g carbohydrate, 19g fat, 2g fiber, 119mg cholesterol, 1333mg sodium

◀ Quick & Easy

Prep Time: 10 minutes

Stand Time: 40 minutes

Cook Time: 10 minutes per batch

Average Rating: ★★★★★

What other cooks have done:
"These waffles have quickly become the family's favorite. They smell so wonderful when cooking. They're truly delicious. I didn't have any self-rising flour so I added 2¾ teaspoons of baking powder to the flour. The kids are fighting to get to the fridge in the morning to get the leftovers."

Cranberry Swirl Coffee Cake

Submitted by: **Laura Owen**

"An old family recipe that's delicious for breakfast on Thanksgiving Day while watching the parade! Plain yogurt can be substituted for sour cream."

½	cup butter	1	teaspoon baking soda
1	cup white sugar	½	teaspoon salt
2	eggs	1	cup sour cream
1	teaspoon almond extract	1	(8 ounce) can whole-berry
2	cups all-purpose flour		cranberry sauce, divided
1	teaspoon baking powder		

1. Preheat oven to 350°F (175°C). Grease and flour a 9 or 10 inch tube pan.
2. In a large bowl, cream together butter and sugar until light and fluffy. Beat in eggs, one at a time, then stir in almond extract. Combine flour, baking powder, baking soda, and salt; stir into the creamed mixture, alternating with the sour cream.
3. Pour one-third of batter into the prepared tube pan. Swirl half of cranberry sauce into batter. Repeat, ending with batter on top.
4. Bake in the preheated oven for 55 minutes or until golden brown.
Yield: 14 servings.

Per serving: About 249 calories, 3g protein, 35g carbohydrate, 11g fat, 1g fiber, 55mg cholesterol, 296mg sodium

◀ Crowd-Pleaser

Prep Time: 20 minutes

Cook Time: 55 minutes

Average Rating: ★★★★★

What other cooks have done:
"It's the best! I added a crumb topping: ⅓ cup flour, ¼ cup packed brown sugar, 3 tablespoons melted butter. Then I drizzled the coffee cake with a glaze made from powdered sugar, vanilla extract, and milk. It was awesome!"

Prep Time: 30 minutes

Cook Time: 1 hour

Average Rating: ★★★★★

What other cooks have done:

"A delicious recipe! I didn't use a springform pan. I used a 12 inch round stone dish. I increased the butter for the topping to ½ cup (one stick), the brown sugar to ¾ cup, cranberries to 1¾ cups, and pecans to ¾ cup. Using stoneware, I had to melt the butter in the microwave (something I wouldn't do using a regular metal pan). This recipe is a keeper. Suggest buying extra cranberries and freezing to have on hand year-round for this recipe."

Cranberry Upside-Down Coffee Cake

(pictured on page 264)

Submitted by: **Marjorita Whyte**
"Cranberries and pecans are baked in the bottom of this cake. Turn the cake over for oohs and ahs."

1½	cups all-purpose flour	½	cup chopped pecans
1½	teaspoons baking powder	½	cup butter, softened
1	teaspoon baking soda	¾	cup white sugar
½	teaspoon ground cinnamon	2	eggs
¼	teaspoon salt	1	teaspoon vanilla extract
⅔	cup packed brown sugar	1	(8 ounce) container sour cream
⅓	cup butter		
1¼	cups cranberries		

1. Preheat oven to 350°F (175°C). Wrap the outside of a 9 inch springform pan with aluminum foil to prevent leaking. Sift together the flour, baking powder, baking soda, cinnamon, and salt. Set aside.
2. In a saucepan over medium heat, combine brown sugar and ⅓ cup butter. Bring to a boil and pour into prepared springform pan. Sprinkle with cranberries and pecans.
3. In a large bowl, cream together the butter and ¾ cup sugar until light and fluffy. Beat in the eggs, one at a time, and stir in the vanilla. Beat in the flour mixture alternately with the sour cream. Pour batter into prepared pan.
4. Bake in the preheated oven for 1 hour or until a toothpick inserted in the center of the cake comes out clean. Cool in pan for 10 minutes; invert onto a serving platter, and carefully remove pan. Serve warm. **Yield:** 12 servings.

Per serving: About 358 calories, 4g protein, 39g carbohydrate, 21g fat, 1g fiber, 78mg cholesterol, 340mg sodium

Cinnamon Rolls

Submitted by: **Kathy Nowell**

"Here's my all-time favorite cinnamon roll recipe. It turns out perfect every time and is so quick and easy to make."

1	cup warm water (110°F/45°C)	1	teaspoon active dry yeast
1	egg	⅓	cup butter
3	cups bread flour	½	cup vanilla ice cream
¼	cup white sugar	½	cup packed brown sugar
3	tablespoons instant non-fat dry milk powder	½	cup butter, softened
1½	teaspoons salt	1	tablespoon ground cinnamon
5	tablespoons butter, softened	½	cup packed brown sugar

1. Place water, egg, bread flour, white sugar, powdered milk, salt, 5 tablespoons butter, and yeast into bread machine pan in the order suggested by the manufacturer. Select Dough setting and press Start.

2. Lightly grease a 9x13 inch pan.

3. In a small saucepan, melt ⅓ cup butter. Add ice cream and brown sugar; bring to a boil and cook for 2 minutes. Pour caramel into the prepared pan.

4. Preheat oven to 350°F (175°C).

5. Turn dough out onto a lightly floured surface. Pat dough into a rectangle. Spread with ½ cup softened butter and sprinkle lightly with cinnamon. Crumble ½ cup brown sugar over the top. Roll up and press edge to seal. Cut into 12 rolls and place in prepared pan of caramel. Allow dough to rise until doubled in size, about 45 minutes.

6. Bake in the preheated oven for 20 to 25 minutes or until golden brown. **Yield:** 1 dozen rolls.

Per serving: About 376 calories, 6g protein, 46g carbohydrate, 19g fat, 1g fiber, 68mg cholesterol, 493mg sodium

◀ **Family Favorite**

Prep Time: 30 minutes

Cook Time: 25 minutes

Average Rating: ★★★★★

What other cooks have done:

"These cinnamon rolls are a hit anywhere I take them—work, family gatherings, etc. I like to prepare them the night before, let them rise (covered and in the refrigerator) while I'm sleeping, and pop them into the oven for fresh, just-out-of-the-oven cinnamon rolls in the morning."

Sweet Dinner Rolls

Submitted by: **Donna West**
"You can use this dough to make wonderful dinner rolls as well as cinnamon rolls. Mix it in your bread machine, but bake the rolls in the oven. They're light, soft, and sweet."

½	cup warm water (110°F/45°C)	1	teaspoon salt
½	cup warm milk	3¾	cups all-purpose flour
1	egg	1	(.25 ounce) package active dry yeast
⅓	cup butter, softened	¼	cup butter, softened
⅓	cup white sugar		

1. Place water, milk, egg, ⅓ cup butter, sugar, salt, flour, and yeast into bread machine pan in the order suggested by the manufacturer. Select Dough/Knead setting and First Rise Cycle; press Start.
2. When cycle finishes, turn dough out onto a lightly floured surface. Divide dough in half. Roll each half into a 12 inch circle and spread 2 tablespoons softened butter on each round. Cut each circle into 8 wedges. Roll up wedges, starting at wide end; roll gently but tightly. Place point side down on ungreased baking sheet. Cover with a clean kitchen towel and let rise in a warm place 1 hour. Preheat oven to 400°F (200°C).
3. Bake in the preheated oven for 10 to 15 minutes or until golden.
Yield: 16 servings.

Per serving: About 192 calories, 4g protein, 27g carbohydrate, 8g fat, 1g fiber, 32mg cholesterol, 222mg sodium

Hawaiian Bread

Submitted by: **Teresa**
"Styled after the classic Hawaiian sweet bread and very good."

½	cup mashed banana	1	teaspoon coconut extract
½	cup crushed pineapple, with juice	½	teaspoon salt
1	egg	⅓	cup white sugar
¼	cup milk	½	cup instant potato flakes
¼	cup butter or margarine, softened	3	cups bread flour
		1½	teaspoons active dry yeast

1. Place all ingredients into bread machine pan in the order suggested by the manufacturer. Select Light setting and press Start. **Yield:** 1 (1½ pound) loaf (15 servings).

Per serving: About 168 calories, 4g protein, 29g carbohydrate, 4g fat, 1g fiber, 14mg cholesterol, 122mg sodium

---

Whole Wheat Honey Bread

Submitted by: **Melinda Halvorson**
"Very moist. This is our family favorite!"

1	cup plus 2 tablespoons water	1	tablespoon instant non-fat dry milk powder
3	cups whole wheat flour	1½	tablespoons shortening
1½	teaspoons salt	1½	teaspoons active dry yeast
⅓	cup honey		

1. Place all ingredients into bread machine pan in the order suggested by the manufacturer. Select Whole Wheat setting and press Start. **Yield:** 1 (1½ pound) loaf (12 servings).

Per serving: About 148 calories, 5g protein, 30g carbohydrate, 2g fat, 4g fiber, 0mg cholesterol, 297mg sodium

Batter White Bread

Submitted by: **Ed**
"Batter bread is a no-knead yeast bread. Hint: All yeast bread doughs rise best at about 85°F. Put the dough in the oven with a bowl of hot water on the bottom shelf."

2	tablespoons shortening	1	(.25 ounce) package active dry yeast
3	cups sifted all-purpose flour, divided	1¼	cups warm water (110°F/45°C)
2	tablespoons white sugar	1	tablespoon butter, melted
2	teaspoons salt		

1. Mix together shortening, 1¼ cups flour, sugar, salt, and yeast. Add warm water and beat by hand about 300 strokes, or 3 minutes with an electric mixer. Add remaining flour, scraping bowl often, and mix all together until smooth.
2. Cover with a clean cloth and let rise until doubled in bulk.
3. Stir dough down gently and spoon into a lightly greased 5x9 inch loaf pan (batter should be sticky). Pat down with floured hands to help shape. Cover again and let rise for about 30 minutes.
4. Preheat oven to 375°F (190°C).
5. Bake in the preheated oven for 45 minutes. Place on a wire rack to cool and brush top with melted butter. **Yield:** 1 (5x9 inch) loaf (12 servings).

Per serving: About 151 calories, 4g protein, 26g carbohydrate, 3g fat, 1g fiber, 3mg cholesterol, 399mg sodium

◀ **Healthy**

Prep Time: 5 minutes
Cook Time: 3 hours
Average Rating: ★★★★★
What other cooks have done:
"Everything about this bread was just right—the texture, the shape, the crust, the rising, the flavor. I will definitely make this one again!"

◀ **Kid-Friendly**

Prep Time: 25 minutes
Rise Time: 1 hour 15 minutes
Cook Time: 45 minutes
Average Rating: ★★★★☆
What other cooks have done:
"Easiest yeast bread recipe I've ever made—and with excellent results. I also made a cinnamon bread by increasing the sugar to ⅓ cup; after the first rise, I sprinkled a mixture of ¼ cup sugar and 1 teaspoon cinnamon over the top, then gently folded it in to make swirls of cinnamon. Yum!"

Dr. Michael's Yeasted Cornbread

Submitted by: **Verla**

"Dr. Michael makes this every year for Christmas gifts. Luckily, we're on his list. Makes wonderful toast. Wrap in foil to store."

3½ cups bread flour	1 cup milk
½ cup cornmeal	2 tablespoons water
1 teaspoon salt	1 egg
3 tablespoons white sugar	2½ teaspoons active dry yeast
3 tablespoons shortening	

1. Place all ingredients into bread machine pan in order suggested by the manufacturer. Select Basic or White Bread setting and press Start.
2. Transfer the bread from the pan to a wire rack to cool. **Yield:** 12 servings.

Per serving: About 222 calories, 7g protein, 37g carbohydrate, 5g fat, 2g fiber, 19mg cholesterol, 212mg sodium

Sidebar

Burger or Hot Dog Buns

Submitted by: **Sally**

"Use this to make hamburger buns or hot dog buns. For hot dog buns, shape each piece into a 4x6 inch rectangle. Starting with the longer side, roll up tightly, and pinch edges to seal. Let rise 20 to 25 minutes. Bake as directed. These buns are pretty big. My husband says they're 'top of the line.'"

1 cup milk	1 (.25 ounce) package active dry yeast
½ cup water	
¼ cup butter	2 tablespoons white sugar
4½ cups all-purpose flour, divided	1½ teaspoons salt
	1 egg

1. In a small saucepan, heat milk, water, and butter until very warm, 120°F (50°C).
2. In a large bowl, mix together 1¾ cups flour, yeast, sugar, and salt. Mix milk mixture into flour mixture, and then mix in egg. Stir in the remaining flour, ½ cup at a time, beating well after each addition. When the dough has pulled together, turn it out onto a lightly floured surface and knead until smooth and elastic, about 8 minutes. Lightly grease a baking sheet.
3. Divide dough into 12 equal pieces. Shape into balls and place on baking sheet. Flatten slightly. Cover and let rise for 30 to 35 minutes.
4. Preheat oven to 400°F (200°C).
5. Bake in the preheated oven for 10 to 12 minutes or until golden brown. **Yield:** 1 dozen buns.

Per serving: About 231 calories, 6g protein, 39g carbohydrate, 5g fat, 1g fiber, 30mg cholesterol, 347mg sodium

Sidebar

Pizza Dough II

Submitted by: **Stephen**

"Makes three hearty pizza crusts that can also be used to make calzones. Dough can be frozen for later use."

1 (.25 ounce) package active dry yeast	2 tablespoons olive oil
1 tablespoon white sugar	½ cup whole wheat flour
2½ cups warm water (110°F/45°C)	5½ cups bread flour, divided
	1 tablespoon salt

1. In a large mixing bowl, dissolve yeast and sugar in warm water. Let stand until creamy, about 10 minutes.

2. Stir together olive oil, whole wheat flour, 4 cups bread flour, and salt into the yeast mixture. Mix in the remaining bread flour, ½ cup at a time, stirring well after each addition. When the dough has pulled together, turn it out onto a lightly floured surface and knead until smooth and elastic, about 8 minutes. Lightly oil a large bowl; place the dough in the bowl and turn to coat. Cover with a damp cloth and put in a warm place to rise until doubled in bulk, about 1 hour.

3. Punch dough down and turn out onto a lightly floured surface. Divide the dough into 3 equal portions and form into rounds. Cover the rounds and let them rest for about 10 minutes.

4. Preheat oven to 425°F (220°C).

5. Use a rolling pin to roll the dough into the desired shape. Cover dough with your favorite toppings and bake in the preheated oven for about 20 minutes or until the crust and cheese are golden brown.

Yield: 3 pizza crusts (12 servings).

Per serving (without toppings): About 226 calories, 8g protein, 45g carbohydrate, 2g fat, 2g fiber, 0mg cholesterol, 589mg sodium

◀ **Company is Coming**

Prep Time: 20 minutes

Rise Time: 1 hour

Cook Time: 20 minutes

Average Rating: ★★★★★

What other cooks have done:

"The best all-around pizza dough I've ever used. Not too crispy, not too chewy, substantial enough to hold the toppings, but not heavy. My kids love it. I froze one third of the batch, which was a little sticky when thawed in the microwave. Next time I'll let it sit at room temperature a little longer before rolling it."

Buttery Soft Pretzels

Submitted by: **Christa Rose**

"After spending so much money on those mall-bought pretzels, I thought I'd try making some. These pretzels are a bit sweeter than other types. Once finished, dip the hot pretzel into melted butter and coat with your favorite flavors—a bit of pretzel salt or a mixture of cinnamon and sugar. Enjoy!"

Prep Time: 30 minutes

Rise Time: 1 hour

Cook Time: 8 minutes

Average Rating: ★★★★★

What other cooks have done:

"I was looking for a new pretzel recipe and found the perfect one! Really, really good. I recommend brushing the pretzels with beaten egg yolk before sprinkling on the salt—it makes a nice, shiny appearance. A real hit on a rainy day!"

4	teaspoons active dry yeast	1½	teaspoons salt
1	teaspoon white sugar	1	tablespoon vegetable oil
1¼	cups warm water (110°F/45°C)	½	cup baking soda
5	cups all-purpose flour	4	cups hot water
½	cup white sugar	¼	cup kosher salt

1. In a small bowl, dissolve yeast and 1 teaspoon sugar in warm water. Let stand until creamy, about 10 minutes.

2. In a large bowl, mix together flour, ½ cup sugar, and salt. Make a well in the center; add yeast mixture and oil. Mix and form into a dough. If the mixture is dry, add 1 or 2 tablespoons water. Knead until smooth, about 7 to 8 minutes. Lightly oil a large bowl; place the dough in the bowl and turn to coat. Cover with plastic wrap and let rise in a warm place until doubled in size, about 1 hour.

3. Preheat oven to 450°F (230°C). In a large bowl, dissolve baking soda in hot water. Lightly grease a baking sheet.

4. Turn dough out onto a lightly floured surface and divide into 12 equal pieces. Roll each piece into a rope and twist into a pretzel shape. Dip each pretzel into the baking soda solution and place on prepared baking sheet. Sprinkle with kosher salt.

5. Bake in the preheated oven for 8 minutes or until browned.

Yield: 1 dozen pretzels.

Per serving: About 237 calories, 6g protein, 49g carbohydrate, 2g fat, 2g fiber, 0mg cholesterol, 4643mg sodium

Desserts

Cookies 'n' Cream Cake

Submitted by: **Suzanne Stull**
"Very good, simple cake to make. It always gets a lot of attention."

1	(18.25 ounce) package white cake mix	3	cups confectioners' sugar, divided
1¼	cups water	¾	cup shortening
⅓	cup vegetable oil	1	teaspoon vanilla extract
3	egg whites	3	tablespoons milk
1	cup chocolate sandwich cookie crumbs	12	chocolate sandwich cookies

1. Preheat the oven to 350°F (175°C). Grease and flour 2 (9 inch) round pans.
2. In a large bowl, mix the cake mix, water, oil, and 3 egg whites with an electric mixer on high speed for 2 minutes. Gently stir in crushed cookies. Pour batter into the prepared pans.
3. Bake in the preheated oven for 25 to 35 minutes or until a knife inserted in the center of the cake comes out clean. Cool 10 minutes in pans. Remove from pans and cool completely on wire racks.
4. In a small bowl, thoroughly blend ½ cup confectioners' sugar, shortening, vanilla, and milk. Beat in remaining confectioners' sugar until creamy. Frost the cake and garnish with remaining cookies.
Yield: 12 servings.

Per serving: About 552 calories, 4g protein, 75g carbohydrate, 27g fat, 1g fiber, 0mg cholesterol, 408mg sodium

Pineapple Upside-Down Cake V

Submitted by: **Donna**
"Double your pleasure with this two-layer pineapple upside-down cake."

¼	cup butter, softened	1	(10 ounce) jar maraschino cherries, drained
½	cup packed brown sugar, divided	1	(8 ounce) can crushed pineapple, drained with juice reserved
½	cup flaked coconut		
1	(8 ounce) can sliced pineapple, drained with juice reserved	1	(18.25 ounce) package yellow cake mix

1. Preheat oven to 350°F (175°C). Butter 2 (9 inch) round pans. Sprinkle ¼ cup brown sugar into each pan.
2. In 1 of the pans, sprinkle coconut over the brown sugar. Place pineapple rings in a single layer on top of coconut. Place a cherry in the center of each ring. In the other pan, spread the drained crushed pineapple.

3. Mix the cake mix as directed on package, substituting reserved pineapple juice for the water. Divide batter between the 2 pans. (Remember which pan has the pineapple rings in it.)
4. Bake in the preheated oven for 40 to 50 minutes or until a toothpick inserted in cake comes out clean. Cool in pans for 20 minutes.
5. While the bottoms of the cake pans are still warm, invert the layer with the crushed pineapple onto a serving dish and gently invert the layer with pineapple rings on top of it. **Yield:** 12 servings.

Per serving: About 320 calories, 2g protein, 57g carbohydrate, 10g fat, 1g fiber, 11mg cholesterol, 337mg sodium

Santa's Favorite Cake

Submitted by: **Debbie Rowe**
"Surprise Santa with this red velvet cake with a peppermint twist— a delicious peppermint cream cheese frosting."

1	(18.25 ounce) package white cake mix	2	tablespoons red food coloring
3	egg whites	1	teaspoon cider vinegar
1⅓	cups buttermilk	1	(8 ounce) package cream cheese, softened
2	tablespoons vegetable oil		
1	(9 ounce) package yellow cake mix	1	cup butter or margarine, softened
½	cup buttermilk	2	(16 ounce) packages confectioners' sugar
1	egg		
1½	tablespoons unsweetened cocoa powder	2	teaspoons peppermint extract

1. Preheat the oven to 350°F (175°C). Grease and flour 3 (9 inch) round pans.
2. In a large bowl, combine white cake mix, 3 egg whites, 1⅓ cups buttermilk, and vegetable oil. Mix with an electric mixer for 2 minutes on high speed. In a separate bowl, combine yellow cake mix, ½ cup buttermilk, 1 egg, cocoa, red food coloring, and vinegar. Mix with an electric mixer for 2 minutes on high speed.
3. Spoon white batter alternately with red batter into the prepared cake pans. Swirl batter gently with a knife to create a marbled effect.
4. Bake in the preheated oven for 22 to 25 minutes or until a toothpick inserted in the center comes out clean. Let cool in pans for 10 minutes before turning out onto a wire rack to cool completely.
5. In a large bowl, beat cream cheese and butter until smooth. Gradually blend in confectioners' sugar until incorporated and smooth. Stir in peppermint extract. Spread frosting between layers and on top and sides of cake. **Yield:** 12 servings.

Per serving: About 810 calories, 7g protein, 127g carbohydrate, 32g fat, 1g fiber, 40mg cholesterol, 710mg sodium

◄ Holiday Fare

Prep Time: 45 minutes
Cook Time: 25 minutes
Average Rating: ★★★★★
What other cooks have done:
"This makes a really festive cake. One suggestion: One teaspoon of peppermint extract goes a long way. Taste it before you add the second."

Prep Time: 30 minutes

Cook Time: 55 minutes

Average Rating: ★★★★★

What other cooks have done:

"Great cake! After trying the recipe as is, I then made another cake with butterscotch instant pudding and substituted ¾ cup of shredded zucchini for the ¾ cup mashed banana. It, too, was wonderful and tasty."

Banana Pudding Cake

Submitted by: **Barbara**

"Very moist banana cake that travels well to potlucks or picnics. It also can be baked in a 9x13 inch pan or an angel food cake pan. It's a family favorite."

1	(18.25 ounce) package yellow cake mix	¾	cup mashed banana
1	(3.4 ounce) package instant banana pudding mix	2	cups confectioners' sugar
4	eggs	2	tablespoons milk
1	cup water		Dash vanilla extract
¼	cup vegetable oil	½	cup chopped walnuts (optional)

1. Preheat the oven to 350°F (175°C). Grease and flour a 10 inch Bundt pan.

2. In a large bowl, stir together cake mix and pudding mix. Make a well in the center and pour in eggs, water, oil, and mashed banana. Beat on low speed with an electric mixer until blended. Scrape bowl and beat 4 minutes on medium speed. Pour batter into prepared pan.

3. Bake in the preheated oven for 50 to 55 minutes or until a toothpick inserted in center of cake comes out clean. Let cool in pan for 10 minutes and turn out onto a wire rack and cool completely.

4. In a small bowl, combine confectioners' sugar, milk, and vanilla. Whisk until smooth and drizzling consistency. When cake is cooled, drizzle icing over cake with a zig-zag motion. Sprinkle with chopped nuts, if desired. **Yield:** 12 servings.

Per serving: About 406 calories, 5g protein, 65g carbohydrate, 15g fat, 1g fiber, 72mg cholesterol, 429mg sodium

Brownie Caramel Cheesecake,
page 314

Butter Pecan Ice Cream, page 330

Blueberry Crumb Bars,
page 337

Margarita Cake, page 91

Chocolate Mug Milkshakes, page 15

Candy Bar Fudge, page 343

Raspberry-White Chocolate Mousse,
page 330

Black and White Cookies, page 334

Mini Cheesecakes, page 313

Fresh Strawberry Pie, page 319

Hot Fudge Ice Cream Bar Dessert,
page 71

Lemon Bundt Cake

Submitted by: **Phyllis**

"Lemon instant pudding and lemon-lime soda make this a very moist and delicious lemon cake."

1	(18.25 ounce) package lemon cake mix	¾	cup vegetable oil
1	(3.4 ounce) package instant lemon pudding mix	4	eggs
		1	cup lemon-lime flavored carbonated beverage

1. Preheat the oven to 325°F (165°C). Grease and flour a 10 inch Bundt pan.
2. In a large bowl, combine cake mix and pudding mix; stir in the oil. Beat in the eggs, one at a time, and stir in the lemon-lime soda.
3. Pour batter into the prepared pan. Bake in the preheated oven for 35 minutes or until a toothpick inserted in the center of the cake comes out clean. Allow to cool in pan, then turn onto a wire rack and cool completely. **Yield:** 14 servings.

Per serving: About 313 calories, 4g protein, 36g carbohydrate, 18g fat, 0g fiber, 70mg cholesterol, 375mg sodium

◀ Quick & Easy

Prep Time: 10 minutes
Cook Time: 35 minutes
Average Rating: ★★★★★
What other cooks have done:

"I used a 'cheater's glaze': Melt a half can of lemon frosting in the microwave for 30 seconds and drizzle over the cake. A garnish of fresh raspberries in the center of the cake looks great."

Chocolate Cavity Maker Cake

Submitted by: **Caitlin Koch**

"Chocolate, chocolate, chocolate. This cake is so moist and rich there's absolutely no need for frosting. It made me an instant star with my clients. I quickly became known as 'that incredible chocolate cake lady!'"

1	(18.25 ounce) package dark chocolate cake mix	3	eggs
1	(3.9 ounce) package instant chocolate pudding mix	⅓	cup vegetable oil
1	(16 ounce) container sour cream	½	cup coffee liqueur
		2	cups semisweet chocolate chips

1. Preheat the oven to 350°F (175°C). Grease and flour a 10 inch Bundt pan.
2. In a large bowl, combine cake mix, pudding mix, sour cream, eggs, oil, and liqueur. Beat until ingredients are well blended. Fold in chocolate chips. (Batter will be thick.) Spoon batter into prepared pan.
3. Bake in the preheated oven for 1 hour or until cake springs back when lightly touched. Cool 10 minutes in pan and turn out to cool completely on a wire rack. **Yield:** 12 servings.

Per serving: About 536 calories, 6g protein, 65g carbohydrate, 28g fat, 3g fiber, 70mg cholesterol, 487mg sodium

◀ Family Favorite

Prep Time: 30 minutes
Cook Time: 1 hour
Average Rating: ★★★★★
What other cooks have done:

"Wow! My family raved. This cake can satisfy anyone's chocolate cravings. I like using the mini-morsels best. Also, I used chocolate syrup instead of the liqueur. I agree that it's definitely rich enough not to need icing, but I couldn't let it go without adding a satiny chocolate glaze. A little whipped cream on the side is the perfect addition. This is an excellent cake for parties."

Black Russian Cake

Submitted by: **Rory Kate**
"Extremely moist and delicious cake. The coffee liqueur gives it an exceptionally rich and unique flavor. It's wonderfully complemented served with coffee drinks as an after-dinner treat."

1	(18.25 ounce) package yellow cake mix	¼	cup vodka
1	(5.9 ounce) package instant chocolate pudding mix	¼	cup coffee liqueur
		¾	cup water
4	eggs	¼	cup coffee liqueur
½	cup white sugar	1	cup confectioners' sugar, divided
1	cup vegetable oil		

1. Preheat the oven to 350°F (175°C). Grease and flour a 10 inch Bundt pan.
2. In a large bowl, combine the cake mix, pudding mix, eggs, white sugar, oil, vodka, ¼ cup liqueur, and water. Beat on medium speed with an electric mixer for 4 minutes. Pour batter into prepared pan.
3. Bake in the preheated oven for 40 minutes or until toothpick inserted in center of cake comes out clean. Cool on a wire rack.
4. Make a glaze by combining ¼ cup liqueur and ½ cup confectioners' sugar. Turn cake out onto a cake plate. Poke cake several times with a fork. Cover with glaze and dust with remaining ½ cup confectioners' sugar. **Yield:** 12 servings.

Per serving: About 542 calories, 4g protein, 68g carbohydrate, 25g fat, 1g fiber, 72mg cholesterol, 502mg sodium

Chocolate Rum Cake

Submitted by: **Suzanne Stull**
"Good for Christmas or anytime!"

½	cup chopped nuts	½	cup water
1	(18.25 ounce) package chocolate cake mix	½	cup white rum
		½	cup butter
1	(3.9 ounce) package instant chocolate pudding mix	1	cup white sugar
		¼	cup white rum
4	eggs	¼	cup water
½	cup vegetable oil		

1. Preheat oven to 325°F (165°C). Grease a 10 inch Bundt pan. Sprinkle chopped nuts in pan.
2. With an electric mixer, beat cake mix, pudding mix, eggs, oil, ½ cup water, and ½ cup rum on high speed for 2 minutes. Pour batter into prepared pan over the chopped nuts.

3. Bake in the preheated oven for 50 to 60 minutes.

4. In a saucepan, combine the butter, sugar, ¼ cup rum, and ¼ cup water. Bring mixture to a boil and cook for 2 minutes. Pour glaze over cake as soon as you remove it from the oven. Let cake stand for 30 minutes, then turn out onto a serving dish. **Yield:** 14 servings.

Per serving: About 450 calories, 5g protein, 49g carbohydrate, 25g fat, 2g fiber, 78mg cholesterol, 502mg sodium

Cream Cheese Pound Cake III

Submitted by: **Nanci**
"A heavy, dense, extremely flavorful pound cake."

1½	cups butter, softened	6	eggs
1	(8 ounce) package cream cheese, softened	3	cups all-purpose flour
3	cups white sugar	1	teaspoon vanilla extract

1. Preheat the oven to 325°F (165°C). Grease and flour a 10 inch tube pan.

2. In a large bowl, cream butter and cream cheese until smooth. Add sugar gradually and beat until fluffy.

3. Add eggs, two at a time, beating well after each addition. Add the flour all at once and mix in. Stir in vanilla.

4. Pour into prepared pan. Bake in the preheated oven for 1 hour and 20 minutes, checking for doneness after 1 hour. A toothpick inserted into center of cake will come out clean. **Yield:** 14 servings.

Per serving: About 526 calories, 7g protein, 64g carbohydrate, 28g fat, 1g fiber, 162mg cholesterol, 276mg sodium

◄ **Classic Comfort Food**

Prep Time: 30 minutes

Cook Time: 1 hour 20 minutes

Average Rating: ★★★★★

What other cooks have done:

"It could probably be the best pound cake I've ever made, but I did tweak it a bit. I used 1¼ cups butter and ¼ cup buttermilk. Buttermilk is a secret ingredient that I like to use in place of regular milk in a recipe. It makes cakes, muffins, and breads very moist. I also added a teaspoon of lemon extract along with the vanilla. The lemon flavor was very light and added a little something special."

Coconut Pound Cake

Submitted by: **Janie Carter**
"My grandchildren love this cake."

2	cups white sugar	3½	ounces flaked coconut
1	cup butter, softened	1	teaspoon coconut extract
5	eggs	1	cup white sugar
2	cups all-purpose flour	¼	cup water
1½	teaspoons baking powder	1	teaspoon coconut extract
½	cup milk	½	cup chopped walnuts

1. Preheat the oven to 350°F (175°C). Grease and flour a 10 inch tube pan.
2. In a large bowl, cream 2 cups sugar and the butter. Fold in the eggs, one at a time, fully incorporating each one before adding another.
3. In separate bowl, mix the flour, baking powder, milk, flaked coconut, and 1 teaspoon coconut extract. Beat into the creamed mixture. Pour the batter into the prepared pan.
4. Bake 1 hour in the preheated oven or until a knife inserted in the center comes out clean. Cool on a wire rack for just a few minutes and turn out onto a serving platter.
5. In a small saucepan, mix together 1 cup sugar, water, 1 teaspoon coconut extract, and walnuts. Boil for 1 minute and pour over warm cake. **Yield:** 14 servings.

Per serving: About 441 calories, 5g protein, 61g carbohydrate, 20g fat, 1g fiber, 112mg cholesterol, 232mg sodium

Pineapple Angel Food Cake

Submitted by: **Donna**
"Delicious and so very easy."

1	(18.25 ounce) package angel food cake mix	1	(12 ounce) container frozen whipped topping, thawed
1	(20 ounce) can crushed pineapple with juice		

1. Preheat oven to 350°F (175°C). Lightly grease a 9x13 inch pan with vegetable cooking spray.
2. In a large bowl, combine cake mix and pineapple (with juice). Mix until well blended.
3. Pour batter into prepared pan. Bake in the preheated oven for 25 minutes or until golden brown. Let cool.
4. Serve with whipped topping. **Yield:** 18 servings.

Per serving: About 183 calories, 3g protein, 32g carbohydrate, 5g fat, 0g fiber, 0mg cholesterol, 252mg sodium

---

Crowd-Pleaser ▶

Prep Time: 20 minutes
Cook Time: 1 hour 1 minute
Average Rating: ★★★★★
What other cooks have done:
"Great cake! I would definitely make it again, using a plain powdered sugar glaze instead."

Healthy ▶

Prep Time: 10 minutes
Cook Time: 25 minutes
Average Rating: ★★★★★
What other cooks have done:
"This cake turned out beautiful! It even tastes great without the whipped topping—making it a guilt-free snack. My family loves this recipe!"

Mandarin Orange Cake

Submitted by: **Ellen**
"Quick and delicious!"

1 (18.25 ounce) package
   yellow cake mix
4 eggs
1 cup vegetable oil
1 (11 ounce) can mandarin
   orange segments with
   juice

1 (8 ounce) container frozen
   whipped topping, thawed
1 (20 ounce) can crushed
   pineapple with juice
1 (3.4 ounce) package instant
   vanilla pudding mix

1. Preheat oven to 350°F (175°C). Grease and flour a 9x13 inch pan.
2. In a large bowl, combine cake mix, eggs, oil, and mandarin oranges with juice. Beat until smooth. Pour batter into prepared pan.
3. Bake in the preheated oven for 35 to 40 minutes or until a toothpick inserted in the center of the cake comes out clean. Cool.
4. In a large bowl, beat together whipped topping, pineapple with juice, and pudding mix until blended. Spread on cake. **Yield:** 18 servings.

Per serving: About 337 calories, 3g protein, 38g carbohydrate, 20g fat, 1g fiber, 48mg cholesterol, 286mg sodium

◄ **Covered-Dish Favorite**

Prep Time: 15 minutes
Cook Time: 40 minutes
Average Rating: ★★★★★
What other cooks have done:
"Try making the icing with mandarin orange slices instead of pineapple. This cake is like a trifle and ambrosia. I didn't use any oil—I substituted applesauce for all of it. Yummy!"

Coconut Poke Cake

Submitted by: **Leslie**
"White cake soaked in sweet creamy coconut milk and smothered in whipped topping and flaked coconut. A real treat for those with a sweet tooth."

1 (18.25 ounce) package
   white cake mix
1 (14 ounce) can cream of
   coconut
1 (14 ounce) can sweetened
   condensed milk

1 (16 ounce) package frozen
   whipped topping, thawed
1 (8 ounce) package flaked
   coconut

1. Prepare and bake white cake mix in a 9x13 inch pan according to package directions. Remove cake from oven. While still hot, using a fork, poke holes all over the top of the cake.
2. Mix cream of coconut and sweetened condensed milk. Pour over the hot cake. Let cake cool completely, then frost with the whipped topping and top with the flaked coconut. Keep cake refrigerated. **Yield:** 18 servings.

Per serving: About 371 calories, 4g protein, 48g carbohydrate, 19g fat, 1g fiber, 8mg cholesterol, 265mg sodium

◄ **Family Favorite**

Prep Time: 30 minutes
Cook Time: 1 hour
Average Rating: ★★★★★
What other cooks have done:
"Awesome coconut cake. I've been making this for a while. However, I recommend adding 1 teaspoon coconut extract to the batter and using homemade whipped cream on top, sprinkled with coconut. Yum!"

Classic Comfort Food ▶

Prep Time: 30 minutes

Cook Time: 40 minutes

Average Rating: ★★★★★

What other cooks have done:

"I made this using cherry pie filling, ½ teaspoon almond extract instead of the cinnamon, and chopped blanched almonds instead of the walnuts. My son and husband begged me to make another one right after they polished it off! It's easy and delicious. Perfect as a coffee cake for the morning!"

Holiday Gift Giving ▶

Prep Time: 25 minutes

Cook Time: 1 hour

Average Rating: ★★★★★

What other cooks have done:

"I recommend increasing the cinnamon and ginger to at least 2 teaspoons each. I baked the cake in a 9 inch springform pan and it was really pretty. You can sprinkle powdered sugar over the top for a nice presentation."

Apple Cake III

Submitted by: **Mary Ann Benzon**
"An old, treasured recipe that's quick and easy."

1	(18.25 ounce) package yellow cake mix	
3	eggs	
1	(21 ounce) can apple pie filling	

¾	cup packed brown sugar
1	tablespoon all-purpose flour
1	tablespoon butter
1	teaspoon ground cinnamon
1	cup chopped walnuts

1. Preheat the oven to 350°F (175°C). Grease and flour a 9x13 inch pan.

2. In a large bowl, mix together the cake mix, eggs, and apple pie filling. Pour into the prepared pan. Combine the brown sugar, flour, butter, cinnamon, and walnuts. Sprinkle over the top of the batter.

3. Bake in the preheated oven for 35 to 40 minutes or until a toothpick inserted in the center of the cake comes out clean. Allow to cool. **Yield:** 24 servings.

Per serving: About 192 calories, 3g protein, 31g carbohydrate, 7g fat, 1g fiber, 28mg cholesterol, 168mg sodium

Favorite Old-Fashioned Gingerbread

Submitted by: **Charles**
"This is everyone's holiday favorite, even the busy cook's, because it's so easy to make."

½	cup white sugar
½	cup butter, softened
1	egg
1	cup molasses
2½	cups all-purpose flour
1½	teaspoons baking soda

1	teaspoon ground cinnamon
1	teaspoon ground ginger
½	teaspoon ground cloves
½	teaspoon salt
1	cup hot water

1. Preheat the oven to 350°F (175°C). Grease and flour a 9 inch square pan.

2. In a large bowl, cream together the sugar and butter. Beat in the egg and molasses.

3. In a bowl, sift together the flour, baking soda, cinnamon, ginger, cloves, and salt. Blend into the creamed mixture. Stir in the hot water. Pour into the prepared pan.

4. Bake in the preheated oven for 1 hour or until a knife inserted in the center comes out clean. Allow to cool in pan before serving. **Yield:** 12 servings.

Per serving: About 275 calories, 3g protein, 47g carbohydrate, 8g fat, 1g fiber, 38mg cholesterol, 349mg sodium

Cake Mixes from Scratch and Variations

Submitted by: **Janet**

"A convenient substitute for commercial mixes. Quick, easy, and yummy. Best of all, you control the ingredients!"

2⅓	cups all-purpose flour	½	cup shortening
1	tablespoon baking powder	2	eggs
¾	teaspoon salt	1	cup milk
1½	cups white sugar	1	teaspoon vanilla extract

1. *For a Yellow Cake:* Preheat oven to 350°F (175°C). Grease and flour a 9x13 inch pan.

2. Sift together flour, baking powder, salt, and sugar. Cut in shortening until fine crumbs are formed. Add eggs, milk, and vanilla. Beat at low speed for 1 minute, then high for 2 minutes, scraping the bowl frequently.

3. Pour batter into prepared pan. Bake in the preheated oven for 25 to 30 minutes.

4. *Variation for a White Cake:* Prepare as for the basic Yellow Cake except use 3 egg whites for the 2 whole eggs. Whites may be beaten separately and folded in for a lighter cake.

5. *Variation for a Chocolate Cake:* Add ¼ cup unsweetened cocoa powder to the basic cake mix prior to adding the milk.

6. *Variation for a Spice Cake:* Add 1 teaspoon ground cinnamon, ¼ teaspoon ground cloves, and ¼ teaspoon ground allspice to the basic cake mix.

7. *Variation for a Pineapple Upside Down Cake:* Melt ½ cup butter in a 9x13 inch pan. Add ⅔ cup brown sugar, stirring into the butter. Arrange pineapple slices in the pan. Top with the basic (Yellow Cake) mix recipe. Bake 30 to 35 minutes, cool 5 minutes, and invert to serve. **Yield:** 24 servings.

Per serving: About 142 calories, 2g protein, 23g carbohydrate, 5g fat, 0g fiber, 19mg cholesterol, 144mg sodium

◀ Crowd-Pleaser

Prep Time: 20 minutes

Cook Time: 35 minutes

Average Rating: ★★★★★

What other cooks have done:

"Love the versatility of this recipe! Don't be afraid to experiment with it! I made the white version with almond extract instead of vanilla. Try it with a fudgelike frosting."

Sunshine S'more Cupcakes

Submitted by: **Lisa**

"Easy cupcakes with graham cracker, marshmallow, and chocolate. Kids really love these."

1	(18.25 ounce) package French vanilla cake mix	24	milk chocolate candy kisses, unwrapped
2	tablespoons graham cracker crumbs	½	cup graham cracker crumbs
1½	cups water	1	(7 ounce) jar marshmallow creme
3	egg whites		

1. Preheat oven to 350°F (175°C). Line muffin pans with paper liners.
2. In a large bowl, combine the cake mix, 2 tablespoons graham cracker crumbs, water, and egg whites. Beat for 2 minutes at high speed with an electric mixer.
3. Divide batter evenly among muffin cups, filling about ⅔ full. Place a chocolate kiss in each cupcake, pressing in lightly. Spoon 1 teaspoon graham cracker crumbs onto each cupcake.
4. Bake in the preheated oven for 18 to 25 minutes. Remove from the oven and top each cupcake with 1 teaspoon marshmallow creme. (Dip spoon into hot water to prevent sticking.) Return cupcakes to oven for about 1 minute to melt slightly. **Yield:** 24 servings.

Per serving: About 151 calories, 2g protein, 28g carbohydrate, 4g fat, 1g fiber, 1mg cholesterol, 162mg sodium

Apple Banana Cupcakes

Submitted by: **Barbara**

"This cupcake smells as good as it tastes. It's an old Polish recipe from some of the best bakers in Milwaukee!"

2	cups all-purpose flour	2	eggs
1	teaspoon baking soda	1	teaspoon vanilla extract
1	teaspoon salt	¼	cup buttermilk
½	teaspoon ground cinnamon	1	cup ripe bananas, mashed
½	teaspoon ground nutmeg	2	apples, peeled, cored, and shredded
⅔	cup shortening		
1¼	cups white sugar		

1. Preheat oven to 375°F (190°C). Grease and flour muffin pans or use paper liners. Sift together the flour, baking soda, salt, cinnamon, and nutmeg. Set aside.
2. In a large bowl, cream together the shortening and sugar until light and fluffy. Beat in the eggs, one at a time; stir in the vanilla and buttermilk. Beat in the flour mixture, mixing just until incorporated.

Fold in the mashed bananas and shredded apples. Fill each muffin cup half full.

3. Bake in the preheated oven for 20 to 25 minutes or until a toothpick inserted in the center of a cupcake comes out clean. Remove from pans immediately to a wire rack. Allow to cool. **Yield:** 24 cupcakes.

Per serving: About 152 calories, 2g protein, 23g carbohydrate, 6g fat, 1g fiber, 18mg cholesterol, 158mg sodium

Mini Cheesecakes *(pictured on page 303)*

Submitted by: **Janice Reesman**
"Easy and so good for holidays, weddings, or whatever the occasion!"

½	(12 ounce) package vanilla wafers	2	eggs
2	(8 ounce) packages cream cheese, softened	1	teaspoon vanilla extract
¾	cup white sugar	1	(21 ounce) can cherry pie filling

1. Preheat oven to 350°F (175°C). Line miniature muffin pans with miniature paper liners.
2. Crush the vanilla wafers and place 1 teaspoon of the crushed vanilla wafers into each muffin cup.
3. With an electric mixer, cream together the cream cheese, sugar, eggs, and vanilla. Fill each muffin cup with mixture, almost to the top.
4. Bake in the preheated oven for 15 minutes. Cool and then top each with a teaspoonful of cherry pie filling. **Yield:** 48 cheesecakes.

Per serving: About 95 calories, 1g protein, 12g carbohydrate, 5g fat, 0g fiber, 19mg cholesterol, 54mg sodium

◀ **Party Food**

Prep Time: 30 minutes
Cook Time: 15 minutes
Average Rating: ★★★★★
What other cooks have done:
"These are always a hit. I actually doubled the batter so the cheesecakes came out a little bigger. I added mini chocolate chips because not everyone likes the fruit topping."

Brownie Caramel Cheesecake *(pictured on page 297)*

Submitted by: **Jackie Meiborg**

"I get compliments whenever I make this dessert. It's very rich and worth the time and calories."

1	(10.25 ounce) package brownie mix	2	(8 ounce) packages cream cheese, softened
1	egg	½	cup white sugar
¼	cup vegetable oil	1	teaspoon vanilla extract
2	tablespoons cold water	2	eggs
1	(14 ounce) package individually wrapped caramels, unwrapped	⅓	cup chocolate fudge topping
1	(5 ounce) can evaporated milk		

1. Preheat oven to 350°F (175°C). Grease the bottom and sides of a 9 inch springform pan.

2. In a small bowl, mix together brownie mix, 1 egg, oil, and water. Spread into the prepared pan. Bake in the preheated oven for 25 minutes. Cool 10 minutes.

3. Melt the caramels with the evaporated milk over low heat in a heavy saucepan. Stir often and heat until mixture has a smooth consistency. Reserve ⅓ cup of this caramel mixture and pour the remainder over the warm, baked brownie crust.

4. In a large bowl, beat the cream cheese, sugar, and vanilla with an electric mixer until smooth. Add eggs, one at a time, beating well after each addition. Pour cream cheese mixture over caramel mixture.

5. Bake cheesecake for 40 minutes. Chill in pan. When cake is thoroughly chilled, loosen by running a knife around the edge and remove the rim of the pan. Heat reserved caramel mixture and drizzle over cheesecake. Drizzle with the chocolate topping. **Yield:** 12 servings.

Per serving: About 513 calories, 8g protein, 69g carbohydrate, 24g fat, 2g fiber, 100mg cholesterol, 353mg sodium

Peanut Butter Frosting

Submitted by: **Suzanne Stull**

"If you like peanut butter, you'll love this frosting. It's great on chocolate cakes, but for a real peanut butter experience, try it on a peanut butter cake. If you don't have cream, you can substitute milk."

½	cup butter, softened	4	cups confectioners' sugar
1	cup creamy peanut butter, divided	¼	cup whipping cream

1. In a large bowl, beat butter and peanut butter until light and fluffy. Slowly beat in 2 cups confectioners' sugar. Mix in ¼ cup cream. Beat in the remaining confectioners' sugar. If necessary, add a little more cream until the frosting is desired spreading consistency. Makes enough to frost 1 (2 layer) cake or 1 (9x13 inch) cake. **Yield:** 3 cups (16 servings).

Per serving: About 280 calories, 4g protein, 33g carbohydrate, 16g fat, 1g fiber, 22mg cholesterol, 136mg sodium

Cool Whipped Frosting

Submitted by: **Shirley**
"A light and cool topping vaguely resembling Bavarian cream."

1 (3.4 ounce) package instant vanilla pudding mix	1 teaspoon vanilla extract
1 cup milk	1 (8 ounce) container frozen whipped topping, thawed

1. In a medium bowl, combine pudding mix with milk and vanilla. Mix until smooth. Gently fold in whipped topping until no streaks remain. Spread evenly over cake. **Yield:** 1½ cups (10 servings).

Per serving: About 121 calories, 1g protein, 16g carbohydrate, 6g fat, 0g fiber, 2mg cholesterol, 159mg sodium

◀ **Quick & Easy**

Prep Time: 15 minutes

Average Rating: ★★★★★

What other cooks have done:
"Versatile recipe. I use many different flavors—whatever is available in instant puddings—butterscotch and coconut have been well received. I have added toasted coconut to it for variety. You couldn't ask for anything simpler."

Cinnamon Coffee Frosting

Submitted by: **Melanie Ditzel**
"My mom has made this cake frosting for as long as I can remember; she has no idea where she got it but it's very unique and absolutely delicious on a chocolate cake. I now make it for my family, and they love it, too."

1 teaspoon instant coffee granules	½ cup butter, softened
½ teaspoon ground cinnamon	1 teaspoon vanilla extract
Pinch salt	3 cups confectioners' sugar
	⅓ cup milk

1. In a small bowl, mash instant coffee with the back of a spoon until powdery. Stir in cinnamon and salt. In a large bowl, beat the butter until smooth and stir in spice mixture and vanilla. Alternately beat in confectioners' sugar and milk until desired spreading consistency. **Yield:** 2 cups (12 servings).

Per serving: About 146 calories, 0g protein, 24g carbohydrate, 6g fat, 0g fiber, 16mg cholesterol, 86mg sodium

◀ **Company is Coming**

Prep Time: 10 minutes

Average Rating: ★★★★★

What other cooks have done:
"This frosting is so yummy! So far I've used it on a chocolate cake and a white cake. It was wonderful on both!"

Caroline's Chocolate Fudge Frosting

Submitted by: **Carrie Reynolds**

"A good fudgy frosting for cake or cupcakes."

½	cup butter	½	teaspoon vanilla extract
3	(1 ounce) squares unsweetened chocolate	¾	cup milk, divided
1	(16 ounce) package confectioners' sugar		

1. Melt butter and chocolate in the microwave or in the top of a double boiler. In a large bowl, combine confectioners' sugar, vanilla, and ½ cup milk. Blend in the melted chocolate mixture. Add remaining milk, a little at a time, until desired consistency.

2. Let stand until spreadable (frosting will thicken as it cools). **Yield:** 2 cups (12 servings).

Per serving: About 260 calories, 1g protein, 40g carbohydrate, 12g fat, 1g fiber, 22mg cholesterol, 87mg sodium

Allspice Cream Cheese Frosting

Submitted by: **v monte**

"Cream cheese frosting with a little extra something. This is a good frosting for spice cakes that contain allspice."

1	(3 ounce) package cream cheese, softened	4	cups confectioners' sugar
⅓	cup butter, softened	1	teaspoon vanilla extract
¾	teaspoon ground allspice	2	tablespoons milk

1. In a medium bowl, blend the cream cheese, butter, and allspice. Gradually mix in the confectioners' sugar, vanilla, and milk until the desired spreading consistency. **Yield:** 3 cups (10 servings).

Per serving: About 274 calories, 1g protein, 48g carbohydrate, 9g fat, 0g fiber, 26mg cholesterol, 90mg sodium

Graham Cracker Crust

Submitted by: **Carol**

"Teams great with many pies."

1½	cups finely ground graham cracker crumbs	6	tablespoons butter, melted
⅓	cup white sugar	½	teaspoon ground cinnamon (optional)

1. Preheat the oven to 375°F (190°C). Mix graham cracker crumbs, sugar, melted butter, and cinnamon until well blended. Press mixture into an 8 or 9 inch pie plate.
2. Bake in the preheated oven for 7 minutes. Cool. **Yield:** 8 servings (1 pie crust).

Per serving: About 176 calories, 1g protein, 21g carbohydrate, 10g fat, 1g fiber, 23mg cholesterol, 183mg sodium

Butter Cookie Crust

Submitted by: **Nona**
"A rich buttery crust that's perfect for just about any filling. It's great for cheesecakes. You can substitute chocolate cookie crumbs for a chocolate crust."

1½	cups finely crumbled vanilla wafers	6	tablespoons butter, melted
¼	cup white sugar	½	teaspoon ground cinnamon

1. Preheat oven to 375°F (190°C).
2. In a medium bowl, combine the cookie crumbs, sugar, butter, and cinnamon; mix until well blended. Press into a 9 inch pie plate.
3. Bake in the preheated oven for 7 minutes. Cool. **Yield:** 8 servings (1 pie crust).

Per serving: About 261 calories, 2g protein, 30g carbohydrate, 15g fat, 1g fiber, 23mg cholesterol, 191mg sodium

◀ **Family Favorite**

Prep Time: 10 minutes
Cook Time: 7 minutes
Average Rating: ★★★★☆
What other cooks have done:
"This is tasty and easy. I used it for banana cream pie, and it was wonderful. I added chopped macadamia nuts (I got this from a favorite restaurant's banana pie) and omitted the cinnamon. It was wonderfully crispy and crunchy."

Quick and Easy Lemon Pie

Submitted by: **April**
"Cool and easy, even your kids can help you make it! They'll love the pudding and cream cheese filling and the graham cracker crust!"

1	(4.6 ounce) package non-instant lemon pudding mix	3	tablespoons lemon juice
1	(8 ounce) package cream cheese	1	(9 inch) prepared graham cracker crust
½	(14 ounce) can sweetened condensed milk	1	(8 ounce) container frozen whipped topping, thawed

1. Cook pudding as directed on package. After pudding thickens, reduce heat to low. Stir in cream cheese, condensed milk, and lemon juice. Stir frequently as mixture may stick to bottom of saucepan.
2. Pour mixture into graham cracker crust. Cover and refrigerate. Serve with whipped topping. **Yield:** 8 servings.

Per serving: About 458 calories, 5g protein, 53g carbohydrate, 24g fat, 1g fiber, 39mg cholesterol, 361mg sodium

◀ **Make-Ahead**

Prep Time: 15 minutes
Average Rating: ★★★★★
What other cooks have done:
"Being calorie conscious, I used a low-fat graham crust, low-fat cream cheese, and low-calorie condensed milk. It was delicious and not as loaded with calories, so I didn't feel guilty having more than one slice!"

Crushed Pineapple Sour Cream Pie

Submitted by: **Diane Hutchinson**

"Here's a quick and easy no-bake pie. Garnish with whipped cream or whipped topping. You can use a prepared graham cracker crust, if you wish."

1 (8 ounce) can crushed pineapple with juice	2 tablespoons white sugar
1 (3.4 ounce) package instant vanilla pudding mix	1 (8 ounce) container sour cream
	1 (9 inch) pie crust, baked

1. In a large mixing bowl, combine pineapple, pudding mix, and sugar. Stir well and add sour cream. Beat on low speed for 2 minutes.
2. Pour mixture into prepared pie crust. Chill before serving. **Yield:** 8 servings.

Per serving: About 216 calories, 2g protein, 28g carbohydrate, 11g fat, 0g fiber, 13mg cholesterol, 294mg sodium

Cindy's Pumpkin Pie

Submitted by: **Cindy**

"Ice cream's the secret ingredient in this pie. The result is delicious. I've never brought home leftovers of this pie. I recommend using fresh pumpkin, but canned pumpkin can also be used."

3 eggs	¼ teaspoon ground ginger
1¾ cups canned pumpkin puree	¼ teaspoon ground nutmeg
¾ cup white sugar	1½ pints vanilla ice cream, softened
½ teaspoon salt	Pastry for 2 (9 inch) single
1 teaspoon ground cinnamon	crust pies

1. Preheat oven to 425°F (220°C).
2. In a large bowl, whisk the eggs. Stir in the pumpkin, sugar, salt, cinnamon, ginger, and nutmeg. Mix in ice cream until smooth. Pour filling into unbaked pie crusts.
3. Bake in the preheated oven for 15 minutes. Reduce temperature to 350°F (175°C) and bake 30 to 40 more minutes or until filling is set. **Yield:** 16 servings (2 [9 inch] pies).

Note: To use fresh pumpkin, preheat oven to 325°F (165°C). Wash and halve pumpkins. Scoop out seeds. Place pumpkin halves, cut sides down, in a baking pan. Bake in the preheated oven for 45 minutes to 1 hour or until pumpkins are soft to the touch. Remove from oven and let cool. Scrape out pumpkin meat and puree in food processor or blender. (This can be done several weeks in advance and the puree stored in the freezer.)

Per serving: About 224 calories, 4g protein, 28g carbohydrate, 11g fat, 2g fiber, 51mg cholesterol, 286mg sodium

Fresh Strawberry Pie *(pictured on page 303)*

Submitted by: **Janice Papola**
"Delicious pie made with fresh strawberries. Top with whipped cream, if you like."

1 cup white sugar	2½ quarts fresh strawberries,
2 tablespoons cornstarch	stems removed
1 cup boiling water	1 (9 inch) pie crust, baked
1 (3 ounce) package	Whipped cream (optional)
strawberry flavored	
gelatin	

1. In a saucepan, mix together the sugar and cornstarch; make sure to blend cornstarch in completely. Add boiling water and cook over medium heat until mixture slightly thickens. Remove from heat. Add gelatin and stir until smooth. Cover and let mixture cool to room temperature.
2. Place strawberries in baked pie crust, pointed ends facing up. Pour cooled gelatin mixture over strawberries.
3. Refrigerate until set. Serve with whipped cream, if desired. **Yield:** 8 servings.

Per serving: About 330 calories, 4g protein, 62g carbohydrate, 10g fat, 4g fiber, 0mg cholesterol, 190mg sodium

Yummy Eggnog Pie

Submitted by: **Rodney**
"This yummy delight has become a holiday tradition in our family, as it will in yours! It's surprisingly easy to prepare. Rum may be omitted or replaced with 1 teaspoon rum extract."

1 (4.6 ounce) package	2 teaspoons rum
non-instant vanilla	2 cups heavy cream
pudding mix	1 (9 inch) pie crust, baked
¼ teaspoon ground nutmeg	Pinch ground nutmeg
1½ cups eggnog	

1. In a medium saucepan, combine pudding mix, ¼ teaspoon nutmeg, and eggnog; mix well. Cook over medium heat, stirring constantly, until thick and bubbly. Remove from heat and stir in rum. Transfer mixture to a large bowl, cover, and refrigerate until thoroughly chilled.
2. In a medium bowl, whip the cream to soft peaks. Remove the cold pudding from the refrigerator and beat until smooth; fold in whipped cream. Spoon into baked pie crust. Sprinkle additional nutmeg over the top for garnish. Refrigerate 4 hours or until set. **Yield:** 8 servings.

Per serving: About 451 calories, 5g protein, 34g carbohydrate, 34g fat, 1g fiber, 110mg cholesterol, 291mg sodium

Prep Time: 30 minutes

Cook Time: 10 minutes

Average Rating: ★★★★★

What other cooks have done:

"Having just finished eating the first slice of this pie, I'm wondering if I've just died and gone to heaven! I used a graham cracker pie crust instead and it turned out great."

Toasted Coconut, Pecan, and Caramel Pie

Submitted by: **Patrice**
"Very rich tasting pie that's easy to prepare. Everyone loves this pie."

¼	cup butter	1	(12 ounce) container frozen whipped topping, thawed
1	(8 ounce) package flaked coconut	2	(9 inch) pie crusts, baked
½	cup chopped pecans	1	(12 ounce) jar caramel ice cream topping
1	(8 ounce) package cream cheese, softened		
1	(14 ounce) can sweetened condensed milk		

1. In a medium skillet, melt butter over medium heat. Add coconut and pecans. Toss well and sauté until coconut is lightly browned. Set aside to cool.
2. In a large mixing bowl, beat cream cheese until fluffy. Add condensed milk and mix until smooth. Fold in whipped topping. Spread ¼ of cream cheese mixture into each pastry shell. Sprinkle ¼ of coconut mixture over each pie. Drizzle ½ of caramel topping over each coconut layer. Follow with remaining cream cheese mixture and remaining coconut mixture. Serve chilled or frozen. **Yield:** 16 servings (2 [9 inch] pies).

Per serving: About 484 calories, 6g protein, 50g carbohydrate, 30g fat, 2g fiber, 32mg cholesterol, 339mg sodium

Prep Time: 15 minutes

Cook Time: 50 minutes

Average Rating: ★★★★★

What other cooks have done:

"Very fudgy! I added 1 tablespoon of bourbon to give it extra flavor. Serve pie with whipped cream or ice cream."

Chocolate Pecan Pie

Submitted by: **Karin Christian**
"Just like a traditional pecan pie, but with chocolate chips. It's always the first dessert to go at our family's Thanksgiving!"

3	eggs	1	cup pecan halves
⅔	cup white sugar	1½	cups semisweet chocolate chips
½	teaspoon salt		Pastry for a 9 inch single crust pie
⅓	cup butter or margarine, melted		
1	cup light corn syrup		

1. Preheat oven to 375°F (190°C).
2. Beat eggs, sugar, salt, butter, and syrup on medium speed with an electric mixer. Stir in pecans and chocolate chips. Pour into pie shell.
3. Bake in the preheated oven for 40 to 50 minutes or until set. Cool. **Yield:** 8 servings.

Per serving: About 735 calories, 7g protein, 92g carbohydrate, 40g fat, 3g fiber, 83mg cholesterol, 424mg sodium

Chocolaty Peanutty Pie

Submitted by: **Maureen Worman**

"A real treat for your taste buds!"

2	cups graham cracker crumbs	2	(3.9 ounce) packages instant chocolate pudding mix
⅔	cup chopped peanuts	2½	cups skim milk
½	cup butter, melted	⅔	cup peanuts
1	(8 ounce) package cream cheese, softened	¼	cup grated semisweet chocolate
⅓	cup peanut butter		
1	cup confectioners' sugar		
1	(16 ounce) container frozen whipped topping, thawed and divided		

1. Preheat oven to 350°F (175°C). Mix together graham cracker crumbs, chopped peanuts, and melted butter. Press mixture into the bottom of a 9x13 inch pan. Bake in the preheated oven for 8 to 10 minutes. Cool.

2. Mix together cream cheese, peanut butter, and confectioners' sugar until creamy. Fold in half of the whipped topping.

3. In another bowl, combine pudding mixes and milk.

4. Spread the peanut butter mixture over the crust. Spoon pudding over peanut butter layer and spread remaining whipped topping over pudding. Sprinkle with peanuts and grated chocolate. Refrigerate overnight. **Yield:** 8 servings.

Per serving: About 881 calories, 17g protein, 83g carbohydrate, 58g fat, 4g fiber, 63mg cholesterol, 823mg sodium

---

◄ **Kid-Friendly**

Prep Time: 30 minutes

Cook Time: 10 minutes

Average Rating: ★★★★★

What other cooks have done:

"I first made this dessert to take to a covered-dish lunch at my church. It was gone in a flash. The second time was for my 10-year-old son's birthday. He asked for it instead of a traditional cake. It was that delicious!"

Chocolate-Hazelnut Mocha Cappuccino Pie

Submitted by: **LV**

"I adapted this recipe from a favorite pie recipe. With just a few substitutions and additions, I had a whole new taste sensation!"

- 1 (3.4 ounce) package instant vanilla pudding mix
- 1½ cups cold milk
- 2 tablespoons instant mocha cappuccino mix
- 2 cups frozen whipped topping, thawed and divided
- 1 (9 inch) prepared chocolate cookie crumb crust
- ½ cup semisweet chocolate chips
- ½ cup chopped hazelnuts

1. Prepare pudding according to package directions using the milk and cappuccino mix. Fold ½ cup whipped topping into pudding, then spread mixture into pie crust. Sprinkle ¼ cup chocolate chips and ¼ cup hazelnuts over pie. Cover and refrigerate for 2 hours.
2. Spread remaining 1½ cups whipped topping on pie and sprinkle remaining chocolate chips and hazelnuts on top. **Yield:** 8 servings.

Per serving: About 377 calories, 6g protein, 40g carbohydrate, 23g fat, 2g fiber, 5mg cholesterol, 282mg sodium

Out-of-the-Ordinary ▶

Prep Time: 10 minutes

Average Rating: ★★★★★

What other cooks have done:

"I substituted white chocolate pudding for vanilla—even better. Next time, I'll use ¼ cup less milk to make it hold up better. I also used mini chocolate chips instead of the regular. I like the appearance better and they disperse the chocolate flavor throughout the whole pie."

Cookies and Cream

Submitted by: **Kimberly**

"A chocolate experience that's creamy and delicious. To cut this pie easily, use a knife dipped in water."

- 1 (3.9 ounce) package instant chocolate pudding mix
- 1 (8 ounce) container frozen whipped topping, thawed
- 1 cup crushed chocolate sandwich cookies
- 1 (9 inch) prepared chocolate cookie crumb crust

1. Prepare pudding as directed for pie filling; let set.
2. When pudding is set, fold in whipped topping and crushed cookies. Pour pudding mixture into crust.
3. Freeze 8 hours or overnight. **Yield:** 8 servings.

Per serving: About 326 calories, 3g protein, 41g carbohydrate, 18g fat, 1g fiber, 0mg cholesterol, 450mg sodium

Quick & Easy ▶

Prep Time: 15 minutes

Freeze Time: 8 hours

Average Rating: ★★★★☆

What other cooks have done:

"This was the first pie to disappear on Thanksgiving. I jazzed up the recipe by adding chocolate cookies that had a peppermint cream filling. The flavor was subtle but definitely gave it more 'zing.'"

Brownie Pie

Submitted by: **Phyllis**

"Yummy brownies topped with chocolate pudding and whipped topping. This is a favorite in my family."

1	(20 ounce) package chocolate brownie mix with pecans	1	(8 ounce) container frozen whipped topping, thawed
1	(3.9 ounce) package instant chocolate pudding mix	¼	cup shaved semisweet chocolate
1	cup milk		Crushed chocolate wafers

1. Make brownies in a 9x13 inch pan according to package directions. Bake and cool.
2. In a small bowl, combine pudding mix and milk. Whisk until smooth. Allow to set up 5 minutes and spread over cooled brownies. Spread whipped topping over pudding layer. Top with shaved chocolate and crushed chocolate wafers immediately before serving. Store leftovers in refrigerator. **Yield:** 12 servings.

Per serving: About 330 calories, 4g protein, 50g carbohydrate, 13g fat, 2g fiber, 2mg cholesterol, 333mg sodium

Fruity Tart

Submitted by: **Jennifer**

"Cutting up all the fruit takes a bit of time, but the rest is easy as pie. Use any fruit of your liking."

1	(4.6 ounce) package non-instant vanilla pudding mix	½	cup fresh blueberries
3	cups milk	1	cup fresh peaches, pitted and sliced
1	(9 inch) pie crust, baked	½	cup fresh raspberries
½	cup fresh strawberries, sliced	1	cup kiwi, sliced
		¼	cup apricot, strawberry, or raspberry jam

1. Combine pudding mix and milk in a medium saucepan. Cook according to package directions. Pour pudding into pastry shell and refrigerate until cool and firm. Arrange fruit on top of pudding layer.
2. Place the jam in a small saucepan over low heat, stirring occasionally until melted. Using a pastry brush, coat fruit with jam. **Yield:** 8 servings.

Per serving: About 248 calories, 4g protein, 43g carbohydrate, 7g fat, 3g fiber, 7mg cholesterol, 274mg sodium

English Butter Tarts

Submitted by: **Priscilla Sullivan**

"This is a recipe my mother had in Scotland. I've saved it since I was a teenager because the tarts are so good."

12	(2 inch) unbaked tart shells	¼	cup shortening
¾	cup raisins	1	egg
½	cup packed brown sugar	1	teaspoon vanilla extract
½	cup light corn syrup	¼	teaspoon salt

1. Preheat oven to 400°F (200°C).
2. Arrange tart shells on a baking sheet. Distribute raisins evenly into shells. In a large bowl, combine brown sugar, corn syrup, shortening, egg, vanilla, and salt. Mix until smooth and pour over raisins in shells.
3. Bake in the preheated oven for 12 to 15 minutes or until set. Be careful not to overbake. **Yield:** 12 tarts.

Per tart: About 270 calories, 3g protein, 42g carbohydrate, 11g fat, 0g fiber, 18mg cholesterol, 146mg sodium

Easy Cream Cheese Danish

Submitted by: **Natalie**

"A real find—this recipe makes the best cream cheese Danish I've ever tasted. It's very simple to make."

2	(10 ounce) cans refrigerated crescent roll dough	1½	teaspoons lemon juice
		1	teaspoon vanilla extract
2	(8 ounce) packages cream cheese, diced and softened	2	teaspoons sour cream
		1	cup confectioners' sugar
¾	cup white sugar	1	tablespoon milk
		1	tablespoon butter, softened

1. Preheat oven to 350°F (175°C). Lightly grease a 9x13 inch pan.
2. Line bottom of pan with 1 can of crescent rolls. Pinch all seams together to seal.
3. In a large bowl, mix together cream cheese, white sugar, lemon juice, vanilla, and sour cream. Spread filling on top of rolls. Place second can of rolls on top of filling.
4. Bake in the preheated oven for 20 to 30 minutes.
5. In a small bowl, stir together confectioners' sugar, milk, and butter. After pastry has cooled, drizzle with icing. **Yield:** 10 servings.

Per serving: About 498 calories, 8g protein, 51g carbohydrate, 29g fat, 0g fiber, 53mg cholesterol, 586mg sodium

Allie's Delicious Baked Dumplings

Submitted by: **Alyson Pray**

"A delicious baked apple dumpling with a crispy crust and a moist and juicy inside! Always a big hit for all occasions and surprisingly easy to prepare."

1 (17.5 ounce) package frozen puff pastry, thawed	1 egg, lightly beaten
1 cup white sugar	4 Granny Smith apples, peeled, cored, and halved
½ cup dry breadcrumbs	1 cup confectioners' sugar
3 tablespoons ground cinnamon	1 teaspoon vanilla extract
Pinch ground nutmeg	3 tablespoons milk

1. Preheat oven to 425°F (220°C). Lightly grease a baking sheet.

2. Roll out each sheet of pastry to measure 12x12 inches. Cut into fourths, to make 8 (6 inch) squares.

3. In a small bowl, combine sugar, breadcrumbs, cinnamon, and nutmeg. Brush a pastry square with beaten egg. Place 1 tablespoon breadcrumb mixture in center. Place 1 apple half, cut side down, over breadcrumbs. Top with another tablespoon of breadcrumb mixture. Pull up 4 corners of pastry and pinch sides together to seal seams completely. Repeat with remaining pastry, breadcrumb mixture, and apples.

4. Brush each dumpling with beaten egg. Bake in the preheated oven for 15 minutes. Reduce heat to 350°F (175°C) and bake 25 more minutes or until lightly browned. Let cool completely.

5. To make icing, combine confectioners' sugar, vanilla, and enough milk to make a drizzling consistency. Drizzle over cooled dumplings. Serve the same day. **Yield:** 8 servings.

Per serving: About 564 calories, 6g protein, 82g carbohydrate, 25g fat, 4g fiber, 27mg cholesterol, 209mg sodium

---

◄ Classic Comfort Food

Prep Time: 15 minutes

Cook Time: 40 minutes

Average Rating: ★★★★★

What other cooks have done:

"I've made this recipe for guests and family and have always received rave reviews. I've learned to look for smaller apples because it's difficult to stretch the quartered puff pastry dough over the larger ones. It's now a staple dessert in my family."

Apple Betty

Submitted by: **Barbara Milam**

"Everyone always raves about this pie. You don't have to make pie crust! You can control the sweetness by the amount of streusel topping you use."

4	cups thinly sliced apples	½	teaspoon ground cinnamon
¼	cup orange juice	¼	teaspoon ground nutmeg
¾	cup all-purpose flour		Pinch salt
1	cup white sugar	½	cup butter

1. Preheat oven to 375°F (190°C). Lightly grease a 9 inch pie plate.
2. Mound sliced apples in the pie plate. Sprinkle with orange juice.
3. In a medium bowl, mix the flour, sugar, cinnamon, nutmeg, and salt. Cut in butter until the mixture resembles coarse crumbs. Sprinkle over the apples.
4. Bake in the preheated oven for 45 minutes. Serve warm. **Yield:** 8 servings.

Per serving: About 282 calories, 2g protein, 44g carbohydrate, 12g fat, 2g fiber, 31mg cholesterol, 166mg sodium

Rhubarb-Strawberry Crunch

Submitted by: **Michelle Davis**

"Ever wonder what to do with that big rhubarb plant in the garden? This is your answer."

1	cup white sugar	3	cups diced rhubarb
3	tablespoons all-purpose flour	1½	cups all-purpose flour
		1	cup packed brown sugar
3	cups sliced fresh strawberries	1	cup rolled oats
		1	cup butter

1. Preheat oven to 375°F (190°C).
2. In a large bowl, mix white sugar, 3 tablespoons flour, strawberries, and rhubarb. Place the mixture in a 9x13 inch baking dish.
3. Mix 1½ cups flour, brown sugar, and oats. Cut in butter until the mixture resembles coarse crumbs. Crumble on top of the rhubarb and strawberry mixture.
4. Bake in the preheated oven for 45 minutes or until crisp and lightly browned. **Yield:** 18 servings.

Per serving: About 252 calories, 2g protein, 38g carbohydrate, 11g fat, 2g fiber, 28mg cholesterol, 111mg sodium

Strawberry Cobbler

Submitted by: **Eleanor Johnson**

"Serve with whipped cream or ice cream."

½	cup white sugar	1	tablespoon white sugar
1	tablespoon cornstarch	1½	teaspoons baking powder
1	cup water	½	teaspoon salt
3	cups strawberries, hulled	3	tablespoons butter
2	tablespoons butter, diced	½	cup heavy whipping cream
1	cup all-purpose flour		

1. Preheat oven to 400°F (200°C). Grease a 2 quart baking dish.
2. Combine ½ cup sugar, cornstarch, and water. Cook over medium heat, stirring constantly, until thick and hot. Stir in strawberries and remove from heat. Pour mixture into the prepared baking dish and dot with 2 tablespoons butter.
3. Sift together the flour, 1 tablespoon sugar, baking powder, and salt. Blend in 3 tablespoons butter. Stir in cream. Mixture should be fairly soft. Spoon on top of berries.
4. Bake in the preheated oven for 25 minutes. **Yield:** 8 servings.

Per serving: About 248 calories, 2g protein, 32g carbohydrate, 13g fat, 2g fiber, 40mg cholesterol, 318mg sodium

◀ **Kid-Friendly**

Prep Time: 15 minutes

Cook Time: 35 minutes

Average Rating: ★★★★★

What other cooks have done:

"I've been looking for this recipe for years! It tastes just like the one served at our local family restaurant. Now I can make it at home. The topping is so delicious—I've never been able to find a recipe that tastes the same. It's crispy on the outside and tender on the inside. My family loved it. Try it with cherry pie filling if you're pressed for time!"

Zucchini Cobbler

Submitted by: **Beverly**

"Let's say you have an abundance of zucchini, but you're fresh out of apples. You can sneak this in on the kids and they'll never know."

5	cups peeled, seeded, and chopped zucchini	½	teaspoon ground nutmeg
		4	cups all-purpose flour
½	cup fresh lemon juice	1½	cups white sugar
¾	cup white sugar	1½	cups butter, chilled
1	teaspoon ground cinnamon	1	teaspoon ground cinnamon

1. Preheat oven to 375°F (190°C). Grease a 9x13 inch baking dish.
2. Place zucchini and lemon juice in a medium saucepan. Cook, covered, over medium-low heat, stirring occasionally, for about 15 minutes or until tender. Stir in ¾ cup sugar, 1 teaspoon cinnamon, and nutmeg. Simmer 1 minute longer; remove from heat and set aside.
3. In a large mixing bowl, combine flour and 1½ cups sugar. Cut in butter until the mixture resembles coarse crumbs. Stir ½ cup crumb mixture into zucchini mixture. Press half remaining crumb mixture into the prepared pan. Spread zucchini evenly over crust. Sprinkle remaining crumb mixture and 1 teaspoon cinnamon over zucchini.
4. Bake in the preheated oven for 35 to 40 minutes or until golden and bubbly. **Yield:** 18 servings.

Per serving: About 341 calories, 4g protein, 48g carbohydrate, 16g fat, 1g fiber, 41mg cholesterol, 158mg sodium

◀ **Out-of-the-Ordinary**

Prep Time: 20 minutes

Cook Time: 56 minutes

Average Rating: ★★★★★

What other cooks have done:

"I've made zucchini apple pie before, but this is the best dessert recipe for zucchini cobbler. I substituted ½ cup oatmeal for ½ cup of the flour and added ½ cup chopped walnuts on top. Absolutely wonderful!"

Chocolate-Banana Bread Pudding

Submitted by: **Gabrielle**

"A local restaurant served a version of this recipe. I went crazy over it and decided to create my own. It's great served warm or cold."

Company is Coming ▶

Prep Time: 20 minutes

Cook Time: 1 hour

Average Rating: ★★★★★

What other cooks have done:

"Yummy! Really good for using up old bread and overripe bananas. I doubled the amount of chocolate chips and used torn up cinnamon raisin bread and half a loaf of day-old French bread. I also added a cup of chopped walnuts and a sprinkle of cinnamon and nutmeg. It's better than homemade, oven-fresh chocolate chip cookies. I'll make this for company."

4	eggs	4	cups cubed French bread
2	cups milk	2	bananas, sliced
1	cup white sugar	1	cup semisweet chocolate
1	tablespoon vanilla extract		chips

1. Preheat oven to 350°F (175°C). Grease a 5x9 inch loaf pan.

2. In a large mixing bowl, mix eggs, milk, sugar, and vanilla until smooth. Stir in bread, bananas, and chocolate chips; let stand 5 minutes for bread to soak. Pour into prepared pan.

3. Line a roasting pan with a damp kitchen towel. Place loaf pan on towel inside roasting pan and place roasting pan on oven rack. Fill roasting pan with water to reach halfway up the sides of the loaf pan.

4. Bake in the preheated oven for 1 hour or until a knife inserted in the center comes out clean. **Yield:** 8 servings.

Per serving: About 441 calories, 11g protein, 76g carbohydrate, 12g fat, 4g fiber, 111mg cholesterol, 385mg sodium

English Trifle

Submitted by: **Teri**

"This dessert recipe came from a friend from England. It's delicious and elegant looking layered in a trifle bowl or individual dessert glasses."

Crowd-Pleaser ▶

Prep Time: 20 minutes

Average Rating: ★★★★★

What other cooks have done:

"Great recipe. I wanted a trifle recipe for an anniversary party and this one really fit the bill. I poured brandy over the cake to make it really special. Yum. I also left out the bananas because I forgot to buy them. Very easy to make, and the end result is very pretty."

2	pints fresh strawberries	2	(8 or 9 inch) white cake
¼	cup white sugar		layers, baked and cooled
2	bananas	1	pint fresh blueberries
¼	cup orange juice	1	cup heavy whipping cream
1	(3.5 ounce) package instant	12	maraschino cherries
	vanilla pudding mix	¼	cup blanched slivered
2	cups milk		almonds

1. Slice strawberries and sprinkle with sugar. Cut the bananas into slices and toss with orange juice. Combine pudding mix with milk and mix until smooth. Cut the cake into 1 inch cubes.

2. Use half of the cake cubes to line the bottom of a large glass bowl. Layer half of the strawberries followed by half of the blueberries, and then half of the bananas. Spread half of the pudding over the fruit. Repeat layers in the same order.

3. In a medium bowl, whip the cream to stiff peaks and spread over top of trifle. Garnish with maraschino cherries and slivered almonds. **Yield:** 14 servings.

Per serving: About 638 calories, 10g protein, 99g carbohydrate, 24g fat, 4g fiber, 29mg cholesterol, 542mg sodium

Vanilla and Chocolate Delight

Submitted by: **Brenda Moore**

"Delicious dessert layered with pecans, cream cheese, and vanilla and chocolate pudding."

1	cup finely chopped pecans	3	cups milk
1	cup all-purpose flour	1	(3.9 ounce) package instant chocolate pudding mix
½	cup butter, melted		
1	(8 ounce) package cream cheese, softened	1	(3.4 ounce) package instant vanilla pudding mix
1	cup confectioners' sugar	2	(1.45 ounce) bars milk chocolate with crispy rice, crumbled
1	(16 ounce) container frozen whipped topping, thawed and divided		

1. Preheat the oven to 400°F (200°C). In a medium mixing bowl, combine pecans, flour, and butter. Press into a 9x13 inch pan. Bake for 25 minutes. Allow to cool.

2. In a large bowl, beat together cream cheese and confectioners' sugar until smooth. Fold in half of the whipped topping. Spread on cooled crust.

3. In a large bowl, combine milk, chocolate pudding mix, and vanilla pudding mix. Beat until thick. Pour over cream cheese layer. Top with remaining whipped topping and sprinkle with crushed chocolate bars. **Yield:** 18 servings.

Per serving: About 351 calories, 4g protein, 34g carbohydrate, 23g fat, 1g fiber, 32mg cholesterol, 286mg sodium

◄ **Covered-Dish Favorite**

Prep Time: 20 minutes

Cook Time: 25 minutes

Average Rating: ★★★★★

What other cooks have done:

"I used this recipe to make 2 pies instead of a 9x13 inch dessert, and they were beautiful! I served them for Thanksgiving dessert and got rave reviews—especially from the children! This recipe is very easy and definitely a keeper! I'll make the pies again for Christmas, but will top them with mini red and green candy-coated chocolate pieces instead of the crushed chocolate candy bar."

Raspberry-White Chocolate Mousse *(pictured on page 302)*

Submitted by: **Stacey Walery**

"This is a light and fluffy mousse with a wonderful raspberry sauce. You can serve additional sauce over the mousse or spoon the sauce over cake."

1 (10 ounce) package frozen raspberries, thawed	6 ounces white chocolate, chopped
2 tablespoons white sugar	6 drops red food coloring
2 tablespoons orange liqueur	
1¾ cups heavy whipping cream, divided	

1. Process berries in a blender or food processor until smooth. Strain mixture into a small bowl and discard seeds. Add the sugar and liqueur and stir until sugar dissolves.

2. In a heavy saucepan on low heat, warm ¼ cup of the cream and the white chocolate, stirring constantly until chocolate melts. Let mixture cool until lukewarm. Stir in 1 tablespoon raspberry sauce and the food coloring. Transfer to a large bowl.

3. In a medium bowl, whip remaining 1½ cups cream to soft peaks. Fold into melted chocolate mixture, ⅓ at a time, until no streaks remain.

4. Serve mousse with raspberry sauce, if desired. **Yield:** 4 cups mousse, 1 cup sauce (8 servings).

Per serving: About 348 calories, 3g protein, 28g carbohydrate, 26g fat, 2g fiber, 76mg cholesterol, 40mg sodium

Butter Pecan Ice Cream *(pictured on page 298)*

Submitted by: **Susan Long**

"Creamy homemade ice cream! Excellent summertime treat!"

1 cup chopped pecans	3 cups half-and-half
½ tablespoon butter	1 cup heavy whipping cream
2 cups brown sugar	2 teaspoons vanilla extract
4 eggs, beaten	

1. In a small skillet over medium heat, sauté pecans in butter until lightly browned, stirring frequently. Set aside.

2. In a medium saucepan over low heat, stir together brown sugar, eggs, and half-and-half until smooth. Bring to a simmer, stirring occasionally, and cook 20 minutes or until a candy thermometer registers 160°F (70°C). Remove from heat and strain mixture. Stir in cream, vanilla, and pecans.

3. Pour into ice cream maker and freeze according to manufacturer's directions. **Yield:** 4 cups (8 servings).

Per serving: About 278 calories, 4g protein, 30g carbohydrate, 16g fat, 0g fiber, 94mg cholesterol, 66mg sodium

White Chocolate-Orange Cookies

Submitted by: **Jennifer**
"These are my new personal favorites!"

1	cup butter, softened	2¼	cups all-purpose flour
½	cup white sugar	¾	teaspoon baking soda
½	cup packed brown sugar	½	teaspoon salt
1	egg	2	cups white chocolate chips
1	tablespoon orange zest	1	cup chopped walnuts

1. Preheat oven to 350°F (175°C).
2. Cream the butter and sugars together until light and fluffy. Beat in the egg and orange zest. Stir together the flour, baking soda, and salt; mix into the creamed mixture. Stir in the white chocolate chips and chopped walnuts. Drop tablespoonfuls of dough onto ungreased baking sheets.
3. Bake in the preheated oven for 10 to 12 minutes. Allow to cool on the baking sheets for 2 minutes before transferring to wire racks to cool completely. **Yield:** 3 dozen.

Per cookie: 174 calories, 2g protein, 18g carbohydrate, 11g fat, 1g fiber, 22mg cholesterol, 123mg sodium

◄ Quick & Easy

Prep Time: 15 minutes
Cook Time: 12 minutes per batch
Average Rating: ★★★★★
What other cooks have done:
"Very unique and flavorful cookie. You could reduce the amount of white chocolate chips to 1½ cups. The orange taste is unexpected and fabulous."

Oatmeal Butterscotch Cookies

Submitted by: **Jolene**
"Great cookies!"

¾	cup butter, softened	1	teaspoon baking soda
¾	cup white sugar	½	teaspoon ground cinnamon
¾	cup packed brown sugar	½	teaspoon salt
2	eggs	3	cups rolled oats
1	teaspoon vanilla extract	1⅔	cups butterscotch chips
1¼	cups all-purpose flour		

1. Preheat oven to 375°F (190°C).
2. In a large bowl, beat the butter, white sugar, and brown sugar together. Add the eggs and vanilla, beating well.
3. Stir together the flour, baking soda, cinnamon, and salt. Gradually add the flour mixture to the butter mixture and stir until blended. Stir in the oats and the butterscotch chips. Drop by teaspoonfuls onto ungreased baking sheets.
4. Bake in the preheated oven for 8 to 10 minutes or until the edges begin to brown. **Yield:** 4 dozen.

Per cookie: About 119 calories, 1g protein, 16g carbohydrate, 5g fat, 1g fiber, 17mg cholesterol, 90mg sodium

◄ Classic Comfort Food

Prep Time: 15 minutes
Cook Time: 10 minutes per batch
Average Rating: ★★★★★
What other cooks have done:
"Yummy cookies! I used 2 cups of butterscotch chips (to finish off the package) and 1 cup of chopped pecans (because my husband loves pecans), and the cookies turned out great."

Chocolate Chip-Pumpkin Cookies

Submitted by: **Diane**

"Delicious cakelike drop cookie. A family favorite and so easy to make."

Holiday Gift Giving ▶

Prep Time: 10 minutes

Cook Time: 15 minutes per batch

Average Rating: ★★★★★

What other cooks have done:

"Chocolate chip and pumpkin—what a combination! I used a bit more cinnamon and nutmeg and also added ground cloves and ginger. I also made them with and without the walnuts, and they're much better with them. They're a great, unusual addition to my Christmas cookie baking and were a hit with everyone who's tried them."

1	cup shortening	1½	teaspoons baking powder
2	cups white sugar	1	teaspoon salt
2	eggs	1	teaspoon ground cinnamon
2	teaspoons vanilla extract		Pinch ground nutmeg
1	(15 ounce) can pumpkin puree	1	cup semisweet chocolate chips
4	cups all-purpose flour	1	cup chopped walnuts (optional)
1½	teaspoons baking soda		

1. Preheat the oven to 375°F (190°C). Grease 2 baking sheets.

2. In a large bowl, cream together the shortening and white sugar until smooth. Beat in the eggs, one at a time. Stir in the vanilla and pumpkin until well blended. Combine the flour, baking soda, baking powder, salt, cinnamon, and nutmeg; stir into the pumpkin mixture. Mix in the chocolate chips. Stir in the walnuts, if desired. Drop by teaspoonfuls onto the prepared baking sheets.

3. Bake in the preheated oven for 12 to 15 minutes or until edges begin to brown. Allow to cool for a few minutes on the baking sheets before removing to wire racks to cool completely. **Yield:** 7 dozen.

Per cookie: About 85 calories, 1g protein, 11g carbohydrate, 4g fat, 1g fiber, 5mg cholesterol, 69mg sodium

Baking with Fresh Pumpkin ▼

When autumn arrives, it brings a pumpkin bonanza! Big pumpkins, small pumpkins, nubby pumpkins, white pumpkins, stringy pumpkins....With all these compelling choices, which kind should you use in baking?

The answer is the sugar or pie pumpkin. The jack-o'-lantern pumpkins you see everywhere in the fall tend to be too large and stringy for baking. But the sugar pumpkin, now there's a pumpkin to sink your teeth into. Small and sweet, with dark orange colored flesh, it's perfect for pies, soups, side dishes, cookies, and breads.

There are three ways to transform an uncooked pumpkin into the puree used in baking. A medium-sized (4 pounds) sugar pumpkin should yield around 1½ cups of mashed pumpkin. This puree can be used in all your recipes calling for canned pumpkin.

Baking Method

Cut the pumpkin in half and discard the stem section and stringy insides. Save the seeds to dry and roast; they make a tasty snack. In a shallow baking dish, place the two halves, cut sides down, and cover with foil. Bake in a preheated 375°F (190°C) oven for about 1½ hours for a medium-sized sugar pumpkin. Once the baked pumpkin has cooled, scoop out the flesh and puree in a food processor or mash with a potato masher or potato ricer.

Boiling Method

Cut the pumpkin in half, discarding the stringy insides. Then peel and cut the pumpkin into chunks. Place in a saucepan and cover with water. Bring to a boil and cook until the pumpkin chunks are tender. Let the chunks cool, then puree the flesh in a food processor or mash.

Microwave Method

Cut the pumpkin in half, discarding the stringy insides. Microwave on high for 7 minutes per pound.

You can refrigerate fresh pumpkin puree up to 3 days or store it in the freezer up to 6 months, enabling you to enjoy the great taste of fall pumpkins for months to come.

For more information, visit **Allrecipes.com**

Chewy Peanut Butter-Chocolate Chip Cookies

Submitted by: **Kathy Bliesner**

"These cookies are really chewy and addictive."

½	cup butter, softened	2	tablespoons water
½	cup peanut butter	2	teaspoons vanilla extract
1	cup packed brown sugar	2½	cups all-purpose flour
½	cup white sugar	1	teaspoon baking soda
2	eggs	½	teaspoon salt
2	tablespoons light corn syrup	2	cups chopped semisweet chocolate

1. Preheat the oven to 375°F (190°C).

2. In a large bowl, cream together the butter, peanut butter, brown sugar, and white sugar until smooth. Beat in the eggs, one at a time, and stir in the corn syrup, water, and vanilla. Combine the flour, baking soda, and salt; stir into the peanut butter mixture. Fold in chocolate chunks. Drop by ¼ cupfuls 3 inches apart onto ungreased baking sheets.

3. Bake in the preheated oven for 12 to 14 minutes or until edges are golden. Allow cookies to cool for 1 minute on the baking sheets before removing to wire racks to cool completely. **Yield:** 2 dozen.

Per cookie: About 246 calories, 4g protein, 34g carbohydrate, 12g fat, 2g fiber, 28mg cholesterol, 176mg sodium

◄ **Kid-Friendly**

Prep Time: 15 minutes

Cook Time: 14 minutes per batch

Average Rating: ★★★★★

What other cooks have done:

"I added 1 cup crunchy peanut butter and decreased the chocolate chips to about 1½ cups. I used a scoop that was a tad over 1 tablespoon and baked the cookies at 350°F (175°C) for 10 to 11 minutes."

Prep Time: 20 minutes

Cook Time: 30 minutes

Average Rating: ★★★★★

What other cooks have done:

"I found this recipe, made the cookies, and felt like I was back in New York City. They came out great. I found out that you should not make the icing until all of the cookies are completely cooled, since it hardens quickly. I do all of my baking on stoneware and the texture was perfect. Thanks for the memories!"

Black and White Cookies *(pictured on page 303)*

Submitted by: **Mary Jane**
"These remind me of New York black and white deli cookies."

1	cup unsalted butter, softened	2½	cups all-purpose flour
1¾	cups white sugar	1	teaspoon baking powder
4	eggs	½	teaspoon salt
1	cup milk	4	cups confectioners' sugar
½	teaspoon vanilla extract	⅓	cup boiling water
½	to 1 teaspoon lemon extract	1	(1 ounce) square bittersweet chocolate, chopped
2½	cups cake flour		

1. Preheat oven to 350°F (175°C). Line 2 baking sheets with parchment paper. Place baking sheets in refrigerator.

2. In a medium bowl, cream together butter and white sugar until smooth. Beat in eggs, one at a time, and stir in the milk, vanilla, and lemon extract. Combine cake flour, all-purpose flour, baking powder, and salt; gradually blend into the creamed mixture. Chill dough 15 minutes. Using a 2½ inch ice cream scoop, drop dough 2 inches apart onto prepared baking sheets.

3. Bake in the preheated oven for 28 to 30 minutes or until edges begin to brown. Cool completely.

4. Place confectioners' sugar in a large bowl. Mix in boiling water, 1 tablespoon at a time, until mixture is thick and spreadable. (Add more than the indicated amount if necessary.)

5. Transfer half of the frosting to the top of a double boiler set over simmering water. Stir in the chocolate. Heat mixture, stirring frequently, until the chocolate melts. Remove from heat.

6. Coat half the cookie with chocolate frosting and the other half with the white frosting. (Black and White cookies are traditionally frosted on the bottom, flat side.) Set on wax paper until frosting hardens. **Yield:** 1 dozen.

Per cookie: About 492 calories, 8g protein, 73g carbohydrate, 19g fat, 1g fiber, 114mg cholesterol, 165mg sodium

Easy Lemon Cookies

Submitted by: **Lissa**

"The basic cake mix cookie with a twist."

1	(18.25 ounce) package lemon cake mix	1	teaspoon lemon extract
2	eggs	⅓	cup confectioners' sugar for decoration
⅓	cup vegetable oil		

1. Preheat oven to 375°F (190°C).

2. Pour cake mix into a large bowl. Stir in eggs, oil, and lemon extract until well blended. Drop teaspoonfuls of dough into a bowl of confectioners' sugar. Roll them around until they're lightly covered. Once sugared, put them on ungreased baking sheets.

3. Bake in the preheated oven for 6 to 9 minutes or until the bottoms are light brown. **Yield:** 3 dozen.

Per cookie: About 87 calories, 1g protein, 12g carbohydrate, 4g fat, 0g fiber, 15mg cholesterol, 106mg sodium

◀ **Quick & Easy**

Prep Time: 10 minutes

Cook Time: 9 minutes per batch

Average Rating ★★★★★

What other cooks have done:

"If you're looking for a fast, easy recipe with few ingredients—probably ingredients you already have in your kitchen—this is the recipe to make. You can put them fairly close on your baking sheet because they flatten only slightly."

Chewy Sugar Cookies

Submitted by: **Cindy**

"I love sugar cookies that are crisp on the outside and very chewy on the inside. Change up this recipe easily by rolling the dough in cinnamon-sugar before baking. I sometimes add almond extract for a different flavor."

2¾	cups all-purpose flour	2	cups white sugar
1	teaspoon baking powder	2	eggs
½	teaspoon salt	2	teaspoons vanilla extract
1¼	cups butter or margarine, softened	¼	cup white sugar for decoration

1. Preheat oven to 350°F (175°C). In a medium bowl, stir together the flour, baking powder, and salt; set aside.

2. In a large bowl, cream together the butter and 2 cups sugar until light and fluffy. Beat in the eggs, one at a time, and the vanilla. Gradually stir in the dry ingredients until just blended. Roll the dough into walnut sized balls and roll in ¼ cup sugar. Place balls 2 inches apart onto ungreased baking sheets and flatten slightly.

3. Bake in the preheated oven for 8 to 10 minutes or until lightly browned at the edges. Allow cookies to cool on baking sheets for 5 minutes before removing to wire racks to cool completely. **Yield:** 2½ dozen.

Per cookie: About 172 calories, 2g protein, 24g carbohydrate, 8g fat, 0g fiber, 14mg cholesterol, 139mg sodium

◀ **Classic Comfort Food**

Prep Time: 10 minutes

Cook Time: 10 minutes per batch

Average Rating: ★★★★★

What other cooks have done:

"These were the best sugar cookies ever! I think they taste the best when just baked, so I keep the dough in a container to have on hand. Also, I added 1 teaspoon of cornstarch. I do this to chocolate chip cookies, too. It makes the cookies more crunchy on the outside and chewy on the inside."

Ultimate Maple Snickerdoodles

Submitted by: **Linda Carroll**

"These have been voted the Number One cookie that I bake (and I bake a lot!), and are loved by all who eat them. They're chewy, mapley good!"

2 cups all-purpose flour	1 cup white sugar
1½ teaspoons baking powder	1 egg
¼ teaspoon baking soda	3 tablespoons maple syrup
1½ teaspoons ground cinnamon	½ cup white sugar
½ cup butter or margarine, softened	¼ cup maple sugar

1. Preheat oven to 350°F (175°C). Stir together the flour, baking powder, baking soda, and cinnamon. Set aside.

2. In a large bowl, cream together the butter and 1 cup sugar until light and fluffy. Beat in the egg and 3 tablespoons maple syrup. Gradually blend in the dry ingredients until just mixed. In a small dish, mix together ½ cup white sugar and the ¼ cup maple sugar. Roll dough into 1 inch balls and roll in the sugar mixture. Place 2 inches apart on ungreased baking sheets.

3. Bake in the preheated oven for 8 to 10 minutes. Cookies will be crackly on top and look wet in the middle. Remove from baking sheets to wire racks to cool. **Yield:** 3 dozen.

Per cookie: About 91 calories, 1g protein, 16g carbohydrate, 3g fat, 0g fiber, 6mg cholesterol, 61mg sodium

Key Lime Cookies

Submitted by: **Pam**

"Lime-flavored rolled cookies make the perfect afternoon snack."

½ cup butter, softened	1½ cups all-purpose flour
1 cup white sugar	1 teaspoon baking powder
1 egg	½ teaspoon salt
1 egg yolk	½ cup confectioners' sugar for decoration
1½ teaspoons grated lime zest	
¼ cup fresh lime juice	

1. Preheat oven to 350°F (175°C). Grease 2 baking sheets.

2. In a large bowl, cream butter, 1 cup sugar, egg, and egg yolk until smooth. Stir in lime zest and lime juice. Combine the flour, baking powder, and salt; blend into the creamed mixture. Form dough into ½ inch balls and arrange on the prepared baking sheets.

3. Bake in the preheated oven for 8 to 10 minutes or until lightly browned. Remove to wire racks. Sift confectioners' sugar over cookies while still warm. **Yield:** 3 dozen.

Per cookie: About 74 calories, 1g protein, 11g carbohydrate, 3g fat, 0g fiber, 19mg cholesterol, 74mg sodium

Cherry Poppy Seed Twinks

Submitted by: **Nancy**

"A great poppy seed version of the thumbprint cookie. These are so good that they are almost addictive."

1	cup butter, softened	2	cups all-purpose flour
1	cup confectioners' sugar	½	teaspoon salt
1	egg	2	tablespoons poppy seeds
1	teaspoon vanilla extract	½	cup cherry preserves

1. Preheat oven to 300°F (150°C).
2. Cream together butter and confectioners' sugar until light and fluffy. Beat in egg and vanilla. Mix in flour, salt, and poppy seeds until well blended. Drop dough by teaspoonfuls onto ungreased baking sheets. Make an indentation in the middle of each cookie with your finger. If the dough is too sticky, dip your finger in water first. Fill each with about ½ teaspoon cherry preserves.
3. Bake in the preheated oven for 20 to 25 minutes or until edges begin to brown. **Yield:** 2½ dozen.

Per cookie: About 121 calories, 1g protein,15g carbohydrate, 7g fat, 0g fiber, 24mg cholesterol, 104mg sodium

◀ Holiday Gift Giving

Prep Time: 25 minutes

Cook Time: 25 minutes per batch

Average Rating: ★★★★

What other cooks have done:

"Here's an idea for a variation: Make walnut size balls and flatten them with a drinking glass. Bake until light golden. When cooled, 'glue' two cookies together with lemon curd or raspberry jam. Dust with confectioners' sugar. Keep in an air-tight tin."

Blueberry Crumb Bars *(pictured on page 299)*

Submitted by: **A. Beavers**

"Cheap and easy to make. Kids love them. Any berry can be used."

1	cup white sugar	1	cup shortening
3	cups all-purpose flour	1	egg
1	teaspoon baking powder	½	cup white sugar
¼	teaspoon salt	3	teaspoons cornstarch
	Pinch ground cinnamon	4	cups fresh blueberries

1. Preheat the oven to 375°F (190°C). Grease a 9x13 inch pan.
2. In a medium bowl, stir together 1 cup sugar, 3 cups flour, and baking powder. Mix in salt and cinnamon. Use a fork or pastry cutter to blend in the shortening and egg. Dough will be crumbly. Pat half of dough into the prepared pan.
3. In another bowl, stir together the sugar and cornstarch. Gently mix in the blueberries. Sprinkle the blueberry mixture evenly over the crust. Crumble remaining dough over the berry layer.
4. Bake in the preheated oven for 45 minutes or until top is golden. Cool completely before cutting into bars. **Yield:** 15 servings.

Per serving: About 318 calories, 3g protein, 45g carbohydrate, 14g fat, 2g fiber, 14mg cholesterol, 79mg sodium

◀ Family Favorite

Prep Time: 15 minutes

Cook Time: 45 minutes

Average Rating: ★★★★

What other cooks have done:

"Delicious! I used a mixture of frozen berries: blueberries, raspberries, and blackberries. I also substituted butter for the shortening and added a small amount of almond extract to the crust. It turned out amazing!"

Becky's Oatmeal Carmelitas

Submitted by: **Robin J.**

"A good friend of mine (and one of the best cooks I know) created this delightfully chewy caramel bar."

1	(14 ounce) package individually wrapped caramels, unwrapped	1	teaspoon baking soda
½	cup evaporated milk	½	teaspoon salt
2	cups all-purpose flour	1	cup butter, melted
2	cups quick cooking oats	2	cups semisweet chocolate chips
1½	cups packed brown sugar	1	cup chopped walnuts

1. Preheat oven to 350°F (175°C). Grease a 9x13 inch pan.

2. In a saucepan over medium heat, melt the caramels with the evaporated milk, stirring frequently until smooth. Set aside.

3. In a medium bowl, stir together the flour, oats, brown sugar, baking soda, and salt. Stir in the melted butter. Press half of the mixture into the bottom of the prepared pan.

4. Bake in the preheated oven for 10 minutes. Remove from the oven and sprinkle with chocolate chips and walnuts. Drizzle the caramel mixture over all. Crumble the remaining oat mixture evenly over the top and pat down lightly.

5. Bake 15 to 20 more minutes or until the top is golden. Cool before cutting into bars. **Yield:** 24 servings.

Per serving: About 353 calories, 5g protein, 49g carbohydrate, 17g fat, 2g fiber, 23mg cholesterol, 232mg sodium

Macaroon Cookie Bars

Submitted by: **Elaine**

"A nice alternative to coconut macaroons."

1	(18.25 ounce) package devil's food cake mix	1	teaspoon vanilla extract
½	cup butter, softened	1	egg
1	egg	1¼	cups flaked coconut
1	(14 ounce) can sweetened condensed milk	1	cup chopped pecans

1. Preheat oven to 350°F (175°C). Grease a 9x13 inch pan.

2. In a large bowl, mix together the cake mix, butter, and 1 egg. (Mixture will be crumbly.) Press into the prepared pan.

3. In another bowl, mix together the sweetened condensed milk, vanilla, and 1 egg until smooth. Stir in 1 cup coconut and pecans. Spread the mixture evenly over the prepared crust. Sprinkle remaining ¼ cup coconut over top.

4. Bake in the preheated oven for 30 to 35 minutes or until golden brown. Cool on a wire rack before cutting into bars. **Yield:** 18 servings.

Per serving: About 319 calories, 6g protein, 36g carbohydrate, 18g fat, 1g fiber, 50mg cholesterol, 311mg sodium

Easy Toffee Bars

Submitted by: **Toni**

"Saltine crackers serve as the base for this salty-sweet treat."

1	cup butter	1	(12 ounce) package semisweet chocolate chips
1	cup packed brown sugar		
1	(10 ounce) package saltine crackers		

1. Preheat oven to 400°F (200°C).

2. In a small saucepan over medium-high heat, melt butter with brown sugar; bring to a boil and remove from heat.

3. Arrange crackers (salt side up) on a 10x15 inch jellyroll pan. Pour butter mixture over crackers.

4. Bake in the preheated oven for 5 minutes.

5. Remove from oven and sprinkle chocolate chips over crackers. Bake for 5 more minutes. **Yield:** 24 servings.

Per serving: About 220 calories, 2g protein, 26g carbohydrate, 13g fat, 1g fiber, 21mg cholesterol, 235mg sodium

Chocolate Mint Dessert Brownies

Submitted by: **Kim Getchell**

"Brownies covered in mint cream and topped with chocolate. Mmmmmm!"

1	cup white sugar	½	cup butter, softened
½	cup butter, softened	2	tablespoons creme de
4	eggs		menthe liqueur
1½	cups chocolate syrup	6	tablespoons butter
1	cup all-purpose flour	1	cup semisweet chocolate
2	cups confectioners' sugar		chips

1. Preheat oven to 350°F (175°C). Grease a 9x13 inch baking dish.
2. In a large bowl, cream together 1 cup sugar and ½ cup of softened butter until smooth. Beat in eggs, one at a time, and stir in the chocolate syrup. Stir in the flour until just blended. Spread the batter evenly into the prepared pan.
3. Bake in the preheated oven for 25 to 30 minutes or until top springs back when lightly touched. Cool completely in the pan.
4. In a small bowl, beat the confectioners' sugar, ½ cup butter, and creme de menthe until smooth. Spread evenly over the cooled brownies; chill until set.
5. In a small bowl over simmering water, or in the microwave, melt 6 tablespoons butter and the chocolate chips, stirring occasionally until smooth. Allow to cool slightly and spread over the top of the mint layer. Cover and chill for at least 1 hour before cutting into squares.
Yield: 24 servings.

Per serving: About 287 calories, 2g protein, 40g carbohydrate, 14g fat, 1g fiber, 64mg cholesterol, 133mg sodium

Caramel Turtle Brownies

Submitted by: **Jessi**

"These are so moist and so fantastic that you won't want to stop eating them! They're a brownie version of a confection called turtles. These are just as good."

1	(14 ounce) package individually wrapped caramels, unwrapped	6	tablespoons butter, melted
		1	cup semisweet chocolate chips
1	(12 ounce) can evaporated milk, divided	¼	pound whole pecans (optional)
1	(18.25 ounce) package chocolate cake mix		

1. Preheat oven to 350°F (175°C). Grease a 9x13 inch pan.
2. Place caramels in a saucepan with 2 tablespoons evaporated milk. Melt over medium to low heat, stirring constantly.

3. In a large bowl, combine the remaining evaporated milk, cake mix, and melted butter. Stir until well blended. Spread half of this mixture in the prepared pan. Bake for 10 minutes.

4. Remove brownies from oven. Sprinkle chocolate chips and drizzle melted caramels over the top. Drop remaining cake mixture by tea-spoonfuls over all. Return to oven and bake for 20 more minutes. Top with whole pecans, if desired. **Yield:** 24 servings.

Per serving: About 265 calories, 4g protein, 35g carbohydrate, 14g fat, 2g fiber, 13mg cholesterol, 263mg sodium

Best Brownies

Submitted by: **Angie**
"These brownies always turn out!"

½	cup butter	¼	teaspoon baking powder
1	cup white sugar	3	tablespoons butter, softened
2	eggs	3	tablespoons unsweetened
1	teaspoon vanilla extract		cocoa powder
⅓	cup unsweetened cocoa	1	tablespoon honey
	powder	1	teaspoon vanilla extract
½	cup all-purpose flour	1	cup confectioners' sugar
¼	teaspoon salt		

1. Preheat oven to 350°F (175°C). Grease and flour an 8 inch square pan.

2. In a large saucepan, melt ½ cup butter. Remove from heat and stir in 1 cup white sugar, eggs, and 1 teaspoon vanilla. Beat in ⅓ cup cocoa, ½ cup flour, salt, and baking powder. Spread batter into pre-pared pan. Bake in the preheated oven for 25 to 30 minutes. Do not overbake.

3. Combine 3 tablespoons butter, 3 tablespoons cocoa, honey, 1 tea-spoon vanilla, and confectioners' sugar. Frost brownies while still warm. **Yield:** 16 brownies.

Per serving: About 183 calories, 2g protein, 26g carbohydrate, 9g fat, 1g fiber, 48mg cholesterol, 133mg sodium

◀ Family Favorite

Prep Time: 25 minutes

Cook Time: 35 minutes

Average Rating: ★★★★★

What other cooks have done:

"The butter (instead of oil) in this recipe makes a huge difference! These brownies were very easy to make and absolutely yummy—the frosting was great, too, although I added a smidgen of milk to smooth it out."

Almond Crunch

Submitted by: **Heather**
"I'm begged for this recipe whenever I serve it. My advice: Invest in a good candy thermometer and always use good ingredients. Don't use margarine as a substitute for the butter because the water content is too high."

1	cup blanched slivered almonds	2	tablespoons light corn syrup
1	cup butter	2	tablespoons water
1¼	cups white sugar	2	cups milk chocolate chips

1. Preheat oven to 375°F (190°C). Arrange almonds in a single layer on a baking sheet. Toast in the preheated oven until lightly browned, approximately 5 minutes. Line a 10x15 inch jellyroll pan with foil.
2. In a heavy saucepan, combine butter, sugar, corn syrup, and water. Cook over medium heat, stirring constantly, until mixture boils. Boil, without stirring, to hard crack stage, 300°F (150°C). Remove pan from heat.
3. Working quickly, stir in almonds and pour mixture into prepared jellyroll pan; tip pan from side to side to spread candy evenly in pan. Sprinkle chocolate chips over candy brittle. Let stand about 5 minutes or until chocolate is shiny and soft. Spread chocolate evenly over candy. Cool to room temperature and refrigerate for 1 hour. Break into bite-size pieces. **Yield:** 16 servings.

Per serving: About 327 calories, 2g protein, 33g carbohydrate, 22g fat, 1g fiber, 36mg cholesterol, 121mg sodium

Holiday Gift Giving ▶

Prep Time: 15 minutes

Cook Time: 30 minutes

Chill Time: 1 hour

Average Rating: ★★★★★

What other cooks have done:

"All our friends who have tried this recipe want it. Instead of almonds, I use chopped pecans. I also put some chopped pecans on top of the melted chocolate (press lightly into chocolate)."

Creamy Peanut Butter Fudge

Submitted by: **Janet Awaldt**
"The creamiest peanut butter fudge ever. Thanks, Mom!"

4	cups white sugar	1	(7 ounce) jar marshmallow creme
1	cup light brown sugar		
½	cup butter	1	(16 ounce) jar peanut butter
1	(12 ounce) can evaporated milk	1	teaspoon vanilla extract

1. Grease a 9x13 inch baking dish.
2. In a medium saucepan over medium heat, combine white sugar, brown sugar, butter, and evaporated milk. Bring to a boil, stirring constantly, and boil for 7 minutes. Remove from heat; stir in marshmallow creme until well incorporated and melted. Stir in the peanut butter and vanilla until smooth; spread in prepared pan. Let cool before cutting into squares. **Yield:** 24 servings.

Per serving: About 355 calories, 6g protein, 54g carbohydrate, 15g fat, 1g fiber, 14mg cholesterol, 150mg sodium

Classic Comfort Food ▶

Prep Time: 10 minutes

Cook Time: 10 minutes

Average Rating: ★★★★★

What other cooks have done:

"I used fat-free evaporated milk and reduced-fat peanut butter in this recipe. Everyone ate it in one day, and I didn't feel bad because I cut down on the fat."

Candy Bar Fudge *(pictured on page 301)*

Submitted by: **Patty Stockton**
"I included fudge in my Christmas treats that I took to the teachers at school. It was the first to go, and I had lots of requests for the recipe!"

½ cup butter	30 individually wrapped caramels, unwrapped
⅓ cup unsweetened cocoa powder	1 tablespoon water
¼ cup packed brown sugar	2 cups salted peanuts
¼ cup milk	1 cup semisweet chocolate chips
3½ cups confectioners' sugar	1 cup milk chocolate chips
1 teaspoon vanilla extract	

1. Grease an 8 inch square pan.
2. In a microwave-safe bowl, combine butter, cocoa powder, brown sugar, and milk. Microwave until mixture boils. Stir in confectioners' sugar and vanilla. Spread into prepared pan.
3. In a microwave-safe bowl, microwave caramels and water until caramels melt. Stir in peanuts. Spread mixture over chocolate layer in the pan.
4. In a small microwave-safe bowl, combine semisweet and milk chocolate chips; microwave until melted. Spread over caramel layer. Chill for 2 hours or until firm. **Yield:** 32 servings.

Per serving: About 204 calories, 3g protein, 29g carbohydrate, 10g fat, 1g fiber, 9mg cholesterol, 131mg sodium

Marshmallow Popcorn Balls

Submitted by: **Kory**
"The marshmallows make these similar to those popular crispy rice cereal bars. They're sweet, crispy, and chewy. Everyone's favorite combination!"

1 tablespoon vegetable oil	5 cups miniature marshmallows
½ cup unpopped popcorn	
6 tablespoons butter	

1. Grease a 9x13 inch baking dish.
2. Add vegetable oil to a 4 quart saucepan and heat over high heat. When oil is hot, add popcorn. Keep pan moving constantly. When corn stops popping, remove from heat. Put popcorn in prepared pan.
3. Melt butter in a medium saucepan over low heat. Stir in marshmallows and cook until melted, stirring constantly. Pour marshmallow mixture over popcorn and mix with a spoon to coat evenly.
4. Let mixture cool slightly. Smear butter on your hands or spray with non-stick cooking spray. Mix popcorn with your hands so that it's evenly coated. Form popcorn mixture into 8 balls. **Yield:** 8 servings.

Per serving: About 237 calories, 2g protein, 35g carbohydrate, 11g fat, 2g fiber, 23mg cholesterol, 103mg sodium

Metric Equivalents

The recipes that appear in this cookbook use the standard United States method for measuring liquid and dry or solid ingredients (teaspoons, tablespoons, and cups). The information on this chart is provided to help cooks outside the U.S. successfully use these recipes. All equivalents are approximate.

METRIC EQUIVALENTS FOR DIFFERENT TYPES OF INGREDIENTS

A standard cup measure of a dry or solid ingredient will vary in weight depending on the type of ingredient. A standard cup of liquid is the same volume for any type of liquid. Use the following chart when converting standard cup measures to grams (weight) or milliliters (volume).

Standard Cup	Fine Powder	Grain	Granular	Liquid Solids	Liquid
	(ex. flour)	(ex. rice)	(ex. sugar)	(ex. butter)	(ex. milk)
1	140 g	150 g	190 g	200 g	240 ml
¾	105 g	113 g	143 g	150 g	180 ml
⅔	93 g	100 g	125 g	133 g	160 ml
½	70 g	75 g	95 g	100 g	120 ml
⅓	47 g	50 g	63 g	67 g	80 ml
¼	35 g	38 g	48 g	50 g	60 ml
⅛	18 g	19 g	24 g	25 g	30 ml

USEFUL EQUIVALENTS FOR DRY INGREDIENTS BY WEIGHT

(To convert ounces to grams, multiply the number of ounces by 30.)

1 oz	=	1/16 lb	=	30 g
4 oz	=	¼ lb	=	120 g
8 oz	=	½ lb	=	240 g
12 oz	=	¾ lb	=	360 g
16 oz	=	1 lb	=	480 g

USEFUL EQUIVALENTS FOR LENGTH

(To convert inches to centimeters, multiply the number of inches by 2.5.)

1 in			=	2.5 cm		
6 in	=	½ ft	=	15 cm		
12 in	=	1 ft	=	30 cm		
36 in	=	3 ft	= 1 yd =	90 cm		
40 in			=	100 cm	=	1 m

USEFUL EQUIVALENTS FOR LIQUID INGREDIENTS BY VOLUME

¼ tsp						=	1 ml
½ tsp						=	2 ml
1 tsp						=	5 ml
3 tsp	=	1 tbls			= ½ fl oz	=	15 ml
		2 tbls	=	⅛ cup	= 1 fl oz	=	30 ml
		4 tbls	=	¼ cup	= 2 fl oz	=	60 ml
		5⅓ tbls	=	⅓ cup	= 3 fl oz	=	80 ml
		8 tbls	=	½ cup	= 4 fl oz	=	120 ml
		10⅔ tbls	=	⅔ cup	= 5 fl oz	=	160 ml
		12 tbls	=	¾ cup	= 6 fl oz	=	180 ml
		16 tbls	=	1 cup	= 8 fl oz	=	240 ml
	1 pt	=	2 cups	= 16 fl oz	=	480 ml
	1 qt	=	4 cups	= 32 fl oz	=	960 ml
					33 fl oz	=	1000 ml	= 1 liter

USEFUL EQUIVALENTS FOR COOKING/OVEN TEMPERATURES

	Fahrenheit	Celsius	Gas Mark
Freeze Water	32° F	0° C	
Room Temperature	68° F	20° C	
Boil Water	212° F	100° C	
Bake	325° F	165° C	3
	350° F	175° C	4
	375° F	190° C	5
	400° F	200° C	6
	425° F	220° C	7
	450° F	230° C	8
Broil			Grill

Common Substitutions

Ingredient	Amount	Substitution
Allspice	1 teaspoon	• ½ teaspoon ground cinnamon, ¼ teaspoon ground ginger, and ¼ teaspoon ground cloves
Arrowroot starch	1 teaspoon	• 1 tablespoon flour OR 1 teaspoon cornstarch
Baking powder	1 teaspoon	• ¼ teaspoon baking soda plus ½ teaspoon cream of tartar OR ¼ teaspoon baking soda plus ½ cup buttermilk (decrease liquid in recipe by ½ cup)
Beer	1 cup	• 1 cup nonalcoholic beer OR 1 cup chicken broth
Brandy	¼ cup	• 1 teaspoon imitation brandy extract plus enough water to make ¼ cup
Breadcrumbs	1 cup	• 1 cup cracker crumbs OR 1 cup matzo meal OR 1 cup ground oats
Broth (beef or chicken)	1 cup	• 1 bouillon cube plus 1 cup boiling water OR 1 tablespoon soy sauce plus enough water to make 1 cup OR 1 cup vegetable broth
Brown sugar	1 cup, packed	• 1 cup white sugar plus ¼ cup molasses and decrease the liquid in recipe by ¼ cup OR 1 cup white sugar OR 1¼ cups confectioners' sugar
Butter (salted)	1 cup	• 1 cup margarine OR 1 cup shortening plus ½ teaspoon salt OR ⅞ cup vegetable oil plus ½ teaspoon salt OR ⅞ cup lard plus ½ teaspoon salt
Butter (unsalted)	1 cup	• 1 cup shortening OR ⅞ cup vegetable oil OR ⅞ cup lard
Buttermilk	1 cup	• 1 cup yogurt OR 1 tablespoon lemon juice or vinegar plus enough milk to make 1 cup
Cheddar cheese	1 cup, shredded	• 1 cup shredded Colby Cheddar OR 1 cup shredded Monterey Jack cheese
Chervil	1 tablespoon, fresh	• 1 tablespoon fresh parsley
Chicken base	1 tablespoon	• 1 cup canned or homemade chicken broth or stock. Reduce liquid in recipe by 1 cup
Chocolate (semisweet)	1 ounce	• 1 (1 ounce) square of unsweetened chocolate plus 4 teaspoons sugar OR 1 ounce semisweet chocolate chips plus 1 teaspoon shortening
Chocolate (unsweetened)	1 ounce	• 3 tablespoons unsweetened cocoa plus 1 tablespoon shortening or vegetable oil
Cocoa	¼ cup	• 1 (1 ounce) square unsweetened chocolate
Corn syrup	1 cup	• 1¼ cup white sugar plus ⅓ cup water OR 1 cup honey OR 1 cup light treacle syrup
Cottage cheese	1 cup	• 1 cup farmers cheese OR 1 cup ricotta cheese
Cracker crumbs	1 cup	• 1 cup breadcrumbs OR 1 cup matzo meal OR 1 cup ground oats
Cream (half-and-half)	1 cup	• ⅞ cup milk plus 1 tablespoon butter
Cream (heavy)	1 cup	• 1 cup evaporated milk OR ¾ cup milk plus ⅓ cup butter

Ingredient	Amount	Substitution
Cream (light)	1 cup	•1 cup evaporated milk OR ¾ cup milk plus 3 tablespoons butter
Cream (whipped)	1 cup	•1 cup frozen whipped topping, thawed
Cream cheese	1 cup	•1 cup pureed cottage cheese OR 1 cup plain yogurt, strained overnight in cheesecloth
Cream of tartar	1 teaspoon	•2 teaspoons lemon juice or vinegar
Crème fraîche	1 cup	•Combine 1 cup heavy cream and 1 tablespoon plain yogurt. Let stand for 6 hours at room temperature.
Egg	1 whole (3 tablespoons)	•2½ tablespoons powdered egg substitute plus 2½ tablespoons water OR ¼ cup liquid egg substitute OR ¼ cup silken tofu pureed OR 3 tablespoons mayonnaise OR ½ banana mashed with ½ teaspoon baking powder OR 1 tablespoon powdered flax seed soaked in 3 tablespoons water
Evaporated milk	1 cup	•1 cup light cream
Farmers cheese	8 ounces	•8 ounces dry cottage cheese OR 8 ounces creamed cottage cheese, drained
Fats for baking	1 cup	•1 cup applesauce OR 1 cup fruit puree
Flour (bread)	1 cup	•1 cup all-purpose flour plus 1 teaspoon wheat gluten
Flour (cake)	1 cup	•1 cup all-purpose flour minus 2 tablespoons
Flour (self-rising)	1 cup	•⅞ cup all-purpose flour plus 1½ teaspoons baking powder and ½ teaspoon salt
Garlic	1 clove	•⅛ teaspoon garlic powder OR ½ teaspoon granulated garlic OR ½ teaspoon garlic salt (reduce salt in recipe)
Ginger (dry)	1 teaspoon, ground	•2 teaspoons chopped fresh ginger
Ginger (fresh)	1 teaspoon, minced	•½ teaspoon ground dried ginger
Green onion	½ cup, chopped	•½ cup chopped onion OR ½ cup chopped leek OR ½ cup chopped shallots
Hazelnuts	1 cup whole	•1 cup macadamia nuts OR 1 cup almonds
Herbs (fresh)	1 tablespoon, chopped	•1 teaspoon chopped dried herbs
Honey	1 cup	•1¼ cups white sugar plus ⅓ cup water OR 1 cup corn syrup OR 1 cup light treacle syrup
Hot sauce	1 teaspoon	•¾ teaspoon cayenne pepper plus 1 teaspoon vinegar
Ketchup	1 cup	•1 cup tomato sauce plus 1 teaspoon vinegar plus 1 tablespoon sugar
Lemon grass	2 fresh stalks	•1 tablespoon lemon zest
Lemon juice	1 teaspoon	•½ teaspoon vinegar OR 1 teaspoon white wine OR 1 teaspoon lime juice
Lemon zest	1 teaspoon, grated	•½ teaspoon lemon extract OR 2 tablespoons lemon juice
Lime juice	1 teaspoon	•1 teaspoon vinegar OR 1 teaspoon white wine OR 1 teaspoon lemon juice
Lime zest	1 teaspoon, grated	•1 teaspoon grated lemon zest
Macadamia nuts	1 cup	•1 cup almonds OR 1 cup hazelnuts
Mace	1 teaspoon	•1 teaspoon ground nutmeg
Margarine	1 cup	•1 cup shortening plus ½ teaspoon salt OR 1 cup butter OR ⅞ cup vegetable oil plus ½ teaspoon salt OR ⅞ cup lard plus ½ teaspoon salt
Mayonnaise	1 cup	•1 cup sour cream OR 1 cup plain yogurt

Ingredient	Amount	Substitution
Milk (whole)	1 cup	• 1 cup soy milk OR 1 cup rice milk OR 1 cup water or juice OR ¼ cup dry milk powder plus 1 cup water OR ⅔ cup evaporated milk plus ⅓ cup water
Mint (fresh)	¼ cup, chopped	• 1 tablespoon dried mint leaves
Mustard (prepared)	1 tablespoon	• Mix together 1 tablespoon dried mustard, 1 teaspoon water, 1 teaspoon vinegar, and 1 teaspoon sugar
Onion	1 cup, chopped	• 1 cup chopped green onions OR 1 cup chopped shallots OR 1 cup chopped leek OR ¼ cup dried minced onion
Orange zest	1 tablespoon, grated	• ½ teaspoon orange extract OR 1 teaspoon lemon juice
Parmesan cheese	½ cup, grated	• ½ cup grated Asiago cheese OR ½ cup grated Romano cheese
Parsley (fresh)	1 tablespoon, chopped	• 1 tablespoon chopped fresh chervil OR 1 teaspoon dried parsley
Pepperoni	1 ounce	• 1 ounce salami
Raisins	1 cup	• 1 cup dried currants OR 1 cup dried cranberries OR 1 cup chopped pitted prunes
Rice (white)	1 cup, cooked	• 1 cup cooked barley OR 1 cup cooked bulgur OR 1 cup cooked brown or wild rice
Ricotta	1 cup	• 1 cup dry cottage cheese OR 1 cup silken tofu
Rum	1 tablespoon	• ½ teaspoon rum extract, plus enough water to make 1 tablespoon
Saffron	¼ teaspoon	• ¼ teaspoon turmeric
Semisweet chocolate chips	1 cup	• 1 cup chocolate candies OR 1 cup peanut butter or other flavored chips OR 1 cup chopped nuts OR 1 cup chopped dried fruit
Shallots (fresh)	½ cup, chopped	• ½ cup chopped onion OR ½ cup chopped leek OR ½ cup chopped green onions
Shortening	1 cup	• 1 cup butter OR 1 cup margarine minus ½ teaspoon salt from recipe
Sour cream	1 cup	• 1 cup plain yogurt OR 1 tablespoon lemon juice or vinegar plus enough cream to make 1 cup OR ¾ cup buttermilk mixed with ⅓ cup butter
Soy sauce	½ cup	• ¼ cup Worcestershire sauce mixed with ¼ cup water
Stock (beef or chicken)	1 cup	• 1 beef or chicken bouillon cube dissolved in 1 cup water
Sweetened condensed milk	1 (14 ounce) can	• ¾ cup white sugar mixed with ½ cup water and 1⅛ cups dry powdered milk (Bring to a boil, and cook, stirring frequently, until thickened, about 20 minutes.)
Vegetable oil (for baking)	1 cup	• 1 cup applesauce OR 1 cup fruit puree
Vegetable oil (for frying)	1 cup	• 1 cup lard OR 1 cup vegetable shortening
Vinegar	1 teaspoon	• 1 teaspoon lemon or lime juice OR 2 teaspoons white wine
White sugar	1 cup	• 1 cup brown sugar OR 1¼ cups confectioners' sugar OR ¾ cup honey OR ¾ cup corn syrup
Wine	1 cup	• 1 cup chicken or beef broth OR 1 cup fruit juice mixed with 2 teaspoons vinegar OR 1 cup water
Yeast (active dry)	1 (.25 ounce) package	• 1 cake compressed yeast OR 2½ teaspoons active dry yeast OR 2½ teaspoons rapid rise yeast
Yogurt	1 cup	• 1 cup sour cream OR 1 cup buttermilk OR 1 cup sour milk

Recommended Storage Guide

IN THE PANTRY

Baking powder and soda	1 year
Flour, all-purpose	10 to 15 months
Milk, evaporated and sweetened condensed	1 year
Mixes	
cake	1 year
pancake	6 months
Peanut butter	6 months
Salt and pepper	18 months
Shortening	8 months
Spices (discard if aroma fades)	
ground	6 months
whole	1 year
Sugar	18 months

IN THE REFRIGERATOR

Butter and margarine	1 month
Buttermilk	1 to 2 weeks
Eggs (fresh in shell)	3 to 5 weeks
Half-and-half	7 to 10 days

Meat	
casseroles, cooked	3 to 4 days
steaks, chops, roasts, uncooked	3 to 5 days
Milk, whole or fat-free	1 week
Poultry, uncooked	1 to 2 days
Sour cream	3 to 4 weeks
Whipping cream	10 days

IN THE FREEZER

Breads	
quick	2 to 3 months
yeast	3 to 6 months
Butter	6 months
Cakes	
cheesecakes and pound cakes	2 to 3 months
unfrosted	2 to 5 months
with cooked frosting	not recommended
with creamy-type frosting	3 months
Candy and fudge	6 months
Casseroles	1 to 2 months
Cheese	4 months

Cookies	
baked, unfrosted	8 to 12 months
dough	1 month
Eggs (not in shell)	
whites	1 year
yolks	8 months
Ice cream	1 to 3 months
Meat	
cooked	2 to 3 months
ground, uncooked	3 to 4 months
roasts, uncooked	9 months
steaks or chops, uncooked	4 to 6 months
Nuts	8 months
Pies	
pastry shell	2 to 3 months
fruit	1 to 2 months
pumpkin	2 to 4 months
custard, cream, meringue	not recommended
Poultry	
cooked	3 to 4 months
parts, uncooked	9 months
whole, uncooked	12 months
Soups and stews	2 to 3 months

Nutritional Analysis

Nutrition Analyses Based on Premier Databases

Allrecipes.com is proud to provide ESHA Research's nutrient databases for recipe nutrition analysis. ESHA Research is the premier nutrition analysis provider for the world's nutrition and health industries, having provided nutrient information to health care providers and the world's top food manufacturing firms for more than 15 years. Its nutrient databases total more than 22,000 foods, track 165 nutrient factors, and combine nutrient data from over 1,200 scientific sources of information. For more information about ESHA Research, visit the website at **http://www.esha.com.**

Using Allrecipes.com Information with Care

Allrecipes.com is committed to providing recipe-based nutritional information so that individuals may, by choice or under a doctor's advice, adhere to specific dietary requirements and make healthful recipe choices. The nutrition values that appear in this book and on **Allrecipes.com** nutrition pages are based on individual recipe ingredients. When a recipe calls for "salt to taste," we calculate sodium based on ¼ teaspoon or 1 gram of salt. While we have taken the utmost care in providing you with the most accurate nutritional values possible, please note that this information is not intended for medical nutrition therapy. If you are following a strict diet for medical or dietary reasons, it's important that you, first, consult your physician or registered dietitian before planning your meals based on recipes at **Allrecipes.com,** and, second, remain under appropriate medical supervision while using the nutrition information at **Allrecipes.com.**

Recipe Title Index

This index alphabetically lists every recipe by exact title.

General Recipe Index

This index lists every recipe by food category and/or major ingredient.

Favorite Recipes Journal

Jot down your family's and your favorite recipes for quick and handy reference.
Remember to include the dishes that drew rave reviews when company came for dinner.

Recipe	Source/Page	Remarks